D0908834

Demographic
Analysis

Demographic
Analysis
Methods, Results, Applications

by Roland Pressat

Institut National D'études Démographiques, Paris

Translated by Judah Matras

Hebrew University, Jerusalem

with a foreword by
Nathan Keyfitz

University of California at Berkeley

Aldine · Atherton

Chicago & New York

Library
I.U.P.
Indiana, Pa.

301.32072   P926d
c. 1

THE AUTHOR

ROLAND PRESSAT received his advanced degree from the Institut National D'études Démographiques in Paris where he is now Professor of Demography. He is a member of the International Union for the Scientific Study of Population and the International Statistical Institute, and has contributed many articles to demographic literature.
The translator, JUDAH MATRAS, received his Ph.D. from the University of Chicago where he was a Research Associate in the Population Research and Training Center. Since 1963 he has taught in the Department of Statistics at the Hebrew University of Jerusalem. He is the author of *Social Change in Israel* (Aldine, 1965) and has contributed many articles to professional journals in the fields of sociology and demography.

This is a translation of *L'analyse Démographique* (Paris, 1961) with the addition of two chapters from the second edition of the same work (Paris, 1969) published by Presses Universitaires de France.

French edition copyright © 1961, 1969 by Presses Universitaires de France.

English edition first published and copyright © 1972 by
Aldine · Atherton, Inc.
529 South Wabash Avenue
Chicago, Illinois 60605

All rights reserved. No part of this publication may be reproduced or transmitted in any form or by any means, electronic or mechanical, including photocopy, recording, or any information storage and retrieval system, without permission in writing from the publisher.

Library of Congress Catalog Card Number 69-11228
ISBN 0-202-30093-5
Printed in the United States of America

Foreword

POPULATION control requires that the birth rate be aimed at the death rate. If it is too low—say 13 per thousand population when the death rate is 14— the population will decline. If it is too high, say 15 per thousand, the population will increase. If either condition persists long enough the population will diminish towards zero or increase towards infinity. Fortunately the birth trajectory does not have to be set once and for all, but can be adjusted within limits during the course of flight. Since birth and death rates determine whether we are heading for population extinction or explosion, they are well designated "vital statistics." Their understanding and use are the central theme of demographic analysis.

Poor countries cannot seriously talk about development without proposing to do something about their rapidly increasing populations. The Mexican death rate is very low—what sign is there that its birth rate has fallen to accord with this? What would be the relative populations of the United States and Mexico in 75 years if the birth and death rates of both as shown in 1970 were to persist? Rich countries are growing more slowly, yet any plan to tackle problems of the environment requires action on their rate of growth and population distribution. Vital statistics can be made to answer other questions than those concerning the growth and decline of populations. By how much do American women outlive American men? Is the difference increasing, and to what causes of death is the male excess mortality due? To what extent is the American pattern of nearly everyone marrying, and marrying young, spreading through the world? What is the chance that a French girl of 20 will be married by the time she is 25? that she will be divorced before she is 30?

Interest in such questions is widespread. But interest is not enough. The important questions cannot be answered by merely counting up the number of births and deaths in successive years and different countries. The raw statistics are indeed the basis of knowledge, but to bring out their implications requires techniques that have been developed over more than a century by scholars in several countries. Europe's great demographer, Alfred Sauvy, who wrote the preface to the French editions of this book, speaks of the originators: Quetelet, Boekh, Kuczynski, Landry; to these might be added Graunt, Euler, Farr, Lexis, Lotka, Whelpton, Notestein, Glass, Coale, Brass, Ryder, Duncan, Goodman, Henry, Sheps, Bourgeois-Pichat, Tabah, and others whose work initiated or extended the techniques expounded by Pressat. Like other disciplines, ours has had a long series of puzzling problems, apparent solutions, errors, and corrections as it evolved the methods that are now standard. To try to dispense with this heritage is to risk repeating the errors of the past.

This volume by Roland Pressat provides those techniques that will most often be called for in the study of today's demographic problems. They fill the gap between the large amounts of data made available by censuses, and the theoretical and practical questions that need to be answered; the techniques of this book effectively bring the data into confrontation with the problems.

Pressat's success reflects his ability to make use of the best of mathematical methods in demography and then to present them with very little of the mathematical apparatus showing. His skill as a teacher is matched by that of the translator, Judah Matras, who is himself a research demographer with a number of papers on methods as well as substance in professional journals. Matras has further enriched the book by adding examples pertaining to the United States and British populations, some of them derived from his study and research at the University of Chicago. The book concentrates the techniques elaborated over more than a century and cumulated in two great centers of population study, Paris and Chicago.

The substance of the book can be presented in a one-semester course of which the largest part would be devoted to its main themes, mortality and fertility. Underlying these as well as nearly every other kind of data with which the demographer deals is the problem of location in time—the relation of vital events to the calendar, and also to the age of the persons undergoing them. Pressat's detailed attention to this problem in Part I forms a solid basis for the subsequent methodology.

In the study of mortality, the technique for locating events in time finds its first application. We know the number of deaths during a year and the population at mid-year; by division we can approximate the death rate, both in total and at individual ages. But we need the probability that a person alive at the beginning of a year will survive to the end; some subtle issues are unavoidably raised in the passage from death *rate* to *probability* of dying. Further issues arise in going from probabilities of dying at several ages to expectations of life, and Pressat deals with them incisively.

The life table provides a model for analysis of nuptiality, the probability of marrying being calculable by somewhat the same methods as the probability of dying. Indeed the formal similarity is shown in later chapters to extend to the probability of having a first child, and other events occurring to the individual.

But demography is less interested in the fate of individuals than in the movement of populations. The procedure for going from death statistics to the life table is valuable because the life table facilitates calculation of prospective survivors in real populations. What in application to an individual of given age is the *probability* of surviving to the next age turns out to be the right factor for estimating the *fraction* of a population surviving from that age to the next. The projected population includes the survivors among those initially alive, plus the survivors among the births during the projection period.

In his treatment of population projection, Pressat applies the methods developed in earlier sections for mortality and fertility. The emphasis given to population projection accords with its usefulness in demographic analysis. The meaning of a demographic rate or trend is brought out by seeing to what condition it would lead if continued. The difference between two rates may be small; projection is like a microscope that enlarges the difference by showing the divergence between the path population would follow at one rate as opposed to the other. No assumption is made that the concrete future will follow either path; the future enters as a way of interpreting the present. Though the usefulness of this section of Pressat's book does not depend on its predictive effectiveness, it contains whatever scientific prediction has so far been attained in the field of population.

Sometimes the projection shows that a rate cannot continue—growth of some capital cities at present rates would lead to their containing the entire population of their countries within less than a century: such counter-predictions, as they may be called, are also an adjunct to demographic analysis.

Finally, the Matras translation introduces explicit mathematics in a section on stable population theory. The inclusion here of the chief addition of Pressat's second edition will give the reader access to some uses of stable theory—for instance, in the inference of birth rates for countries that lack registrations—and it will also prepare him for further reading in the mathematics of population.

This English translation may be expected to extend further the success Pressat's *L' analyse Demographique* has had in Spanish, Russian, and other languages.

Nathan Keyfitz

Preface
to the English Edition

THIS felicitous translation by Professor Judah Matras of Hebrew University is, in fact, a revised and augmented version of the original work: besides supplementary illustrative materials drawn from American demographic sources, an entirely new chapter on mathematical demography has now been added to the first French edition.

This work was intended to answer the need of as many as possible of the numerous people interested in demography and especially in the latest techniques of statistical demographic analysis. On this side of the Atlantic Ocean we often praise American textbooks because, in a great variety of fields, they do such an excellent job of stressing the practical aspects of the subjects they discuss. That is the very spirit in which this book was written: it embodies the author's own experiences as he acquired his present familiarity with the tools of analysis. We hope that the English-speaking reader will here discover those very qualities that he has come to expect in his literature, and we much look forward to his response.

Translator's Preface

PREPARATION of the English translation of Professor Pressat's important and influential treatise, *L'analyse démographique*, was first undertaken early in 1967, six years after its publication, and after it had already achieved wide acceptance in France and French-speaking countries, after Russian- and Polish-language editions had already appeared, and as preparation of a Spanish-language edition was in its final stages. The present translation was undertaken at the initiative of the publisher, and with the often strategic encouragement of Professor Nathan Keyfitz, who has also contributed a *Foreword*.

The June, 1967, war in Israel and its immediate aftermath seriously interrupted the work and delayed completion of the translation. Subsequently the decision to expand and update in a modest way some of the examples contained in the original French edition, ensuing editorial and production problems, as well as other commitments of the author and translator converged to force further delays. In 1969 Professor Pressat published a second French edition of the book. The major addition to this revised edition consists of two entirely new chapters on Mathematics and Demographic Analysis, and it was decided to incorporate these into the present English-language version of Professor Pressat's work. Thus this translation, *Demographic Analysis*, consists of Professor Pressat's original book translated in its entirety, and Part V from his second edition.

Translation and preparation of this work has turned out to be rather more complicated and difficult than initially envisaged, and the knowledge, skills, and abilities commanded by the translator have not always sufficed to give the present version the clarity and precision which the original text deserved. In any case the present version could well have benefited from some rewriting and recasting of sentences. But rather than delay its appearance further, it was decided to publish the translation in its present form in the hope that the reader will find the substantive, methodological, and technical rewards of braving the prose more than sufficient to merit the effort.

Judah Matras

Contents

PART II

VITAL EVENTS

PART IV

POPULATION PROJECTIONS

PART V

MATHEMATICS AND DEMOGRAPHIC ANALYSIS

Part I
PRELIMINARY CONSIDERATIONS

CHAPTER ONE

Subject Matter and Sources of Data

DEMOGRAPHY is the discipline that seeks a statistical description of human populations with respect to (1) their demographic structure (the number of the population; its composition by sex, age and marital status; statistics of families, and so on) at a given date, and (2) the demographic events (births, deaths, marriages and terminations of marriage) that take place in them.

Accordingly, a demographer's attention is sometimes focused upon the structure of *groups of people*, which is in turn determined by demographic events that occurred to these groups in the past (for example, marriages and terminations of marriage in the past determine the current composition of the population by marital status). Sometimes, on the other hand, it is *groups of events* that are the focus of the study (for example, deaths in a given year), but with reference to the structure of the population that experiences these events (for example, one might study the frequency of deaths in the part of a population having a given age).

These two aspects of statistical description of population require two types of demographic statistics, which should be carefully distinguished from each other:

1. Statistics of the size and structure of the population, obtained from population censuses and permitting description of the demographic structure of the population at a given instant;[1]

2. Statistics of demographic (or vital) events, obtained from civil (or vital) registers and classifying, by various criteria, the demographic events occurring in a population in a given period of time, usually a year.

1. We shall see later that the census may also be instructive about the past history of populations.

Population Census

A history of censuses and a review of census techniques may be found in other books. We list here only a brief inventory of the various types of information provided by a modern population census. We should remember that in France, the United States, Great Britain, and elsewhere most of these data derive from responses to questions enumerated on schedules by households for which the ultimate source of information is the householder himself (or his representative).

In the past the census played an exclusively administrative role: it gave the number of citizens and households in a given territory, the total population of military age, etc. Our current periodic censuses still retain that role. Most of the information they provide helps in the understanding of the economic and social structure of the country (and thus serves it indirectly), but certain of the census data are of more direct interest to the administrative authorities. These are the data indicating the population of the various administrative units. In the United States, for example, this geographic division of the population (the population of regions, states, counties, townships, cities, urbanized areas, Standard Metropolitan Statistical Areas) is complemented by distinctions between the population living in households and those in institutions; between the urban, the rural nonfarm,

TABLE 1.1. *Kankakee County, Illinois: Population of Minor Civil Divisions, 1940, 1950, and 1960*

County and Minor Civil Division	1960	1950	1940
Kankakee County	92,063	73,524	60,877
Aroma Township	4,222	1,255	1,465
Aroma Park Village	744	544	497
Kankakee City (pt.)	687	—	—
Bourbonnais Township	16,677	9,114	5,418
Bourbonnais Village	3,336	1,598	771
Bradley Village	8,082	5,699	3,689
Kankakee City (pt.)	133	119	127
Essex Township	795	744	799
Essex Village	328	284	211
Union Hill Village (pt.)	—	25	—
Ganeer Township	2,980	2,191	1,970
Momence City (pt.)	1,261	1,059	970
Kankakee Township	36,090	33,844	30,022
Kankakee City (pt.)	26,846	25,737	22,114
West Kankakee	3,197	2,784	—
Limestone Township	2,507	1,250	964

and the rural farm population, etc.[2] Table 1.1 shows how information on population in counties and minor civil divisions is presented in the 1960 United States Census.

But the main interest in the information provided by a population census lies elsewhere.

The Census as Portrait of the Population

The population census provides a portrait as of a given instant of a population constantly changing under the influence of the events—births, marriages, and deaths—that occur in it. Thus the census tells us the size of the population by sex, age, marital status, and citizenship, at the date of the census. All the various kinds of information that have been collected can be combined in many ways, and they can concern an entire country or some given part of the country (region, state, province, county, or city). Multiple cross-tabulations could lead to very detaiied (but very bulky) tables such as the distribution, by broad age-groups and sex, of foreigners by major nationalities, by state of residence. Such detail is not necessarily desirable.

The list of statistical tables varies from one census to another and from one country to another. Their number depends both on the depth of information given on each questionnaire or schedule and on the intensity of its exploitation. In the developed countries the variety of possible relationships and associations is so great that the number of published tables is very much less than the number possible: delays, costs, and limits to interest mean that a selection has to be made. Conversely, in the under-developed countries the quality of responses and the limited number of schedules limit the possibilities of statistical tabulation and analysis.

The Census as History of the Population

A population census gives more, however, than the structure of the population at a given instant. Certain questions asked permit, in effect, the study of the past history of all or part of the population.

This is especially true of family statistics. For if women are asked appropriate questions about the birth of their children, it is possible to arrive at a description of family formation in any specified group of the population. In particular, it is possible to study the spacing between births of different orders, if the dates of birth of each mother's live-born children are obtained

---

2. For definitions of such categories of population in France, see the census volumes giving this type of statistics. The annual abstracts of national statistics usually recapitulate these definitions.

at the census. The simple figure of the total number of live births to any group of mothers aged 50 years or over (the age limit of fertility) gives us at once the completed family size of the group. By combining this information with data on economic or social status (occupation, place of residence, age at marriage), one may undertake quite detailed analyses.

Statistics of internal migration are very often deficient, even in countries where demographic statistics are otherwise quite complete. One partial remedy for this deficiency is to question those enumerated about their changes of residence during a certain interval of time (usually one year) preceding the census. In the case of censuses in underdeveloped countries, this form of inquiry is used extensively. It substitutes, to a certain extent, for the nonexistent vital register by questioning persons about vital events during the preceding year (births, marriages, deaths). Delving further into the past, we may reconstruct the demographic characteristics of the population even more extensively.

By-Products of the Population Census

During periodic population censuses it is customary to collect information —sometimes quite extensive—about educational achievement, occupations, dwellings and residential structures, industrial establishments, farms, etc.

Population Changes

Statistics concerning population changes should account for physical movement, that is to say for international and internal migrations as well as for vital events. But inadequate counting at the frontiers and the absence of community population registers allow only very approximate measures of international migrations and even less information on internal migration. We shall consider under the term 'vital events' only those changes introduced in the number and structure of population by births, deaths, marriages, and terminations of marriage—all events that are registered. The statistics of population changes in developed countries are characterized by great precision thanks to the excellent operation of the vital registers.[3]

Even when the annual totals of births and of deaths are well known, certain breakdowns remain in doubt; there are certificates of births, marriages, and deaths where the various details concerning the person in question and his kindred are not always exactly or completely submitted.

3. Divorce statistics are an exception. Divorce results from a judgment; this judgment is generally (but not always) followed by an entry in the civil register; in addition, there are delays, of varying duration, between the judgment and the entry. As a result, divorce statistics taken from the civil registers are, in France at least, both incomplete and inaccurate.

It follows that, after statistical processing of these details, the tables that are derived must contain a 'no response' or 'unknown' category, the magnitude of which varies according to the country and the nature of the tables. Thus, a certain number of deaths, for example, cannot be classified by age. But this number is very small in a well-developed country such as France.

We summarize here the variety of statistical tables that can be worked out in a developed country, taking as examples natality and mortality.

Natality

Besides the summary statistics giving the number, sex, legitimacy or illegitimacy, and month of birth of newborn infants, there are statistics permitting analysis of the fertility of couples: births by age of mother, by duration of marriage, and by order of birth (that is, according to the number of children previously born). These details for the administrative subdivisions of a territory (county or township, for example) will be found in greater or lesser degrees of completeness.

The births in any single year are to mothers of all ages and of diverse durations of marriage. This heterogeneity of the group makes demographic analysis difficult. But comparison of the observations for consecutive years permits following the development of fertility within groups that are homogeneous with respect to age, duration of marriage, etc. For example, by comparing the births registered each year to women married in 1946, one may follow the evolution of the total fertility of that group of women.

Mortality

Most current mortality statistics report numbers of deaths classified by sex and age. Monthly statistics have been established that also permit taking account of sex and age. The latter permit study of the seasonal character of mortality.

The statistics go into great detail about mortality in the first year of life (infant mortality) because of its great importance.

Statistics of cause of death have one important feature; the different causes are detailed according to the characteristics given earlier (age, sex, month of the year).

Extension of the Field of Study and of the Sources

Thus far, our presentation of the subject matter of demography and of its methods of statistical observation has been concentrated on what is usually done in the developed countries at the level of large human groups. In fact, the science of demography was until very recently interested only in large, territorially well-defined groups.

Little by little, the field of investigations has been extended. It has become apparent that demographic considerations have their place in groupings much smaller and much more specific than the usual national aggregates. This involves studies not only at the level of small administrative or other units (cities, villages, natural regions), but also at the level of human categories that are not territorially well defined (for example, the agricultural population).

Social and occupational groups and the like are also of concern to demography: one may speak of the population of an industrial enterprise, consider its age structure, and study its history as affected by accessions to employment (analogous to natality) and by deaths and retirement from employment (analogous to mortality). In fact, in all human groupings, whatever the reasons for considering them, there is always a place for demographic observation and analysis. Data useful for such analysis exist only rarely in official statistics. The peculiar character of the specific problems raised requires the collection of appropriate information through special inquiries or surveys.

Demographic Inquiries

Demographic inquiries (or surveys) usually involve the collection of data on a small scale, based on individual questionnaires. Such studies may also be based upon statistical material that already exists, but in a somewhat latent state, e.g., quantitative information that certain official or professional organizations (social security, family allocation funds, professional organizations, large offices, and so forth) can give. These statistics only rarely give the information that is sought in a precise fashion; to extract the desired information it is necessary to make certain adjustments or to undertake certain estimations requiring a sophistication that only practical demographic experience and a statistical sense can give.

But sometimes the demographer's statistical sense will not be able to produce useful figures when the available information is too meager or inappropriate. National or local administrations ought not to be content to play the restricted role for which they were established, but should seek to exploit their information in a manner that would permit a better understanding of the human society in which they function.

An inquiry carried out by a study of existing documents (but which have not been statistically processed) or by interview requires work that may be as extensive at the collection phase as at the processing phase. Soon, individual energy is not enough; above a certain size of the area or of the population studied, the inquiry requires collective effort and the use of modern methods of processing (machine tabulation).

We cannot go into detail about types of possible inquiries, which vary with the nature of the problem studied, the detail of description and analysis that is sought, etc. Often interview inquiries have no demographic purpose per se; demographic data are obtained simply as a background to certain aspects of economic and social life, analysis of which constitutes the principal theme of the inquiry.

As a general rule, demographic inquiries seek to ascertain, as precisely as possible, some of the details that statistics carried out on a large scale ordinarily leave aside: migratory movements, demographic history of families, etc. Although they are limited in the extent of the field covered, the workman-like character of the majority of these inquiries is well suited to work in depth, so that a large period of past history can be studied with great profit even from quite a modest inquiry.

Aside from exhaustive inquiries concerning small human groups, of the kind that often leads to a thesis or a monograph, there are types of data collection that try to obtain information valid for the entire population on the basis of data obtained from only a fraction of the larger population. The latter are sample survey inquiries.

Sample Surveys

In a sample survey it would appear necessary that the fraction of the population that is interviewed be chosen "judiciously." We will not discuss the exact meaning of "judicious choice," for we would be entering the domain of an autonomous field of study that, like others, requires systematic training. It is necessary to know at least that "samples" of the population taken for the inquiry must be determined in one of two ways:

1. By purposive choice. One seeks to form a "subpopulation" that will be a reduced model of the total population, in the sense that the subpopulation and the total population have identical structures with respect to certain characteristics: sex, age, social and occupational categories, etc. The choice of common characteristics must be limited; a priori considerations will lead to a decision about which characteristics ought to determine inclusion in the sample, given the information sought. This procedure is called *quota sampling*.

2. At random. In fact, many precautions must be taken to achieve random samples, and they are quite different from sample surveys carried out haphazardly. Besides, there are many schemes of randomization that can variously take into account questions of the cost of the inquiry, its

precision, etc. These are called *probability samples*, because the mathematical theory of probability is used in the design and in the processing to permit evaluation of the precision of the results obtained.

Sample surveys are studies on limited numbers of individuals, somewhat similar to those carried out in studies for a monograph; but, because of the way in which the sample was chosen, the results obtained are not so much of interest in themselves but as a means of inferring findings valid for a much larger population.

A sample survey may be carried out in many ways. For example, instead of making an exhaustive inquiry, only a small part of the total number of persons questioned (say, in a census), may be retained in the sample to furnish information on a specific point. Thus, in the French census of 1954, only 50,000 women were asked questions about the birth of their children; in this manner information was obtained that was still sufficiently representative, but with less expense, owing to the size of the sample and the manner in which it was chosen. One may even anticipate that better information is obtained in such a partial inquiry, since the relatively restricted number of persons questioned permits better control of operations and more care in filling out questionnaires.

The sample survey may also be used during processing. In the French census of 1954, one schedule in twenty was counted during preliminary processing. Results were thus obtained rapidly which had great precision for large groupings.

In underdeveloped countries the sample survey contributes much to demographic knowledge. It gives information where complete inquiries are impossible because they are impracticable or too costly.

Parish Registers

Neglected until recently as a means of demographic investigation, parish registers in France, England, and certain other Western countries sometimes give information valuable for both its completeness and its precision. In France, these parish registers fulfilled the function of vital registration until 1792. But these scattered records, relating to populations that were mobile and not enumerated in a census, did not get any attention because the work of processing them was cumbersome and difficult.

Following initial attempts, a methodology has been developed that should routinize methods of collection as well as analytical procedures quite distinct from the traditional ones. Once demographic phenomena are placed in the framework of the family, the type of information available is close to that which may be obtained in the monographic inquiry. Such studies, aside from their intrinsic historical interest, can thus serve as models for the limited inquiries that modern demography recognizes are useful.

Published Sources of Demographic Statistics

As a general rule, demographic statistics are found (1) in publications devoted to censuses of population, (2) in publications of annual vital statistics, and (3) in statistical yearbooks.

The specific conventions in each country lengthen this list to varying extents. We first discuss French demographic statistics in more detail.

French Demographic Statistics

The French censuses were formerly quinquennial and took place in years ending in "1" or "6." (However, the census of 1871 was replaced by that of 1872, and the censuses of 1916 and 1941 never took place.)

There was a census in 1946, but the one that was supposed to have been taken in 1951 was not taken until 1954, the necessary budgetary allocations having been delayed. In the future, in accordance with international recommendations, the trend will be to take decennial censuses.

The processing of a census is very complicated, and occupies the entire intercensal period. The object is the publication of a dozen volumes, which can total several thousand pages. A characteristic of the most recent censuses has been the processing by sample survey of a fraction of the census schedules, so that fairly detailed information could be obtained about each of the ninety French *départements* at very early dates. In the recent censuses, numerous data have been published in regional statistical bulletins (about which more is said below) prior to being compiled in national summaries.

Statistics of vital events are the subject of numerous publications:

1. One may follow closely the trend of vital events in the monthly bulletins of statistics edited by the French National Institute of Statistics and Economic Studies (INSEE), which give total statistics of marriages, births, and deaths (at all ages and at under one year), for each quarter, as soon as they are available. For the Seine *département* and for 110 cities, the same statistics are given monthly, indicating the current situation even more promptly.

2. In each December issue of the monthly bulletin of statistics, a first summary sheet is set up (in part provisional, since at the date of publication the year is not finished and some delay is necessary anyway for compilation of the statistics). Figures are given for births, deaths, and net migration for the year that is ending, as well as forecasts of the population by age and sex on January 1 of the coming year.

3. Each year. in one of the numbers of the quarterly supplement to the monthly bulletin of statistics (this supplement is called *Études Statistiques* after 1956). detailed statistical information is given concerning the demographic situation during the previous year. Until the first number (January March) of 1956, the delay was a little longer than one year; the supplement dated January–March. 1956. giving statistics of population changes in 1954. Since the fourth number (October–December) of 1956 the presentation of statistics has been more prompt; that supplement gave statistics of population changes in 1955.

4. Complete statistics of population changes are published in a special volume. At present (1961). findings for two years are compiled in a single volume (of about 350 pages). but its publication is long after the events take place; at the end of 1958 the most recent volume concerned the years 1950 and 1951.

5. Finally, regional statistical bulletins follow the situation in the *départements* and are prepared under the supervision of the INSEE. These statistics are concerned essentially with totals for given geographic units (cities. wards. districts. etc.). Details by age. by periods. and so forth are less frequent. Many of the data obtained by regional branches of the INSEE are not published but can often be obtained directly from these branches. However. in the statistical commentaries and the miscellanies of the regional bulletins and their annual supplements. supplementary details are given concerning some aspect or another of local demography. as decided by the regional statistical authorities. These additions are not concerned only with vital events; sometimes census data not yet released for the whole nation are available for certain *départements*[4] in the regional bulletins.

The different publications devoted to vital statistics generally contain population estimates by age or by the age groups necessary for calculation of rates.

The French statistical year book *(Annuaire statistique)* presents a collection of statistics concerning essentially the economic and social life of the country; under this heading certain data from the censuses and the vital statistics are recapitulated in the yearbooks. In the statistical yearbooks are found also the most recent estimates of the population by sex. age. and marital status as of each January 1.

Sometimes material not published elsewhere is found in the statistical yearbook; e.g.. the French life table for the years 1950–1951. The statistical yearbooks also contain valuable retrospective demographic statistics for France and occasionally for foreign countries.

4. Besides statistics of vital events. the INSEE publishes statistics of causes of death. amounting cumulatively to a volume of about 200 pages of statistics for each year.

American and British Demographic Statistics

The population censuses of the United States are taken each decade in years ending in "0." We shall not undertake a review of the contents of the publications presenting census findings; with modern means of statistical summary and analysis, data have tended to increase from one census to the next, and for the latest census filled several thousand large-format pages.

Complementing these voluminous publications of census results are the *Current Population Reports*. These include, in particular, Series P-20 *(Population Characteristics)*, Series P-25 *(Population Estimates)*, and Series P-28 *(Special Censuses)*, all giving various findings on population size and structure derived from partial censuses, sample surveys, and annual population estimates carried out by the United States Bureau of the Census.

Population censuses of England and Wales, Scotland, and Northern Ireland are carried out simultaneously, always in years ending in "1," but their results and findings are published separately except for the *Summary Tables* for Great Britain. The publication for England and Wales and for Scotland of the very valuable volume of data entitled *Fertility Tables* is especially noteworthy; this volume contains the statistics of fertility derived from the census.

In the United States, vital statistics are found primarily in the volumes entitled *Vital Statistics of the United States*. At present these include Volume I, Natality; Volume II, Mortality, Parts A and B; and Volume III, Marriage and Divorce.

In the *Monthly Vital Statistics Report*, current provisional or summary demographic statistics are presented. Finally, other data on vital events not included in previously cited publications appear in the series formerly entitled *Vital Statistics, Special Reports*, which currently are Series 20–23 of the United States Public Health Service Publication No. 1000.

In Great Britain there are separate publications for England and Wales and for Scotland. The data concerning vital events in England and Wales are published under the general title *The Registrar General's Statistical Review of England and Wales* and are presented in two volumes of statistics *(Part I: Tables, Medical,* and *Part II: Tables, Population)* and one volume of analysis *(Part III: Commentary)*. For Scotland there is a single annual volume: *Annual Report of the Registrar General for Scotland*.

International Demographic Statistics

The use of collections of demographic statistics for different countries is often difficult. For comparative studies, the data may require considerable correction and adjustment, as well as a great deal of handling. The existence of international summaries of statistics, while not entirely eliminating the necessity for researches in national collections of statistics, considerably facilitates the work in cases where the details required are not too extensive.

In France there are several volumes of international statistics of population change available *(Statistiques internationales du mouvement de la population)*; the first and second volumes cover, respectively, the periods 1749–1901 and 1901–1910, and are edited by the Statistique Génerale de la France (the French national statistical bureau); the third is entitled *Le mouvement naturel de la population dans le monde 1906 à 1936* (World Natural Increase from 1906 to 1936) and is edited by the National Institute of Demographic Studies of France.

The existence of international organizations (the League of Nations formerly; then, the United Nations, the World Health Organization, etc.) has permitted the development of world statistical yearbooks. Until 1944 certain general demographic findings could be found in the *Statistical Yearbook of the League of Nations*. Since 1948, the United Nations has issued a voluminous *Demographic Yearbook* (between 400 and 800 pages, depending on the year) giving quite extensive data. Each year a particular subject is treated in detail; thus the yearbook for 1954 emphasizes natality; that of 1955, general characteristics described in population censuses; that of 1956, the economic characteristics obtained in censuses; that of 1957, mortality.

The World Health Organization likewise issues a *Yearbook of Epidemiological and Vital Statistics*, which, for the most part, does not duplicate the United Nations' *Demographic Yearbook*.

Demographic Knowledge and Statistical Information

Every activity in demographic analysis must be derived from statistical information obtained basically by familiarity with tables of numbers. For the beginner there is a long period of apprenticeship, involving close contacts with raw data. Moreover, the study of statistics always requires a real effort, regardless of the experience one possesses. Examination of a table consisting of numerous classifications and detailed definitions (contained in headings and subheadings) demands concentration, a type of "sorting power" that precludes any intellectual untidiness. The study of summaries of demographic statistics and of the commentaries that accompany them, besides being one of the best introductions to a knowledge of demographic facts, is also part of statistical apprenticeship.

CHAPTER TWO

Location in Time

TO BE analyzed, the data produced concerning population structure and vital events must be classified according to certain criteria, especially by criteria involving time (age, duration, etc.). The population is classified by age; legitimate births in a given year are classified by the duration of marriage of the parents or by the interval since the preceding birth, and so on. The national statistics of developed countries make extensive use of standard classifications that are highly detailed, and the analyst may generate still finer distinctions and groupings from them. In underdeveloped countries, where the data are frequently approximate, such refined distinctions are often impossible. This is also the case in Western countries for certain older statistics or for regional statistics, which may not go into as much detail as the corresponding national statistics.

These limitations do not diminish the weight of the considerations of this chapter. Even though the statistics may be imperfect or incomplete, the analyst, in order to extract a maximum of information from them, must make numerous approximations that presuppose a very precise grasp of the phenomena studied. Without such precise knowledge, the approximations made may be unwarranted, frivolous, or seriously misleading.

Theories, that are the basis of thought in demography, cannot be conceived without precise representation of the phenomena studied. In this chapter, however, we are entering into technical details quite distant from actual demographic theory. Geometric notation will play an important role in what follows.

Geometric Representation of Time Instants and Time Intervals

Consider a straight line and, on that line, a succession of points located equidistantly and numbered 0, 1, 2, 3, etc. (Fig. 2.1a). A natural procedure would be to associate with each of these points each of the successive instants:

0 seconds (instant of origin), 1 second, 2 seconds, 3 seconds, etc.
0 months (instant of origin), 1 month, 2 months, 3 months, etc.
0 years (instant of origin), 1 year, 2 years, 3 years, etc.

With such a scale of time instants, the intervals are measured as lengths. Thus, in Figure 2.1b, where instants are expressed in years, the length *AB* represents an interval of 2 years, the length *CD* an interval of 1 year, 9 months (2 years, 6 months–0 years, 9 months). This location of time instants is, of course, made with calendar dates (Figure 2.1c).

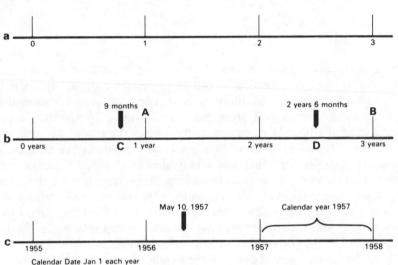

Figure 2.1

A Terminological Convention

The scale of intervals and ages employed in demography may be large or small, depending upon the phenomena under study. Mortality, for instance, is currently studied by age in *days* up to age 1 month, then in *months* up to age 1 year, and, finally, in *years* over age 1 year. We do not, then, attempt to distinguish all the events occurring between two time instants on the scale. We consider as a whole, for instance, the total number of children dying between the exact age of 3 months and the exact age of 4 months. For these deaths we do not take the exact age at the moment of death but the number of complete months lived by the child; and we speak of deaths occurring at the age of *3 complete months*, that is to say, between the successive exact ages 3 months and 4 months. Similarly, for a man dying at age 37 years, 5 months, and 10 days, we would say that he died at 37 *complete years* of age (if it had been decided not to distinguish among deaths occurring in the interval between the 37th and 38th birthdays).

The generalization of this convention of terminology, which is of great convenience, may be the source of errors for the careless student. He may not see, for example, that, where ages or intervals are expressed in complete years in statistical tables, the figures do not refer to exact instants but to time intervals.

To give examples:

1. As we have seen, the total number of deaths indicated at 37 complete years includes deaths occurring between the 37th and the 38th birthday. We cite an exact age, but in fact refer to an interval between two consecutive exact ages.

2. In a classification of the population by age or by age groups in complete years:

    a. The group 0 years includes those children between age 0 (exact age, that is to say, at the instant of birth) and 1 year (exact age) during the period considered. We speak also of the group "under 1 year of age."

    b. The group 0–4 years includes those children between 0 and 5 years during the period under consideration.

    c. The group 5–9 years includes those children between 5 and 10 years during the period considered.

3. In France there is compulsory school attendance beginning with exact age 6 years to exact age 14 years; that is to say, for the group 6–13 years in complete years.

4. In terms of complete years, we speak of births that have taken place:

    a. In the interval or duration of 0 years of marriage, i.e., between marriage (instant 0) and the first anniversary of marriage. This 0 interval is also called "under 1 year."

    b. In the interval or duration of 1 year of marriage, i.e., between the first and the second anniversaries of marriage.

To avoid any ambiguity, it is best to say in the text and in statistical tables whether or not one means ages, intervals and durations in complete years. One thus speaks of births occurring at 7 years of marriage *in complete years* or *during* the 8th year of marriage (which is the same thing).

Introduction to the Lexis *Diagram*

Let us consider a vital event occurring on May 10, 1956; for example, a birth. With the two perpendicular straight lines of Figure 2.2 as axes (one

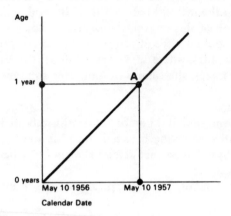

Figure 2.2

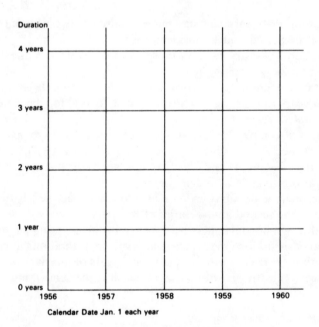

Figure 2.3

indicating the calendar dates and the other the ages), a child at his birth is located by the intersection point of the two axes or lines. On the horizontal axis this point indicates that we are at May 10, 1956, and on the vertical axis it indicates that on that date the infant is aged exactly 0 years. In proportion to the time elapsed, the point representing the child moves on the bisector of the right angle, because the intervals elapsed since birth and measured on the two straight lines are necessarily always equal. Thus, when the child is 1 year old, the point representing him will be at A. It is usual to call the line described by the child his *life line* (it terminates when the individual dies).

In the *Lexis* diagram this mode of representing demographic events is systematized, where elapsed intervals (or ages, which are the intervals elapsed since birth) and dates are combined. We shall now review several applications of this representation.

The Lexis *Grid*

Let us take the time instants January 1, 1956, January 1, 1957, etc., on the horizontal line; and the instants of 0 years (coinciding with January 1, 1956), 1 year, 2 years, etc., on the vertical straight line. Through these points we draw lines parallel to the two straight lines serving as axes (Figure 2.3). (The choice of dates on the horizontal axis obviously depends on the location in time of the phenomenon being studied.)

The instants on the vertical axis correspond to what we shall call *intervals*. In particular cases these may be ages (see Figure 2.2), durations of marriage, etc., that is, intervals elapsed since some initial event (birth, marriage, etc.). The horizontal lines passing through these points are, then, "birthday" or "anniversary" lines.

Generation or Cohort Life Lines

As a first application we shall determine the location of the life lines of a generation, or birth cohort (the group of persons born during one calendar year), in the *Lexis* diagram (Figure 2.4). We shall consider the 1957 birth cohort; that is, all the children born from January 1, 1957, to December 31, 1957.

At the instant of their birth their points are located on the horizontal axis along that portion of it which lies between the indicated dates (*AB*). We now follow the children born on January 1, 1957, through time: their common life line is the diagonal beginning at point *A*. Similarly, the diagonal beginning at point *B* is the common life line of all children born on December 31, 1957. Thus it becomes clear that the life lines of the 1957 generation will be located in the cross-hatched band of Figure 2.4[1]

The grid in Figure 2.4 may be used also for the group married in 1957 (we call it the *cohort* of those married in 1957, or marriage cohort). The dates of the various marriages are all located on the segment *AB*; as time

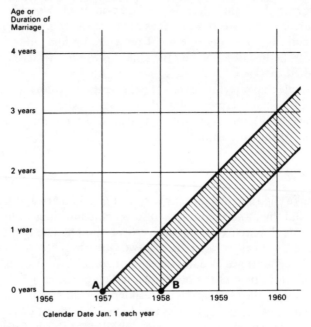

Figure 2.4

elapses, the point that represents each couple moves within the cross-hatched band parallel to the borders, continuing until the marriage is dissolved by death or divorce. The expression "life line" is no longer very appropriate; "survival line" can be substituted, implying survival in the state of marriage. The termination of the survival line, then, may result not only from the death of one of the two partners but also from divorce.

1. There is a minor difficulty in presentation (and in illustration). Each individual really has an autonomous life line, however little the differences between instants of birth may be for permitting their location with sufficient precision. Only life lines sufficiently distant from one another on the paper are, strictly speaking, distinguishable *graphically;* moreover (considering the nature of the phenomena studied), distinctions between persons born one minute or one hour apart make no sense *practically.* It is convenient and sufficient here to treat all the newborn of a single day as a group, without distinguishing among its elements. It also follows that a diagonal in the *Lexis* grid is really a *bound,* and, strictly speaking, it is therefore incorrect to assign it to the newborns of December 31st (it would be just as legitimate to assign it to the newborns of January 1st); but these, again, are distinctions without practical importance, which only encumber the presentation.

In a general way, the representation of Figure 2.4 lets us follow the path in time of any cohort, that is, of any group of individuals who have lived through some similar type of event during a given time period (most often a year)—marriage cohort, cohort of widows, cohort of women giving birth to their third child, etc. We shall see the convenience of this representation presently.

Ages and Cohorts

In this section we consider only the ages of individuals at different dates. By simple extension one can see the general character of what follows, although in the examples chosen we deal with mortality only.

1. Let us consider first the children at the age of 2 complete years at any given moment in the year 1959. As shown in Figure 2.5, their life lines

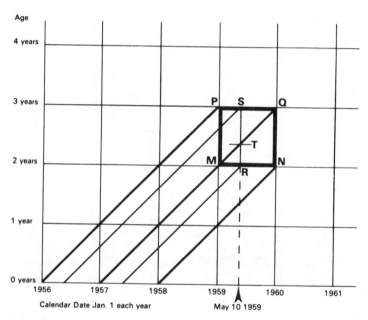

Figure 2.5

must pass through the square *MNPQ*, formed by the intersection of the horizontal band (2 complete years) and the vertical band (1959).

At any given instant in the year 1959, these children belong to two birth cohorts: 1956 and 1957. In Figure 2.5 the time instant chosen is May 10, 1959.

The only exception to the rule is for January 1st: on January 1, 1959, children aged 2 complete years *all* belong to the 1956 cohort. The children of this cohort have life lines that cross the vertical on January 1, 1959, at segment *MP*. Similarly, we see that on January 1, 1960, children aged 2 complete years *all* belong to the cohort of 1957; their life lines cross the vertical on January 1, 1960, at segment *NQ*

2. We go on to a different application of the *Lexis* diagram: let us consider the 1957 cohort during the year 1959. The corresponding life lines are in the parallelogram *HIJK* of Figure 2.6, where the 1957 generation band intersects with the band for the year 1959. Persons of this cohort reach their second birthday when their life lines cross the horizontal segment *JI*.

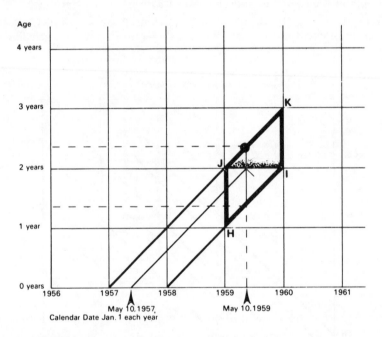

Figure 2.6

At any moment in the year the cohort is separated into two age groups: (1) those aged 2 complete years and (2) those aged 1 complete year. As an example we have shown in the diagram a cross section for May 10, 1959, which shows the situation at that time. The proof of this is graphical. In the 1957 generation children born prior to May 10, 1957, are aged two complete years on May 10, 1959, and children born between May 10 and December 31, 1957, are aged 1 complete year on May 10, 1959. Within the same cohort, exact ages and the ages calculated by the differences between the dates of the year of observation (here 1959) and the year of birth (1957, a difference of 2 years) are thus not the same at a given instant for all persons. There is always one important exception: on January 1 in any year, exact ages and ages calculated by the difference between dates coincide, as Figures 2.5 and 2.6 show. This observation is of practical utility; it implies that birth cohort groups coincide with age groups on January 1 each year (see Figures 2.7a and 2.7b).

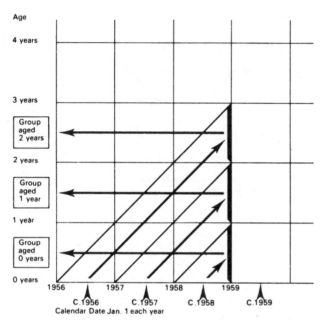

Figure 2.7a

We conclude with a concrete example taken from a census of population. The date for the census is chosen so that it will be taken under the best possible conditions. Periods of great population mobility (the summer months and holiday seasons), or of difficulty for rural enumerators (the winter months) and the like are generally avoided. In Western countries it is not therefore practicable to take a census on January 1, the date when birth cohort groups and age groups coincide.

If the distribution of the population by year of birth (that is to say, by cohort) is given at the census date, that distribution will not coincide with the distribution by age at the same period. To obtain the latter it would be necessary to make a distinction, in each cohort, between persons who have already had their birthdays before the census and those who will have them after the census.

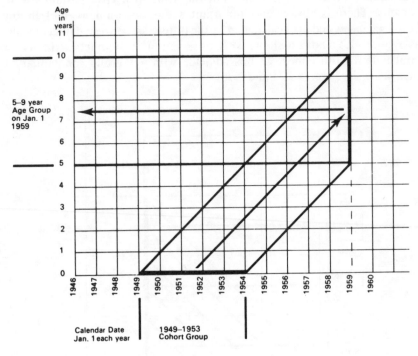

Figure 2.7b

Data from the French census of 1946 are shown in Table 2.1. This census gives the flow of life lines crossing the vertical line at March 10, 1946, on the axis of calendar dates. (See Figure 2.8.)

TABLE 2.1.   *France: Total Enumerated Population, March 10, 1946*

Year of Birth	Age in Completed Years on January 1, 1946	Population
1946: January 1 to March 9	...	146,573
1945: March 10 to December 31	0	481,602
1945: January 1 to March 9	0	112,514
1944	1	565,593
1943	2	524,307

For the 1945 cohort we have the distribution of children born before March 10 and of those born March 10 or after. The group aged 0 complete years before March 10, 1946, can then be constructed (146,573 + 481,602 = 628,175). We have here a first example of double classification (by age and by cohort), the importance of which we shall see later. This double classification stops at the 1944 cohort, and it is not possible to get the distribution by year of age on March 10, 1946, except for the class aged 0 years.

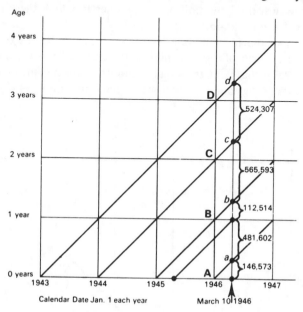

Figure 2.8

In fact, it is common to reconstruct the population as of the January 1st preceding the census (in this case, January 1, 1946) when ages and cohorts coincide, and so estimate the flow across *ab*, *bc*, *cd*, etc., and the flow across *AB*, *BC*, *CD*, etc., which takes into account deaths and migratory movements shown in the parallelograms *ABab*, *BCbc*, *CDcd*, etc.

Double Classification in Demography

In demography, events (births, marriages, deaths, etc.) are generally observed over the calendar year. It is of interest to classify these events according to two criteria: (1) the *interval* elapsed since a previous or initial event, e.g., deaths according to the duration of life (or age), widowhood according to duration of marriage, third births according to interval elapsed since the second birth, etc., and (2) the *cohort* of individuals to which it is natural to relate the person who has experienced the event, e.g., deaths as related to the birth cohort, widowhood related to the marriage cohort, women giving birth to their third infant as related to the cohort of women having their second child.

In our graphic representation a vital event is shown by the termination of the life line (or survival line) at the interval and date at which that event takes place. The event is in a sense made concrete by the point of termination. We now turn our attention to the manner in which these points are placed in the *Lexis* diagram.[2]

Again we take the life line as a simple example. It begins on May 10, 1957, the date of birth of a given child. If the death of this child occurs on October 10, 1959—that is, at age 2 years 5 months—the life line is terminated at the corresponding point, sometimes called the mortality point (see Figure 2.9).

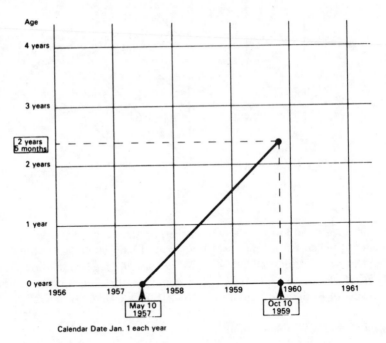

Figure 2.9

Let us see how the distribution of mortality points corresponds to the double classification of deaths by age and by cohort. We reproduce a

2. The life lines or survival lines of individuals are never traced in practice. Interest is centered on the termination points of these lines, the number of which is marked in the various triangles of the *Lexis* diagram.

Library
I.U.P.
Indiana, Pa.

301.32072 P926d

C. 1

section from the table giving the double classification of male deaths in
1955 (Table 2.2). Reading this table carefully, we derive Figure 2.10.

TABLE 2.2.   *France: Male Deaths in 1955, by*
Year of Birth and by Age

Year of Birth	Age in Completed Years	Number of Deaths
1955	0	11,400
1954	0	4,359
1954	1	986
1953	1	705
1953	2	325
1952	2	275
1952	3	218
1951	3	204
1951	4	162
...	...	...

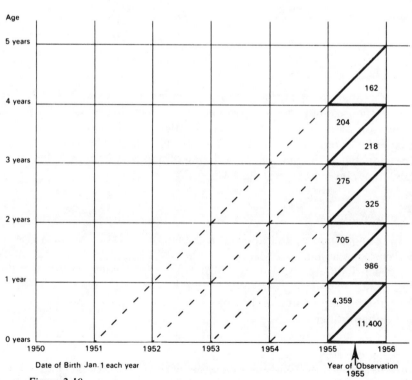

Figure 2.10

Our second example comes from fertility statistics. Table 2.3 gives some statistics of first births (or births of first order), according to the year of marriage and the duration of marriage. From these data Figure 2.11 is obtained.

TABLE 2.3. *France: First Order Live Births in 1955, by Year of Marriage and by Duration of Marriage*

Year of Marriage	Duration of Present Marriage in Completed Years	Number of Births
1955	0	39,449
1954	0	78,615
1954	1	37,454
1953	1	26,575
1953	2	12,266
1952	2	11,431
1952	3	6,530
1951	3	6,533
1951	4	4,246
...	...	...

In the analysis of fertility, statistics similar to those of Table 2.3 are frequently used, but without specifying birth order. Many points may then appear on the line of the *Lexis* diagram that represents a given woman, each point corresponding to the live birth of a child. This particular case does not change the rule for transcription of numbers from the table to the *Lexis* diagram (compare Table 2.4 and Figure 2.12).

General Remarks

In certain French publications (the demography text of Michael Huber, earlier demographic publications of the INSEE), the *Lexis* diagram is constructed differently. However, the principle of construction and the uses of the diagram are exactly the same in both cases. We have departed from the usual presentation because it seems to us difficult to understand and rather artificial.

In the chapters to come, the *Lexis* diagram will serve constantly as a support for our analytical presentation of phenomena. Frequently in practice the data to which the demographer has access are too gross or too approximate for use in a diagram. But even then the diagram will often be a

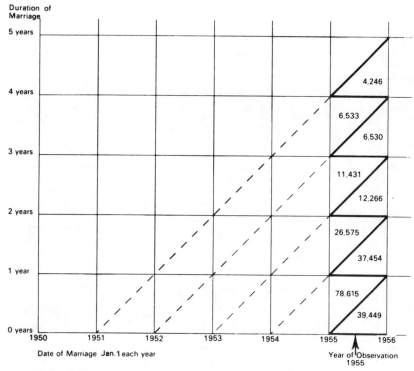

Figure 2.11

TABLE 2.4. *France: Live Births (of all Birth Orders) in 1955, by Year of Marriage and by Duration of Marriage*

Year of Marriage	Duration of Present Marriage in Completed Years	Number of Births
1955	0	40,292
1954	0	80,407
1954	1	47,068
1953	1	46,522
1953	2	37,113
1952	2	40,415
1952	3	31,985
1951	3	35,706
1951	4	27,616
...	...	...

valuable guide that determines the possible approximations and indicates the best treatment to be applied to raw data in order to carry out the analysis.

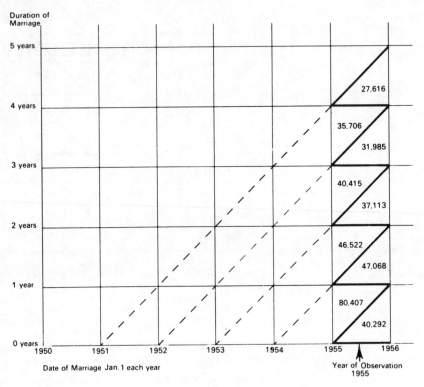

Figure 2.12

CHAPTER THREE

Rates in Demography

IN THIS chapter we show the different ways of calculating the various rates used in demography. There is sufficient unity in the principles and procedures for us to bring together everything concerning techniques of computation. We shall keep our consideration of rates as tools of analysis for the chapters on methodology.

Crude Rates

The main idea that leads to the formulation of a rate is the idea of getting a measure that relates to a phenomenon and that permits comparisons in time and in space.

In order to compare the level of mortality in Great Britain in 1871 and in 1921, absolute numbers of deaths (606,000 and 560,000, respectively) do not suffice, for the population of Great Britain grew from 27,431,000 inhabitants to 44,027,000 inhabitants in the same period. In order to neutralize the effect of this variation in population, corresponding numbers of deaths per given number of inhabitants, most often per 1,000 inhabitants, are computed for the two dates. In this way *crude death rates* are obtained. Thus the crude death rate of 22.1 per 1,000 in 1871 is compared with 12.8 per 1,000 in 1921.

This need to base the number of deaths on a given number of inhabitants appears again when one wants to compare mortality in countries with quite different populations. In 1850 there were 93,000 deaths in Belgium compared with 762,000 deaths in France. But these correspond to a crude death rate of 21.2 per 1,000 for Belgium, compared with the French crude death rate of 21.4 per 1,000 in 1850.

Computation of Crude Rates

Crude rates are generally calculated for single calendar years. There is a crude death rate, a crude birth rate, and a crude marriage rate. More specifically, the crude death rate (or birth rate) is obtained by dividing the annual number of deaths (or births) by the mean population of the country or territory in question and multiplying the quotient by 1,000.[1]

By *mean population* is meant the population on June 30 of the year in question. When estimates of the population for that date are not available, it is customary to compute the arithmetic mean of the populations for the two January 1 dates that bound the year in question. It is frequently this arithmetic mean that is given as the mean population in statistical publications.

Example—France, 1954:
Estimated population on January 1, 1954   42,785,000
Estimated population on January 1, 1955   43,117,000
Arithmetic mean (estimate of the population
   on June 30, 1954):

$$\frac{42,785,000 + 43,117,000}{2} = 42,951,000.$$

Crude Death Rates per 1,000 (515,346 deaths)	Crude Birth Rates per 1,000 (807,206 births)
$\dfrac{515,346 \times 1,000}{42,951,000} = 12.0$ per 1,000	$\dfrac{807,206 \times 1,000}{42,951,000}$ 18.8 per 1,000

The crude marriage rate is determined in a similar manner. However, the computation may be made either on the basis of the number of *marriages* or on the basis of the number of *newly married persons* (which is double the number of marriages). According to the latter convention, followed in Western populations, the crude marriage rate is of an order of magnitude comparable to that of the crude birth rate.

Example—France, 1954:
Crude marriage rate (314,453 marriages, 628,906 newly married persons):

$$\frac{628,906 \times 1,000}{42,951,000} = 14.6 \text{ per } 1,000.$$

In England and Wales and in the United States, where annual estimates of the population on July 1 are made each year, the mean population is

1. A "rate per 1,000" is thus obtained. One may also multiply the quotient by 10,000, for example; thus obtaining a rate per 10,000. But it is the rate per 1,000, with a single digit after the decimal point, that is conventionally employed.

obtained directly. The population of the United States on July 1, 1961 was estimated to be 182,953,000 (excluding U.S. Armed Forces personnel stationed overseas). In 1961 there were 1,701,522 deaths, 4,268,326 births, and 1,548,000 marriages (that is, 3,096,000 newly married persons), whence the crude rates:

Crude death rate: $\dfrac{1,701,222 \times 1,000}{182,953,000} = \; 9.3$ per 1,000.

Crude birth rate: $\dfrac{4,268,326 \times 1,000}{182,953,000} = 23.3$ per 1,000.

Crude marriage rate: $\dfrac{3,096,000 \times 1,000}{182,953,000} = 16.9$ per 1,000.

Specific Rates

The crude rates measure the frequency of phenomena in the total population. Certain refinements suggest themselves immediately. For example:

1. Would it not be more satisfactory to calculate a birth rate restricted to that part of the population which may in fact give birth to children?

2. Mortality varies with age a great deal. Would it not be better to calculate different rates for different age groups in the population?

Thus we enter into the realm of specific rates, by which we mean rates calculated for a subpopulation, which is often just some specific age group. We shall consider different rates of this type, in each case indicating the manner of its calculation.

Rates by Age

We are going to show how to calculate age-specific rates, using mortality as an example—say, the calculation of the death rate of French males aged 40 complete years in 1954. We are therefore measuring the frequency of deaths between the 40th and 41st birthdays.

We give in Tables 3.1, 3.2a, and 3.2b the extracts from the annual vital statistics and estimates of the population of France on January 1 that will be used for these computations.[2]

2. Statistics of population structure and vital events usually include some unknown or not reported categories, that is to say, individuals or events (deaths, births, etc.) that cannot be classified by age or by other characteristics. Utilization of these statistics most often assumes a previous distribution of these unknowns. The manner in which one obtains these distributions is illustrated by the example in Table 3.10.

TABLE 3.1. *France: Deaths in 1954, by Year of Birth and Age*

Year of Birth	Age in Completed Years	Male Deaths
...	...	...
1915	39	396
1914	39	532
1914	*40*	*589*
1913	*40*	*604*
1913	41	685
1912	41	623
1912	42	752
...	...	...

TABLE 3.2a. *Estimated Population of France, by Sex and Age, January 1, 1954*

Year of Birth	Age in Completed Years	Males
...	...	...
1914	39	289,301
1913	*40*	*298,299*
1912	41	302,208
...	...	...

TABLE 3.2b. *Estimated Population of France, by Sex and Age, January 1, 1955*

Year of Birth	Age in Completed Years	Males
...	...	...
1914	*40*	*287,970*
1913	41	296,710
1912	42	300,623
...	...	...

The elements used in the calculations are shown in the *Lexis* diagram in Figure 3.1a. These are: (1) the total male population aged 40 complete years on January 1, 1954 (the flow across the segment *AB*); (2) the total male population aged 40 complete years on January 1, 1955 (the flow across segment *A'B'*), and (3) the number of males dying who were aged 40 complete years at the time of their deaths (number of mortality points in the square *AB A'B'*).

All these elements appear in Tables 3.1, 3.2a, and 3.2b; we have placed them in the *Lexis* diagram in Figure 3.1b. Computing the arithmetic mean of the total of the two populations, we obtain the mean population required for computing the rate, that is:

$$\frac{(298,299 + 287,970)}{2} = 293,134.$$

The number of deaths at age 40 complete years in 1954 is $589 + 604 = 1,193$. From this we derive the male death rate at age 40 years:

$$\frac{1,193 \times 1,000}{293,134} = 4.1 \text{ per } 1,000.$$

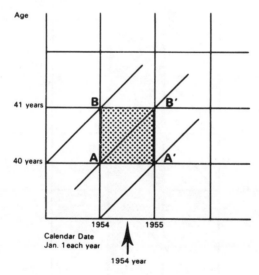

Figure 3.1a

Rates by Age Groups

Calculation of mortality rates is usually carried out for groups of several years of age. Working with five-year age groups, a description of mortality

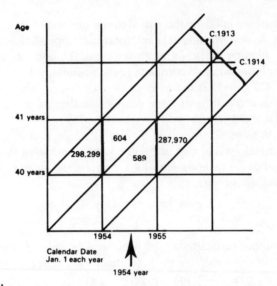

Figure 3.1b

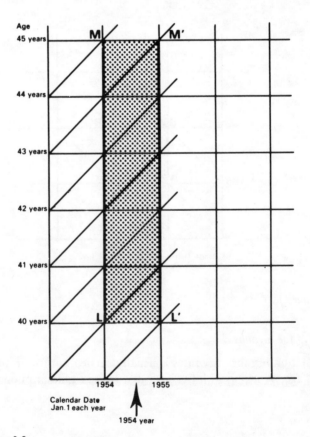

Figure 3.2a

by age is obtained with the aid of some 20 rates, while nearly 100 rates would be needed if rates for single years of age were used.

Let us calculate the male mortality rate for the 40–44-year age group in 1954. We are therefore measuring the frequency of death between the 40th and 45th birthdays.

In Tables 3.3, 3.4a, and 3.4b, we give the extracts from the annual vital statistics and estimates of the population of France on January 1, that will

TABLE 3.3. *France: Male Deaths in 1954, by Year of Birth and Age*

Year of Birth	Age in Completed Years	Male Deaths
...	...	...
1915	39	396
1914	39	532
1914	40	589
1913	40	604
1913	41	685
1912	41	623
1912	42	752
1911	42	755
1911	43	739
1910	43	801
1910	44	820
1909	44	909
1909	45	989
1908	45	1,009
...	...	...

TABLE 3.4a. *Estimated Population of France by Sex and Age-groups, January 1, 1954*

Year of Birth	Age Group in Completed Years	Males
...	...	...
1918–1914	35–39	977,002
1913–1909	40–44	1,488,072
1908–1904	45–49	1,492,613
...	...	...

TABLE 3.4b. *Estimated Population of France by Sex and Age-groups, January 1, 1955*

Year of Birth	Age Group in Completed Years	Males
...	...	...
1919–1915	35–39	890,565
1914–1910	*40–44*	*1,468,344*
1909–1905	45–49	1,485,639
...	...	...

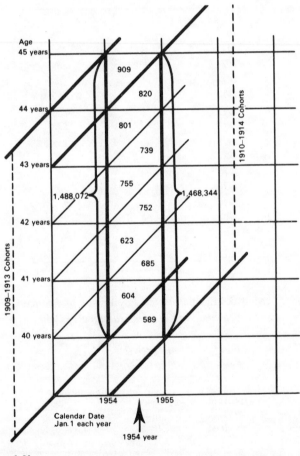

Figure 3.2b

be used for these calculations; they are shown in the *Lexis* diagram in Figure 3.2a. These are: (1) the total male population aged 40–44 complete years on January 1, 1954 (the flow across segment *LM*); (2) the total male population aged 40–44 complete years on January 1, 1955 (the flow across *L'M'*), and (3) the number of males dying who were aged 40–44 complete years at the time of their deaths (number of mortality points in the rectangle *LM L'M'*). All these elements are shown in Tables 3.3, 3.4a, and 3.4b; we have placed them in the *Lexis* diagram in Figure 3.2b.

Computing the arithmetic mean of the totals of the two populations, we obtain the mean population required for computation of the rate, which is:

$$\frac{1,488,072 + 1,468,344}{2} = 1,478,208.$$

The number of deaths at 40–44 complete years of age in 1954 is:
$$589 + 604 + 685 + 623 + 752 + 755 + 739 + 801 + 820 + 909 = 7,277.$$
From this we derive the male mortality rate at age 40–44 years:

$$\frac{7,277 \times 1,000}{1,478,208} = 4.9 \text{ per } 1,000.$$

Specific Fertility Rates

It is common to calculate rates restricted to all or part of the female population of reproductive age. These rates are called *fertility rates*.[3]

To distinguish among the different types, we use a standardized terminology, which should be observed scrupulously.[4] A distinction might be made between fertility measured for all births (live births and stillbirths) and fertility measured for live births only, but, since only fertility measured for live births will concern us in what follows, we shall not pursue this distinction.

When we relate the aggregate of live births in one year to all women of reproductive age, we obtain a *general fertility rate*. The reproductive ages are usually taken as running from 15 to 49 complete years. In particular cases these limits may be modified. For example, we might take all women aged 10 years and over. It is then necessary to state the modification explicitly.

If the aggregate of legitimate live births only is considered and is related

---

3. One ought to specify "female fertility rate," for nothing prevents definition of male rates; the latter, however, are not common.

4. For all questions of terminology the student may usefully consult the *Multilingual Demographic Dictionary*, published by the United Nations. For the idea behind this dictionary, we may refer the reader to the article of P. Vincent, author of the French version, appearing in *Population*, No. 1, January–March, 1953: "Conception d'un dictionnaire démographique."

to the total number of married women of reproductive age, the marital general fertility rate (or *legitimate general fertility rate*) is obtained. By similar reasoning and corresponding data (live illegitimate births and unmarried women of reproductive age), the *illegitimate general fertility rate* is defined.

All these concepts are retained when rates restricted to specifically delineated age groups of the female population are calculated. The adjective "general" is then dropped, and we speak, for example of the fertility rate at 20–24 years, the marital fertility rate (or legitimate fertility rate) at 30–34 years, or the illegitimate fertility rate at 15–19 years.

General Fertility Rates

We collect and present in Table 3.5 the various elements for calculation of three general fertility rates for the United States in 1960.

TABLE 3.5. *General Fertility Rates in the United States in 1960*

General Fertility Rate	Marital (Legitimate) General Fertility Rate	Illegitimate General Fertility Rate
Mean Female Population Aged 15–49 Years:	Mean Married Female Population Aged 15–49 Years:	Mean Unmarried Female Population Aged 15–49 Years:
36,085,000	25,801,000	10,284,000
Live Births: 4,258,000	Legitimate Births: 4,033,700	Illegitimate Births: 224,300
General Fertility Rate:	Marital General Fertility Rate:	Illegitimate General Fertility Rate:
118.0 per 1,000	155.5 per 1,000	21.8 per 1,000

For these three calculations we have taken the live births (first all of them, then legitimate only, and finally illegitimate only) irrespective of the age of the mother, but have related them only to females 15–49 years of age; for, practically speaking, all births are produced within this age grouping. The only exceptions would be the births to girls under 15 years of age and to women over 50, which are very few; in France in 1949 there were 87 births to mothers under 15, and 26 to mothers over 50.

Age-Specific Fertility Rates

The method of calculation of age-specific fertility rates is completely analogous to that employed for determining the mortality rates by age or age groups. We shall confine the discussion to explaining the calculation for rates by age groups. The extracts from the published vital statistics and population structure that are needed to calculate the fertility rate at age 20–24 years for France in 1949, are shown in Tables 3.6, 3.7a and 3.7b.

The mean female population aged 20–24 years of age in 1949 is given by:

$$\frac{(1,614,849 + 1,612,471)}{2} = 1,613,660.$$

The births used in the computation are placed in the *Lexis* diagram in Figure 3.3.

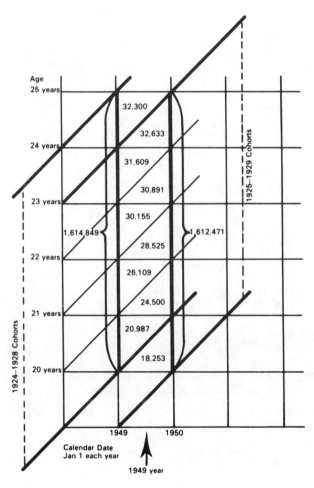

Figure 3.3

TABLE 3.6. *France: Live Births in 1949, by Mother's Year of Birth and Year of Age*

Year of Birth	Age in Completed Years	Live Births
...	...	...
1929	19	14,275
1929	20	18,253
1928	20	20,987
1928	21	24,500
1927	21	26,109
1927	22	28,525
1926	22	30,155
1926	23	30,891
1925	23	31,609
1925	24	32,633
1924	24	32,300
1924	25	30,649
...	...	...

TABLE 3.7a. *Estimated Female Population, by Age Groups, January 1, 1949*

Year of Birth	Age Group in Completed Years	Females
1933–1929	15–19	1,590,845
1928–1924	20–24	1,614,849
1923–1919	25–29	1,546,336

TABLE 3.7b. *Estimated Female Population, by Age Groups, January 1, 1950*

Year of Birth	Age Group in Completed Years	Females
1934–1930	15–19	1,577,936
1929–1925	20–24	1,612,471
1924–1920	25–29	1,657,470

The total number of live births to women aged 20–24 years is thus:
18,253 + 20,987 + 24,500 + 26,109 + 28,525 + 30,155 + 30,891 + 31,609 + 32,633 + 32,300 = 275,962.

The age-specific fertility rate at 20–24 years in France in 1949 is therefore:

$$\frac{275,962 \times 1,000}{1,613,660} = 171 \text{ per } 1,000.$$

The computations of legitimate fertility and of illegitimate fertility by age groups are carried out in the same fashion. It is necessary to have access to quite detailed data for both births and population structure. Such data are shown in Tables 3.8, 3.9a, and 3.9b.

TABLE 3.8. *France: Live Births in 1949 by Legitimacy, and by Mother's Year of Birth and Year of Age*

Year of Birth	Age in Completed Years	Live Births Legitimate	Live Births Illegitimate
...	...	...	...
1929	19	12,332	1,943
1929	20	16,162	2,091
1928	20	18,780	2,207
1928	21	22,430	2,070
1927	21	23,972	2,137
1927	22	26,505	2,020
1926	22	28,099	2,056
1926	23	29,145	1,746
1925	23	29,697	1,912
1925	24	30,980	1,653
1924	24	30,688	1,612
1924	25	29,145	1,504
...	...	...	...

TABLE 3.9a. *France: Estimated Female Population by Age and by Marital Status, January 1, 1949*

Year of Birth	Age in Completed Years	Single	Married	Widowed	Divorced
...	...	...	...	...	...
1933–1929	15–19	1,492,433	97,942	336	134
1928–1924	20–24	793,076	811,971	3,774	6,028
1923–1919	25–29	332,955	1,167,905	14,911	30,565
...	...	...	...	...	...

TABLE 3.9b.   *France: Estimated Female Population by Age and by Marital Status, January 1, 1950*

Year of Birth	Age in Completed Years	Single	Married	Widowed	Divorced
...	...	...	...	...	...
1924–1930	15–19	1,482,063	95,580	179	114
1929–1925	20–24	786,507	817,410	3,216	5,338
1924–1920	25–29	342,829	1,271,107	13,219	30,315
...	...	...	...	...	...

Table 3.10 shows how these data are processed in order to yield marital and illegitimate fertility rates.

TABLE 3.10.   *France, 1949: Fertility Rates for Women aged 20–24 Years (computation procedure)*

Marital Fertility Rate	Illegitimate Fertility Rate
Mean Married Female Population: $(811,971 + 817,410): 2 = 814,690$	Mean Unmarried Female Population: $(793,076 + 3,774 + 6,028 + 786,507 + 3,216 + 5,338): 2 = 798,969$
Number of Legitimate Live Births $16,162 + 18,780 + 22,430 + 23,972 + 26,505 + 28,099 + 29,145 + 29,697 + 30,980 + 30,688 = 256,458$	Number of Illegitimate Live Births: $2,091 + 2,207 + 2,070 + 2,137 + 2,020 + 2,056 + 1,746 + 1,912 + 1,653 + 1,612 = 19,504$
Marital Fertility Rate at age 20–24 years $\dfrac{256,458}{814,690} = 315 \text{ per } 1000$	Illegitimate Fertility Rate at age 20–years $\dfrac{19,504}{798,969} = 24.4 \text{ per } 1000$

Age-Specific Marriage Rates

The definitions and calculations are obvious extensions of those carried out for mortality and fertility.

It must be noted that (1) the calculations of frequencies of marriage at each age or age groups are made separately for each sex; (2) in addition to the general marriage rates (calculated on the basis of marriages in all categories, and so including at the same time the marriages of persons previously single, widowed, and divorced), marriage rates can be constructed that are restricted to single persons, or widowed persons, or divorced persons.

We give a single example in detail. Let us calculate the marriage rate for widowers aged 30–34 years in 1949. The data used are contained in Tables 3.11, 3.12a, and 3.12b.

TABLE 3.11.   *France: Marriages in 1949 by Groom's Year of Birth, Age and Previous Marital Status*

Year of Birth	Age in Completed Years	Single	Previous Marital Status Widowed	Divorced
...	...	...	...	...
1919	29	3,750	119	434
1919	30	2,870	81	397
1918	30	2,649	82	356
1918	31	2,506	107	425
1917	31	1,986	68	365
1917	32	1,998	93	346
1916	32	1,718	73	339
1916	33	1,702	100	332
1915	33	1,636	88	323
1915	34	2,188	122	486
1914	34	2,259	214	561
1914	35	2,195	173	725
...	...	...	...	...

TABLE 3.12a.   *France: Estimated Male Population by Age and Marital Status, January 1, 1945*

Year of Birth	Age-Group in Completed Years	Single	Married	Widowed	Divorced
...	...	...	...	...	...
1923–1919	25–29	576,906	999,145	4,360	13,735
1918–1914	30–34	225,562	761,011	5,577	21,545
1913–1909	35–39	244,276	1,224,124	15,628	43,981
...	...	...	...	...	...

TABLE 3.12b.   *France: Estimated Male Population by Age and Marital Status, January 1, 1950*

Year of Birth	Age-Group in Completed Years	Single	Married	Widowed	Divorced
...	...	...	...	...	...
1924–1920	25–29	605,389	1,089,336	4,376	14,043
1919–1915	30–34	208,298	707,398	4,754	18,935
1914–1910	35–39	237,018	1,213,586	14,033	44,826
...	...	...	...	...	...

We get 1,028 marriages $(81+82+107+68+93+73+100+88+122+214 = 1,028)$ of widowers between 30 and 35 years old in a mean population of 5,165 male widowers of the same age $(5,577+4,754 \div 2 = 5,165)$. The marriage rate for widowers is therefore:

$$\frac{1,028 \times 1,000}{5,165} = 199 \text{ per } 1,000.$$

Notice that the various marriage rates by age are calculated by relating the appropriate number of marriages to the appropriate number of marriageable persons, that is, to persons who are "exposed" to the possibility of marriage. This is so whether the marriage rates are calculated for single persons, for widows and widowers, or for divorced persons; when a general marriage rate is calculated, it follows that the total number of marriages is related to the total population of persons single, widowed, and divorced (that is, the total population in whatever age groups are being studied, but excluding those that are married).

Limitations of Age-Specific Rates

If we want to calculate an age-specific mortality rate, the first necessity is to have a very accurate count of the number of deaths occurring at the age under consideration during the year studied.[5] A similar need also arises if we want to calculate any of the other age-specific rates.

In order to get a relative measure of reality this absolute number of deaths occurring at the indicated age must be related to the *mean number of the population studied*, which is, however, a fairly fluid concept. It arises from the need to know how many persons could possibly die at the age in question during the course of the calendar year. But even if the number of persons who are alive and at that age varies but little during the course of the year, the group of persons who are exposed to the mortality risk in question does not remain the same throughout the course of the year. Individuals are continually leaving our field of observation because they have reached the maximum age in which we are interested, while other individuals are continually entering the field of observation because they have attained the minimum age required for being so included and observed. This is shown quite clearly in the *Lexis* diagram.

Thus, in Figure 3.4 (a reproduction of Figure 3.1b), the oldest persons of the 1913 birth cohort and the youngest persons of the 1914 birth cohort

5. Age in complete years: we may recall that this refers to deaths between two successive birthdays. Accordingly, the deaths at age 40 are deaths that occur between the 40th and 41st birthdays.

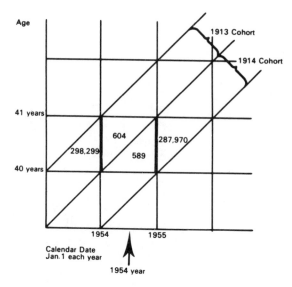

Figure 3.4

are observed for only a short time (Figure 3.5a); those who are born a little before or a little after January 1, 1914, are observed for the longest period of time (Figure 3.5b).

These exits and entries during the period of observation, and the resulting ambiguity in the definition of the mean number of population, occur in the course of work on age groups as well, though to a lesser extent; there are entries and exits only for the two extreme birth cohorts, although six annual cohorts are required in order to observe the vital events of interest for a five-year age group (see Figure 3.2b).

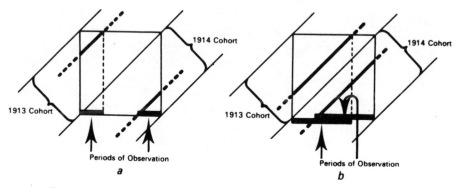

Figure 3.5

One way of avoiding this inconvenience consists in observing vital events by birth cohort, but then it is necessary to forego measurements of mortality, fertility, and marriage between exact ages.

Rates by Birth Cohort

Let us develop the idea of a cohort rate for the case of mortality. What is meant by "the cohort mortality rate at age 40 years in 1954"? All persons attaining their 40th birthday in the year 1954 belong to the 1914 birth cohort. (These are those whose life lines cross the segment *LN* in Figure 3.6.)

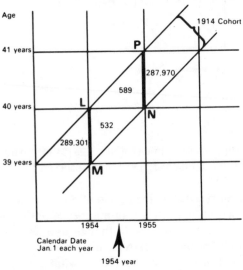

Figure 3.6

The deaths in this cohort during the calendar year 1954 occur both before the 40th birthday (that is, at age 39 complete years and in the triangle *LMN*) and after the 40th birthday (at age 40 complete years and in triangle *LNP*). We might say that "on the average" they occur at 40 years of age, that is, a little before and a little after the 40th birthday.

In the cohort rate, deaths in the parallelogram *LMNP* are related to the mean of the populations at segments *LM* and *PN* (the mean number in the cohort during the course of the period). The numerical data used are shown in Figure 3.6. We find for the mean number of the cohort during the course of the period:

$$\frac{289{,}301 + 287{,}970}{2} = 288{,}635.$$

and for the number of deaths:

$$532 + 589 = 1,121.$$

The corresponding rate from these figures is:

$$\frac{1,121 \times 1,000}{288,635} = 3.9 \text{ per } 1,000.$$

Mortality is thus studied at an "age" less strictly defined than is the case for rates between exact ages.[6] But, on the other hand, it is studied in precisely defined human groups that are kept in observation throughout the course of the calendar year chosen for study. This advantage is particularly marked when one wishes to study mortality (or fertility) for a single year of age. It is less marked when the study concerns several years of age.

Rates by Groups of Birth Cohorts

We draw again upon our example of mortality. To substitute a cohort group rate for the rate for the age group 40–44 years, the male cohorts to be considered are those attaining ages 40–44 years during the course of the year studied. These cohorts will be "on the average" 40–44 years of age during the course of the calendar year 1954.

Obviously this refers to the 1910–1914 birth cohorts. Therefore, we substitute for deaths in the rectangle $LML'M'$ the deaths in the parallelogram $PQL'M'$ (compare Figure 3.7).

For the calculation it is necessary to know: (1) the number in the 1910–1914 cohort group as of January 1, 1954 (the group aged 39–43 complete years on that date), which is 1,476,246, and (2) the number in the 1910–1914 cohort group on January 1, 1955 (those in the age group 40–44 complete years at that date), which is 1,468,344.

From (1) and (2) one can compute the mean number during the course of the period:

$$\frac{1,476,246 + 1,468,344}{2} = 1,472,295.$$

6. It may be noticed, however, that for a given age the deaths taken in the computation of a cohort rate occur at ages a little younger than deaths entering the computation of rates between exact ages. Consequently cohort rates will be a little higher than corresponding rates between exact ages for the period of life where mortality diminishes with age (between 0 and 11 years, approximately), and a little less in the period where it increases with age (over 11 years). In fact, here the rate at 40 years equals 4.1 per 1,000 if it is computed in exact ages and 3.9 per 1,000 if it is computed by cohorts.

We must also know (3) the deaths in the 1910–1914 cohort group during the course of the year 1954:

$$532 + 589 + 604 + 685 + 623 + 752 + 755 + 739 + 801 + 820 = 6,900.$$

From these data, the corresponding rate is:

$$\frac{6,900 \times 1,000}{1,472,295} = 4.7 \text{ per } 1,000,$$

a lower rate than by the previous definition (4.9 per 1,000). The application of these procedures to calculation of fertility and marriage rates is obvious.

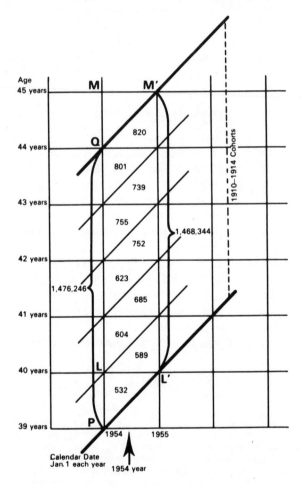

Figure 3.7

Choice of Rates

We ourselves prefer cohort rates or cohort group rates, with which there is never any ambiguity concerning the population being studied. The definition is more satisfactory theoretically, and it also avoids certain difficulties sometimes encountered in using rates between exact ages. To illustrate this, let us calculate the legitimate fertility rates at 29, 30, and 31 years of age in France for 1949. We label these rates f_{29}, f_{30}, and f_{31}. The data used are shown in Figure 3.8a.

$$f_{29} = \frac{(26{,}017 + 17{,}795)\,1{,}000}{\dfrac{164{,}641 + 278{,}213}{2}} = \frac{(43{,}812) \times (1{,}000)}{221{,}427} = 198 \text{ per } 1{,}000.$$

$$f_{30} = \frac{(12{,}028 + 12{,}615)\,1{,}000}{\dfrac{148{,}434 + 167{,}776}{2}} = \frac{(24{,}643) \times (1{,}000)}{158{,}105} = 156 \text{ per } 1{,}000.$$

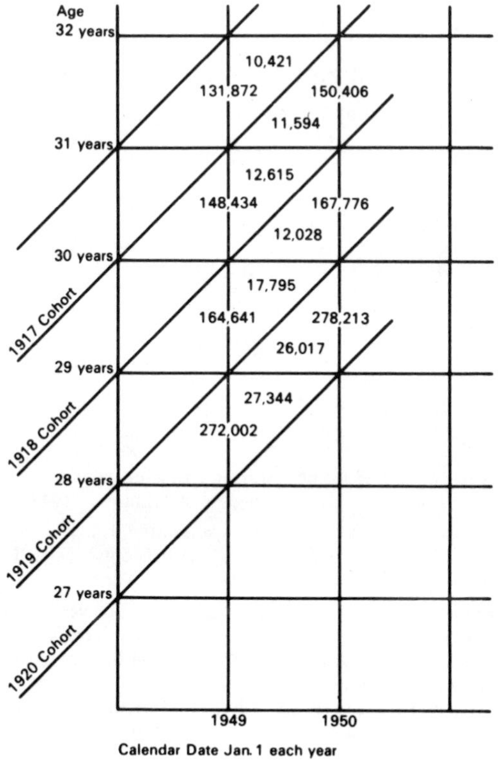

Figure 3.8a

$$f_{31} = \frac{(11,594+10,421)\,1,000}{\dfrac{131,872+150,406}{2}} = \frac{(22,015)\times(1,000)}{141,139} = 156 \text{ per } 1,000.$$

According to these indices, the fertility seems stationary between ages 30 and 31, but it decreased just prior to age 30 years.

In fact, we arrive at a net underestimate of actual fertility at age 29 years, for in our calculation we mix married women in two adjacent cohorts.[7] These two cohorts of women are unequal in size (164,641 and 278,213), and the more numerous group has—all other things being equal— a slightly higher fertility rate because it is a little younger on the average.[8] Similarly, and for the same reasons, we overestimate, but much less, the fertility rate at ages 30 and 31 years.

To this first cause of bias another is added: the births in the 1919 generation, studied in 1949, are unequally distributed in the two triangles of the *Lexis* diagram (17,795 and 12,028).[9] In the calculation of rates between exact ages, other things being equal, this distribution minimizes the fertility at age 30 years.

When we calculate cohort rates, which we may denote by f'_{29}, f'_{30}, and f'_{31}, all these disadvantages disappear. We obtain:

$$f'_{29} = \frac{(27,344+26,017)\,1,000}{\dfrac{272,002+278,213}{2}} = \frac{(53,361)\,1,000}{275,108} = 194 \text{ per } 1,000.$$

$$f'_{30} = \frac{(17,795+12,028)\,1,000}{\dfrac{164,641+167,776}{2}} = \frac{29,823\,(1,000)}{166,209} = 179 \text{ per } 1,000.$$

$$f'_{31} = \frac{(12,615+11,594)\,1,000}{\dfrac{148,434+150,406}{2}} = \frac{(24,209)\,1,000}{149,420} = 162 \text{ per } 1,000.$$

7. This has reference to cohorts of women born in the same calendar year, here in 1919 and in 1920, of whom we consider only those married as of January 1, 1949, and January 1, 1950.

8. To clarify this explanation let us specify that legitimate fertility in populations practicing birth control diminishes consistently with age. For a specific analysis of this phenomenon, see the chapter on natality.

9. This fact is not peculiar to the year 1949; it is observed in each year for the cohort of women born in 1919. This fact is true because the births of 1919 were largely concentrated at the end of the year (35 percent of the births in the last three months, instead of 25 percent, which would have been the case in a uniform distribution), a result of the return home of men mobilized during World War I. Thus, in this cohort a larger than usual fraction of the women would be having babies each year prior to their birthdays; thus, we have a large accumulation of births in the lower triangle of the *Lexis* diagram (17,795 births as contrasted with 12,028 births).

For the 1915 cohort we see the inverse phenomenon for the opposite reasons: a large accumulation of births in the first three months of the year.

and our description is free of the anomalies indicated above. It becomes clear that the female legitimate fertility rate at *exactly* 29 years of age (f_{29}) in 1949 is plainly less than 198 per 1,000; the rate $f'_{29} = 194$ per 1,000 furnishes an upper bound for f_{29}.[10] Conversely, $f_{30} = 156$ per 1,000 is too low, for it is lower than $f'_{31} = 162$ per 1,000, which gives a lower bound.[11]

Not only are cohort rates sometimes better measuring instruments, they are also better analytical tools. Because they detail perfectly the role of the different cohorts in determining, for example, the fertility in a calendar year, they also permit partitioning the fertility into one part that may be ascribed to the conditions of the calendar year studied, and another part that may be ascribed to the nature of the different cohorts observed.

In practice, a choice between the two categories of indices is only rarely possible. In the first place, data permitting this choice (double classification of vital events by cohorts and by duration in units of time elapsed) exist for only a few countries. They are not available in England or in the United States. In any case, the question of choice does not arise in numerous studies where such refined treatment of the data is beyond the purpose of the study. However, when making comparisons among countries, it is important to verify which type of rate has been used. Thus, the French rates that are given in statistics of vital events published by the INSEE are rates by cohort groups; they differ from the rates of most other countries, which are rates by age groups.

American and British Statistics

Most of the considerations in the preceding sections have no direct application in the many countries—including the United States and Great Britain—that do not practice double classification of vital events by duration or age as well as by cohort. In these countries the available data correspond to those required for the calculation of conventionally defined rates.

Thus if we wish to compute the age-specific fertility rate at ages 25–29 years for the United States in 1961,[12] we have:

number of births to women aged 25–29
    complete years: 1,081,706
female population aged 25–29 complete years
    on July 1, 1961:   5,489,000.

---

10. Since f_{29} is related to women aged 29 years on the average and f'_{29} is related to women aged 29.5 years on the average, and taking account of note 8.

11. Which is seen by reasoning identical to that of note 10 above.

12. See *Vital Statistics of the United States* 1961, Vol. I., Natality.

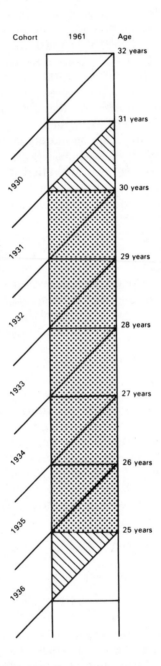

Figure 3.8b

From these figures we derive the rate:

$$\frac{(1,081,706) \times 1,000}{5,489,000} = 197.1 \text{ per } 1,000.$$

This presentation of statistics leads to difficulties when it is desirable, for purposes of longitudinal analysis (see p. 66), to identify and collect all the vital events characterizing a well-defined group of cohorts. Thus, the births noted above pertain to the 1931 to 1936 cohorts inclusively, as shown in Figure 3.8b. But we can readily see that the 1936 cohort also participated in the births occurring in 1961 to women in the 20–24 year age group (cross-hatched area); similarly, the 1931 cohort participated in the births in the 30–34 year age group. In short, difficulties occur because age groups and birth cohort groups do not coincide.

Quotients and Probabilities

Quotients give a measure of mortality, fertility, and nuptiality in cohorts between two exact ages, which need not be consecutive. This type of measure derives from a probabilistic approach to vital events. We can show how it works by taking mortality again as an example.

Let us consider a birth cohort of individuals; for example, the cohort of males in France that was born in 1914. Let us enumerate those who reach their 40th birthdays; some of them will die before their 41st birthday. The quotient of mortality at age 40 years in this cohort is defined as the proportion among males reaching their 40th birthday who die prior to their 41st birthday. The quotient of mortality at 40 years of age thus measures very precisely the risk of death between exact ages 40 and 41 years in the group being studied. In fact, it is the probability that any particular person who reached age 40 died before he reached 41.

The 1914 cohort reached 40 years of age during the year 1954, and 41 years of age during the year 1955 (Figure 3.9). The proportion defining the probability of mortality at 40 years of age is given by the ratio:

$$\frac{\text{deaths in the parallelogram } LL'MM'}{\text{the total number in } LL'}$$

All that has been said thus far presumes that the population has no migratory exchanges with foreign countries. The type of refinements that must otherwise be made to the calculation will be examined in connection with the construction of life tables.

We have no means of knowing directly the size of a cohort attaining any given exact age (the number in LL'). Under the conditions of actual statistical observation, we only know the size of a cohort (and, more generally, of a population) at a given instant (by census or estimate); in other words, we only know the flow across vertical segments of the *Lexis* diagram, such as *L'M*. In this case, the flow refers to the size of the 1914 male cohort on January 1, 1955, which is 287,970 men according to the estimates of the INSEE.

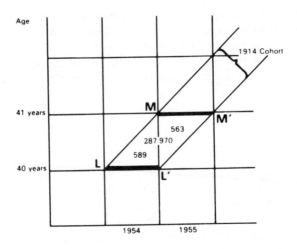

Figure 3.9

If the population is closed, the flow across the segment *LL'* (i.e., the number of males in the cohort reaching 40 years) can be obtained by adding to 287,970 the number of deaths in the triangle *LML'* (i.e., by adding the deaths at 40 complete years of age in the 1914 cohort during the year 1954). According to the data for vital events in 1954, these male deaths total 589. The initial total with reference to which we measure the risk of death is thus:

$$287,970 + 589 = 288,559 \text{ males.}$$

In order to get a figure for deaths at 40 complete years of age in this group, it is necessary to add to 589 the deaths in the triangle *L'MM'* (i.e., the deaths at 40 complete years in the 1914 cohort during the year 1955). According to the data for vital events in 1955, these male deaths were 563 in number. The total is therefore: $589 + 563 = 1,152$ deaths.

The quotient of mortality for males aged 40 years in the 1915 cohort then comes to:

$$\frac{1,152}{288,559} = 0.004 \text{ or } 4.0 \text{ per } 1,000.$$

We have just calculated an annual quotient; we can similarly calculate five-year, ten-year, etc., quotients that measure the risks during age intervals of five years, ten years, etc. The five-year quotient at 40 years of age measures the risk of dying between the 40th birthday and the 45th birthday for persons having attained the age of 40.

As we have defined them, quotients are probabilities that require calculations for cohorts that are observed during two consecutive calendar years (in the case of annual quotients), during six calendar years (for five-year quotients), etc. The problem of definition of a quotient (annual, five-year, etc.) on the basis of vital events in a single calendar year will be studied below.[13]

These definitions and methods of calculation are in principle transferable to quotients of fertility and of marriage. Often the measurement of "risks" of fertility and of marriage in the pure state demand certain supplementary precautions, which will be indicated in the corresponding chapters.

Concern with quotients or probabilities is particularly shown in the construction of tables, life tables being the most familiar and having the longest history. The idea of probability arises also in the conventional measure of infant mortality.

Infant Mortality Rates

The infant mortality rate is intended to measure mortality between 0 and 1 year of age. Despite its name, it is in fact the annual quotient of mortality at 0 years of age.

The correct method of calculating this index is the same as that shown in the preceding section. This time the flow across LL' (Figure 3.10) is known directly, since it concerns live births in the year 1954 (807,208). The last deaths amongst this birth cohort under 1 year of age occur at the end of 1955. Examining the data on vital statistics for the years 1954 and 1955, we know that the number of deaths at age 0 (in complete years) in 1954 to children born in 1954 (in the triangle LML') is 21,286 deaths.

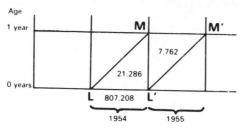

Figure 3.10

13. We take up this problem below in connection with study of infant mortality rates.

Deaths at age 0 (in complete years) in 1955 to those born in 1954 ($L'MM'$) total 7,762.

For the 1954 generation there was thus a total of:

$$21,286 + 7,762 = 29,048 \text{ deaths under 1 year of age.}$$

The infant mortality rate is then:

$$\frac{29,048 \times 1,000}{807,208} = 36.0 \text{ per } 1,000.$$

But 36.0 per 1,000 measures neither the 1954 nor the 1955 infant mortality rate. We must modify the above computation, though the procedure is in principle irreproachable, in order to obtain a period measure infant mortality.

It is evident that all the deaths under one year of age that occurred in 1954 must be included in this measure (deaths in the square $LPML'$, Figure 3.11). We now recall a difficulty mentioned before with reference to rates: to what size of population should these deaths be related?

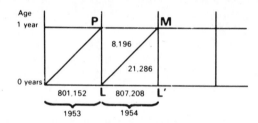

Figure 3.11

Methods of calculating the Infant Mortality Rate

The most common method of calculating the infant mortality rate is to relate infant deaths in the calendar year to live births in the same year. Thus, with the data of Figure 3.11, the conventional infant mortality rate derived for 1954 is:

$$\frac{(21,286 + 8,196)\, 1,000}{807,208} = 36.5 \text{ per } 1,000.$$

Though somewhat unsatisfactory in principle (it relates certain deaths—those in the triangle LMP—to births of a different period), this method quite often gives completely acceptable results. Nevertheless, if variations in the number of births from one year to the next are considerable (as they were, for example, in France from 1945 to 1946), the results can be gravely in error.

The number of deaths in the triangle *LMP* obviously depends upon the number of births in the calendar year 1953. Nevertheless, these deaths depend less on the 1953 births than do the deaths in 1954, for mortality amongst infants is ordinarily (other things being equal) much greater the younger the infants are, and the children of the 1954 cohort are (obviously) younger in 1954 than the children of the 1953 cohort are in 1954.

These considerations, extended by appropriate calculations, lead to the construction of the divisor required to compute the infant mortality rate in 1954, for example, in the following manner:

1/3 of the births in 1953+2/3 of the births in 1954,[14]

which gives

$$\frac{801,152+2\times807,208}{3} = 805,189$$

and leads to a slight correction of the rate initially computed:

$$\frac{29,482\times1,000}{805,189} = 36.6 \text{ (instead of 36.5) per 1,000.}$$

In this case the correction is of no significance; however, it is justified for the year 1946, where the deviations are of quite a different magnitude (see Figure 3.12).

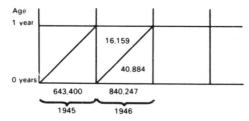

Figure 3.12

First computation:

Divisor:	840,247 births.
Dividend:	40,884+16,159 = 57,043 deaths.
Infant mortality rate:	$\dfrac{(57,043)\,1,000}{840,247} = 67.9 \text{ per 1,000.}$

14. The coefficients 1/3 and 2/3 are approximate. In fact, these coefficients depend on the distribution of deaths during the first year of life, a distribution that varies according to the level of mortality. For a quite low level of infant mortality the coefficients 1/4 and 3/4 would be more appropriate. But fairly wide variability in the choice of coefficients is acceptable, since it does not entail any sizable errors in the determination of the rates. In France the National Statistics Institute has adopted the coefficients 1/4 and 3/4.

Second computation:

Divisor:
$$\frac{643,400 + 2 \times 840,247}{3} = 774,631 \text{ births.}$$

Dividend: $40,884 + 16,159 = 57,043$ deaths.

Infant mortality rate:
$$\frac{(57,043)\,1,000}{774,631} = 73.6 \text{ per } 1,000.$$

This method of constructing the divisor is called the method of the *weighted mean*, and is quite common in demographic computations.

The calculation of infant mortality rates for periods shorter than a year (the quarter or the month) also requires weighting of births, but the details will be described in the chapter on mortality.[15]

Note that when we are fortunate enough to have a double classification of deaths of the kind indicated in Figure 3.12, a more correct method of calculation can be used. This method relates the two categories of deaths respectively to the categories of births that correspond to them. In the case of the data of Figure 3.12 we have

$$\frac{(16,159)\,1,000}{643,400} + \frac{(40,884)\,1,000}{840,247} = 25.1 + 48.7 = 73.8 \text{ per } 1,000.$$

This is a rigorous method, if the mortality during the calendar year of birth is the same in the two cohorts. The weighted mean method, presented above, is only a substitute for this method.

Conversion of Rates to an Annual Basis

All the indices—rates or quotients—that we have introduced in this chapter have been calculated on the basis of an interval of observation of a single year: they are annual rates or quotients. Conditions of observation or the requirements of analysis may demand calculation of rates or quotients for periods longer or shorter than a year. The order of magnitude of the indices is thus affected, and immediate comparison with annual rates or quotients is impossible.

In what follows we restrict ourselves to the usual problem of the comparison of rates constructed for different periods of observation: this is resolved by conversion to a rate on an annual basis. For example: suppose we wish to calculate the crude death rate in France for the first quarter of 1949.

15. In our computations of infant mortality rates we have not taken account of misclassified stillbirths; that is, infants born alive but dying prior to a registration of the birth (which, in France, may take as long as three days), which for this reason are registered as stillbirths. This correction will be described in the chapter on mortality.

During the first quarter there were 198,138 deaths. The mean population was estimated at 41,468,950.[16] By division we get:

$$\frac{198,138 \times 1,000}{41,468,950} = 4.78 \text{ per } 1,000,$$

a rate that is markedly lower than the annual rate, since it is calculated on a period about one-fourth as long.

Conversion of this rate to an annual rate comprises calculating a rate from the deaths that would occurr in 365 days at the same intensity of mortality as during the 90 days $(31 + 28 + 31)$ of the first quarter of 1949. The number of deaths based on a full year will be equal to:

$$\frac{198,138 \times 365}{90} = 803,741 \text{ deaths.}$$

From the annual rate (retaining the same mean population) is:

$$\frac{803,741 \times 1,000}{41,468,950} = 19.4 \text{ per } 1,000.$$

This rate may be compared with the crude rate for the year 1949 (13.7 per 1,000), a comparison that indicates the higher levels of mortality characteristic of the winter.[17]

Notice a useful idea implied in the preceding computations: *the mean daily number of events*, during a given period—here, the mean daily number of deaths during the first quarter of 1949. This is equal to:

$$\frac{198,138}{90} = 2,202.$$

It is by multiplying this mean daily number by 365 that one finds the number 803,741 for annual deaths (with an error of a few units, since the mean daily number is rounded off). Use of the mean daily number of events is a convenient way of measuring seasonal changes in demographic phenomena.

General Considerations and Suggestions

We will postpone an examination of rates and probabilities as tools of demographic analysis for the methodological chapters that follow. Here

16. The volume of statistics concerning vital events for the years 1949 and 1950 gives population estimates only for January 1, 1949, and January 1, 1950, which are 41, 424, 500 and 41,780,100, respectively. Assuming regular (linear) growth between the two dates, we arrive at the number 41,468,950 as the mean population in the first quarter of 1949.

17. If the year had been a leap year it would have been necessary to calculate what would have been the number of deaths on the base of a year having 366 days, including 91 days in the first quarter.

the intention is to furnish the practical means of computing a number of common indices. We have also attempted to present these techniques by drawing as much as possible upon examples taken from actual statistics.

The reader will find it profitable to check the sources, since the practical problems begin with the collection of appropriate data from the various statistical tables. He could extend the work of checking by computing rates and quotients for different years and different countries. In summary, it is important to study this chapter yery carefully in order to acquire the techniques that are simple yet indispensable to any demographic work.

Part II
VITAL EVENTS

CHAPTER FOUR

Analysis of Vital Events

BY *vital events* we mean births, deaths, marriages, and termination of marital unions. Let us recall that the main body of quantitative information concerning vital events is the subject of the statistics of *population change*. In general, it is also possible to reconstruct facts concerning past vital events on the basis of censuses or surveys of the population in question. We present here some general observations concerning methods of analysis of vital events.

Demography as a Science of Rates

The study of vital events made such consistent use of rates in the past that these rates may still appear to some people to be the most refined tools available for demographic analysis. In the present volume, we have ourselves devoted several pages to their definition and calculation.

In fact, however specific and detailed they may be, demographic rates do not as a rule provide the best description of demographic data; their analytical power is often weak, and they are sometimes highly abstract. Without rejecting their use, we should be wary of automatic recourse to these indices, which may sometimes be advantageously replaced by other methods or analytical tools.

Rates and Their Limits

Crude rates (crude death rates, crude birth rates, etc.), for which computation is generally easy, permit somewhat broad but nevertheless very useful comparisons. They cannot themselves analyze correctly the phenomena of mortality, natality, etc., but they measure the relative numbers of deaths and of births in the human population groups investigated and permit comparison from one year to the next within the same population. In certain cases, these are the essential characteristics of the demographic situation.

A first refinement consists in the calculation of rates by age: it recognizes that the age of individuals plays an essential role in the explanation of the phenomenon investigated. In fact, such rates are very appropriate in the study of mortality. In the study of fertility and of nuptiality their use is more limited; without rejecting them arbitrarily, it is necessary to recognize that numerous other measures are sometimes better adapted and have greater meaning.

Rates can be refined further: the subpopulations for which it is possible to calculate this type of measure are very numerous. Let us restrict ourselves to nuptiality. Having distinguished female and male nuptiality, it is possible to calculate rates by age. To continue refinement of the analysis, it is possible to restrict the calculation to first marriages, i.e., to calculate rates of marriage for single (never married) persons. The study of re-marriages leads similarly to calculation of marriage rates (by age) of widowed persons and marriage rates (by age) of divorced persons.

The procedure seems logical. However, all has not yet been said about nuptiality. For certain facets of nuptiality, the preceding analysis would lead to serious shortcomings. For example, such an analysis does not permit a response to the following type of question, which is indeed an obvious one: what is the effect of age at widowhood upon the remarriage of widows?

Quotients and Tables

By definition, quotients differ markedly from rates. They are tied to a probabilistic conception of vital events. Quotients measure a risk: for example, the risk among persons attaining 20 years of age of dying between the ages of 20 and 21 years or between the ages of 20 and 25 years. Their use is primarily in that they comprise the basis for construction of *synthetic tables*, sometimes describing the phenomenon investigated in a very striking way, e.g., life tables, nuptiality tables.

Period Observations and Cohort Observations

We now introduce an essential distinction to which we will return constantly when studying methods of analysis of vital events. The conditions of statistical observation lead us quite naturally to events that occur during a given interval of time (most often a single year or a group of calendar years) in a given population group. We will call these *period* observations, e.g., the observation of deaths in France in 1956.

With such data it is possible to compute various rates. However, certain concepts, which enter naturally into a study of demographic phenomena, cannot be introduced without using special procedures. We do not see, for instance, how to define and compute the average length of life in 1956[1] until we have more data than the deaths by age in 1956.

On the other hand, if our observations concern a birth cohort—that is, a group of persons born in a given calendar year until the complete disappearance of that cohort by death—then the notion of an average length of life comes readily to mind, and the notion of rate has no natural place in our description.

Observation by birth cohorts (or *generation*) is a special case of the mode of observation by *cohort*. We understand by *cohort* a group of persons experiencing the same vital event during the same interval of time, usually during the same calendar year. For example, when referring to newborns of the year 1956, we may speak readily of "the 1956 birth cohort." But we may speak also of the cohort married in 1956 or of the cohort of women giving birth to their third child in 1956, etc.

Hypothetical Cohorts

The deaths in a calendar year—for example, the deaths in the year 1956 in France—involved persons belonging to about a hundred birth cohorts. Let us imagine a hypothetical cohort of 10,000 or of 100,000 newborn children, and let us follow this cohort through all the ages of life, assuming that the deaths occurring therein at the various ages occur with the intensity that was observed at the various ages in France in 1956.[2]

By thus transposing data derived from observations actually made upon about a hundred real and distinct cohorts onto one hypothetical cohort, the mortality situation of a single year can be stated in terms applicable to a single cohort. It is hence possible to say that in the years 1950–1951 the mean length of life of a male in France was 63.6 years.

Similarly, we may construct hypothetical cohorts of women married in the same year, to whom are applied the observed fertility characteristics of the whole group of women during a given calendar year according to the different durations of marriage. We can then say that in 1950, on the average, 2.35 children were born per marriage in France.

1. It is not, however, the mean age of persons dying in France during that year. When we present life tables we will indicate why this notion is very seriously in error.
2. We do not indicate more for the time being; a concise examination of this problem of transposition will be undertaken in connection with the presentation of life tables.

   This transposition is not always effected without difficulty, and one of the objects of analysis is to specify how to do it.

Study of Real Cohorts

   With modern statistics, observations upon real cohorts usually come from relating observations made during successive calendar years. Let us show how such a comparison may be carried out by reconstructing the mortality losses sustained by the 1950 male birth cohort (the total of boys born in 1950). Table 4.1 indicates what is assumed to hold for all of the annual statistics of population change (from 1950 to 1957). These data are shown in the *Lexis* diagram in Figure 4.1.

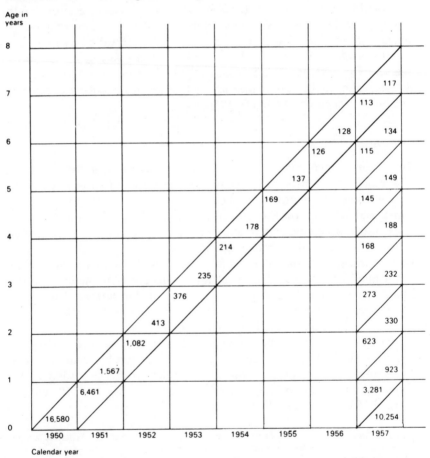

Figure 4.1

TABLE 4.1.   *France: Deaths in the 1950 Male Generation*

Year for which Vital Statistics used	Age at Death (in completed years)	Deaths
1950	0	16,580
1951	{ 0 (before birthday)	6,461
	{ 1 (after birthday)	1,567
1952	{ 1 (before birthday)	1,082
	{ 2 (after birthday)	413
1953	{ 2 (before birthday)	376
	{ 3 (after birthday)	235
1954	{ 3 (before birthday)	214
	{ 4 (after birthday)	178
1955	{ 4 (before birthday)	169
	{ 5 (after birthday)	137
1956	{ 5 (before birthday)	126
	{ 6 (after birthday)	128
1957	{ 6 (before birthday)	113
	{ 7 (after birthday)	117

SOURCES: 1950–1951, I.N.S.E.E.—Statistique du mouvement de la population, Paris 1956.

1952–1957.—Various quarterly supplements of the Monthly Statistical Bulletin.

This mode of reconstruction of the events affecting cohorts is quite general. In analogous fashion, the composition of the offspring of a cohort of married females can be followed, or the nuptiality of a cohort of males can be studied. Notice that, on the basis of censuses and surveys, questions bearing upon the history of individuals (e.g., the birth of children in a single family) permit direct observation of cohorts or, at least, of that part of cohorts surviving to the time of the census or survey inquiry.[3]

Cohort Analysis and Period Analysis

When a demographic analysis applies to events happening to a single cohort, we speak of a *cohort* analysis. In the preceding paragraph, for instance, we assembled data permitting a cohort analysis of the mortality of the 1950 male birth cohort. We may speak also of *longitudinal* or *generation* analysis.

---

3. Nevertheless, this observation is biased to the extent that persons not remaining in the population (dying, emigrating) have characteristics different from those persons reached by the census or survey. We shall detail some examples when we study fertility.

When the analysis applies to a category of events experienced by a group of cohorts during a given year (or in a period of years), we then speak of a *period* analysis. For instance, we may be interested in deaths in the year 1957; these deaths take place among about a hundred different birth cohorts; we may speak also of *current* or *cross-sectional* analysis.

Events assembled for a cohort analysis are indicated in an "oblique column" in the *Lexis* diagram; those assembled for a period analysis are indicated in a "vertical column" (see Figure 4.1).

A Paradigm in Demography

We owe to Louis Henry a very fruitful mode of analysis of vital phenomena. In demography it is always of interest to relate the observed event to an event that *necessarily* precedes it. Thus it is possible to think of: (1) death as logically dependent upon birth; (2) first marriage as dependent upon birth (or upon survival to the minimal age for marriage); (3) remarriage as dependent upon termination of a marriage (distinguishing here between widowhood and divorce); (4) birth of a first child as dependent upon marriage; birth of a second child as dependent upon the birth of a first child; (5) birth of a child of the order $(n+1)$ as dependent upon birth of a child of the nth order, etc.

This indicates the great generality of the paradigm. We will explain it for each of the above cases in connection with the methodological study of the corresponding demographic phenomena. Let us illustrate here the kind of description sought by taking as an example the nuptiality of widowed persons.

The study of the remarriage of widows as an event logically following and consequent upon their widowhood brings us to the question: among 1,000 women who are widowed in a given year, how many remarry? The immediate answer will not be very meaningful because of variation in the age at widowhood: a first stage in the analysis will be to study the proportion of remarriages among women widowed *at a given age*. Thus, for example, what is the proportion remarrying among women widowed between the ages of 25 and 30 years? A previous study (*Population*, January–March, 1956) gave 69 percent as the proportion.

A complementary question: among women widowed at ages 25 to 29 and who do remarry, what is the distribution of durations of widowhood (intervals between widowhood and remarriage)? In terms less exact but more immediately intelligible: how long does it take women widowed at ages 25 to 29 years to remarry?

The complete study of remarriage shows that among women widowed under 45, at whatever age they were widowed, there is no great difference in the distribution of intervals between widowhood and remarriage. Among every 100 women widowed between ages 20 to 45 years:

  5   remarried in the first year of widowhood,
 18   remarried in the second year of widowhood,
14.5 remarried in the third year of widowhood,
12.0 remarried in the fourth year of widowhood,
 9.3 remarried in the fifth year of widowhood,
 7.2 remarried in the sixth year of widowhood, etc.

We can continue (imperfectly) the distribution of these intervals and then calculate the mean: the mean interval between widowhood and remarriage is 5.5 years (see Figure 4.2).

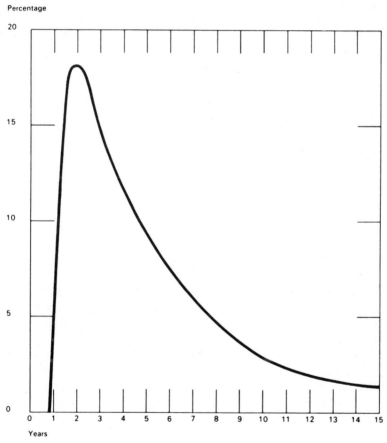

Figure 4.2. Distribution of Widowed Persons by Duration of Widowhood (per 100 total remarriages of females widowed at ages 20–45 years).

Let us isolate the idea of the study presented above and discuss it in rather general terms. It is possible to study any vital event B (here, the remarriage of widows) as logically following or dependent on an appropriately chosen prior event A (here, widowhood).

The complete description of the movement from A to B requires knowledge of: (1) the proportion of persons who, having undergone event A, experience event B (here the proportion of a group of widows who remarry, by age at widowhood); (2) the distribution of the intervals between event A and event B (here the distribution of the intervals between widowhood and remarriage).

Notice that this description uses the language of cohort analysis. Just as all the deaths in a single year can eventually give us the mean length of life characteristic of the mortality of that year, we can similarly analyze other demographic data for a given year and arrive at syntheses formally similar to the model we have just presented for widowhood and remarriage.

This mode of description is very expressive. The results to which it leads us for the remarriages of widows are more significant than any that can be obtained by employing even the most elaborate of rates. Let us take the tables of nuptiality for the years 1925–1927: What is the meaning of a marriage rate of 13.9 per 1,000 for widows aged 22 years (age of the maximum rate), even when compared with the marriage rate of 21.6 per 1,000 for single women at the same age (also the age of the maximum rate)?

CHAPTER FIVE

Mortality

THE STUDY of mortality has long served as a model for the study of other vital phenomena (nuptiality, natality). A simple identity of analytical methods is not made here, but it is no less true that certain elementary treatments of data are common to the study of mortality and other phenomena. Since the study of mortality does not require a very complex methodology, it seems appropriate to begin with it.

The Crude Death Rate: Its Variations in Time and Space

We may recall that the crude death rate in a given human population group is the relationship between deaths at all ages during a given period (usually a single year) and the mean population during the same period (see p. 30). For the prestatistical era, before the year 1800, it is difficult to determine exact levels of mortality. Even the best sources of information (parish registers) yield only partial information on this point.

It is certain that an *average* crude rate of about 45 to 50 per 1,000 must have been the upper limit of mortality that could obtain without threatening the survival of the species. What we know about fertility suggests that the maximum limit of the birth rate is about 45 to 50 per 1,000 and, very exceptionally, 55 per 1,000. But we are speaking of an *average* crude death rate, the outcome of fluctuations between "normal" or "non-catastrophic" mortality, which ought to have reached 30 to 35 per 1,000, and the exceptionally high mortality of years of epidemics, wars, and famine, which could have reached extremely high rates. These very considerable fluctuations are the dominant characteristics of historical mortality. They were observed in Western countries at the beginning of the statistical era and may still be observed in underdeveloped countries.

71

The decline of mortality in the West was the dominant demographic feature of the nineteenth century. There was, first of all, a decline in the frequency and a lessening of the severity of famine (which in France disappeared in the eighteenth century) and of epidemics: the curve of the trend in the crude rate became smooth because of the disappearance of occasional excessive mortality,[1] indicating at the same time a general downward movement in the rates. This downward movement has accelerated since 1900, although it is slowed by the progressive ageing of Western populations. To illustrate the general pattern of development, we may turn to Figure 5.1 where the trend of Swedish mortality (which can be followed since 1749) is traced.

The decline took place much later in the central and eastern Mediterranean countries of Europe, where it had barely begun at the close of the nineteenth century. Finally, the underdeveloped world, last to undergo this change, has seen its mortality decline since World War I; from levels of 30 per 1,000 and more, mortality has declined so that at present it rarely exceeds 20 per 1,000. It is plain that the change has been much more rapid than in the West.

While the continuing decline of mortality in France, England, and other countries is the outcome of joint progress in science, the economy, medical-social facilities, and the cultural level of the population, the decline in underdeveloped countries has resulted essentially from external medical help. In underdeveloped countries, modern medicine has succeeded in prolonging the life of individuals, though the level of living is virtually unchanged. This is because those causes of death that entail considerable loss of human life (notably, the serious epidemic diseases: plague, cholera, smallpox, and malaria) have become relatively easy to fight, and modern therapeutic methods (vaccinations, DDT, etc.) make the struggle less expensive. Table 5.1 makes a rapid review of the recent situation (1958 and 1965).

We have reproduced in this table only the figures from countries where the data are fairly reliable. Underregistration of deaths is too great to let us include the Moslem countries, for which we can estimate a general rate of about 20 per 1,000, or the countries of sub-Saharan Africa, which would appear to be at present the areas with the highest mortality. Nevertheless, we may cite the results of a sample survey in Guinea — then, French Guinea — in 1954–1955, giving a rate of 27 per 1,000 in the urban centers and 36 per 1,000 in the bush. For India, rates close to 20 per 1,000 in 1958, declining to about 14 per 1,000 in 1964, appear probable.

Leaving aside the underdeveloped countries where high mortality has persisted, the crude rates indicate, in general, a relatively narrow dispersion.

---

1. Aside from excess mortality due to wars.

Rate per
1,000 Population

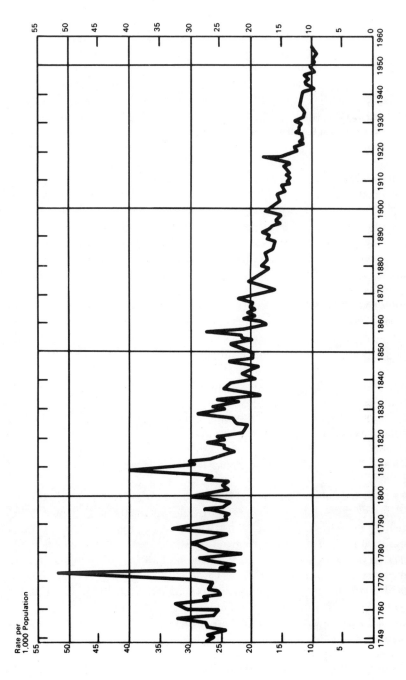

Figure 5.1.   Trend of Crude Death Rates in Sweden.

TABLE 5.1. *Crude Death Rate in 1958 and 1965 (per 1,000)*

	1958	*1965*
AFRICA		
Union of South Africa		
European Population	8.6	9.1
Colored Population	17.0	15.8
Asiatic Origin Population	8.2	8.1
NORTH AMERICA		
Canada	7.9	7.5
United States	9.5	9.4
Guatemala	21.3	16.8
Jamaica	8.8	7.9
Mexico	12.5	9.5
Panama	8.7	7.1
Puerto Rico	6.9	6.6
El Salvador	13.5	10.5
SOUTH AMERICA		
Argentina	8.1	8.2
Uruguay (1956) (1962)	7.0	7.8
Chile (1961)	12.1	11.2
Colombia (1964)	12.8	10.0
Ecuador (1964)	15.2	12.1
Venezuela (1964)	9.4	7.2
ASIA		
Israel	5.9	6.2
Japan	7.5	7.1
Ceylon	9.7	8.6
China (Mainland)	13.0	—
Taiwan	7.6	5.5
Hong Kong	7.5	4.6
Singapore	7.0	5.6
EUROPE		
West Germany	10.8	11.2
Austria	12.2	13.0
Belgium	11.7	12.1
Denmark	9.2	10.1
Finland	8.9	9.7
France	11.2	11.1
Great Britain	11.7	11.5
England and Wales	11.7	11.5
Scotland	10.8	12.1
Northern Ireland	12.0	10.6
Ireland	12.0	11.5
Norway	8.9	9.1
Netherlands	7.5	8.0
Sweden	9.6	10.1

TABLE 5.1 *(continued)*

	1958	*1965*
Switzerland	9.5	11.5
Spain	8.7	8.7
Greece (1964)	7.1	8.2
Italy	9.4	10.0
Portugal	10.2	10.3
Yugoslavia	9.2	8.7
Albania	9.3	9.0
East Germany	12.5	13.4
Bulgaria (1964)	7.9	7.9
Hungary	9.9	10.7
Poland	8.4	7.4
Rumania	8.7	8.6
Czechoslovakia	9.3	10.0
U.S.S.R.	7.2	7.3
OCEANIA		
Australia	8.4	8.8
New Zealand	8.9	8.7

France (11.2 per 1,000) ranks low relative to countries where the state of sanitation is notoriously poorer (for example, certain Mediterranean countries: Spain, 8.7 per 1,000; Greece, 7.1 per 1,000; Portugal, 10.2 per 1,000; Yugoslavia, 9.2 per 1,000—all in 1958). It may seem equally surprising that the United States (9.4 per 1,000) ranks below Puerto Rico (6.9 per 1,000). We shall touch here upon the limits of the crude rate and upon its inability to summarize the "risks of mortality" owing to variations in the *age composition of populations.*

The Composition of Mortality by Age and Sex

Current observation leads to the association of mortality with age; to specify this relationship, it is natural to compute rates by age or by age groups. For a given age, a separate calculation for each sex will show the differences between males and females. The correct calculation of these rates requires an appropriate classification of persons dying in the year under study and an estimate of the population by age. The necessary statistics and the technique of calculation have already been presented in detail (see p. 31). Let us give an idea of composition of mortality by age by showing the French, American, British, Canadian, Japanese, and Indian rates for recent years (Table 5.2).

TABLE 5.2. Age-Specific Mortality Rates (per 1,000) by Sex, and Index of Excess Male Mortality, Selected Countries

Age (years)	France, 1955			United States, 1964			Great Britain, 1966		
	Males	Females	Index of Excess Male Mortality	Males	Females	Index of Excess Male Mortality	Males	Females	Index of Excess Male Mortality
0	38.2	30.1	127	27.8	21.5	129	5.3	4.1	129
1–4	1.9	1.7	112	1.0	0.9	111	0.5	0.3	167
5–9	0.5	0.4	130	0.5	0.4	125	0.4	0.3	133
10–14	0.5	0.3	164	0.5	0.3	167	1.0	0.4	250
15–19	1.0	0.5	206	1.3	0.5	260	1.1	0.5	220
20–24	1.6	0.8	207	1.8	0.7	257			
25–29	1.9	1.0	181	1.8	0.9	200	1.1	0.7	157
30–34	2.3	1.4	169	2.2	1.3	169			
35–39	3.1	1.9	161	3.0	1.9	158	2.5	1.8	139
40–44	4.7	2.8	166	4.7	2.8	168			
45–49	7.5	4.2	179	7.4	4.2	176	7.4	4.5	164
50–54	11.8	6.2	192	12.0	6.4	188			
55–59	17.7	8.9	200	18.7	9.2	203	21.8	10.5	208
60–64	26.0	13.6	191	27.9	14.1	198			
65–69	38.2	22.0	174	42.4	22.3	190	54.0	29.2	185
70–74	74.9	49.7	151	59.1	34.4	172			
75–79				83.5	56.0	149	121.6	82.2	148
80–84	18.3	14.7	124	124.3	95.7	130	261.0	206.7	126
85				212.0	192.3	110			

Age	Canada, 1960			Japan, 1959			India, 1958–1959		
0	7.7	5.9	131	37.0	30.6	121	198.0	182.5	108
1– 4	0.7	0.4	175	3.0	2.6	115	42.6	45.4	94
5– 9	0.6	0.3	200	1.1	0.9	122	5.5	5.5	100
10–14	1.3	0.5	260	0.7	0.5	140			
15–19	1.5	0.6	250	1.2	0.8	150	3.5	5.4	65
20–24	1.5	0.7	214	2.2	1.4	157			
25–29	1.6	0.9	178	2.3	1.7	135	4.2	6.4	66
30–34	2.4	1.5	160	2.5	2.0	125			
35–39	3.3	2.1	157	3.0	2.4	125			
40–44	6.0	3.5	171	4.2	3.2	131	5.8	5.4	107
45–49	9.4	5.4	174	6.4	4.5	142			
50–54	15.5	8.1	191	10.2	6.8	150	12.8	8.0	160
55–59	24.3	13.3	183	16.8	10.3	163			
60–64	35.7	21.7	165	25.9	15.7	165	32.2	21.0	153
65–69	55.1	35.6	155	41.8	26.6	157			
70–74	83.5	59.6	140	67.5	45.9	147			
75–79	131.6	106.3	124	107.6	77.7	138	72.9	54.7	133
80–84	237.8	219.7	108	162.5	123.6	131			
85				241.0	200.9	120			

It is understood that the rates may be calculated by single years of age, but rates calculated for quinquennial age groups – or, indeed, for decennial age groups – usually suffice for current analyses. Exceptions must be made for infant mortality because it is particularly important.

Mortality begins at quite a high level at 0 years of age and then diminishes rapidly. It reaches its lowest level somewhere in the age group 10 to 14 years. After that, the increase is uninterrupted, and the new-born child's level of mortality is reached again at approximately 70 years of age.

At all ages, male mortality is higher than female mortality. This is the phenomenon of *male excess mortality*, which is measured by dividing the male rate by the female rate and multiplying the result by 100. The index thus obtained is easy to interpret. In the French example, the index 164 for the group aged 10 to 14 years[2] indicates that the male rate is 64 per cent greater than the female rate, or, alternatively, that for male and female populations of the same size (and at age 10 to 14 years) for every 100 female deaths there are, on the average, 164 male deaths.

Male excess mortality varies with age and among the different countries;[3] later, we shall reconsider male excess mortality in France. Let us note that the concept of excess mortality is quite general; it is applied to any population group in which general mortality, or mortality from some specified cause, is greater than that of one or several other population groups. Thus, we can speak of excess French mortality in general (relative, for example, to Dutch mortality or to Swedish mortality, etc.) just as we can speak of excess mortality of students owing to tuberculosis (relative to, for example, the mortality owing to tuberculosis of the total number of young persons of the same age who are not students).

A somewhat more detailed discussion of mortality by age in the different countries and the examination of its historical trends would require too great a digression here, but these questions are partly considered in connection with the presentation of life tables. We shall confine ourselves here to some brief remarks concerning the recent trends of mortality in the West.

1. Let us examine the case of France, comparing the year 1955 with the period 1935–1937. The crude rate went from 15.3 per 1,000 to 12.1 per 1,000, a decline of 21 per cent. At the same time, *at all ages* the age-specific rates underwent an even greater decline, ranging from 27 to 76 per cent (see Table 5.3). There is no contradiction between these two statements. The growth between 1935–1937 and 1955 in the proportion of aged persons in the French population was what held back the decline in the crude death

2. The result of the computation: $0.470/0.286 \times 100$.
3. The phenomenon is not absolutely general. In particular, there was excess female mortality for certain young age groups until the beginning of the twentieth century in several European countries.

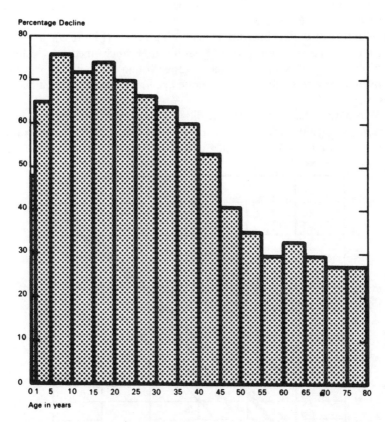

Figure 5.2. Percentage Decline in Mortality in France by Age (both sexes).

TABLE 5.3. *Percentage Decline in French Mortality Rates between 1935–1937 and 1955—Both Sexes*

Age (in years)	Decline (in %)	Age (in years)	Decline (in %)	Age (in years)	Decline (in %)
0	48	25–29	66	55–59	29
1– 4	65	30–34	64	60–64	33
5– 9	76	35–39	60	65–69	29
10–14	72	40–44	53	70–79	27
15–19	74	45–49	41	80 and over	27
20–24	70	50–54	35		

rate (for example, the proportion of the group "age 60 years and over" changed from 14.6 per cent to 16.2 per cent of the population).

The extent of the decline differs according to age (Figure 5.2 and Table 5.3), and the pattern does not only apply to France: medium decline of infant mortality, very great decline at other young ages and among young adults, and progressively more moderate declines at successively advancing ages.

The progress that is observed at older ages is even less apparent in the more recent period, for example, between 1947 and 1955. We shall examine the reasons for this when we study causes of deaths.

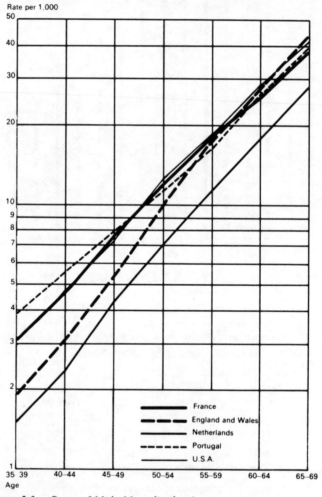

Figure 5.3.   Rates of Male Mortality by Ages.

2. Even in the case of comparable total levels of mortality, the composition of mortality by sex and by age may be quite different in different countries. Let us note the present differences in the West, as compared with the French level, summarized in Figures 5.3 and 5.4.

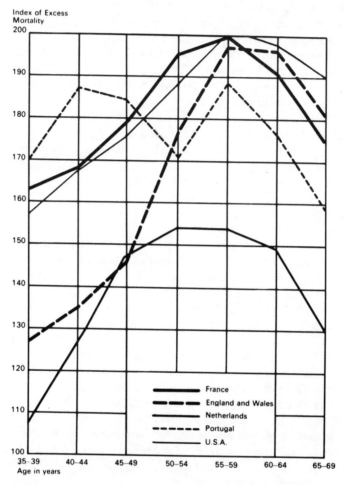

Figure 5.4. Male Excess Mortality by Age.

Figure 5.3 represents only male mortality between the ages of 35 and 65 years during the year 1955, in selected European countries:

a. In England and Wales, where mortality of young persons is quite low, the situation deteriorates with age and becomes even worse than that of France;

b. Italy has a pattern of mortality by age that tends the other way: high infant and juvenile mortality, relatively low mortality after 40 years of age (it has not been included in the diagram because of the absence of recent data); Spain and Portugal have a somewhat less favorable total level, but indicate the same pattern;

c. The Netherlands has much lower mortality—at all ages—than any of the countries previously cited. The Scandinavian countries have comparable levels: Denmark, Norway, Sweden (but not Finland, which very much resembles France);

d. West Germany and Belgium, which are not shown in Figure 5.3, are quite similar to France.

Figure 5.4 shows male excess mortality. This excess mortality, quite high in Italy, Portugal, France, and England and Wales, is shown according to age. The Netherlands is distinguished by quite a moderate excess mortality for the entire age range.

Causes of Death

As well as the purely statistical analysis of mortality, there is analysis by cause of death. This analysis is usually difficult, largely because of the high proportion in these statistics of deaths from unknown or unspecified causes, and because of the existence of multiple causes among which it is necessary to choose: does the alcoholic who dies of a broken thigh-bone following a fall while inebriated die of alcoholism or of an accident? Alcoholism would appear to be the first cause, with the accident being defined as the type of death, but there may be confusion.

But the complexity of the situation can be even greater, for a nursing infant may die of bronchial pneumonia following a case of measles. One may blame the death on bronchial pneumonia, but it is more correctly imputed to measles. One could also seek the fundamental cause: this might be the ignorance of the wet nurse, the distance from the doctor, or the difficulties encountered by the mother living in a city, which oblige her to put the child out to nurse, etc. However, here we are only concerned with statistics of direct causes.

Hidden causes of death, and extra causes that are not included in the statistics, are even more pernicious. Amongst these, we may indicate the alcoholism of a considerable part of the population of France as a cause of general excess mortality and of male excess mortality; for the excess mortality arising from alcoholism is not correctly measured simply on the basis of the statistics of death from alcoholism or cirrhosis of the liver. Quite refined statistical methods, which we shall not explain here, are required for arriving at some evaluation of the real damage caused by alcoholism.

Elementary statistical analysis by sex and age extends to causes of death. Using techniques already described, it is possible to calculate rates of mortality from tuberculosis, cancer, accidents, etc., by sex and by age groups. We shall dwell little on this type of statistics. The quality of the data is often mediocre, which makes it difficult to compare countries or to analyse changes in time.

In France at the present time unknown causes or failures to report causes of death make up about 10 percent of deaths recorded in the statistics, and about 7 percent comprise deaths attributed to "senility," an insufficiently precise category. The majority of deaths are due to old age: vascular lesions, diseases of the heart and of the circulatory system, and cancer. This pattern is found in all countries where mortality has greatly declined; the decline is largely the outcome of the reduction of the dangers of infection (thanks to hygiene, vaccinations, antibiotics, etc.). A greater proportion of individuals now therefore attains any particular advanced age, at which they are more frequently victims of the diseases of age. This partly explains the increase in mortality owing to cancer; but improvement in the diagnosis of cases, as well as a real increase in the frequency of the disease, play a role that is difficult to appraise. Such a general pattern of distribution of causes of death does not hold for earlier periods nor for the majority of underdeveloped countries at present, where infectious diseases are still the major cause of deaths.

In countries with low mortality, influenza remains the only well-known form of mortality owing to an epidemic disease, and it also provides an example of an ill-defined cause of death, as numerous deaths attributed to influenza occur among persons also afflicted with respiratory and circulatory diseases. In France, an epidemic of medium magnitude is represented by some 10–12,000 declared deaths and probably by double or triple that number of actual deaths. In Western nations, influenza is the principal cause of the fluctuations in mortality from one year to another.

Let us return to the French example: the recent sharp decline in mortality from tuberculosis (8,795 deaths in 1956 as opposed to 20,131 deaths in 1946) contrasts with the considerable rise in mortality owing to *declared* alcoholism (that is to say, acute alcoholism or cirrhosis – almost all of which is of alcoholic origin – 20,279 deaths in 1956 against 3,244 in 1946); with the sharp rise in mortality owing to accidents (27,472 in 1956 against 18,734 in 1946); and the rise, already mentioned, in the mortality from cancer (from 59,266 deaths in 1946 to 78,949 in 1956, with cases of leukemia not included). These are the major causes of death that, in France, have shaped the net development of mortality in the last 10 years. We shall not undertake a study of the various causes according to their rates by age.

For France, the publications of the INSEE are quite complete on this point.

Endogenous Mortality and Exogenous Mortality

In our general presentation of causes of death, we have distinguished between deaths due to ageing of the organism (essentially, diseases of the heart and of the circulatory system, and cancer) and deaths from infections or accidents. Let us now be somewhat more specific.

We begin with the individual at the time of his birth. Up to about one year of age, the child runs a substantial risk of mortality. Some of these risks derive from the infant's constitution, from congenital malformations, and from circumstances of the delivery: these are causes that the infant carries within himself, so to speak, or that he undergoes—in the case of accidents during delivery—inevitably, at least in the present state of medical science. The notion of *endogenous mortality* corresponds to this intrinsic non-viability.

The newborn child is also exposed to numerous external perils, if care is not taken: bodily accidents (suffocation, fire, etc.), food poisoning, respiratory accidents, and the dangers of infection in general, which sufficient attention, good hygiene, good preventive care—and, eventually, curative means—can reduce very considerably. The notion of *exogenous mortality* corresponds to the fatal accidents that may come about in these exterior ways.

This exogenous risk is virtually the only one to which the child aged 1 to 10 years is exposed. Then, little by little, biological mortality due to ageing appears and increases steadily with age: biometric measures indicate an incidence increasing in geometric progression from year to year; this is the case with mortality owing to intracranial lesions of vascular origin, diseases of the heart and the coronary arteries, angina pectoris, diabetes, nephritis, cancer, etc. This *endogenous* mortality is juxtaposed upon the *exogenous* mortality met earlier in life, which originates basically from infection or accidents.

The decline of mortality has taken place almost exclusively by the diminution of exogenous mortality, which has retreated because of the prevention, hygiene, and care possible with modern medicine. Despite the extension of the mean length of life, the permanence of the endogenous risk renders the maximum length of human life unchanged; it seems to be in the neighborhood of 110 years.

This distinction between endogenous causes and exogenous causes arose from the very fruitful biometric methods for analyzing mortality. We shall test these methods in connection with the study of infant mortality.

Infant Mortality

Mortality among infants is measured by the infant mortality rate, which is in reality a mortality quotient. Calculated on a given birth cohort, the rate of infant mortality is the ratio (usually multiplied by 1,000) of the number of deaths between birth and one year of age in the cohort to the total size of the cohort at birth (see p. 55).

To measure infant mortality in a given year, we divide the number of persons dying during the year at less than one year of age by the number of live births during the year (see p. 56). To take account of the fact that infant deaths in a given year occur to the newborn of two adjacent generations, in certain cases it is necessary to construct a weighted average of the two numbers of births: the births in the year studied (weighted by 2/3 or by 3/4) and the births in the preceding year (weighted by 1/3 or by 1/4) (see p. 37).

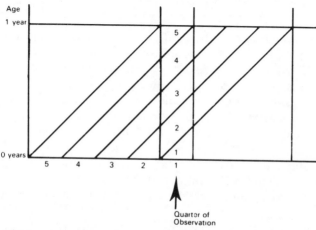

Figure 5.5

The method of weighting has some extensions: let us suppose that one wishes to calculate the infant mortality rate for a quarter (see Figure 5.5). The deaths observed in this quarter (numbered 1 in the diagram) derive from the births in the first quarter and in the four preceding quarters, numbered 2, 3, 4, and 5 (in Figure 5.5, the correspondence between quarters of births and infant deaths may be established with the aid of these numbers). This time, it is necessary to weight the births of five quarters: here are the coefficients proposed by Paul Viencent[4] (see *Population,* Number 1, 1946, p. 56).

In the case of the calculation of a monthly rate, it may be seen that the births that must be taken into account occur in the month being studied and in the 12 preceding months. The same author proposed the series of

4. See *Population,* No. 1, 1946, p. 56.

coefficients shown below (as previously, the numbering adopted goes backward in time, the month studied being number 1).

Quarter of Birth	5	4	3	2	1
Weight	0.054	0.126	0.167	0.266	0.387

Month of Birth	13	12	11	10	9	8	7
Weight	0.017	0.036	0.039	0.042	0.045	0.049	0.055

Month of Birth	6	5	4	3	2	1
Weight	0.062	0.069	0.080	0.097	0.162	0.247

In both cases the sum of the coefficients is, of course, equal to one.[5]

We have seen (p. 58) that the use of weighting is justified only when there are fairly large variations in the number of births in the different periods. This is often the case when calculating quarterly or monthly rates, because of possible seasonal variations in the number of births (the inequality of the lengths of the months is also a factor in the variations).

Measurement of infant mortality is often made difficult by the incompleteness of the death statistics for young children. This incompleteness is chronic in underdeveloped countries, where sometimes a considerable proportion of infant deaths (and births) are not registered. In any case, the distinction between stillborn children and live-born children is not always easy, and, regardless of the apparent completeness of statistics, it is a source of inaccuracy that legislative acts can aggravate. In France, for instance, the compulsory declaration of a birth in the vital register must take place during the three days following the birth. If the child dies before this declaration is made (and in the first days of life the risk of mortality is greatest), the child is considered stillborn: it is included neither in the statistics of live births nor in those of deaths. The resulting error in the data concerning live births is relatively minor, but that in the data for infant deaths is quite significant.

In France the INSEE tries to distinguish between true and erroneous stillbirths; for this reason, it is asked in the stillbirth declaration if the child ever breathed. Some uncertainty remains, and the response to this question is not always given. The way these statistics appear for 1955 is shown in Table 5.4.

5. Let us also observe that the quarterly and monthly rates we have just presented need not necessarily be converted to an annual basis, which would have been necessary with rates computed for the total population (of all ages or of a given age group).

TABLE 5.4 *France, 1955: Registration of Stillbirths*

Total	Experienced Breathing	No Breathing Experienced	Breathing Unknown
17,689	3,614	13,478	597

The number of erroneous stillbirths is then between 3,614 and 3,614 + 597 = 4,211; and the number of live births is between 802,303 + 3,614 = 805,917 and 802,303 + 4,211 = 806,514. The two limits result from the addition of all the "no information about breathing" cases to the numbers of true and of erroneous stillbirths, respectively. The registered infant deaths initially indicated (27,516) must, in consequence, be corrected and increased according to these two hypotheses by 3,614 deaths or by 4,211 deaths. The new figures are then 27,516 + 3,614 = 31,130 and 27,516 + 4,211 = 31,727. The two corresponding rates are derived from the computations of Table 5.5.[6]

TABLE 5.5. *France, 1955: Infant Mortality Rates (per 1,000)*

	Live Births	Infant Deaths	Infant Mortality Rate (per 1,000)
Uncorrected Births, Deaths and Rate	802,303	27,516	34.3
Minimum Number of Erroneous Stillbirths	3,614	3,614	
Corrected Births, Deaths and Rate	805,917	31,130	38.6
Maximum Number of Erroneous Stillbirths	4,211	4,211	
Corrected Births, Deaths and Rate	806,514	31,727	39.3

Without the correction, we would get a rate of 34.3 per 1,000 as against 38.6 per 1,000 or 39.3 per 1,000, a rate increase of some 4 or 5 points; before World War II, with a higher level of infant mortality, this increase was of the order of 5 to 10 points. At the present time, it varies according to the *départements*, with varying procedures for declaration in the vital registry generating considerable variation in the proportion of erroneous stillbirths. To make appropriate comparisons of the level of infant mortality in France in relation to that of other countries, the correction of the French rate for erroneous stillbirths must not be omitted.

Past Trends and Present Level of Infant Mortality

The past trends of infant mortality present certain similarities with the trends of total mortality. The very high infant mortality of past periods

6. In the computation we take into account only births in 1955, the number of which is quite close to the number of births in 1954.

appears to have been at a mean level of about 250 to 300 per 1,000. Whatever is known about the composition of mortality by age permits us to surmise that mortality from age 1 to age 20 was of about the same order of magnitude as infant mortality. Thus, a generation that lost about one quarter of its total number between birth and one year of age was reduced by an additional quarter (of its total at birth), between age 1 and 20 years. At 20 years of age, 400 to 600 survived out of every 1,000 births, and they were responsible for the perpetuation of the species. Under such conditions, it is readily apparent that however high the fertility of that period, it could not provide any considerable growth of population. The very high levels of infant mortality sometimes asserted (without proof) seem to be negated by all available evidence. Infant mortality as high as 500 per 1,000 is sometimes mentioned, but, if a rate of such an order of magnitude held permanently, only a small fraction of the cohort (less than 10 percent) could survive to adulthood.

What was said about human mortality in general holds here as well: 250 to 300 per 1,000 defines a mean order of magnitude of the rate of infant mortality. This mean would have resulted from the balance between rates of the order of 200 to 250 per 1,000 when there were no epidemics, famines, etc., and the exceptionally high infant mortality rates during the frequent catastrophes in those times.

Infant mortality in the West was formerly, therefore, characterized by both a high average level and peaks of excess mortality that could have been very high indeed. Infant mortality in underdeveloped countries was similarly characterized until quite recently. Since about 1950, it has diminished in quite an uneven fashion, depending on the country.

In the West, the decline of infant mortality in the nineteenth century was quite moderate, more moderate than the decline of total mortality: the rate that was 185 per 1,000 between 1805 and 1820, still reached 165 per 1,000 between 1880 and 1900. Developments were not spectacular until after 1900; in the 40 years from 1900 to 1939, the decline was considerable.

Table 5.6 gives rates of infant mortality for the same countries (except Ecuador and Greece) as were shown in Table 5.2. The values for the rates are accurate for most of the countries cited. However, the rate of infant mortality is often in error in underdeveloped countries, where under-registration of deaths between birth and one year is particularly common. To complete the data in Table 5.6, we may say that in Islamic countries infant mortality seems to be about 150 per 1,000; during the survey carried out in French Guinea in 1954–1955, it was 160 1,000 in urban centers and 200 per 1,000 in the bush.

Assuming that registration of births and of deaths is complete, the infant mortality rate is an excellent index of the state of hygiene; it has the

TABLE 5.6. *Infant Mortality Rates in 1958 and 1964 (per 1,000 Live Births)*

	1958	1964
AFRICA		
Union of South Africa		
European Population	29	34
Colored Population	132	116
Asiatic Population	68	50
NORTH AMERICA		
Canada	30	25
United States	27	25
Guatemala	104	92
Jamaica	62	40
Mexico	81	64
Panama	58	43
Puerto Rico	54	52
El Salvador	89	66
SOUTH AMERICA		
Argentine	61	60
Uruguay (1956)	73	—
Chile	127	114
Colombia	100	83
Venezuela	66	49
ASIA		
Israel	35	28
Japan	35	20
Ceylon (1957) (1962)	68	53
China (Mainland)	100	—
Taiwan	36	24
Hong Kong	54	26
Singapore	43	29
EUROPE		
West Germany	36	25
Austria	41	29
Belgium (1965)	30	24
Denmark (1957)	23	19
Finland	24	19
France	32	23
Great Britain	23	21
England and Wales	22	20
Scotland	28	24
Northern Ireland	28	26
Ireland	35	27
Norway (1957)	20	17
Netherlands	17	15
Sweden	16	14
Switzerland	22	19

TABLE 5.6 *(continued)*

	1958	1964
Spain	47	38
Italy	48	36
Portugal	84	69
Yugoslavia	86	—
Albania	68	82
East Germany	44	30
Bulgaria	52	33
Hungary	58	40
Poland	73	48
Rumania	70	49
Czechoslovakia	30	21
U.S.S.R.	41	29
OCEANIA		
Australia	20	19
New Zealand	23	19

advantage over the crude death rate of not being influenced by the age composition of the population.

The most detailed studies that have been undertaken concerning factors of infant mortality have emphasized the importance of social and economic conditions and, even more, of cultural factors. Medico-social organization is an important factor in the decline of infant mortality. It acts by dispensing care and aid and perhaps still more by giving health education to mothers; since medical help is established more easily in the cities than in the countryside, this explains the greater decline of the urban rates.

Rates greater than 150 per 1,000 are becoming quite exceptional. In the West, infant mortality greater than 50 per 1,000 represents a backward situation. France, which in 1958 reached the rate of 32 per 1,000, has a medium position.[7] At the present time (1961), the countries in the highest position have rates of about 20 per 1,000. But the situation of infant mortality and the variations among countries are best judged after separation into endogenous and exogenous causes. It is to the examination of a biometric method permitting this distinction that we now turn.

Biometric Analysis of Infant Mortality

Precise statistics showing the causes of death permit a distinction, in the deaths of the newborn, to be made between deaths caused by accidents during delivery and by congenital malformations—which we consider

7. In the 32 per 1,000 rate shown in Table 5.6, the correction for erroneous stillbirths has been applied.

endogenous deaths—and deaths owing to respiratory diseases, digestive disorders, accidents, and, exterior dangers in general, infectious or otherwise—which we denote *exogenous* deaths. In fact, only rarely are statistics of causes of death appropriately organized (or readily accessible when they exist); the distinction would most often be impracticable unless there were access to a simple biometric method that requires only knowledge of the age structure of mortality within the first year of life.[8]

Such a method is due to J. Bourgeois-Pichat.[9] Careful examination of exogenous deaths in the first year of life convinced Bourgeois-Pichat that they are distributed by age in a manner virtually independent of the level of mortality. In other words, the distribution of these deaths is uniquely a function of age.

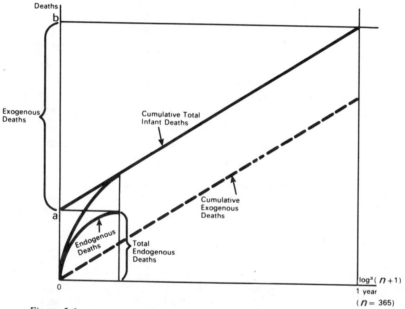

Figure 5.6

Locating age on the abscissa, with an appropriate scale, and the number of exogenous deaths cumulated since birth on the ordinate, according to the different ages, the statistics of exogenous infant deaths can be associated with a series of points that form a straight line (Figure 5.6).

8. For a biometric analysis of mortality as a whole, the reader may usefully refer to the study of J. Sutter and L. Tabah. "La mortalité, phénomène biométrique." *Population*, No. 1, January–March, 1952.

9. See especially *Population*. No. 2, April–June, 1951, and No. 3, July–September, 1951.

If we do not restrict ourselves to plotting the exogenous deaths but include *all* the infant deaths, the points will no longer be located on a straight line. However, the line is straight after the first month of life, because beyond that age the endogenous deaths, which until then had disturbed the linearity, are no longer encountered; sometimes the linearity even begins in the third week.

We thus see the emergence of a graphical method for determining exogenous deaths (and, consequently, endogenous deaths): We locate on a system of axes (see Figure 5.6) all infant deaths cumulated since birth (measured on the ordinate), according to age (measured on the abscissa with an appropriate scale, which we will specify later). We determine graphically the straight line on which the points relating to the cumulative deaths beyond the first month line up. Extension of this straight line to the vertical axis at point *a* gives the endogenous deaths (*Oa*) and, by subtraction, the exogenous deaths in the first year (*ab*).

Various trials led Bourgeois-Pichat to take the function $\log^3 (n+1)$ for the abscissa where *n* is the time (counted in days from the time of birth) prior to which death occurred. For practical applications, we give the values $\log^3 (n+1)$ corresponding to the usual values of *n* (Table 5.7).

As the linearity typically begins in the third week, we show the value of the function for $n = 21$, and since either four weeks (28 days) or one month (31 days) are often used, both corresponding values of $\log^3 (n+1)$ have been calculated. The other values, which nearly correspond to the successive months, are those of the present French statistics.

TABLE 5.7.   *Values of the Function* $\log^3 (n+1)$

n	$n+1$	$\log (n+1)$	$\log^3 (n+1)$
days			
0	1	0	0
21	22	1.34242	2.42
28	29	1.46240	3.13
31	32	1.50515	3.41
61	62	1.79239	5.76
91	92	1.96379	7.57
121	122	2.08636	9.08
151	152	2.18184	10.39
181	182	2.26007	11.54
211	212	2.32634	12.59
241	242	2.38382	13.55
271	272	2.43457	14.43
302	303	2.48144	15.28
333	334	2.52375	16.07
365	366	2.56348	16.85

As a first application, we show the graph (Figure 5.7) corresponding to deaths in France in the first year of life for the three years 1953, 1954, and 1955 combined. The exact values are given in Table 5.8. The fit of the points is quite satisfactory. The point for the second month (61st day) is a little

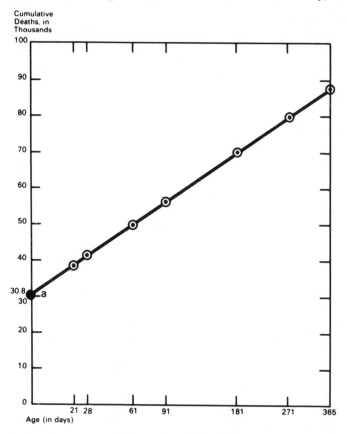

Figure 5.7. Biometric Analysis of Infant Mortality (France: 1953–1955).

TABLE 5.8. *Cumulated Infant Deaths at Ages under One Year*
(1953–1955)

	Deaths Under the Age Indicated						
	21 days	*28 days*	*61 days*	*91 days*	*181 days*	*272 days*	*365 days*
France, Total	38,830	41,324	49,745	56,502	70,514	80,255	87,191
Corsica	247	256	286	319	386	434	475

below the derived line; that for the 365th day, which is not in a straight line with the two points preceding it (which is often the case), pulls down the curve describing the last points of the first year. Indeed, the adjustment of Bourgeois-Pichat holds only for the cumulated deaths in the first year, with the last point often being slightly off the line.

In the present case, the inaccuracy of the adjustment is slight, and the deviations (vertical, from the point *a*) in the estimates of endogenous mortality are small. According to the graph in Figure 5.7, of 87,191 first-year deaths, 30,800 were endogenous deaths; and, by subtraction (87,191—30,800), 56,391 were exogenous deaths. We have, then, for the entire period 1953 to 1955:

the *exogenous* infant mortality rate:

$$\frac{56,391 \times 1,000}{2,410,663} = 23.4 \text{ per } 1,000;$$

the *endogenous* infant mortality rate:

$$\frac{30,800 \times 1,000}{2,410,663} = 12.8 \text{ per } 1,000.$$

Stillbirths and Perinatal Mortality

It must, however, be recognized that in the number 30,800 we do not have all the endogenous deaths. The "erroneous stillbirths" we mentioned previously are mostly deaths owing to endogenous mortality, the mortality of the very first days of life being almost exclusively of this type. It is therefore better to add these both to the number of live births and to the number of endogenous deaths.

We remove the uncertainty about infants declared stillborn, but about whom it is not known whether breathing occurred, by considering them as true stillbirths (which, according to the INSEE, is probably the case). These figures and corrections are shown in Tables 5.9a and 5.9b.

TABLE 5.9a.   *France: Registration of Live Births and Stillbirths*

Year	Live Births		Stillbirths	
	(children declared alive)	*Experienced Breathing*	*No Breathing Experienced*	*Breathing Unknown*
1953	801,152	3,544	14,336	589
1954	807,208	3,546	13,843	591
1955	802,303	3,614	13,478	597
1953–1955	2,410,663	10,704	41,657	1,777

TABLE 5.9b. *Corrected Statistics of Live Births and Stillbirths*

Year	Live Births	Stillbirths	Erroneous Stillbirths
1953	804,696	14,925	3,544
1954	810,754	14,434	3,546
1955	805,917	14,075	3,614
1953–1955	2,421,367	43,434	10,704

Adding the erroneous stillbirths, the total number of endogenous deaths becomes equal to: $10,704 + 30,800 = 41,504$; and the *correct rate of endogenous mortality* is

$$\frac{41,504 \times 1,000}{2,421,367} = 17.1 \text{ per } 1,000.$$

It is usual to define the stillbirth rate as the ratio, for a given year, of the number of stillbirths to the number of live births. Here the rate is

$$\frac{43,434 \times 1,000}{2,421,367} = 17.9 \text{ per } 1,000.$$

The reasons for the nonviability of a foetus are very similar to those causing endogenous deaths. Accordingly, we are led to the notion of *perinatal mortality*, which includes both stillbirths and endogenous mortality. The corresponding rate is the sum of the two preceding numbers or, equivalently, the ratio of the number of stillbirths and endogenous deaths to the number of live births. Here we have:

$$\frac{(43,434 + 41,504)\,1,000}{2,421,367} = \frac{(84,938)\,1,000}{2,421,367} = 35.1 \text{ per } 1,000$$

(the 35.1 differs from $17.1 + 17.9 = 35.0$ because of the rounding of one digit).[10] We group these various ideas in Table 5.10.

TABLE 5.10. *France, 1953–1955: Rates, per 1,000*

	Conventional Infant Mortality 41.3	
Stillbirth 17.1	Endogenous Mortality 17.9	Exogenous Mortality 23.4
	Perinatal Mortality 35.0	

10. Let us observe that, with perinatal mortality encompassing the total of stillbirths and endogenous deaths, the disadvantage of using statistics containing "erroneous stillbirths" disappears in the computation of a perinatal mortality rate, since the number of live births derived from statistics containing "erroneous stillbirths" is only slightly underestimated; the error in the stillbirth rate that results from this is quite negligible (on the order of one per 1,000).

Examples of Biometric Analysis of Infant Mortality

Let us apply the graphic method of analysis to the case of Corsica (for the same period 1953–1955; see Table 5.8).

The seven points would not fit a single straight line. Three points (21 days, 28 days, 61 days) form a first straight line, and five points (61 days, 91 days, 181 days, 271 days, and 365 days) form a second straight line. This exception to the rule of Bourgeois-Pichat is rather frequent and calls for explanation. The noteworthy fact is the break in the adjustment curve (formed by the two segments of the line), which is located at varying ages— quite often at two months, sometimes at three months, more rarely at four months. The line fitting the last points, however, is always situated *above* the extension of the line fitting the first points.

Returning to the direct examination of causes of deaths, we may put this anomaly in relation to the exogenous excess mortality in the last two or three quarters of the first year of life. This is encountered in the warm (Mediterranean) countries and is related to excess mortality due to digestive impairments and associated with weaning and artificial feeding. It is much less important among very young babies, who are generally breast fed, so that mortality in the first week follows the Bourgeois-Pichat rule well.

Accordingly, if the predicted linearity is not observed by biometric analysis, the adjustment of the curve of cumulative deaths requires the study of two lines: that of deaths at the youngest ages, which will yield an estimate of exogenous deaths in the whole group in the first year, *without excess mortality;* and that of the last points, taking account of *exogenous excess mortality* and, by reference to the first line, permitting its measurement.

Let us clarify this by examining the data for Corsica. The line defining normal exogenous mortality would be that drawn from the 28-days point to the 61-days point, a line that is slightly above the point for 21 days. Drawing a line between the points for 28 days and 91 days would leave the point for 61 days well below it; the point for 91 days, however, would be in line with those following it. Following such a procedure, we would estimate that there are 220 endogenous deaths and there is an exogenous excess mortality of 475–413 = 62 deaths.

Let us make the computations of rates for Corsica that we have already made for France as a whole (without its always being possible—as in this case—to use the distinction between true and erroneous stillbirths, because of the absence of the necessary statistics). During the course of the three years 1953, 1954, and 1955, there were 166 stillbirths registered (true or erroneous) and 8,337 live births. Accordingly:

1. The conventional rate of infant mortality:

$$\frac{475 \times 1,000}{8,337} = 57.0 \text{ per } 1,000.$$

2. The rate of exogenous mortality:

$$\frac{(475 - 220)\, 1,000}{8,337} = \frac{255 \times 1,000}{8,337} = 30.6 \text{ per } 1,000.$$

3. The rate of endogenous mortality:

$$\frac{220 \times 1,000}{8,337} = 26.4 \text{ per } 1,000.$$

4. The rate of stillbirths (including erroneous stillbirths):

$$\frac{166 \times 1,000}{8,337} = 19.9 \text{ per } 1,000.$$

5. The rate of perinatal mortality (sum of the two previous rates):

$$26.4 + 19.9 = 46.3 \text{ per } 1,000.$$

Exogenous mortality is thus higher in Corsica than in France as a whole (30.6 compared to 23.4).

At the end of the graphic analysis it appears to us that exogenous excess mortality—probably of digestive origin—was the cause of 62 deaths. If these deaths had been prevented, the rate of mortality would have been diminished by

$$\frac{62 \times 1,000}{8,337} = 7.4 \text{ per } 1,000.$$

The rate of exogenous mortality would then have been

$$30.6 - 7.4 = 23.2 \text{ per } 1,000$$

(a rate comparable to that for France as a whole).

The complete analysis we have just undertaken is not always possible: it assumes quite a detailed knowledge of the age structure of infant deaths. But *if the line-fitting procedure of Bourgeois-Pichat is carried out, the separation of exogenous and endogenous deaths is possible even using less complete information.*

It is evident that the graphic method gives us an estimate of endogenous deaths by measurement of the ordinate at the origin of the fitted line (point *a*, Figure 5.8a). The determination of the line itself requires knowledge of only two points. Transposing this argument: (in terms of deaths) it is enough to know the cumulative number of deaths up to two ages: for example, at 365 days (which is necessary for the calculation of the conventional rate) and at some previous age.

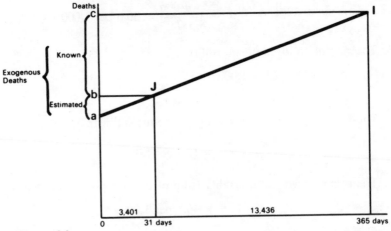

Figure 5.8a

In order that the determination of the line (from only two points) will be fairly precise, it is necessary that the points (that is, the ages) should be sufficiently separated. The cumulative deaths until one month of age are particularly suitable for the earlier point since, in the theory of Bourgeois-Pichat, the fit of the line begins at that point.

Consider Figure 5.8a, where the second point is the point 31 days exactly. Beginning with the known exogenous deaths shown by *bc* (exactly the total of infant deaths from 31 to 365 days, which are nearly all exogenous deaths), we can estimate the exogenous deaths of the first 30 days, from *ab*. The relationship of segment *ab* to segment *bc* is similar to the relationship, on the axis of abscissa, to the lengths (measured according to the scale adopted; see Table 5.7) 0 to 31 days and 31 to 365 days, that is,

$$\frac{3{,}401 \times 100}{13{,}436} = 25.4 \text{ per cent,}$$

commonly rounded to 25 per cent.[11]

11. The lengths in question here (3.401, 13.436, 3.127, and 13.718), which are shown in Figures 5.8a and 5.8b, are derived from rounding off numbers with a large number of decimal places. For this reason they differ slightly from the corresponding lengths given in Table 5.7 (3.41, 13.44, 3.13, and 13.72), and 3.401 + 13.436 is not precisely equal to 3.127 + 13.718.

Thus, when the line-fitting procedure of Bourgeois-Pichat is carried out, *the exogenous deaths of the first 30 days are about 25 percent of the deaths from the 31st through the 365th day of the first year of life;* or again, what is equivalent, the total number of exogenous deaths in the first year is obtained by taking 5/4 of the deaths in the period 31 to 365 days.

It is necessary to revise this percentage if the deaths of the first month (counted here as having 30 days) are actually the deaths of the first four weeks. This is the standard procedure currently used in international statistics, and the procedure used in France since 1949. Dividing 3.127 by 13,718, we get 22.8 percent (see Figure 5.8b). Consequently, *the exogenous deaths of the first 28 days represent approximately 22.8 percent of the deaths between the 29th and 365th day of the first year of life.*

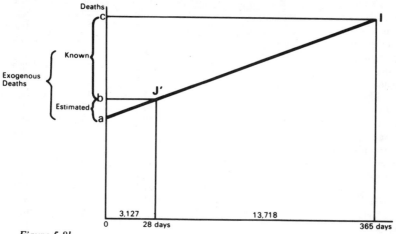

Figure 5.8b

By way of verification, let us apply this rule to the two cases treated previously:

(1) France, 1953–1955

Deaths from the 29th to the 365th day: $87,191 - 41,423 = 45,867$.
$$45,867 \times 22.8\% = 10,458.$$

Total exogenous deaths: 56,325

as opposed to 56,391 by the graphic method. This quite insignificant deviation (66 deaths) indicates that the line-fitting procedure is quite satisfactory.

(2) Corsica, 1953–1955

Deaths from the 29th to the 365th day: $475 - 256 = 219$.
$$219 \times 22.8\% = 50.$$

Total exogenous deaths: 269

as opposed to 255 by the graphic method. The deviation is somewhat larger (+5 percent), and fitting of one line to the whole range was not possible, as we noticed above.

TABLE 5.11. *Infant Mortality in 1954 (Rate per 1,000)*

| | Infant Mortality | | |
	Endogenous	Exogenous	Total
Egypt (Localities with health bureaus)	3	176	17.9
Canada	16.3	15.4	31.7
United States (White population)	16.4	7.5	23.9
Puerto Rico	19.4	38.2	57.6
Venezuela	20.9	47.6	68.5
Japan	19.5	25.1	44.6
West Germany	25.8	17.0	42.8
England and Wales	16.0	9.5	25.5
Austria	23.9	24.4	48.3
Belgium	18.3	23.1	41.4
Denmark	15.9	11.0	26.9
Finland	16.7	13.9	30.6
France	17.3	23.4	40.7
Norway	9.6	11.8	21.4
Netherlands	13.2	7.9	21.1
Sweden	12.7	6.0	18.7
Switzerland	18.3	8.9	27.2
Italy	21.5	31.5	53.0
Portugal	15.9	69.6	85.5
Yugoslavia	25.0	76.6	101.6
East Germany	22.3	28.0	50.3
Bulgaria	24.8	61.5	86.3
Hungary	24.9	35.8	60.7
Poland	19.0	63.6	82.6
Czechoslovakia	14.0	22.8	37.2
Australia	14.8	7.7	22.5
New Zealand	13.1	6.9	20.0

Sources: Annual Epidemiological and Demographic Statistics of the World Health Organization

This standard method has quite a broad application. It still yields quite satisfactory results even in an unfavorable case.

Present Level of Endogenous and Exogenous Infant Mortality

Because of their nature, endogenous deaths diminish little under the influence of medical care, progress, or preventive methods, and levels in the different countries are not dissimilar;[12] in contrast, exogenous deaths have greatly diminished, and differences between countries are quite substantial. Exogenous mortality is a mortality that is readily reduced and ought to disappear through the full utilization of present medical resources. It is already quite low in the most advanced countries.

Table 5.11 has been compiled for the year 1954. The computations were made by the simple arithmetic method of taking an increase of 25 percent— or 22.8 percent—over the number of deaths in the last 11 months.

Endogenous mortality is in the neighborhood of 20 per 1,000; it approaches 10 per 1,000 in countries with the highest levels of health and sanitation. Certain endogenous rates are of doubtful quality; that of Egypt is grossly in error because of deficiencies in the registration of infant deaths at the youngest ages. It is necessary to raise the figure by 20 points at least, so that the total level of infant mortality is about 200 per 1,000. Similarly, the rates for Puerto Rico and Venezuela are probably rather too low.

Differences in national situations are emphasized by the exogenous rates. Just within western Europe, the rate in Portugal is 12 times that of Sweden.

Comparison of Mortality Levels

We have seen the inadequacy of the crude death rate for measuring the "risk of mortality" for the total population: the frequency of human death in a population varies considerably—other things being equal—with the population's age composition.

Heretofore, we have found no means of overcoming the influence of age structure other than the calculation of rates by age or by age groups, which gives us a collection of some 10 or 20 measures accurately describing the mortality situation in a population. But comparisons using such a collection of rates quickly become awkward when they involve several countries. Unless there is a steady difference at all ages, a collection of rates does not let us rank a pair of countries. For this it is necessary to derive synthetic measures summarizing the total of mortality risks at the various ages.

Use of a Standard Population

The variation in composition by age is an obstacle to the comparability of crude death rates in different countries. The direct method of standardi-

---

12. At least this is the case when some minimal level of obstetric progress has been achieved; but there is a considerable gap between current endogenous infant mortality in European countries and such mortality in the eighteenth century or in present-day underdeveloped countries.

zation applies the age-specific rates observed in the countries that are being compared to a *single population of given age structure*. This *standard population* yields a series of numbers of deaths by age corresponding to each set of age-specific rates used, and so permits the computation of a *comparative death rate*.

The choice of the standard population is an arbitrary matter. The rates obtained have no other use than to make the desired comparisons; they have no significance with respect to the countries they represent.

We shall illustrate this method by comparing mortality for white and non-white males in the United States. For the year 1965 the crude death rates were:

White males: 10.85 per 1,000.
Nonwhite males: 11.14 per 1,000.

For the reader not forewarned, it would appear that the sanitary and health conditions are almost identical for nonwhites and whites, which would belie virtually all the age-specific rates. In order to neutralize the effect of age structure, we need to choose a standard population. No exact rule is applicable here, but one possibility is to take one of the two populations as the standard population and apply the rates of the other population to it.[13] Thus, applying the white male age-specific rates to the nonwhite male population (which here plays the role of the standard population) we see to what level the crude rate would diminish if the United States white male population had an age structure as young as that of the nonwhite males: the rate obtained is, then, directly comparable to the nonwhite male rate. The computations for the year 1952 are given in Table 5.12.

They result in a "standardized" rate of

$$\frac{93,602 \times 1,000}{11,190,000} = 8.36 \text{ per } 1,000,$$

which would be the rate for white males if the age structure of its population were the same as that of nonwhite males. The rate of 8.36 per 1,000 is what should be compared with the nonwhite male rate of 11.14 per 1,000.

Notice that our calculations do not necessarily presume that the age-

13. One may do the same again in comparing the mortality in more than two populations; in this way the actual number of deaths in the population chosen as standard population serves directly for the comparison without it being necessary to make such a computation, as would be the case if the standard population were not one of the populations in question.

Sometimes we take as standard population (without this being necessarily required) a population with an age structure "intermediate" between the different populations in question. Sometimes the choice of an "intermediate" population results from addition of the numbers at the different ages in the populations in which mortality is to be compared. Thus, comparing 50 states, we might take the total population of the United States as standard population.

TABLE 5.12. *Computation of Expected Number of Deaths in United States Nonwhite Male Population, Based upon Age-Specific Mortality Rates of White Male Population, 1965*

Age Group in Years	Est. Mean 1965 (July 1) Nonwhite Male (Standard Population)	1965 White Male Age-Specific Mortality Rates (per 1,000)	Expected Deaths in the Nonwhite Male Population with White Male Mortality Rates Col. (2) × Col. (3) ÷ 1,000
Col. (1)	Col. (2)	Col. (3)	Col. (4)
Total – All Ages	11,190,000	10.85	93,602
Under 1 year	322,000	23.74	7,644
1–4 years	1,327,000	0.89	1,181
5–9 years	1,487,000	0.47	699
10–14 years	1,316,000	0.49	645
15–19 years	1,071,000	1.31	1,403
20–24 years	780,000	1.72	1,342
25–29 years	631,000	1.57	991
30–34 years	607,000	1.79	1,087
35–39 years	615,000	2.57	1,581
40–44 years	615,000	4.11	2,528
45–49 years	536,000	6.82	3,656
50–54 years	493,000	11.44	5,640
55–59 years	404,000	18.10	7,312
60–64 years	345,000	27.16	9,370
65–69 years	227,000	41.26	9,366
70–74 years	184,000	59.41	10,931
75–79 years	118,000	85.03	10,034
80–84 years	71,000	127.77	9,072
85 and over	41,000	222.43	9,120

Source: Vital Statistics of the United States, 1965, Vol. II, Part A, Table 1–9 and 6–2.

specific rates of nonwhite males are known; it is only necessary to know the size of the population by age. The comparison may be extended to more than two countries. In the preceding example, if we had wanted to extend our comparison to, say, white female mortality, it would have been necessary to apply the white female age-specific rates to the nonwhite male population, which would have allowed calculation of a "standardized" rate for white females.

This method of comparison of total mortality is particularly useful when one wishes to compare the situations in many countries or regions. It permits, for example, calculation of "standardized" comparative rates for the 50 states on a base of a standard population given by the total population of the United

States (see note 12). It is, however, necessary to have age-specific rates for each state, which presumes a knowledge of both the population by age and the number of deaths by age.

The indirect method of comparison based on the use of a standard mortality schedule is more easily employed, for it requires only knowledge of the population by age in the countries to be compared (and, of course, the total number of deaths).

Use of a Standard Mortality Schedule

Let us take up again the problem of comparing white male and nonwhite male mortality in 1965. Indirect standardization consists of choosing a standard schedule of age-specific death rates and applying this schedule successively to the two populations for which mortality is being compared.

The repeated application of this standard schedule of mortality yields two figures for total deaths, in the white male and in the nonwhite male population. These are then compared with the two figures for the actual number of deaths respectively observed in 1965.

The two ratios:

$$I_n = \frac{\text{actual deaths in nonwhite male population}}{\text{expected deaths in nonwhite male population}}$$

and

$$I_w = \frac{\text{actual deaths in white male population}}{\text{expected deaths in white male population}}$$

yield two indices permitting the ordering of the two populations, the larger index indicating the one having the higher mortality.

As in the application of the standard population method, it is possible to take the age-specific mortality rates of one of the populations being compared as the standard mortality schedule. To compare white and nonwhite male mortality in 1965, let us then take the schedule of white male age-specific rates as the standard schedule. Application of this schedule to the white male population to get the total number of deaths is easy: the number of deaths in question is simply the number of deaths actually observed. In other words, having chosen as the standard mortality schedule that of white males, the actual number of deaths and the expected number of deaths are identical for the white male population. The index, I_w is by definition equal to unity (or to 100, if one multiplies the ratio by 100).

The expected number of nonwhite male deaths in 1965, as based on the white male age-specific rates, totals 93,874 (following the computations of

Table 5.12).[14] The actual total number of deaths registered in 1965 was 124,689. Accordingly,

$$I_n = \frac{124,689}{93,874} = 1.33$$

or 133 if one takes as an index $100 \times I_n$.

In 1965, on the base for white males of 100, the index of mortality for nonwhite males equals 133.

This index has meaning only in relation to the standard schedule of mortality chosen. If the standard schedule of mortality varies, I_w and I_n may vary in a manner such that I_n/I_w need not remain constant.

The utility of this method becomes apparent when it is a question of carrying out comparisons of mortality for a large number of different populations. For example, applying the rates by age and sex for the whole United States to each of the populations of the 50 states for a given year, we obtain expected numbers of deaths which, compared with actual numbers of registered deaths (the relationship consisting always in dividing the registered [or real] deaths by the calculated [or expected] number of deaths), yield indices of mortality for each state, by sex, relative to the United States as a whole. To apply this method it is enough to know for each of the states only the age structure of the population and the total number of deaths.

This indirect method of standardization is particularly appropriate when one wishes to locate the relative level of mortality of quite a small human group, for which calculation of age-specific rates would make no sense because of the small numbers involved. Let us take the study of Frank G. Dickinson and Leonard W. Martin on mortality among American doctors from 1949 to 1951 as an example,[15] even though the relatively large number of persons observed (more than 200,000) does not really represent a typical case where recourse to indirect standardization is the only solution to the problem of comparison.

The standard mortality schedule used is that of white males in the United States in the same period. Comparison between the expected deaths (on the basis of the standard mortality schedule) and the observed deaths in any given age group may be insignificant if the total number of doctors is small in the age group considered. But the effects of small numbers disappear for the

---

14. Let us observe that we are here carrying out computations different from those undertaken during the application of direct standardization. The 93,602 expected deaths do not yield a death rate but define an index for comparison with the actual number of deaths. Of course, we could have taken the nonwhite male mortality rate schedule as standard and applied it to the white male population; nonwhite male mortality would then have comprised the base, 100, and white male mortality, relative to this base, would have had an index of less than 100.

15. Frank G. Dickinson and Leonard W. Martin, "Physician Mortality, 1949-1951," *Journal of the American Medical Association*, No. 162, December, 1955, pp. 1462–1468.

population as a whole, and the total registered deaths (10,738) becomes significant in comparison with the total expected deaths (11,513.8). In the example shown, one arrives at a general index, I, of mortality for American doctors relative to the mortality conditions for white males:

$$I = \frac{10,738}{11,513.8} \times 100 = 93.3.$$

TABLE 5.13

Age Group (in completed years)	Deaths Among Physicians in 1949–1951	Expected Deaths Based on Standard Mortality Schedule
20–24	12	14.2
25–29	75	116.7
30–34	120	154.2
35–39	165	248.3
40–44	328	383.6
45–49	448	484.9
50–54	599	636.2
55–59	751	819.7
60–64	1,130	1,099.8
65–69	1,458	1,441.1
70–74	1,834	1,857.2
75–79	1,680	1,852.1
80–84	1,268	1,381.5
85–89	580	679.0
90–94	240	274.9
95–99	45	64.8
100 and over	5	5.6
All ages	10,738	11,513.8

CHAPTER SIX

Life Tables

LIFE tables—called "mortality tables" in many countries—provide the most complete statistical description of mortality. The computation of life tables is one of the oldest techniques in demography. The technique has been extended to other phenomena with varying degrees of success. Nonetheless, it is a fact that the life table provides a descriptive model amenable to certain useful extensions.

Presentation of the Life Table

Let us suppose that we were able to observe a given part of a cohort or of a group of cohorts (a group of individuals born during the same year or the same span of calendar years) from birth until all members have died, that is, over about 100 years. We would have a good statistical description of mortality in this group if we knew the number of survivors at ages sufficiently close together to be comparable; for example, if we have the total number of survivors at successive complete years of age: 0 years (birth), 1 year, 2 years, . . . , 95 years, etc.

Delaporte[1] gives these details for different cohorts born in Europe in the previous century as well as in the eighteenth century; apparently, these do not derive from direct observations but from reconstructions (about which we will not go into detail). We know that in forming a group of 10,000 French males, born around 1880, it would have been possible to observe, on the average:

8,200 survivors at 1 year of age
7,815 survivors at 2 years of age
7,580 survivors at 3 years of age

1. *Evolution de la mortalité en Europe depuis l'origine des statistiques de l'état civil*, Paris, 1941

7,435 survivors at 4 years of age

..................,...........................

5,529 survivors at 45 years of age
5,466 survivors at 46 years of age

....

Here exact ages are involved; in other words, 8,200 persons reached their first birthday, 7,815 reached their second birthday, and so on. It is clearly equivalent to know that, in the group of 10,000 Frenchmen in question,

1,800 died between 0 and 1 year of age
385 died between 1 and 2 years of age
235 died between 2 and 3 years of age
145 died between 3 and 4 years of age

....

63 died between 45 and 46 years of age[2]

....

To these two types of data a third, more elaborate type can be added, which measures the risks of death between the various consecutive ages: such data yield mortality probabilities.

Following the definition of probability given previously (see p. 53), the probabilities from the figures just given are these:

The probability at 0 years is equal to

$$\frac{1,800}{10,000} = 0.180, \text{ or } 180 \text{ per } 1,000.$$

The probability at 1 year of age is equal to

$$\frac{385}{8,200} = 0.047, \text{ or } 47 \text{ per } 1,000.$$

....

The probability at 45 years of age is equal to

$$\frac{63}{5,529} = 0.011, \text{ or } 11 \text{ per } 1,000.$$

....

It is possible to group these three sequences of values in a table, according to the conventional format of life tables (Table 6.1).

2. It is in this way, by recording successive human attrition, that the most effective direct observation of mortality in a group is carried out.

TABLE 6.1. *Life Table for French Male Cohorts Born Around 1880*

Age x (in years)	Survivors to Age x	Deaths Between x and x+1	Probability of Mortality Between Ages x and x+1 (per 1,000)
x	l_x	d_x	q_x
0	10,000	1,800	180
1	8,200	385	47
2	7,815	235	30
3	7,580	145	19
4	7,435		
...	...	...	...
45	5,529	63	11
46	5,466		
...	...	...	...

We may note the conventional notation, introduced in that table:

x exact age corresponding to a number of complete years;
l_x total number of survivors to exact age x;
d_x the number of deaths between exact ages x and $x+1$;
q_x annual probability of mortality at age x.

Here, for example: $l_{45} = 5,529$; $d_{45} = 63$; $q_{45} = 11$ per 1,000.

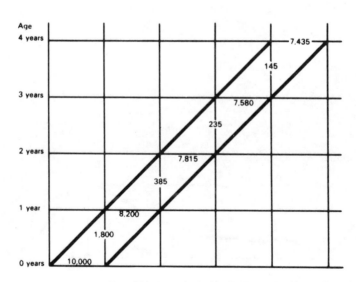

Figure 6.1. Survivors and Deaths in a Life Table.

Clearly, we must have:

$$d_x = l_x - l_{x+1},$$

and, consequently,

$$l_{x+1} = l_x - d_x$$

$$q_x = \frac{d_x}{l_x},$$

and, consequently,

$$d_x = l_x q_x.$$

Let us observe, finally, that if the data in Table 6.1 concern a single generation, they are placed in a *Lexis* diagram according to the representation in Figure 6.1.

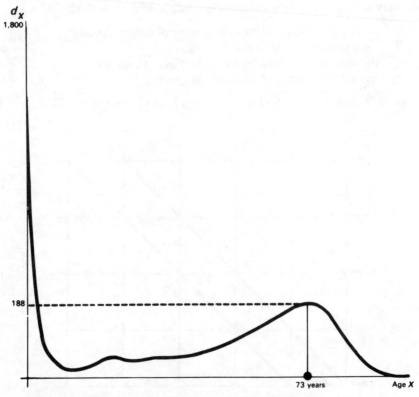

Figure 6.2.   Distribution of Deaths by Age in a Life Table.

Life Table Description of Mortality

Knowledge of the sequence of deaths in a life table leads to a description of mortality as a demographic phenomenon following natality, in accordance with the paradigm we have presented above (see p. 68). In Table 6.1, 10,000 males are born (event *A*), which exposes them to the subsequent phenomenon of mortality (event *B*):

1. What is the proportion of persons having experienced event *A* who experience the subsequent event *B*? The response is apparently 1 (or 100 per cent), for all men are mortal . . . .

2. What is the distribution of intervals between event *A* and event *B*? This question concerns lengths of life, and the distribution sought is nothing more than the distribution by age of death in the table. For the entire life table, of which Table 6.1 gives only certain extracts, this distribution is that shown in Figure 6.2. It is similar to the distribution of Figure 4.2, p. 69, given in connection with the general presentation of this mode of description.[3]

Construction of Life Tables

A life table can be completed with knowledge of any one of the following three sequences:

$$[l_x], [d_x], [q_x].$$

We have just seen this with respect to $[l_x]$. It is quite evident in the case of $[d_x]$ from which $[l_x]$ and, hence, also $[q_x]$ can be derived.

Let us show how it is possible to derive $[l_x]$ and $[d_x]$ if $[q_x]$ is known. This problem is important, for it occurs each time we construct a period (or "current" or "cross sectional") life table. Let us treat it concretely by starting the construction of Table 6.1 beginning with:

$$q_0 = 180 \text{ per } 1,000$$
$$q_1 = 47 \text{ per } 1,000$$
$$q_2 = 30 \text{ per } 1,000$$
$$q_3 = 19 \text{ per } 1,000$$
$$\dots\dots\dots\dots\dots\dots\dots\dots$$

Let us fix the number of survivors at 0 years, that is l_0, which will be called the *radix* of the table. The choice is more or less arbitrary; by convention some power of 10 is employed 1,000, 10,000, 100,000, 1,000,000, etc.

1. Let $l_0 = 10,000$ here. Following the notation of a mortality probability, and since q_0 equals 180 per 1,000:

$$d_0 = \frac{10,000 \times 180}{1,000} = 1,800.$$

3. Since the 1880 generation could not be observed to its extinction, beyond a certain age, the distribution of deaths in Figure 6.2 is based upon extrapolation (see Delaporte, *op. cit.*, p. 62).

Among the 10,000 survivors to 0 years, 1,800 die between ages 0 and 1 year; there are, accordingly:

$l_1 = 10,000 - 1,800 = 8,200$ survivors at 1 year of age.

2. We multiply the 8,200 survivors to age 1 year by a mortality probability at that age, here $q_1 = 47$ per 1,000. This results in:

$$d_1 = \frac{8,200 \times 47}{1,000} = 385 \text{ deaths between 1 and 2 years of age.}$$

This yields, accordingly:

$l_2 = 8,200 - 385 = 7,815$ survivors at 2 years of age, and so forth.

Thus, we reconstruct the mortality table of Table 6.1.

Cohort Life Tables and Period Life Tables

The only natural way of introducing the notion of a life table is to follow a birth cohort (or a group of cohorts) through time. However, life tables for cohorts are of only limited practical interest. Attention is more usefully given to conditions of mortality obtaining during a single year or given period of years than to the effect of mortality throughout the history of a generation. There are many reasons for this:

1. The phenomenon studied occurs over a quite long period of time—about a century—which renders observation difficult.

2. The trends characterizing different cohorts do not seem to have many implications for their future; in other words, the effect of selection by mortality seems slight in comparison with other contributing factors.[4] Thus the study of the mortality of a cohort does not clarify the analysis; by contrast, in the case of nuptiality, for example, it is not possible to separate the behavior of any given cohort at a given date from its past history (recovery of deferred marriages, etc.).

3. Finally, there is obviously considerable interest in observing the state of mortality in a given year in order to measure the effects of different economic, social, epidemiological, or climatic factors and to follow the changes from year to year. Such measurement will be facilitated by the fact just stated—that past conditions do not appear to have implications for the present situation, which appears rather to depend almost exclusively on current conditions.

To summarize briefly: in the study of mortality, period analysis always takes priority. We must, therefore, confront the problem of construction of period life tables.

---

4. This could be otherwise when only late endogenous deaths remain.

The construction of a period life table rests on the derivation of an hypothetical cohort, which is taken through all the ages of life and, at each of the various ages, is subjected to the mortality conditions observed for real cohorts in the year (or group of years) studied.

The essential element for construction of these tables is the series of mortality probabilities $[q_x]$ observed in the period studied. These probabilities are then applied according to the process indicated above.

Let us, therefore, turn our attention now to different problems posed by the derivation of mortality probabilities.

Review of Mortality Probabilities

We consider here only the computation of annual probabilities, i.e., indices giving for a single cohort (or group of cohorts) the probability that persons in that cohort (or group of cohorts) reaching age x will die before reaching age $x + 1$.

Defined for a cohort, the probability is obtained from the formula:

$$q_x = \frac{d_x}{l_x}$$

Defined for several cohorts (two in order to illustrate the ideas), which we will distinguish in the notation by superscripts 1 and 2, the probability is equal to:[5]

$$q_x = \frac{d_x^1 + d_x^2}{l_x^1 + l_x^2}. \tag{F}$$

The data used are placed on the *Lexis* diagram as shown in Figures 6.3a and 6.3b.

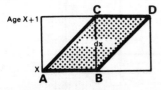

Figure 6.3a

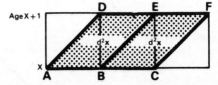

Figure 6.3b

5. We could also define this probability as the arithmetic mean of

$$q_x^1 = \frac{d_x^1}{l_x^1} \text{ and } q_x^2 = \frac{d_x^2}{l_x^2},$$

a mean that differs somewhat from the q_x defined in equation (F). The difference can be substantial if the numbers of the two cohorts are very different; in equation (F) the mortality levels of the two cohorts are weighted by the respective cohort totals. Since these mortality levels concern different periods, we might prefer – to obtain a more correct measure of period mortality – to take the arithmetic mean of the probabilities, thus giving equal weight to the two cohorts.

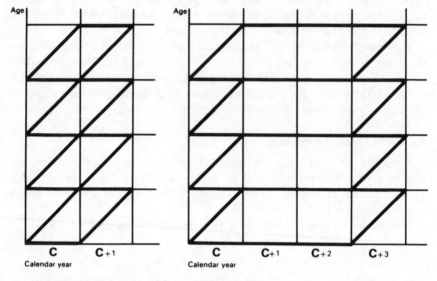

Figure 6.4a   *Figure 6.4b*

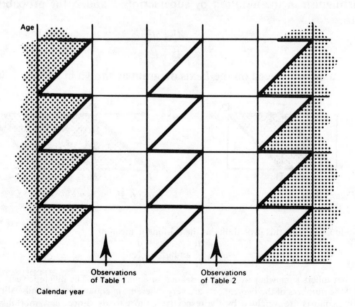

Figure 6.5

Let us return to the problem initially presented: determining the probabilities of mortality at different ages, based upon *all* the deaths occurring in a given calendar year (or group of years) in the populations studied. If we were to study the mortality of calendar year C (Figure 6.4a), we would have to take into account all the deaths included in the corresponding vertical column of the *Lexis* diagram. But, according to the strict definition, the probabilities are derived from the computations in the parallelograms, which requires taking into consideration the deaths of at least two consecutive calendar years, C and $C+1$ (or $C-1$ and C). Thus, in keeping the computation of mortality probabilities consistent with the definition, it becomes impossible to make these computations with the deaths of a single calendar year or to define a period table for a single year.

Of course, it is possible to compute the mortality probabilities with the deaths of two or more calendar years, but it is never possible to take into account *all* the deaths in the period studied. If the period covers two years, about half the deaths are not taken into account (Figure 6.4a); if it covers four years, about a quarter of the deaths are neglected (Figure 6.4b).

No doubt a computation of successive mortality tables that uses the deaths "enclosed" quite exactly in a *Lexis* diagram (Figure 6.5) does not neglect any quantitative data about the mortality of a country. But the problem of the exact determination of the current (period) conditions is avoided.

Before studying how mortality probabilities can be determined on the basis of the deaths of a single calendar year, we shall undertake the complete computation of a mortality table based on the conventional derivation of each cohort probability.

Life Table for French Males, 1954–1955

This title is somewhat misleading since, as we have just seen, the method of computation that will be used omits approximately half of the deaths in the period 1954–1955. The statistical data necessary are the following: 1) the population by year of age as of January 1, 1955, such as is given, for example, in the *Statistical Abstract of France*, 1956, pp. 9–10, and 2) statistics of deaths by sex and by age (cross classified) for the years 1954 and 1955 (see *Statistical Studies*, No. 1, January–March, 1956, p. 22, for the deaths of 1954; and No. 4, October–December, 1956, p. 22, for the deaths of 1955).

The deaths that we shall use are located in the series of stacked parallelograms as shown in Figure 6.6. The population that we have represents the movement across the diagonal line common to all these parallelograms: the vertical line for January 1, 1955. With these data, we can compute for each parallelogram the corresponding mortality probability.

1. If the population studied is closed, that is, if there is no migration, we

may relate quite simply the number at each age x in the population P, on January 1, 1955 (see Figure 6.7a), to the total number of persons (l) in the cohort who reached age x^6; d and d' being the deaths in the two triangles in the *Lexis* diagram, it is then quite clear that: $l = P + d$, and, consequently:

$$q = \frac{d + d'}{P + d}. \qquad (F)$$

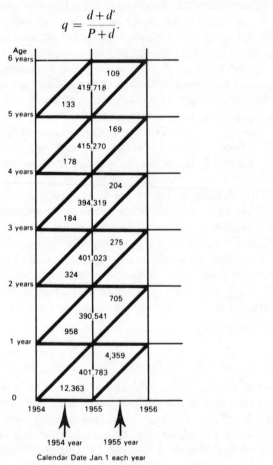

Figure 6.6

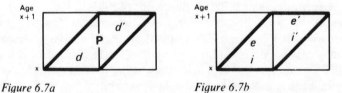

Figure 6.7a   *Figure 6.7b*

6. Since there is no ambiguity here, we drop the index x in order to simplify the notation.

2. If the population studied is subject to migration, the formula (F) still holds *under certain conditions*.

Let us introduce now the totals e, e', i, i' of emigrants and immigrants in the two triangles of the *Lexis* diagram (Figure 6.7b). Let q be the probability sought, which we assume to be the same for all categories of population (migrants and nonmigrants).

Without migration, the l survivors to age x will yield lq deaths. In fact, we record deaths as $d+d'$, which it is necessary to correct: (a) deaths that would occur if the (e, e') emigrants had not left the observed population; but it may be supposed that if the migratory movements are regular enough, so that these $(e+e')$ emigrants are gone on the average half a year, they would then yield

$$\frac{q(e+e')}{2} \text{ deaths;}$$

(b) deaths that could not have been produced without the arrival of $(i+i')$ immigrants; by a reasoning similar to that of paragraph (a) it is seen that these would thus yield

$$\frac{q(i+i')}{2} \text{ deaths.}$$

The sum $(d+d')$ having been corrected,[7] we arrive at the equation:

$$lq = d+d'+\frac{q(e+e')}{2} - \frac{q(i+i')}{2}. \tag{I}$$

On the other hand:

$$l = P+d+e-i.$$

Substitution of this value for l in equation (I) yields:

$$(P+d+e-i)q = d+d'+q\left(\frac{e+e'}{2}\right)-q\frac{(i+i')}{2}. \tag{2}$$

$$q\left(P+d+e-I-\frac{e}{2}-\frac{e'}{2}+\frac{i}{2}+\frac{i'}{2}\right) = d+d'.$$

$$q\left(P+d+\frac{e-e'}{2}-\frac{i-i'}{2}\right) = d+d'.$$

$$q = \frac{d+d'}{P+d+\left(\dfrac{e-e'}{2}\right)-\left(\dfrac{i-i'}{2}\right)}.$$

7. This correction is not entirely rigorous for reasons whose explanation would be unduly lengthy. We shall limit ourselves to the computation that follows, whose accuracy matches that of the data to which we ordinarily have access.

We obtain the equivalent of equation (F) if

$$\frac{e-e'}{2} - \frac{i-i'}{2} = 0,$$

or, in particular, if $e = e'$ and $i = i'$, which is the case when migratory movements do not vary over time.

If they vary but little, or if they are small, the value of the correction term

$$\frac{e-e'}{2} - \frac{i-i'}{2}$$

is very small, and equation (F) is approximated closely enough. This was the case for France in the 1954–1955 period.

Let us go on to the actual computations. Let us distinguish the preparatory computations leading to mortality probabilities from the computations—based on these mortality probabilities—carried out in construction of the actual life table. The two are shown together in Table 6.2.

Columns 1, 2, and 3 simply assemble the data in the format of Figure 6.6, used in the computation of the different mortality probabilities.[8] In columns 4 and 5, the quantities $P+d$ and $d+d'$ are computed, serving in turn for the derivation of q in column 6, according to the formula

$$q = \frac{d+d'}{P+d}.$$

Finally, the probabilities $[q_x]$ are applied in accordance with the procedure indicated above, on page 111, for obtaining the series

$$[l_x] \text{ and } [d_x].$$

---

8. Let us observe that the number of deaths in 1954 of boys under 1 year of age, in the 1954 cohort, differs in Figure 6.6 (12,363) and Table 6.2 (14,563). This is because in the latter we have included erroneous stillbirths following proportional distribution of those with "respiration unknown" as indicated in the following table:

	Respiration Known	Respiration Unknown
No respiration experienced (true stillbirths)	13,843	470
Respiration experienced (erroneous stillbirths)	3,546	121
	17,389	591

Thus, we arrive at 3,667 erroneous stillbirths (3,546 + 121) for the two sexes together. Taking account of the sex ratio at birth, 105/100, of male excess mortality, and of excess male infant mortality (index on the order of 125), we have estimated that 6/10 of these erroneous stillbirths were males. Since in 1954 they practically all belonged to the 1954 generation, we add 3,667 × 0.6 = 2,200 male erroneous stillbirths in 1954 to the number in the 1954 generation; and to the 1954 deaths of males under 1 year of age and in the 1954 generation, 12,363 + 2,200 = 14,563 deaths.

The table is completed by two columns, 9 and 10, that require fairly extensive explanations.

Expectation of Life

A natural way of summarizing the mortality at different ages in one cohort is to compute the mean age of those in the cohort who die, which is also their mean length of life. This idea is transposed without modification when what is concerned are hypothetical cohorts generated during construction of period life tables. Besides, it is the only way of associating the concrete idea of "mean length of life" with the conditions of mortality of a given year or period of years.

This can be explained verbally.

1. *What is the mean length of life of the l_0 newborn persons in a life table?*

If the years lived by the group of l_0 newborn were equally distributed among each of them, each newborn child would reach the mean length of life of the group. Such a definition leads directly to the method of calculating the mean length of life. Let us compute, then, the sum of the years lived by the l_0 newborn. On the one hand: (a) in living through the first complete year of life, the l_1 individuals who reach their first birthday have lived a total of l_1 years, and (b) in living through the second complete year of life, the l_2 individuals who attain their second birthday have lived a total of l_2 years; and so on.

We thus arrive at the total number of years lived:

$$l_1 + l_2 + \ldots + l_\omega{}^9.$$

On the other hand, it is necessary to take account of the fraction of years lived after the last birthday reached. Until this point, for an individual dying at 2 years 3 months, two entire years of life were counted, allowing him to be included in the totals l_1 and l_2, but not in l_3; his three months of life after the two complete years were neglected. To make the necessary correction, we assume that deaths are distributed linearly between successive birthdays,[10] so that the persons dying between age x and $x+1$ (totaling d_x) have each lived a half year on the average, or $0.5\,d_x$. The total correction is equal to:

$$0.5d_1 + 0.5d_2 + 0.5d_3 + \ldots + 0.5d_\omega,$$

9. We denote by ω the last birthday reached by persons in the (real or fictitious) cohort considered; following this definition of ω, $l_{\omega+1} = l_{\omega+2} = \cdots = 0$. Naturally, ω is not perfectly determined; let us recall that it would not at the present be greater than 110 years (see P. Vincent; "La mortalité des vieillards," *Population*, No. 2, April–June, 1951).

The sum $l_1 + l_2 + \cdots + l_\omega$ is, then, written in the usual condensed form:

$$\sum_{i=1}^{\omega} l_i$$

10. This is never exactly the case.

TABLE 6.2. France: Male Life Table for 1954–1955

	Preliminary Computations						Life Table				
Age x	Deaths at Age x in the (1954–x) Generation		Population as of Jan. 1, 1955	Number of Persons reaching x-th Birthday	Number of Deaths at Age x in the (1954–x) Generation	Probability of Mortality (per 10,000) q_x	Survivors l_x	Deaths d_x	e_x	$\sum\limits_{i=x+1}^{\omega} l_i$	Age x
	in 1954	in 1955									
	(1)	(2)	(3)	(4) $(3)+(1)$	(5) $(1)+(2)$	(6) $(5)\div(4)$	(7)	(8)	(9)	(10)	
0	14563.	4359.	401783.	416346.	18922.	454.	10000.	454.	645976.	65.1	0
1	958.	705.	390541.	391499.	1663.	42.	9546.	40.	636430.	67.2	1
2	324.	275.	401023.	401347.	599.	15.	9506.	14.	626924.	66.5	2
3	184.	204.	394319.	394503.	388.	10.	9492.	9.	617432.	65.5	3
4	178.	169.	415270.	415448.	347.	8.	9483.	8.	607949.	64.6	4
5	133.	109.	419718.	419851.	242.	6.	9475.	6.	598474.	63.7	5
6	122.	92.	418146.	418268.	214.	5.	9469.	5.	589005.	62.7	6
7	103.	90.	415658.	415761.	193.	5.	9464.	5.	579541.	61.7	7
8	89.	89.	402766.	402855.	178.	4.	9459.	4.	570082.	60.8	8
9	76.	53.	302581.	302657.	129.	4.	9455.	4.	560627.	59.8	9
10	64.	60.	292495.	292559.	124.	4.	9451.	4.	551176.	58.8	10
11	68.	52.	294796.	294864.	120.	4.	9447.	4.	541729.	57.8	11
12	53.	70.	273913.	273966.	123.	4.	9443.	4.	532286.	56.9	12
13	78.	64.	245797.	245875.	142.	6.	9439.	6.	522847.	55.9	13
14	60.	82.	260220.	260280.	142.	5.	9433.	5.	513414.	54.9	14
15	90.	104.	283998.	284088.	194.	7.	9428.	7.	503986.	54.0	15
16	136.	100.	285373.	285509.	236.	8.	9421.	8.	494565.	53.0	16
17	153.	146.	289212.	289365.	299.	10.	9413.	9.	485152.	52.0	17
18	207.	176.	294154.	294361.	383.	13.	9404.	12.	475748.	51.1	18
19	193.	186.	296875.	297068.	379.	13.	9392.	12.	466356.	50.2	19
20	240.	237.	312239.	312479.	477.	15.	9380.	14.	456976.	49.2	20
21	200.	192.	309898.	310098.	392.	13.	9366.	12.	447610.	48.3	21
22	256.	256.	324398.	324654.	512.	16.	9354.	15.	438256.	47.4	22
23	284.	272.	326919.	327203.	556.	17.	9339.	16.	428917.	46.4	23
24	302.	309.	334961.	335263.	611.	18.	9323.	17.	419594.	45.5	24
25	293.	293.	316339.	316632.	586.	19.	9306.	18.	410288.	44.6	25

26	43.7	401000.	18.	9288.	19.	615.	322256.	321914.	273.	342.	26
27	42.8	391730.	16.	9270.	17.	547.	319617.	319348.	278.	269.	27
28	41.8	382476.	18.	9254.	19.	621.	323185.	322866.	302.	319.	28
29	40.9	373240.	19.	9236.	21.	671.	322987.	322636.	320.	351.	29
30	40.0	364023.	20.	9217.	22.	702.	317818.	317461.	345.	357.	30
31	39.1	354826.	20.	9197.	22.	705.	317083.	316732.	354.	351.	31
32	38.2	345649.	22.	9177.	24.	753.	319171.	318802.	384.	369.	32
33	37.3	336494.	21.	9155.	23.	783.	333552.	333143.	374.	409.	33
34	36.3	327360.	26.	9134.	28.	950.	340972.	340492.	470.	480.	34
35	35.4	318252.	27.	9108.	30.	626.	205768.	205511.	369.	257.	35
36	34.5	309171.	26.	9081.	29.	545.	185035.	184745.	255.	290.	36
37	33.6	300116.	30.	9055.	33.	537.	160569.	160317.	285.	252.	37
38	32.8	291091.	31.	9025.	34.	511.	152046.	151763.	228.	283.	38
39	31.9	282097.	31.	8994.	35.	659.	188625.	188229.	263.	396.	39
40	31.0	273134.	36.	8963.	40.	1152.	288559.	287970.	563.	589.	40
41	30.1	264207.	39.	8927.	44.	1313.	297395.	296710.	628.	685.	41
42	29.2	255319.	43.	8888.	48.	1455.	301375.	300623.	703.	752.	42
43	28.4	246474.	47.	8845.	53.	1491.	283640.	282901.	752.	739.	43
44	27.5	237676.	48.	8798.	54.	1640.	300960.	300140.	820.	820.	44
45	26.7	228926.	57.	8750.	65.	1938.	299998.	299009.	949.	989.	45
46	25.8	220233.	63.	8693.	73.	2188.	300330.	299234.	1092.	1096.	46
47	25.0	211603.	67.	8630.	78.	2311.	296325.	295114.	1100.	1211.	47
48	24.2	203040.	72.	8563.	84.	2502.	298450.	297194.	1246.	1256.	48
49	23.4	194549.	80.	8491.	94.	2776.	296542.	295088.	1322.	1454.	49
50	22.6	186138.	87.	8411.	104.	3065.	293554.	292010.	1521.	1544.	50
51	21.9	177814.	95.	8324.	114.	3321.	291601.	289909.	1629.	1692.	51
52	21.1	169585.	101.	8229.	123.	3609.	294173.	292391.	1827.	1782.	52
53	20.4	161457.	109.	8128.	134.	3855.	287021.	285164.	1998.	1857.	53
54	19.6	153438.	118.	8019.	147.	4015.	273160.	271147.	2002.	2013.	54
55	18.9	145537.	122.	7901.	155.	4101.	263970.	261912.	2043.	2058.	55
56	18.2	137758.	134.	7779.	172.	4178.	243124.	240990.	2044.	2134.	56
57	17.5	130113.	137.	7645.	179.	4137.	231013.	228981.	2105.	2032.	57
58	16.8	122605.	142.	7508.	189.	4126.	218077.	216046.	2095.	2031.	58
59	16.1	115239.	154.	7366.	209.	3809.	182210.	180376.	1975.	1834.	59
60	15.5	108027.	167.	7212.	231.	4144.	179104.	177058.	2098.	2046.	60
61	14.8	100982.	175.	7045.	249.	4422.	177727.	175537.	2232.	2190.	61
62	14.2	94112.	179.	6870.	260.	4279.	164627.	162453.	2105.	2174.	62
63	13.6	87421.	190.	6691.	284.	4730.	166676.	164342.	2396.	2334.	63
64	12.9	80920.	198.	6501.	304.	4714.	155275.	152882.	2321.	2393.	64
65	12.3	74617.	205.	6303.	325.	5183.	159459.	156903.	2627.	2556.	65

TABLE 6.2 *(continued)*

	Preliminary Computations						Life Table				
Age x	Deaths at Age x in the (1954-x) Generation		Population as of Jan. 1, 1955	Number of Persons reaching x-th Birthday	Number of Deaths at Age x in the (1954-x) Generation	Probability of Mortality (per 10,000) q_x	Survivors l_x	Deaths d_x	e_x	$\sum\limits_{i=x+1}^{\omega} l_i$	Age x
	in 1954 (1)	in 1955 (2)	(3)	(4) = (3)÷(1)	(5) = (1)+(2)	(6) = (5)÷(4)	(7)	(8)	(9)	(10)	
66	2655.	2711.	149384.	152039.	5366.	353.	6098.	215.	68519.	11.7	66
67	2789.	2947.	145698.	148487.	5736.	386.	5883.	227.	62636.	11.1	67
68	2938.	3105.	136925.	139863.	6043.	432.	5656.	244.	56980.	10.6	68
69	3033.	3234.	133529.	136562.	6267.	459.	5412.	248.	51568.	10.0	69
70	3161.	3400.	125909.	129070.	6561.	508.	5164.	262.	46404.	9.5	70
71	3163.	3358.	116353.	119516.	6521.	546.	4902.	268.	41502.	9.0	71
72	3389.	3606.	111160.	114549.	6995.	611.	4634.	283.	36868.	8.5	72
73	3402.	3832.	103132.	106534.	7234.	679.	4351.	295.	32517.	8.0	73
74	3417.	3569.	93258.	96675.	6986.	723.	4056.	293.	28461.	7.5	74
75	3670.	3994.	90299.	93969.	7664.	816.	3763.	307.	24698.	7.1	75
76	3666.	4044.	84313.	87979.	7710.	876.	3456.	303.	21242.	6.6	76
77	3668.	4148.	78881.	82549.	7816.	947.	3153.	299.	18089.	6.2	77
78	3752.	4116.	71843.	75595.	7868.	1041.	2854.	297.	15235.	5.8	78
79	3511.	3963.	62619.	66130.	7474.	1130.	2557.	289.	12678.	5.5	79
80	3371.	3883.	53294.	56665.	7254.	1280.	2268.	290.	10410.	5.1	80
81	3124.	3435.	45198.	48322.	6559.	1357.	1978.	268.	8432.	4.8	81
82	2886.	3363.	38822.	41708.	6249.	1498.	1710.	256.	6722.	4.4	82
83	2371.	2390.	26387.	28758.	4761.	1656.	1454.	241.	5268.	4.1	83
84	2196.	2391.	24051.	26247.	4587.	1748.	1213.	212.	4055.	3.8	84
85	1857.	2099.	19293.	21150.	3956.	1870.	1001.	187.	3054.	3.6	85
86	1535.	1776.	13223.	14758.	3311.	2244.	814.	183.	2240.	3.3	86
87	1340.	1468.	9924.	11264.	2808.	2493.	631.	157.	1609.	3.0	87
88	1126.	1228.	8228.	9354.	2354.	2517.	474.	119.	1135.	2.9	88
89	813.	891.	5526.	6339.	1704.	2688.	355.	95.	780.	2.7	89
90							260.		520.	2.5	90

which is

$$0.5(d_0 + d_1 + d_2 + \ldots + d_\omega),$$

or

$$0.5\, l_0,$$

since what is contained within the brackets gives the sum of the total number of deaths, that is, the total of the group at birth.

The mean duration of life, which we denote e_0, is thus equal to

$$e_0 = 1/2 + \frac{l_1 + l_2 + \ldots + l_\omega}{l_0},$$

which is conventionally called *expectation of life at birth*.

2. *What is the mean length of survival of the l_x persons who reach age x in a life table?*

Clearly this is a generalization from Question 1. The mean length of survival at age x is conventionally called the *expectation of life at age x*, and is denoted e_x. Following the method used in Question 1, a computation of the years of life remaining to the l_x survivors of the table leads to the formula

$$e_x = 1/2 + \frac{l_{x+1} + l_{x+2} + \ldots + l_\omega}{l_x}. \tag{E}$$

Calculating the expectation of life at a given age x requires the summation of all the survivors beginning with the last age of the table until $x + 1$. This summation is made in column 9 of Table 6.2.

A certain difficulty arises in beginning this summation: mortality probabilities beyond 89 years of age are unknown, and it is not possible to reach the last age ω and consequently to know the sum $l_{90} + l_{91} + \ldots + l_\omega$. In all ways, the estimation of the mortality of very old persons presents quite considerable statistical difficulties.[11] Here we take that mortality into account only to have a correct estimate of the expectation of life at other ages.

To take account, in some acceptable fashion, of years lived beyond the age of 90, we will adopt a reasonable value for expectation of life at that age. In accordance with formula (E), and letting $x = 90$,

$$l_{90} = 1/2 + \frac{l_{91} + l_{92} + \ldots + l_\omega}{l_{90}}$$

It can be easily deduced:

$$l_{91} + l_{92} + \ldots + l_\omega = (e_{90} - 0.5)l_{90}.$$

11. See P. Vincent, "La mortalité des vieillards," *Population*, No. 2, April–June, 1951.

Thus, if we adopt 2.5 years as the value for e_{90}, the sum $l_{91} + l_{92} + \ldots + l_\omega$ represents, in the case of Table 6.2, twice the number of survivors at 90 years: $2 \times 260 = 520$ survivors.

The choice of e_{90} is clearly in part arbitrary, but the effects of this arbitrariness are quite insignificant: (1) in the first place, according to the most careful studies (see the study of P. Vincent already cited), the life expectancy at the oldest ages varies but quite little by country and over time; (2) 3.2 years and 2.0 years, which represent the extreme values in the West during the past 100 years, would imply deviations from our calculations, based on $e_{90} = 2.5$ years), of an order of magnitude of one-tenth of a year in the derivation of e_{85} and of e_{80}; at earlier ages, the difference is virtually unnoticeable.

Thus, step by step, by dividing the sum of cumulative survivors from ω to $x + 1$ (column 9) by the number of survivors at age x (column 7), and then increasing the result by 0.5 (see the correction factor of formula [E]), we obtain the expectation of life at age x (column 10). Among other results, we see that the expectation of life at birth for males in France in 1954–1955 was 65.1 years.

Description of Mortality Using Life Table Functions

We shall examine the variations with age in the quantities

$$q_x, \quad l_x, \quad d_x, \quad e_x,$$

adding certain new ideas where appropriate. We return to the diagram in Figure 6.8.

The mortality probability q_x. This probability, which at 0 years of age is confounded with the infant mortality rate, diminishes very rapidly at first, to reach a rather steady minimum between 10 and 15 years of age;[12] the increase is subsequently uninterrupted until the most advanced ages. In the example of the table for French males for 1954, the variations in q_x by age are not perfectly continuous (in the graphic sense). This absence of continuity, especially noticeable for years where the probabilities are quite low, derives from the random deviations related to the use of small numbers, from the possible errors of registration (the deaths of soldiers registered as civil deaths), possibly from migratory movements, etc. This is why, for example, q_{21}, q_{27}, q_{32} are smaller, respectively, than q_{20}, q_{26}, q_{31}.[13]

12. The location of this minimum could be specified better by computing the probabilities with a larger number of significant digits and smoothing the end of the values obtained (see note 13); generally, the minimum is located at around 10 or 11 years.
13. There are different techniques for smoothing the values of the probabilities; the most simple and most elementary is a graphic adjustment of the curve of the probabilities. This technique suffices for the demographer in countries with good statistics.

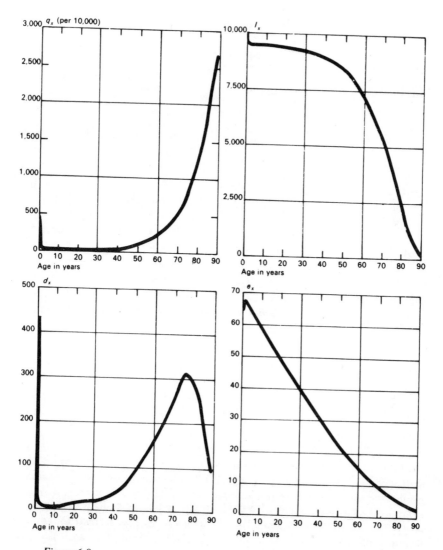

Figure 6.8

Similarly, at each exact age x the probability p_x of survival until the following birthday is defined. With this definition:

$$P_x = \frac{l_{x+1}}{l_x}.$$

This is also the complement of the probability of dying q_x:[14]

$$p_x = 1 - q_x$$

The number of survivors l_x of initial total l_0 (here, 10,000) and the series of l_x or *survival table*. The curve is usually called the *survival curve*. Let us observe that if the annual number of births as well as the conditions of mortality do not vary in a population, the quantities l_x give the number of persons attaining the different ages x in each year. It is in this way that the notion of the *stationary population* is introduced (see Chap. 10).

The study of l_x leads to defining the probability of survival from one age to another. Any l_x gives the proportion of the l_0 newborn who survive to attain their xth birthday; for example, $l_{20} = 9,380$, meaning that 9,380 persons of the 10,000 born reach the age of 20 years. Thus, 0.9380 is termed the *probability of survival from birth to 20 years*; or, more simply, since there is no ambiguity possible, the *probability of survival to 20 years* (under the conditions of mortality of the table).

The quotient

$$\frac{l_{x+k}}{l_x}$$

gives the probability of survival from age x to age $x+k$. The probability of survival from the 20th birthday ($l_{20} = 9,380$) to the 50th birthday ($l_{50} = 8,410$) is then equal to:

$$\frac{8,410}{9,380} = 0.897.$$

A characteristic average (also called a characteristic central tendency) of mortality is sometimes attached to the series of l_x: it is termed the *median length of life* or the *probable length of life*, the length of life that a newborn infant has one chance in two of attaining. This is then the age, x, where l_x

14. The equivalence of the two equations is easily shown:

$$p_x = \frac{l_{x+1}}{l_x}, \text{ but } l_{x+1} = l_x - d_x$$

therefore:

$$p_x = \frac{l_x - d_x}{l_x} \text{ or } 1 - \frac{d_x}{l_x} = 1 - q_x$$

is equal to exactly one half of l_0, here being 5,000. In the table for French males in 1954–1955, this age is between 70 years ($l_{70} = 5,163$) and 71 years of age ($l_{71} = 4,901$).[15]

One can also speak of the *probable length of life at age* x, which is determined by the number of years that an individual located at age x in the life table has one chance in two of living. Thus, 9,380 individuals attained age 20 years: this total of survivors will be reduced by half (to 4,690) between 71 years ($l_{71} = 4,901$) and 72 years ($l_{72} = 4,633$); the probable length of life at age 20 is then between 51 years ($71 - 20$) and 52 years ($72 - 20$).[16]

The number of deaths d_x. This number, excluding infant deaths (d_0), reaches its maximum in Western countries today at a little over 70 years—between ages 75 and 76 years (307 deaths) in the case of Table 6.2. Of course, the risk of mortality continues to increase beyond these ages, but the increasing mortality probabilities affect progressively smaller numbers of survivors, so that the annual number of deaths is lower at the more advanced ages. In the stationary population (see Chap. 10) associated with the life table, the 76th year of life represents the age at which the maximum number of deaths occurs (apart from the period 0 to 1 year of age). This age of the maximum number of deaths is called *the modal age of death*.

Expectation of life e_x. In this figure the maximum is located at 1 year of age, after which the decline continues, the level of e_0 being reached again between 3 and 4 years of age. The fact that the newborn child has an expectation of life lower than that of the child at 1, 2, or 3 years of age is due to the considerable risk of mortality he runs during the first year of life.

In those countries where mortality is higher, and where infant and child mortality in particular are high, the maximum of the expectation of life comes at a more advanced age (4 or sometimes 5 years), and the child 10 years of age has an expectation of life often close to that of the newborn infant. In the French example of 1954–1955, a simple computation shows that, taking into account mortality at other ages, infant mortality must be below 15 per 1,000 for e_0 to be equal to or greater than $e_1 = 67.2$ years.

The expectation of life is the index most often used when one wishes to summarize the risk of mortality in a country. It is worth remarking that the mean length of life in a population is not, in general, identical to the mean age of those dying; this mean age depends considerably on the number of deaths

15. There is sometimes interest in defining an exact age, which requires *interpolation*. We assume that the decline in the number of survivors between 70 and 71 years is regular (in more precise language, we speak of *linear* decline; we speak of carrying out a *linear interpolation*). Thus, ageing one year (between 70 and 71 years) entails the attrition of $5,163 - 4,901 = 262$ individuals: to what amount of ageing (beginning with 70 years) does the loss or attrition of $5,163 - 5,000 = 163$ individuals correspond? With our linearity hypothesis, the answer is evidently $163/262$ of a year or, in decimal form, 0.62 years; the exact median length of life is 70.62 years.

16. A computation of the previous type yields more precisely 51.79 years.

at different ages; and the absolute number of deaths at a given age depends, other things being equal, on the *relative size of the cohort that is exposed to the risk of mortality*. The size of the cohort at the period of study depends on its size at birth, on past mortality, and sometimes on migration. In order for the mean duration of life and the mean age at death to be identical, the population studied must be a "stationary" population. It would then be identical to the population deduced from the survivors in a life table; and in such a table the expectation of life at birth is identical to the mean age at death. A still more serious error consists in identifying the mean length of life and the mean age of the population.[17]

Mean Length of Life in Different Periods and in Different Countries

We shall see below that in a "stationary" population the crude death rate is equal to the inverse of the expectation of life.[18] This property permits us to make two remarks:

1. What we know about human fertility leads us to consider a crude birth rate of 50 per 1,000 as a maximum that may be surpassed only in exceptional cases; under these conditions, a crude death rate of 50 per 1,000 also appears as an extreme rate, above which any population would decline and in the long run would disappear. The inverse of this rate gives 20 years as the lower bound for the expectation of life at birth.

17. In the special case of a stationary population, this identification consists *approximately* in confounding the two quantities:

$$\frac{\sum_{i=0}^{\omega} i l_i}{\sum_{i=0}^{\omega} l_i} \quad \text{and} \quad \frac{\sum_{i=0}^{\omega} l_i}{l_0}$$

18. We could show this result approximately by observing that in a stationary population where the annual number of births (and consequently of deaths) equals l_0, the total population is clearly equal to

$$\sum_{i=0}^{\omega} l_i;$$

therefore, the crude death rate m can be expressed

$$\frac{l_0}{\sum_{i=0}^{\omega} l_i}$$

which is the inverse of

$$\frac{\sum_{i=0}^{\omega} l_i}{l_0}$$

which, in turn, is very close to the expression for e_0 (see equation [E], p. 120).

In fact, all of the conventional computations that might be carried out for historical populations or present day underdeveloped populations have given mean lengths of life greater than 20 years. For example, Duvillard's table for the French population of the second half of the eighteenth century gives 28.8 years. The tables for India at the beginning of the present century give just over 20 years: 23.8 years in 1891–1901, 22.9 years in 1901–1911, 20.15 years in 1911–1921.

2. The control of exogenous causes of deaths (violent accidents, infectious diseases) leads to the definition of a biological maximum age that preventive medicine, hygiene, and the use of present-day therapeutic techniques render accessible.[19] The expectation of life would then be about 77 years. Certain countries are already quite close to this limit: in 1956–1960 the mean length of life in Norway was 71.3 years for males and 75.6 years for females.

The stationary state toward which human populations move sooner or later would, if accompanied by the mortality limit defined above, be translated into a crude death rate (equal to the crude birth rate) of $1/77 = 13$ per 1,000.

At the present time, between the extreme levels for mean lengths of life— from scarcely over 25 years to almost 75 years—all the intermediate positions may be observed. They result from the progress from more or less ancient beginnings, and occur with varying rhythms, faster or slower. French mortality, like that of the majority of countries of western Europe, has had a slow development, which began around 1750 or perhaps a little earlier, leading to an expectation of life that was of the order of magnitude of 30 years during the Ancien Régime, to 47 years in about 1900, to 59 years at the end of World War II, and close to 70 years by 1958. In the United States, expectation of life at birth rose from 47.3 years in 1900 to 70.2 years in 1964. At the other extreme, Ceylon is a long-retarded country (the mean length of life was still only 32 years in 1920–1922) that has recently achieved very rapid progress: from 43 years in 1946, the expectation of life reached close to 60 years in 1954.

In Table 6.3, recent data on expectation of life in several countries are given. It must be noted that the computation of expectation of life in a country presumes relatively good statistical data on mortality: also, it is in the countries of highest mortality that the data are most often deficient. Precise comparisons among countries are difficult, as the periods for which the tables are computed often do not coincide.

Comparison of expectations of life for males and females shows a virtually universal male excess mortality (only five countries[20] are exceptions to this generalization, as is seen in Table 6.3); this excess mortality is indicated by a difference in mean lengths of life, varying generally from three years (for example, 2.9 in the Netherlands and in Sweden) to more than six years

19. See J. Bourgeois-Pichat, "La mortalité biologique de l'homme," *Population*, 1952, No. 3.
20. The Union of South Africa's population of Asiatic origin, Guatemala, Bolivia, Ceylon, and India.

TABLE 6.3.   *Expectation of Life at Birth (in years)*

Country	Date	Males	Females
AFRICA			
Algeria			
Moslems	1948–1951	44	49
Non-Moslems	1948–1951	60	67
Belgian Congo	1950–1952	37.6	40.0
French Guinea	1954–1955	26	28
Reunion	1951–1955	47.5	53.4
Union of South Africa			
European Population	1945–1947	63.8	68.3
	1950–1952	64.6	70.1
Colored Population	1945–1947	41.7	44.0
	1950–1952	44.8	47.8
Asiatic-Origin Population	1945–1947	50.7	49.8
	1950–1952	55.8	54.8
NORTH AMERICA			
Canada	1950–1952	66.3	70.8
	1960–1962	68.4	74.2
United States			
White Population	1956	67.3	73.7
	1964	67.7	74.6
Non-White Population	1956	61.1	65.9
	1964	61.1	67.2
Costa Rica	1949–1951	54.7	57.1
Guadaloupe and Martinique	1951–1955	55.4	59.2
Guatemala	1949–1951	43.8	43.3
Haiti	1950	32.6	
Jamaica	1950–1952	55.7	58.9
	1960	63.0	67.2
Mexico	1950	46.7	49.9
	1960	56.9	60.4
Panama	1952–1954	60.4	63.1
El Salvador	1949–1951	49.9	52.4
	1951–1961	44.7	47.4
Trinidad and Tobago	1954–1956	59.8	63.1
	1959–1961	62.1	66.3
SOUTH AMERICA			
Argentina	1947	56.9	61.4
	1959–1961	63.1	68.9
Bolivia	1949–1951	49.7	49.7
Brazil	1940–1950	39.3	
Chile	1952	49.8	53.9
Venezuela	1950–1951	56.3	58.8
	1960	61.2	65.6

TABLE 6.3 *(continued)*

Country	Date	Males	Females
ASIA			
Israel	1957	68.0	71.4
	1963	70.9	73.0
Japan	1957	63.2	67.6
	1963	67.2	72.3
Ceylon	1954	60.3	59.4
India	1941–1950	32.5	31.7
	1951–1960	41.9	40.6
Philippines	1946–1949	48.8	53.4
Thailand	1947–1948	48.7	51.9
EUROPE			
West Germany	1955	66.0	70.6
	1963–1964	67.3	73.1
Austria	1949–1951	61.9	67.0
	1959–1961	65.6	72.0
Belgium	1946–1949	62.0	67.3
	1959–1963	67.7	73.5
Denmark	1951–1955	69.9	72.6
	1962–1963	70.3	74.4
Finland	1951–1955	63.4	69.8
	1956–1960	64.9	71.6
France	1958	66.7	73.1
	1964	68.0	75.1
Great Britain			
England and Wales	1961–1963	67.9	73.9
	1961–1963	68.0	73.9
Scotland	1954–1956	67.4	71.1
	1961–1963	66.0	71.9
Northern Ireland	1955–1957	65.9	71.1
	1961–1963	67.6	72.5
Ireland	1950–1952	64.5	67.1
	1960–1962	68.1	71.9
Iceland	1941–1950	66.1	70.3
	1951–1960	70.7	75.0
Norway	1951–1955	71.1	74.7
	1956–1960	71.3	75.6
Netherlands	1953–1955	71.0	73.9
	1956–1960	71.4	74.8
Sweden	1951–1955	70.5	73.4
	1962	71.3	75.4
Switzerland	1948–1953	66.4	70.9
	1959–1961	69.5	74.8

TABLE 6.3 *(continued)*

Country	Date	Males	Females
Spain	1950	58.8	63.5
	1960	67.3	71.9
Italy	1955	66.2	70.4
Portugal	1955–1956	58.8	63.8
	1959–1962	60.7	66.4
Yugoslavia	1960–1961	62.2	65.3
Croatia	1952–1954	59.1	63.5
East Germany	1954–1955	66.2	70.2
	1960–1961	67.3	72.2
Bulgaria	1956–1957	63.5	67.9
	1960–1962	67.8	71.4
Hungary	1955	64.7	68.7
	1959–1960	65.2	69.6
Poland	1952–1953	58.6	64.2
	1960–1961	64.8	70.5
Czechoslovakia	1956	66.7	71.6
	1963	67.5	73.4
U.S.S.R	1955–1956	63	69
	1962–1963	70	
OCEANIA			
Australia	1953–1955	67.1	72.8
New Zealand	1960–1962	68.4	73.8
Europeans	1950–1952	68.3	72.4
	1960–1962	69.2	73.8
Maories	1950–1952	54.1	55.9
	1960–1962	59.0	61.4

(6.4 years in France and in Finland, 6.4 years in the white population of the United States).

Abridged Life Tables

The life table we have just presented is based upon computation of annual mortality probabilities, and, consequently, it gives the number of survivors at each successive birthday and the number of deaths between these birthdays. For various reasons, it is sometimes desirable to construct a table in which birthdays are given, for example, in five-year groups: (a) when one wishes to summarize a complete table; (b) when one has access only to approximations or estimates of elements that do not permit construction of a complete table. To present these tables, we shall construct the abridged table resulting from the French males' table for 1954–1955 (Table 6.4).

We have reproduced the number of survivors, l_x, in the complete table in five-year groups, that is, l_0, l_5, l_{10}, l_{15}, ..., l_{90}. In order to give a precise representation of infant mortality, we have also reproduced l_1.

By successive subtractions, we obtain the number of deaths, $_n d_x$ between the x and $x+n$ birthdays, usually x and $x+5$ (except for $x = 0$ and $x = 1$, where n equals 1 and 4, respectively). Finally, the quotient $_n q_x$ results[21] from the formula:

$$_n q_x = \frac{_n d_x}{l_x}.$$

The information contained in Table 6.4 is thus much more condensed than that in Table 6.2. Very often it is sufficient and even more convenient for effecting comparisons.

TABLE 6.4. *Abridged Life Table for French Males, 1954–1955*

Age x	l_x	$_n d_x$	$_n q_x$ (per 10,000)
0	10,000	454	454
1	9,546	71	74
5	9,475	24	25
10	9,451	23	24
15	9,428	48	51
20	9,380	74	79
25	9,306	89	96
30	9,217	111	120
35	9,106	144	158
40	8,962	213	238
45	8,749	339	387
50	8,410	510	606
55	7,900	689	872
60	7,211	909	1,261
65	6,302	1,139	1,807
70	5,163	1,401	2,714
75	3,762	1,494	3,971
80	2,268	1,267	5,586
85	1,001	741	7,403
90	260		

n is equal to 5 years, except in the first line ($n/A = 1$ year) and in the second line ($n/A = 4$ years).

If we had only this information concerning French male mortality in 1954–1955, would we be able to compute a mean length of life? This question is primarily of interest when no other data can be obtained and when the abridged table is the only one that can be constructed on the basis of available data concerning mortality in a given country. It is always possible to

21. Most often this refers to quinquennial probabilities, as is indicated by the lower left index a, which almost always has the value 5; obviously $_1 q_x$ is equivalent to q_x.

try to estimate the quantities l_x that are missing from the abridged life table by graphic interpolation and, subsequently, to apply the formula (E) already given. It is also possible to make do with only the data in the abridged table by modifying formula (E); the resulting estimation of a mean length of life is still a very good one.

Let us, then, carry out the computation of the number of years lived by the 10,000 newborn of Table 6.4, using the l_x and the $_nd_x$ of this table. The hypothesis at the basis of this computation is always that the deaths between ages x and $x+n$ are equally distributed—a hypothesis somewhat more approximate in the case of the abridged table than in the case of a complete table of mortality. Here are the elements of the computation:

(1) the sum of the years lived until the last birthday shown in the abridged table:

$$l_1 + 4l_5 + 5[l_{10} + l_{15} + \cdots + l_{\omega'}];^{22}$$

(2) the sum of the years lived between the last birthday of the table attained and the instant of death:

$$0.5d_0 + 2_4d_1 + 2.5[_5d_5 + _5d_{10} + \cdots].$$

The bracketed number is clearly equal to l_5, and $d_0 = l_0 - l_1$; and $_4d_1 - l_0$;

(3) finally, the sum of the years lived may be expressed

$$0.5l_0 + 2.5l_1 + 4.5l_5 + 5[l_{10} + l_{15} + \cdots],$$

and

$$e_0 = 1/2 + \frac{2.5l_1 + 4.5l_5 + 5[l_{10} + l_{15} + \cdots]}{l_0} \qquad \text{(E')}$$

Applying this formula to the data in Table 6.4,[23] we find that $e_0 = 65.1$ years, a result identical to that found using the complete life table. This indicates the precision of formula (E').

Approximate Tables

Often the abridged life table is derived from approximate computations based on incomplete and sometimes unstable documentation. In this case, the abridged table is no longer a contraction of a previously existing complete life table, but represents the end result of successive approximations carried out for all of the available data.

22. ω' is the last year of age divisible by 5 that can be attained.
23. Ignoring the quantity $5(l_{95} + l_{100} + \cdots)$.

In such a case, the quinquennial mortality probabilities are estimated directly on the basis of available data concerning mortality by age.

Relationship Between Mortality Rates and Mortality Probabilities

We have seen how precise the notion of mortality probability is and how detailed the data required for its computation must be. In practice, it is rare that we have access to data in such great detail; either the statistics of deaths and of population structure are only estimates, or the human groupings studied are small, and the computation of annual mortality probabilities is meaningless, given the random variation associated with the small numbers. In both of these cases, we are obliged to employ more gross indices, such as quinquennial or decennial mortality rates.[24] The problem is then to convert these rates into mortality probabilities.

Let us observe that there are some approximate functional relationships between rate and probability. We work first with an annual probability, q_x:

$$q_x = \frac{d_x}{l_x}. \tag{I}$$

If the population studied does not deviate too much from the stationary population generated in the life table,[25] we may assume that the mean population in the *age group* between x and $x+1$, that is, P_x, is equal to

$$P_x = \frac{l_x + l_{x+1}}{2}.$$

Since

$$l_{x+1} = l_x - d_x,$$

we have

$$l_x + l_{x+1} = 2l_x - d_x,$$

and

$$P_x = l_x - \frac{d_x}{2}.$$

24. Let us observe that, regardless of the data available, a quinquennial or decennial probability could not be computed directly on periods of observation of less than 6 years and 11 years, respectively. It is necessary to have an observation period of at least six years to compute a quinquennial probability in accordance with the definition; but then we would be working with the deaths of only a single cohort, while 11 cohorts have generated the deaths during this period (this can be verified with the aid of the *Lexis* diagram).

25. For this it is necessary in any case to choose a radix of the table l_0 that is clearly consistent with the annual number of births in the population.

With this expression for the mean population, the mortality rate at age x, m_x, can be written:

$$m_x = \frac{d_x}{P_x} = \frac{d_x}{l_x - \dfrac{d_x}{2}}. \qquad (II)$$

By substituting the expression $l_x q_x$ for d_x taken from equation (I) in equation (II), the relationship between m_x and q_x is established. In equation (I) $d_x = l_x q_x$. Substituting this in equation (II) we have

$$m_x = \frac{l_x q_x}{l_x - \dfrac{l_x q_x}{2}} = \frac{q_x}{1 - \dfrac{q_x}{2}}. \qquad (R)$$

which is the relationship sought and can be manipulated to yield q_x as a function of m_x:

$$q_x = m_x\left(1 - \frac{q_x}{2}\right) = m_x - \frac{q_x m_x}{2}$$

$$q_x + \frac{q_x m_x}{2} = m_x; \quad q_x\left(1 + \frac{m_x}{2}\right) = m_x$$

$$q_x = \frac{m_x}{1 + \dfrac{m_x}{2}} = \frac{2m_x}{2 + m_x}. \qquad (R')$$

Applying the same hypothesis to the population studied, we may assume that, in the case of five-year rates

$$_5P_x = 5\left(\frac{l_x + l_{x+5}}{2}\right)$$

by means of which we arrive at the relationship

$$_5q_x = \frac{10\,_5m_x}{2 + 5\,_5m_x},$$

and, more generally,

$$_nq_x = \frac{2n\,_nm_x}{2 + n\,_nm_x}.$$

Actually, to the extent that the structures of real populations deviate from stationary structures, the relationships between rates and probabilities deviate more or less from those defined by the approximate formulas presented above.[26]

The observation of real populations, in which rates and probabilities could be calculated properly, can yield elements permitting empirical study of the relationship between the $_nq_x/n$ and the $_nm_x$. This is what Reed and Merrell[27] did with the population of different states in the United States for 1910, 1920, and 1930. They constructed graphs locating:

on the abscissa, $m_0, {}_4m_1, {}_5m_x, {}_{10}m_x$;

on the ordinate, $q_0, {}_4q_1, {}_5q_x, {}_{10}q_x$.

The groupings of points so obtained were then fitted to curves defining the functional relationships between the $_nq_x$ and the $_nm_x$ more satisfactorily because they were more realistic than those defined by the formulas established previously.[28]

The fact that these relationships were established on the basis of only the experience in different states of the United States between 1910 and 1930 somewhat limits their applicability. It is certain that all the possibilities are not represented and that the relationships run the risk of not reflecting the "mean relationship" existing between rates and probabilities for all countries at all periods. Particularly in present-day underdeveloped countries there are structures and rates of deaths by ages that surely do not correspond to those observed in states of the United States that had the same level of mortality 30 to 50 years ago.

Despite these restrictions, the relationships between rates and probabilities established by Reed and Merrell retain great interest. If one excludes the relationships between m_0 and q_0 and between $_4m_1$ and $_4q_1$, which take into account the underregistration of quite young children in the censuses of the American states in 1910, 1920, and 1930, the relationships that permit converting

from $_5m_x$ to $_5q_x$ for any x

from $_{10}m_x$ to $_{10}q_x$ for any x

26. However, the equation

$$q_x = \frac{2m_x}{2 + m_x}$$

is acceptable often enough in present-day Western populations that are not too different from stationary structures. It provides a means of directly computing annual mortality probabilities when death statistics are given by age but without double classification, as in the case, for instance, of those published in England and Wales and in the United States.

27. See "A Short Method for Constructing an Abridged Life Table," *The American Journal of Hygiene*, Vol. 30, No. 2, September, 1939.

28. In this way $_5q_x$ and $_5m_x$ were connected by the equation $_5q_x = 1 - e^{-(5_5m_x + 0.008(5)_5^3 m_x^2)}$.

are largely acceptable; in addition, Reed and Merrell have calculated tables of this relationship that eliminate nearly all calculations.

Construction of the Abridged Life Tables by the Reed-Merrell Method

The methods to apply in computing the complete mortality table for the single year 1954 are detailed on page 115. We propose here using the five-year age group mortality rates of this year to obtain, with the aid of the Reed and Merrell tables, the corresponding quinquennial mortality probabilities.

These computations are purely illustrative; they permit us to explain the use of the Reed and Merrell tables and to verify their validity.

Always remembering the reservation we have made in connection with the use of these tables for relating m_0 to q_0, we apply the formula

$$q_0 = \frac{2m_0}{2+m_0}. \tag{R''}$$

Here $m_0 = 480$ per 10,000; this results in $q_0 = 469$ per 10,000.[29]

In fact, it will very often be possible to compute q_0 directly as a conventional rate of infant mortality, since this computation uses only the total number of deaths between age 0 and 1 year (which we had to have if we were able to calculate m_0), and the births of that year. In this way we find as the correct value for q_0, for boys in France in 1954, $q_0 = 462$ per 10,000, indicating the degree of accuracy of the formula (R'').[30]

As the relationships established by Reed and Merrell between $_4m_1$ and $_4q_1$ are not as suitable, we furnish in an appendix a corrected table that does not take account of the underregistration of young children in censuses.

Let us present in detail the conversion from $_5m_{60}$ to $_5q_{60}$ with the aid of the Reed-Merrell tables. Taking the computation to five decimal places,[31] we find $_5m_{60} = 0.02680$ (see Table 6.6). The Reed-Merrell tables contain all of the $_5m_x$ from 0.001 to 0.450. Table 6.5 gives the appropriate extract.

TABLE 6.5. *Extract from the Reed-Merrell Table*

$_5m_x$	$_5q_x$	Δ .00
...	...	...
.026	.122498	4423
.027	.126921	4402
...	...	...

29. Evidently it is necessary to write $m_0 = 0.045$ to apply the equation.
30. The Reed-Merrell tables gave a much poorer result: $q_0 = 435$ per 10,000.
31. With $_5m_x$ being of an order of magnitude of 1/5 that of the corresponding $_5q_x$, it is also useful to compute $_5m_x$ carrying to one decimal place more than is wanted for $_5q_x$.

Δ gives the difference between consecutive values of $_5q_x$. By linear interpolation we find that we must add to 0.122498 the value corresponding to $_5m_x = 0.026$.

$$0.004423 \times 0.80 = 0.003538.$$

Thus,

$$_5q_{60} = 0.122498 + 0.003538 = 0.126036,$$

rounded off at 1,260 per 10,000.

Table 6.6a assembles all of the mortality probabilities computed on the one hand by the method of Reed and Merrell,[32] and, on the other hand, with all the care and detail permitted by French statistics, according to a method that will be presented below. The agreement between the numbers of the two series varies according to the ages, but remains satisfactory on the whole.

As in the transformation of rates into mortality probabilities—we had especially in mind the computation of specific elements of a life table, such as the series of the survivors $[l_x]$ or the mean length of life—it is especially important to evaluate the Reed-Merrell approximation in terms of these same elements.

TABLE 6.6a. *Rates and Probabilities of Mortality for French Males in 1954*

Age x in years	$_am_x$ (per 100,000)	$_aq_x$ (per 10,000)		Age x in years	$_am_x$ (per 100,000)	$_aq_x$ (per 10,000)	
		Reed-Merrell Table	Complete Table			Reed-Merrell Table	Complete Table
0	425	469	462	45	811	398	398
1	195	78	80	50	1,253	609	611
5	53	26	29	55	1,819	872	880
10	49	24	25	60	2,680	1,260	1,262
15	107	53	52	65	3,973	1,815	1,816
20	151	75	77	70	6,228	2,704	2,710
25	189	94	96	75	9,887	3,960	3,968
30	240	119	120	80	15,551	5,514	5,572
35	332	165	164	85	25,154	7,331	7,367
40	492	243	244				

a is equal to 5 years, except for the first line ($a = 1$ year) and the second line ($a = 4$ years).

In Table 6.6b we have assembled the series of survivors computed according to the two series of probabilities; it can be seen how close they are. The corresponding mean lengths of life are identical—64.9 years in both cases.

32. Except at 0 years; as far as $_4q_1$ is concerned, it is computed with the aid of the corrected table presented in the Appendix.

TABLE 6.6b.   *Survival Table for French Males in 1954*

Age x in years	L_x Reed-Merrell Table	L_x Complete Table	Age x in years	L_x Reed-Merrell Table	L_x Complete Table
0	10,000	10,000	45	8,725	8,724
1	9,531	9,538	50	8,378	8,377
5	9,457	9,462	55	7,868	7,865
10	9,432	9,435	60	7,182	7,173
15	9,409	9,411	65	6,277	6,268
20	9,359	9,362	70	5,138	5,130
25	9,289	9,290	75	3,749	3,740
30	9,202	9,201	80	2,264	2,256
35	9,092	9,091	85	1,016	999
40	8,942	8,942	90	272	263

The method of Reed and Merrell is useful especially in the construction of approximate tables based on abbreviated and approximate information. For this reason, its use is indicated in underdeveloped countries, along with other methods that we cannot present here.

Let us indicate that in underdeveloped countries it is easier and more immediately useful to establish an acceptable census than it is to ramble among the various methods of vital registration.[33]

This raises the question of the derivation of life tables based on only the data from successive censuses (even if these censuses include no indication at all of vital registration). It is conceivable that the comparison of totals for the same group of cohorts in two successive censuses may provide a measure of human losses due to mortality (with the reservation that migrations are not too numerous). In this way life tables for India since the end of the nineteenth century, and life tables for Brazil, calculated by G. Mortara, have been derived. We will not go into the technical aspect of these methods.

Strictly Period Life Tables

We have seen that it is impossible, if we retain the rigorous definition of mortality probability, to construct period life tables that take into account the total number of deaths in a given period (see p. 115 and Figures 6.4a and 6.4b). In particular, it is impossible to compute the mortality probability on the

33. Besides, as we have already noted, to compensate for the neglect of vital registers, sometimes the census in underdeveloped countries seeks information concerning not only population size and structure but also births and deaths occurring in an interval (usually a year) preceding the census.

basis of deaths of a single year; thus it is also impossible to construct annual period life tables.

Only by broadening the rules for computation of mortality probabilities is it possible to succeed in defining and computing strictly period life tables.

Mortality Probabilities Based on Deaths of a Single Calendar Year

Suppose we wish to compute q_{50} for males in France in 1954. The data for this year and at this age are those in Figure 6.9a: 1,537 deaths in the 1903 male cohort, which totaled 293,238 on January 1, 1954; 1,544 deaths in the 1904 male cohort, which totaled 292,010 on January 1, 1955. Let us use the symbolic data in Figure 6.9b.

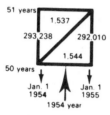

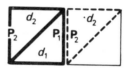

Figure 6.9a   *Figure 6.9b*

We have, then, the two categories of deaths d_1 and d_2 and the two populations P_1 and P_2.

The idea that governs the construction of a mortality probability based on these data is that of the reconstruction of the *Lexis* parallelogram, which contains the data for the computation of the conventional probability. For this, it suffices to replace, by translation, the top triangle of the square and to couple it with the bottom triangle (shown by the dotted line in Figure 6.9b).

But in this parallelogram, the two populations of the same age do not have the same totals: P_1 for one, and P_2 for the other. We may "reconcile" P_2 to P_1, using a rule of three for the deaths: since the number of deaths in P_2 is d_2, the number of deaths that would correspond for P_1 is

$$d_2 \times \frac{P_1}{P_2}$$

deaths (see Figures 6.10a and 6.10b).

Altogether there are, in the parallelogram so constructed,

$$d_1 + d_2 \times \frac{P_1}{P_2} \text{ deaths,}$$

which are related to the number l_1 of survivors at the initial age.[34] Clearly, $l_1 = P_1 + d_1$.

---

34. Here the indices attached to the letter *l* denote cohorts, and not ages; l_1 and l_2 denote the total number of survivors to the same age in the two cases.

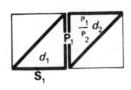

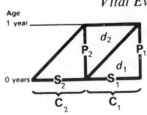

Figure 6.10a   *Figure 6.10b*

Finally, the probability sought is expressed:

$$q = \frac{d_1 + \dfrac{d_2 \times P_1}{P_2}}{l_1}$$

This formula can be transformed, and written successively:

$$q = \frac{d_1 P_2 + d_2 P_1}{P_2 l_1} = \frac{d_1 P_2 + d_2 (l_1 - d_1)}{P_2 l_1}$$

$$[\text{Since } P_1 = l_1 - d_1]$$

where

$$q = \frac{d_1 P_2 + d_2 l_1 - d_1 d_2}{P_2 l_1} = \frac{d_1 P_2}{P_2 l_1} + \frac{d_2 l_1}{P_2 l_1} + \frac{d_1 d_2}{P_2 l_1}$$

and, finally,

$$q = \frac{d_1}{l_1} + \frac{d_2}{P_2} - \frac{d_1}{l_1} \times \frac{d_2}{P_2}. \qquad (Q)^{35}$$

35. In particular, equation (Q) can be applied to the computation of the *infant mortality rate*. Thus for 1954 we find that for boys, $q_0 = 461.9$ per 1,000 (see Table 6.7). Working always with q_0 we may note that equation (Q) can be written

$$\left(d_1 + d_2 \frac{P_1}{P_2} \right) \bigg/ l_1.$$

Consequently,

$$q_0 = \frac{d_1}{l_1} + \frac{d_2}{P_2} \times \frac{P_1}{l_1}$$

Provided that infant mortality varies but little from one year (C_1) to the other (C_2),

$$\frac{P_1}{l_1} \cong \frac{P_2}{l_2}$$

which permits writing equation (Q) in the form

$$q_0 = \frac{d_1}{l_1} \times \frac{d_2}{P_2} \times \frac{P_2}{l_2} \quad \text{or} \quad q_0 = \frac{d_1}{l_1} + \frac{d_2}{l_2}.$$

The infant mortality rate for one year may in this way be obtained by adding the ratios of the two categories of deaths, d_1 and d_2, to the numbers of newborn in the corresponding generations, l_1 and l_2.

Let us observe that very often the product

$$\left(\frac{d_1}{l_1} \times \frac{d_2}{P_2}\right)$$

is negligible. The two quantities d_1/l_1 and d_2/P_2 are, in effect, of an order of magnitude of half of the annual death rate. At 50 years of age, where the rate is of the order of 10 per 1,000 (among males in France), i.e., 0.01, the quantities d_1/l_1 and d_2/P_2 are 0.005, and their product is on the order of 0.000025, or 0.025 per 1,000.

Thus, very often,

$$q = \frac{d_1}{l_1} + \frac{d_2}{P_2} \qquad (Q')$$

will be an appropriate approximate formula.[36]

We present below a number of extracts from the computations for male mortality probabilities in France in 1954 by formula (Q). We see that the value of the correction introduced by the term

$$\frac{d_2}{P_2} \times \frac{d_1}{l_1}$$

is null at many ages (at the degree of precision with which we work, i.e., at

---

36. We can also prove equation (Q) by noting the flow from l to l' by P in the *Lexis* diagram (Figure 6.11a).

Figure 6.11a

Figure 6.11b

The survival rate in the flow from l to P is $f = P/l$. The survival rate in the flow from P to l' is $f' = l'/P$. Consequently, the survival rate, p, the complement of the probability sought, is $p = f \times f'$, whence $q = 1 - ff'$. With the elements of Figure 6.11b

$$f = 1 - \frac{d_1}{l_1} \quad \text{and} \quad f' = 1 - \frac{d_2}{P_2}$$

and we substitute to obtain

$$q = 1 - \left(1 - \frac{d_2}{P_2}\right)\left(1 - \frac{d_1}{l_1}\right) = \frac{d_1}{l_1} + \frac{d_2}{P_2} - \frac{d_1}{l_1} \times \frac{d_2}{P_2}.$$

Finally, let us remark that, if we can determine l_2 (see Figure 6.10a), this time the indices apply to any age interval $(x, x+1)$; with the same proviso as in the preceding note, we have again

$$q_0 = \frac{d_1}{l_1} + \frac{d_2}{l_2}$$

an equation more exact than (Q').

TABLE 6.7.   *France: Mortality Probabilities for Males in 1954 (computation procedure)*

Age x	d_2	P_2	d_1	P_1	$l_1 = P_1 + d_1$	$\dfrac{d_2}{P_2}$ (per 10,000)	$\dfrac{d_1}{l_1}$ (per 10,000)	$\dfrac{d_2}{P_2} + \dfrac{d_1}{l_1}$ (per 10,000)	$\dfrac{d_2}{P_2} \cdot \dfrac{d_1}{l_1}$ (per 10,000)	q_x (per 10,000)
0	4,592	395,918	14,563	401,783	416,346	116.1	349.8	465.9	4.0	461.9
10	76	294,760	64	292,495	292,559	2.6	2.2	4.8	0.0	4.8
40	604	298,299	589	287,970	288,559	20.2	20.4	40.6	0.0	40.6
60	2,075	179,793	2,046	177,058	179,104	115.4	114.2	229.6	1.3	228.3
70	3,255	122,772	3,161	125,909	129,070	265.1	244.9	510.0	6.5	503.5
80	3,604	51,929	3,371	53,294	56,665	694.0	594.9	1,288.9	41.3	1,247.6

TABLE 6.8.   *France: Life Table for Males, 1954*

Age x	Life Expectancy		Relative Error Due to Use of Approximate Probabilities with Equation (Q')
	With Exact Probabilities [Equation (Q)]	With Approximate Probabilities [Equation (Q')]	
Years	Years	Years	Percent
0	64.9	64.8	+ 0.9
20	49.2	49.0	+ 0.0
50	22.6	22.5	+ 0.3
70	9.5	9.4	+ 1.3
80	5.1	4.9	+ 3.3
85	3.6	3.4	+ 5.3

one per 100,000). It is never of great importance and has only the weakest implications on the expectation of life, as is shown in Table 6.8.

Projective Mortality Probabilities

Projective mortality probabilities will be particularly useful when computing survivors in the construction of population projections. It is from this application that these probabilities take their name. The projective probabilities can also furnish a good approximation of the conventional probabilities. Here, for example, is the way in which they are determined.

We will consider, again, the French male mortality in 1954. Let us note the 1903 cohort (Figure 6.12a), in which all the members (survivors) are aged 50 complete years on January 1, 1954. In this cohort, $1,537 + 1,692 = 3,229$ deaths occurring in 1954.

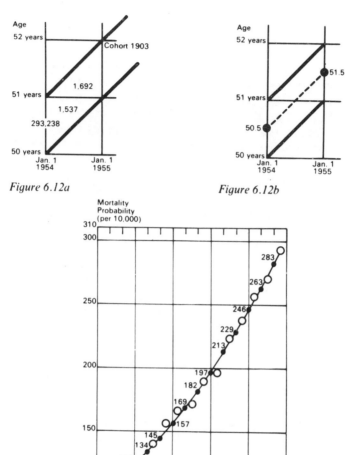

Figure 6.12a

Figure 6.12b

Figure 6.13a

Relating these deaths to the 293,238 survivors of the cohort as of January 1, 1954, we obtain an index equal to

$$\frac{3,229}{293,238} = 0.110, \text{ or } 110 \text{ per } 1,000.$$

Its computation resembles that of the conventional mortality probabilities: in effect, a certain number of events are related to the initial total of persons who risk undergoing these events in the course of a single year. Always, the "initial total" is not that of persons reaching a given birthday, but that of a cohort (or group of cohorts) at a given instant. (The movement across the vertical segment in the *Lexis* diagram and not across a horizontal segment.)

In comparing the total of persons in the cohort to a group of men aged exactly 50.5 years on January 1, 1954, and 51.5 years on January 1, 1955 (Figure 6.12b), which are the mean extremes of the exact ages at the two dates considered, it can be seen that the projective probability is none other than $_1q_{50.5}$—the conventional mortality probabilities between 50.5 years and 51.5 years.

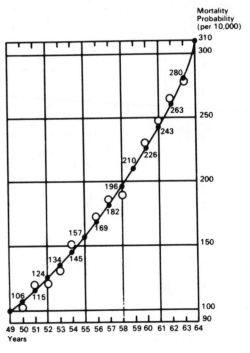

Figure 6.13b

Nothing prevents the computation of a life table using probabilities of the form $_1q_{x+0.5}$. Nevertheless, it may be preferable to construct a life table on the basis of mortality probabilities for complete ages $_1q_x$ for the sake of comparison alone. It is then necessary to interpolate—graphically, for example—among the series of probabilities $_1q_{x+0.5}$; this is the object of the diagram in Figure 6.13a. Similarly, the series of $_1q_x$ obtained is "smoothed," while that resulting from the computations of Table 6.7 was crude; it is possible to "smooth" the latter graphically, as we have done in Figure 6.13b.

We obtain, then, the adjusted probabilities of Table 6.9, which are often identical and, in any case, are always very close to the values drawn from projective probabilities.

TABLE 6.9. *France: Mortality Probabilities for Males*

Age x	Computations of Table 6.7		Based on Projected Probabilities	Age x	Computations of Table 6.7		Based on Projected Probabilities
	Unadjusted	Adjusted			Unadjusted	Adjusted	
50	105	106	107	57	184	182	182
51	117	115	114	58	190	196	197
52	122	124	124	59	210	210	213
53	131	134	134	60	228	226	229
54	151	145	145	61	248	243	246
55	157	157	157	62	263	263	263
56	172	169	169	63	279	284	283

The projective probabilities are the only ones that can be computed directly when the only data available are those giving the deaths classified by birth cohort (in the absence of double classification).

Strictly Period Life Tables for Multiple-Year Periods

According to Figure 6.4a, constructing a period life table for an interval of several years by the conventional method of computation of mortality probabilities[37] entails a loss of information: the deaths in the triangles at the extremities are neglected.

A solution to this deficiency in the conventional method is to obtain at each age the arithmetic mean of the probabilities, computed each time in a square of the *Lexis* diagram according to the two procedures we have already indicated.

Life Table for Children Under One Year of Age

Complete life tables have been defined as giving, for example, the number of survivors at successive birthdays. The term *complete* is largely arbitrary; it is not necessary to rule out the construction of tables giving even more detailed descriptions of mortality than so-called complete mortality tables.

---

37. Either we compute each probability by equation (F) or take the arithmetic mean of the probabilities at the same age for each of the observed cohorts; we prefer the latter solution (see note 5).

More detailed life tables are sometimes constructed concerning mortality in the first year of life; this is justified by the importance of this mortality and the diversity of its structure by age.

The first year of life is thus partitioned into periods expressed in months or in days, for which the conventional elements of a life table are computed. To examine this, we review the technique of computation applied at present in French national vital statistics. By way of example we reproduce in Table 6.10 the data of the French table for the year 1957 for both sexes. Here monthly mortality probabilities are involved.

TABLE 6.10.   *France, 1957: Life Table for Infants under 1 Year of Age (Both Sexes)*

Age (x)		l_x	d_x	$_nq_x$ (per 100,000)
Birth		100,000	1,492	1,492
1 month	(30 days)	98,508	259	263
2 months	(60 days)	98,249	208	212
3 months	(90 days)	98,041	173	176
4 months	(120 days)	97,868	139	142
5 months	(150 days)	97,729	116	119
6 months	(180 days)	97,613	107	110
7 months	(210 days)	97,506	105	108
8 months	(240 days)	97,401	90	92
9 months	(270 days)	97,311	85	87
10 months	(301 days)	97,226	77	79
11 months	(332 days)	97,149	71	73
12 months	(365 days)	97,078		

Note: Figures refer to exact age attained. No correction is made for erroneous stillbirths.
Source: "The Demographic Situation in 1957," *Études Statistiques*, No. 4, Oct.–Dec. 1958.

Model Life Tables

A brief review of existing life tables shows that for a level of mortality at a given age, say, 40 years, there is some corresponding level at a different age, say, 50 years. Systematizing this observation, the Population Branch of the United Nations detailed the linkages between successive probabilities of mortality, basing the work on the experience furnished by 158 national life tables covering the period 1900–1950.

This work was carried out on tables applying to both sexes. Initially, the relationship between the mortality probability at age zero, q_0, and the quinquennial mortality probability $_5q_0$ was studied. Locating the first quantity on a horizontal axis and the second on a vertical axis, a set of 158 points was obtained (each representing a given country at a given period), establishing a strong relationship between the two probabilities. A curve was fitted to this set of points, defining a functional relationship between the two mortality probabilities.[38]

Plotting the set of points representing the empirical relationship between the quinquennial mortality probabilities $_5q_0$ and $_5q_5$ led to a new curve, defining a functional relationship between these two probabilities, and so forth. Once this set of connections was defined and established analytically, it was possible to relate the infant mortality rates to the series of quinquennial mortality probabilities and also to construct the resulting abridged life table. Thus, corresponding to an infant mortality rate of 50 per 1,000, it is possible to derive the mortality probabilities

$$_5q_0 = 65.07 \text{ per } 1,000 \qquad _5q_5 = 5.62 \text{ per } 1,000$$
$$_5q_{10} = 4.35 \text{ per } 1,000 \qquad _5q_{60} = 91.64 \text{ per } 1,000, \text{ etc.}$$

From the table constructed with this series of mortality probabilities, one can derive an expectation of life at birth of 66.42 years.

This work has been carried out for infant mortality levels ranging from 20 per 1,000 to 330 per 1,000, in steps of 5 per 1,000 up to 100 per 1,000, and thereafter in steps of 10 per 1,000. In this way, 40 model life tables were obtained, applicable for the total of both sexes, with the expectation of life ranging from 71.71 years to 18.83 years.[39]

In a subsequent work[40] intended to facilitate the computation of numbers of survivors in population forecasts, the Population Branch of the United Nations derived from these model life tables (corresponding to infant mortality rates in round numbers) other model life tables corresponding to expectations of life at birth in round numbers (from 20 years to 55 years by steps of $2\frac{1}{2}$ years, and from 55 years to 73.9 years by more irregular steps or intervals).

The study of 158 male and female mortality tables also has permitted construction of life tables applicable to each sex separately, corresponding to each of the tables for both sexes together.

Use of Model Life Tables

The model life tables describe varying structures of mortality by age, corresponding to different levels of total mortality (defined by the expecta-

38. This functional relationship is described by the equation $_5q_0 = 23,832 + 1,349406(q_0 - 20) + 0.000844(q_0 - 20)^2$. By this equation, the $_5q_0$ corresponding to a given q_0, say, 50 per 1,000, is $_5q_0 = 65.07$ per 1,000.
39. See *Population Studies*, No. 22, Patterns of Variation in Mortality by Age and Sex. Model Life Tables for Underdeveloped Countries.
40. See *Population Studies*, No. 25, Methods of Population Estimation. Manual III: Methods of Population Projections by Sex and by Age.

tion of life at birth). These are the average structures resulting from comparisons of various life tables for human groups living under quite different economic and social conditions.[41] The living conditions (hygienic, medical, economic, sociological) that assured the French in 1900 of a mean length of life of 45 years are quite different from those permitting the Moslems living in North Africa today to attain, on the average, the same age. This expectation of life, seemingly the same in the two cases, may result from quite different age compositions of mortality, though it leads to the same mean in the aggregate.

Despite these reservations, the model mortality tables remain of great value:

1. The reference to average structures of mortality by age permits classification of the nature of mortality in a given country. Let us compare the French male mortality of 1954 with the model life table closest to it.

In comparing the expectations of life, we use Model Table 6 ($e_0 = 65.2$ years, while in the French table, $e_0 = 64.9$ years). For comparisons of infant mortality, we use Model Table 5 ($q_0 = 45.0$ per 1,000; in the French table $q_0 = 46.2$ per 1,000).

Let us compare the mortality probabilities at each age in the French table and in Model Table 5, as shown in Table 6.11.

Following the levels of infant mortality, which are comparable, are shown the mortality levels of young Frenchmen (under 25 years of age), which are notably lower than those in the model life table, especially between 5 and 10 years of age. Between 5 and 15 years of age the model table, with a higher expectation of life ($e_0 = 69.3$ years) has mortality probabilities higher than the French probabilities: $_5q_5 = 3.1$ per 1,000 against 2.9 per 1,000, and $_5q_{10} = 2.6$ per 1,000 against 2.5 per 1,000.

For ages over 30 years, the French life table shows a consistent excess mortality as compared with the model life table; the excess mortality is especially marked between 40 and 55 years of age. Thus, the structure of male mortality peculiar to France, which is suggested by other studies based on the comparison of numerous countries,[42] appears quite clearly by comparison with model mortality tables.

2. We have seen that the determination of expectation of life supposes numerous computations based on detailed information. This information is often of doubtful quality. Thus, infant mortality rates are little known in underdeveloped countries, where the registration of deaths of young children is quite incomplete; the registration of adult deaths, however, is more reliable.

41. Let us add that these are period conditions and not conditions to which real cohorts were subjected throughout their lives.

42. See, for example, "Vues générales sur la mortalité française despuis la guerre," *Population*, No. 3, 1954.

By contrast, in historical populations that can be studied on the basis of parish registers, it is possible to ascertain quite well the mortality up to the ages of 15 or 20 years, those ages where it is possible to specify the total observed; conversely, the study of mortality of adults and elderly persons is much more problematic.

TABLE 6.11. *Comparison of Life Table for French Males with Model Male Life Table No. 5*

Mortality Probabilities (per 1,000)			
Ages	*French Male Life Table 1954 (e₀ = 64.9)*	*Model Life Table No. 5 (e₀ = 66.0)*	*Percent Differences Between French Life Table and Model Life Table (Base)*
			percent
0– 1	46.2	45.0	+ 3
1– 5	8.0	12.6	−37
5–10	2.9	·5.2	−44
10–15	2.5	4.1	−39
15–20	5.2	6.9	−25
20–25	7.7	9.3	−17
25–30	9.6	9.6	—
30–35	12.0	9.8	+22
35–40	16.4	12.2	+34
40–45	24.4	17.4	+40
45–50	39.8	27.1	+47
50–55	61.1	42.2	+45
55–60	88.0	64.5	+36
60–65	126.2	100.2	+26
65–70.	181.6	153.5	+18
70–75	271.0	234.1	+16
75–80	396.8	347.9	+14
80–85	557.2	493.5	+13

On the basis of fragmentary results concerning the mortality of a country, it is possible, by comparing these data with the corresponding data in the model mortality table closest to it, to construct an approximate life table and to estimate the expectation of life. An example of such a use of model life tables is furnished in the chapter devoted to population projections (Chapter 13). In that example (see p. 395) we will see the use of model life tables as a procedure for estimating the expectation of life and as a means of computing survivors in the projected populations.

3. The Population Branch of the United Nations has interpolated, as was indicated above, among the first 40 model life tables to develop 24 other life tables corresponding to expectations of life at birth (for both sexes) in

round numbers. Various transformations have been effected on these tables in order to render them usable in numerous ways. In particular, they can be used immediately for the computations of survivors in the projection of populations. We will return to this usage in the chapter on population projections, p. 394, in which the example shown in paragraph 2 above is treated.

4. Finally, with the new sets of model life tables computed by Ansley J. Coale and Paul Demeny (*Regional Model Life Tables and Stable Populations*, Princeton, N.J.: Princeton University Press, 1966), we can arrive at a better match between observed data and model tables. For this purpose there are now available four groups of model tables, in each of which the expectation of life for females at birth varies in steps of $2\frac{1}{2}$ years from 20 years to $77\frac{1}{2}$ years; age composition and associated male life tables are different for each group. In short, we need no longer seek a single pattern with which to identify actual mortality; we can now seek instead to characterize different possible structures by sex and age corresponding to a given over-all level of female mortality.

Thus, there are available now some 96 tables for each sex, in four groups of 24 model life tables. Finally, many quantities associated with these tables have been computed, including the complete range of stable populations, providing data of great use in estimating various demographic characteristics in countries with insufficient statistics.

CHAPTER SEVEN

Marriage

THIS chapter considers the various demographic phenomena associated with formation or termination of marital unions. It is concerned with first marriages, remarriages, widowhood, and divorce.

Crude Marriage Rates

In addition to the crude marriage rate already defined (see p. 30), there is a *crude divorce rate*, the ratio of the number of divorces (or sometimes the number of persons divorced, a number that is double the preceding one) in a given year to the mean population.[1] Involved are crude indices reporting differences between countries, when these are considerable, or the change over time in a single given country, when such a change is well documented. Their use is extremely limited.

In what follows we shall pay particular attention to first marriages (marriages of single persons); then we shall show how terminations of marriages and remarriages can be investigated.

First Marriages

A simple global measure of the marriages of single persons in a population is furnished by the proportion, for each sex, of single persons at different ages. This is actually the complement of the proportion that directly measures the relative frequency of marriages. But it is generally preferable to work with the proportion single since the fluctuations are in general more significant.

1. Sometimes a divorce rate for married persons is also computed, relating the number of divorces to the number of married couples.

Table 7.1a gives these proportions at different ages for France, the United States, Canada, and Japan, as of 1956–1960. Computed for quinquennial age groups, proportions clearly do not give a very precise description of the ages at which marriage is most frequent. A computation by single years gives the percentages, shown in Table 7.1b, for France in 1956 and for the United States in 1960.

It must not be forgotten that these proportions are computed for different cohorts, each of which has its own pattern of development: if, in the past of certain of these cohorts, events have been unfavorable to marriage (war, economic crisis, etc.), the present proportion of single persons may be affected. Differential mortality also plays a role: since mortality is higher among single persons,[2] all other things being equal, it reduces the relative size of the proportions single. Nevertheless, this factor has real weight only at quite advanced ages.

If these reservations are kept in mind, Tables 7.1a and 7.1b give an expressive description of nuptiality that, as we shall see, lends itself to comparisons among the cohorts of the same country and among different countries.

From about the ages 35–39 years, we are not far from the final proportions: strictly speaking, there is no age at which the proportions may be considered final (except for the variations in proportions due to differential mortality), but even the crudest observation shows us that beyond a certain age the relative frequency of marriages of single persons becomes negligible. The measurement of the relative frequency of final celibacy in a given cohort is usually taken as at about age 50 years. Considerably beyond that age – at about 70 years, for example – differential mortality has, as was already indicated, a very positive intervening role; thus, among males 70–74 years of age in France as of January, 1956, the proportion of single persons declines or diminishes to 6.2 percent. This corresponds neither to the particular history of the generations in question nor to marriage among the 35 percent of males who were still single at age 50 years (close to 10 percent of the total of their cohort).

These proportions give simultaneously a measure of the *precocity* and of the *intensity* of nuptiality in a given country. We shall verify this by making some comparisons.

Some Comparisons

In Table 7.2a we compare the situation in France with that of various countries in different parts of the world. The differences between the pro-

2. This excess mortality is not due only to the *condition* of bachelorhood, but equally to a selection process in marriage that rejects certain among the physically and mentally deficient bachelors. This excess mortality is more marked among bachelors than among spinsters.

TABLE 7.1a. *Percent Single, by Sex and Age Groups, Selected Countries, and Dates*

Sex and Age Groups	Males							Females						
	20–24	25–29	30–34	35–39	40–44	45–49	50–54	20–24	25–29	30–34	35–39	40–44	45–49	50–54
France January 1, 1956	77.5	32.6	18.0	12.9	11.6	10.7	9.4	50.5	20.2	12.7	10.3	9.4	9.7	10.4
United States April, 1960	53.1	20.8	11.9	8.8	7.3	7.2	7.6	28.4	10.5	6.9	6.1	6.1	6.5	7.6
Canada June 1, 1961	69.3	29.6	17.3	13.0	10.9	10.6	10.4	40.5	15.4	10.5	9.2	8.9	8.7	10.4
Japan October 1, 1960	91.7	46.2	9.6	3.4	2.0	1.3	1.4	68.6	21.2	9.6	5.6	3.0	1.9	1.6

TABLE 7.1b. *Percent Single by Sex and Selected Ages: France, January 1, 1956, and United States, April 1, 1961*

	Age in years												
	18	19	20	21	22	23	24	25	26	27	28	29	30
France													
Males	99.4	97.8	94.4	89.6	85.1	65.4	54.8	43.6	36.3	30.9	27.2	24.5	22.1
Females	92.2	84.5	73.3	60.4	48.9	39.3	32.9	26.4	22.4	19.2	17.1	15.8	14.4
United States													
Males	94.6	87.1	75.8	63.4	51.6	40.5	33.4	27.9	23.5	19.8	17.5	16.0	
Females	75.6	59.7	46.0	34.6	25.6	19.4	15.7	13.1	11.4	10.2	9.2	8.7	

portions single are evident at all ages. Precocity and intensity of nuptiality are clearly higher in underdeveloped countries than in France, where, however, they are somewhat more marked than in certain neighboring countries. The difference is particularly marked among women: in the group aged 20–24 years there are 10 times as many single women in France as in India, and 20 times more in France than in Korea. In these two countries, virtually all women were married eventually, wheareas in France close to 10 percent were never married.[3]

TABLE 7.2a.   *Selected Countries and Dates: Percent Single, by Sex, for Selected Age Groups*

	Males			Females		
	20–24 years	30–34 years	40–44 years	20–24 years	30–34 years	40–44 years
France 1956	77.5	18	12	50.5	13	9
Algeria 1948	68	18.5	6.5	23	5	2.5
India 1931	35	8.5	4.5	4.5	1.5	1
Korea 1930	33.5	4	1.5	2.5	ε	ε

TABLE 7.2b.   *United States, 1960 and Selected European Countries in 1950–1956: Percent Single by Sex for Selected Age Groups*

	Male			Female		
	20–24 years	30–34 years	50–54 years	20–24 years	30–34 years	50–54 years
France 1956	77.5	18	9.5	50.5	13	10.5
Sweden 1950	84.5	27	15	59.5	16	20
United Kingdom 1951	76	19	8.5	52	14.5	15
Switzerland 1950	90.5	28	12.5	74	23	19
Italy 1951	90.5	28.5	8	68	21.5	14.5
Portugal 1950	84	23	10.5	65	24.5	17
United States 1960	53.1	11.9	7.6	28.4	6.9	7.6

Among males the differences between France and the other three countries are closely less marked, especially in respect to the precocity of marriage. The greater precocity and the greater intensity of French nuptiality as compared with that of neighboring countries is shown in the proportions of Table 7.2b. Nevertheless, the final celibacy is (at ages 50–54 years) greater in France than in the United Kingdom or in Italy, where male emigration plays a role.

3. Referring, of course, to the proportion ascertained without taking mortality into account.

Female nuptiality was particularly low in Sweden and in Switzerland, where some 20 percent of the women, double the proportion in France, remained single at ages 50–54 years. The apparent anomaly of a lower proportion of single women in Sweden and in England among those aged 30–34 years (16 percent and 14.5 percent, respectively) than among women aged 50–54 years (20 percent and 15 percent) is due to the fact that these proportions are for different birth cohorts, among which the youngest married in greater proportions. Male and female nuptiality in the United States is both much more intense and much more precocious than in any of the European countries.

Besides specific historical reasons, such as wars and economic crisis that interfere with the nuptiality of certain generations and leave lasting effects, certain profound developments may occur that are marked by a continuing rise or a continuing decline of nuptiality. It is thus that a continuing increase is observed since about 1940 in Switzerland and in the countries of northern Europe. In particular, in Sweden and in the United Kingdom around 1950, the proportion of women unmarried by the age of 30–34 years was lower in the youngest cohorts of females than the proportion among women who had reached the ages of 50–54 years.

Within a given country the disparities can be quite large. Thus, in 1960, in the United States the percentage of women remaining single at 50–54 years of age varied from 5.2 percent in the West to 10.5 percent in the Northeast; and in 1950 the percentage single among American women aged 45–54 ranged from 4.5 percent among women with one to four years of school completed to 24.2 percent among women completing four or more years of college.

Nuptiality by Cohorts

A satisfactory statistical analysis and theory of nuptiality must be able to describe how the totals of opposite sexes and with given age compositions are paired off and matched in a manner leading to marital unions. Theory in this sphere is virtually nonexistent. Nevertheless, the study of nuptiality by birth cohorts is of considerable interest in this respect.

In every explanation of nuptiality it is necessary to consider the relative sizes of the available groups prior to marriage. It is because of this that the total number of marriageable persons is sometimes computed, comprising single persons, widowed persons, and divorced persons of each sex.

But the age of marriageable persons matters a great deal. All other things being equal, advancing age, at first increasing the chances of marriage, eventually becomes an unfavorable factor, especially among women; at the individual level, one has the feeling that "lost opportunities" lead to the risk of final spinsterhood.

If statistical observation does not permit precise measurement of the importance of lost opportunities, it does sometimes present evidence of situations in which opportunities for marriage become less numerous — on the average, for one of the two sexes — because of the imbalance between the totals of marriageable males and females. This is notably the case when the totals, represented schematically by the cross-hatched areas of Figure 7.1, are widely unequal, following some demographic dip affecting only one of the two sexes,[4] or because at the age of most intense nuptiality a large part of one of the two groups is not available for marriage (in time of war, for example). Under these conditions, marriage in the smaller group has every chance of being more intense than if there were no disequilibrium, that in the larger group being, by contrast, less intense.

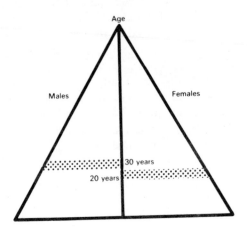

Figure 7.1

In these analyses it is not possible to separate first marriages from re-marriages: the relative number of remarriages of divorced persons and, especially, of widowed persons (notably females) must be expressed in terms of the nuptiality of single persons. Thus, in a period of full nuptiality among males, females are in the minority in the matrimonial market, and there are supplementary opportunities for remarriages among widowed women; conversely, an inverse situation would be unfavorable to them.

But all of these remarks, suggested by common sense, have not yet led to sufficiently elaborate analytical methods. For want of other methods, the

4. A dip that may derive, for example, from a deficit of births affecting only one of the two groups of cohorts represented in Figure 7.1.

construction of nuptiality tables – which derive from mortality tables – may be of some use.

Nuptiality Tables for First Marriages

We place ourselves in the perspective of a given cohort, say, a cohort of women, in order to determine these ideas. To sketch the manner in which first marriages occur in this cohort, we first compute a series of *nuptiality probabilities*, measuring the "risk of marriage" between two successive ages, x and $x+1$.

This "risk" is measured by relating first marriages (or marriages of single persons) that occur between ages x and $x+1$, denoted $m(x, x+1)$, to the total number of single persons having attained exact age x, denoted S_x[5]; this gives:

$$n_x = \frac{m(x,x+1)}{S_x}. \tag{F}$$

The analogy with the mortality probability q_x is evident (see Figure 7.2). Nevertheless, there is a fundamental difference between n_x, which is defined

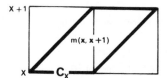

Figure 7.2

by equation (F), and q_x: n_x does not measure the risk of marriage strictly, for among the S_x single persons attaining age x, some will die before reaching age $x+1$, in which case they are not exposed to the risk of marriage throughout the year. But this objection has no great practical consequences; equation (F) is a sufficient approximation of the correct probability of marriage at ages with low mortality, which is the case during the period in which the chance of marriage among single persons is great.

Nevertheless, it is possible to correct equation (F) to take account of mortality. Among the S_x single persons attaining exact age x, there will be d_x who will die between age x and age $x+1$. There are, accordingly, $S_x - d_x$, who run the risk of nuptiality throughout the entire year. We may assume that the d_x persons dying will have lived, on the average, approximately one-half of the year, and consequently will have been exposed to the chance of marriage

5. We use a notation that is in principle reserved exclusively for data in nuptiality tables; in doing so we are able to make the verbal presentation somewhat lighter.

for an average of one-half year each. Overall, this is equivalent to the chances of marriage of $d_x/2$ single persons during a complete year. *Altogether, the risk of marriage is run by a total of:*

$$S_x - d_x + \frac{d_x}{2} = S_x - \frac{d_x}{2}.$$

It is to this total that we must relate the $m(x, x+1)$ marriages of single persons in order to have the correct formula (F'):

$$n_x = \frac{m(x, x+1)}{S_x - \frac{d_x}{2}} \tag{F'}$$

but the amount of the correction is quite small.

But we see that the phenomenon of nuptiality is not observed directly in a pure state. It is juxtaposed with the phenomenon of mortality (and, possibly, with the phenomenon of migration — which we are not considering here — another intervening and sometimes very important phenomenon), whose parasitic effects require, in principle, a correction in formula (F) if they are to be overcome.

It is possible, then, as was done in the case of mortality probabilities, to compute nuptiality tables on the basis of nuptiality probabilities and to define functions analogous to those encountered in life tables. In particular, it is possible to define a table of numbers remaining single, which is analogous to the survivors column in the life table.[6]

The number of single persons living to age 50 will give, to all intents and purposes,[7] the proportion of permanent bachelors or spinsters in the genera-tion. Complements of this proportion will give the proportion of persons who have been married (leaving aside mortality). The corresponding marriages are distributed according to age, as are the series of persons married in the nuptiality table (the analogue of the series of deaths in a life table).

We are coming to a description of nuptiality of single persons consistent with the scheme already presented. According to this scheme, we determine:

1. What is the proportion of persons who, having experienced an initial event *A* (here, the attainment of a minimum legal age of marriage; for example, 15 years for girls), will experience the subsequent event *B* (here, a first mar-riage). In a word, what will be the proportion of 15-year-old single persons who (in the absence of mortality) will marry at least once?

6. The reader will note that it is the constant intervention of mortality that prevents construction of the cohort nuptiality table by "direct" study of the cohort, as one could do in the case of mor-tality (in a closed population).

7. Theoretically it would be necessary to take the number of never married persons beginning with the age at which the probability of nuptiality is nil. But beyond 50 years of age these prob-abilities become very small, and the error committed is insignificant.

2. How are the intervals between events *A* and *B* distributed. In other words, how are marriages distributed in a cohort by age, in the absence of mortality?

Construction of a Cohort Nuptiality Table

We will work with the 1931 French female cohort, in which the first marriages began to take place in 1946. The raw data are given in the annual vital statistics for the years 1946–1951.[8] They are placed in the *Lexis* diagram in Figure 7.3.

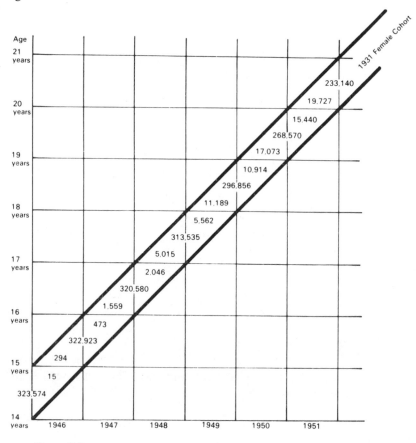

Figure 7.3

8. These statistics (they are the final statistics, which should not be confused with provisional statistics published each year in a quarterly bulletin of the National Statistics Institute) are the subject of three volumes: one appearing in 1953 for the years 1946 and 1947; one in 1954 for the years 1948 and 1949; and one in 1956 for the years 1950 and 1951.

These raw data include: (1) the total number of single persons in the cohort on successive January 1sts and (2) the number of marriages of single females in each of the triangles of the *Lexis* diagram.

Neglecting mortality and migrations, we move from these raw data to data usable for computing nuptiality probabilities by the operations indicated. The results are shown in the diagrams, Figure 7.4, *a* to *e*.

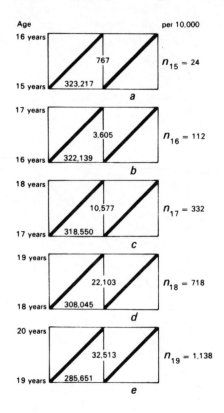

Figure 7.4

Thus, $S_{15} = 322{,}923 + 294 = 323{,}217$ and $m(15{,}16) = 294 + 473 = 767$, from which it follows that:

$$n_{15} = \frac{767}{323{,}217} = 0.0024, \text{ or } 24 \text{ per } 10{,}000.[9]$$

[9] A correction to take account of mortality should involve the deaths to single persons, between 15 and 16 years of age, in the cohort studied, i.e., $d_{15} = 359$. The divisor in the computation giving n_{15} must be diminished by $359/2 \cong 180$ units, which is of no consequence for n_{15}.

Similarly, we find:

$$n_{16} = 112 \text{ per } 10,000.$$
$$n_{17} = 332 \text{ per } 10,000.$$
$$n_{18} = 718 \text{ per } 10,000.$$
$$n_{19} = 1,138 \text{ per } 10,000.$$

For computation of probabilities at 20 years of age and over it will be necessary to await the statistical data of the years 1952 and beyond.[10]

With these probabilities we can determine the proportions of women in the generations still single at 16, 17, 18, 19, and 20 years.

At 16 years, this proportion is obviously $1 - 0.0024 = 0.9976$.

At 17 years, it is obtained by multiplying 0.9976 by $(1 - 0.0112)$, or $0.9976 \times 0.9888 = 0.9864$, etc.

At 20 years, we find

$$0.9976 \times 0.9888 \times 0.9668 \times 0.9282 \times 0.8862 = 0.7845;$$

at this age, 78.45 percent of the women in the generation are still single, which can be written $(1 - n_{15})(1 - n_{16})(1 - n_{17})(1 - n_{18})(1 - n_{19})$, a form that can be extended to all ages. Terminating the multiplication at $(1 - n_{50})$ or at $(1 - n_{60})$, we are close to having the percentage of final spinsters (or bachelors) in the cohort.

We can place a nuptiality table alongside a life table to compute the complete nuptiality table for single persons (to be exact, until age 55). This computation can be carried out for either a cohort (cohort table) or for a given period (period table).

The cohort nuptiality table requires a long and consistent series of appropriate statistics. Nevertheless, by using census data giving the distribution of the population by sex, age, and marital status, as suggested by J. Hajnal[11] and as we have done at the beginning of this chapter, it is possible to obtain cohort tables both more easily and more reliably. We reproduce (see Table 7.2c) the interesting findings of N. B. Ryder concerning nuptiality characteristics of American cohorts, which show the trends of both increasing intensity and increasing precocity of marriage among both males and females in the United States.[12]

10. These data were not yet available at the time of writing. In this cohort we have ignored 15 marriages occurring (by special licence) prior to 15 years of age.

11. See J. Hajmnal, "Age at Marriage and Proportions Marrying," *Population Studies*, VII, No. 2, November, 1953.

12. See N. B. Ryder, "Measures of Recent Nuptiality in the Western World," in *Proceedings of the International Congress on Population*, New York, 1961, Vol. II.

TABLE 7.2c. *Cohort Groups Born in the United States, 1870–1929: Percent Ever Marrying* and Mean Age at First Marriage*

| Cohort Group | Females | | Males | |
	Percent Marrying	Mean Age at First Marriage	Percent Marrying	Mean Age at First Marriage
1870–1874	90.5	23.36	88.1	27.12
1875–1879	90.7	23.30	88.3	26.90
1880–1884	91.0	23.11	88.6	26.66
1885–1889	91.2	22.89	88.7	26.36
1890–1894	91.6	22.73	89.6	26.14
1895–1899	92.0	22.68	90.8	26.11
1900–1904	92.4	22.76	91.7	26.04
1905–1909	92.6	22.79	92.2	25.92
1910–1914	93.8	22.83	92.9	25.69
1915–1919	95.0	22.61	93.4	25.24
1920–1924	96.0	22.01	92.3	24.60
1925–1929	96.2	21.42	92.0	24.25

*Percent computed among Males surviving to 18 years of age, among Females surviving to 15 years of age

Nuptiality Table for Single French Women, 1950–1951

The observation of different female cohorts between two exact consecutive ages in 1950–1951 gives us the period probabilities n_x for this period, with the restriction already made—in constructing the male life table for 1954–1955—that only half the marriages of single persons in the two years are included in the computation of the table.[13] We apply this series of probabilities (n_x) successively to 10,000 15-year-old girls ($S_{15} = 10,000$), thus obtaining simultaneously the series of marriages of single girls $m(x, x+1)$ and the series of those remaining single (S_x). Table 7.3 results from these computations.

From a formal point of view this table is distinguished from the life table essentially by the fact that the sum of the marriages is not equal to $10,000 = S_{15}$: not all girls attaining 15 years of age marry. In other words, S_x is never zero.

An important question is: among all girls subject to event A (attaining the minimum age for marriage, 15 years), what proportion experience event B (marriage)? Here the proportion is .9251, or 92.51 percent. The distribution of marriages (distribution of events B subsequent to events A) is given by

13. Nothing would prevent taking account of *all* the first marriages of these two years, defining strict period nuptiality probabilities, just as we defined strict period mortality probabilities (see p. 141).

the series $m(x, x+1)$. Let us observe, finally, that the series (S_x), like the series $m(x, x+1)$, has been computed without taking account of the effects of mortality.[14]

TABLE 7.3. *France, 1950–1951: Nuptiality for Single Women*

Age x	S_x	Nuptiality Probability n_x (per 10,000)	Marriages $m(x, x+1)$	Age x	Single Women S_x	Nuptiality Probability n_x (per 10,000)	Marriages $m(x, x+1)$
15	10,000	23	23	36	1,038	396	41
16	9,977	109	109	37	997	367	37
17	9,868	322	318	38	960	298	29
18	9,550	716	684	39	931	292	27
19	8,866	1,138	1,009	40	904	241	22
20	7,857	1,480	1,163	41	882	222	20
21	6,694	1,856	1,242	42	862	176	15
22	5,452	1,875	1,022	43	847	171	14
23	4,430	1,812	803	44	833	153	13
24	3,627	1,703	618	45	820	148	12
25	3,009	1,529	460	46	808	126	10
26	2,549	1,433	365	47	798	113	9
27	2,184	1,253	274	48	789	105	8
28	1,910	1,088	208	49	781	86	7
29	1,702	954	162	50	774	82	6
30	1,540	854	132	51	768	66	5
31	1,408	741	104	52	763	68	5
32	1,304	649	85	53	758	61	5
33	1,219	579	71	54	753	48	4
34	1,148	508	58	55	749		
35	1,090	478	52				
							9,251

Period Nuptiality Tables in the Study of Marriage

It is usually impossible to observe the strict period conditions when dealing with marriage. Inevitably, at the end of a long period of stable nuptiality, which no political or economic event has disturbed, the appearance of unfavorable conditions in a given year will affect nuptiality at all ages; and the period table properly will take account of the actual effects in the

14. By this we understand that the table accounts for the distribution of first marriages by age in a group of 10,000 15-year-old girls, all of whom would survive until age 55 years.

Besides, it must be noted that we have not introduced corrections to take account of the disturbing effect of mortality in the computation of the probabilities n_x (see equation [F′]), but this is unrelated to the first point and is justified by the fact that the correction thus introduced is very small.

year being studied. But it is rare that the marriage conditions in a given period result only from current conditions; more often, results of past events affect the different cohorts differentially, with each reacting to the conditions of a given year according to the cohort's past history.

These remarks reduce the applicability of period tables as far as nuptiality is concerned: the summary indices that they render must be interpreted with prudence and in relationship to past history. Let us remember that, with respect to mortality, period tables have a special interest because the situation of a given year seems not to depend, in any obvious way, upon the situation of previous years (in the absence of marked selection).

The percentage of spinsters at age 55 years (quite close to the percentage of final spinsters),[15] according to characteristics of French female nuptiality for 1950–1951, appears at 7.49 percent. This percentage is quite clearly lower than that observed fairly consistently at the same age during censuses (about 10 percent), indicating that the period 1950–1951 remains a period of quite substantial recovery of marriages postponed by World War II (1939–1945).

Some Simple Parameters of the Nuptiality Table

We base this description upon the distribution of marriages connected with the nuptiality table for single women for 1950–1951. The distribution

TABLE 7.4a. *France, 1950–1951: Distribution of Female First Marriages by Age at Marriage, Based on Nuptiality Table*

Age x	Marriages Between Age x and x+1	Age x	Marriages Between Age x and x+1	Age x	Marriages Between Age x and x+1	Age x	Marriages Between Age x and x+1
15	25	25	497	35	56	45	13
16	118	26	395	36	44	46	11
17	344	27	296	37	40	47	10
18	739	28	225	38	31	48	9
19	1,091	29	175	39	29	49	8
20	1,257	30	143	40	24	50	6
21	1,343	31	112	41	22	51	5
22	1,105	32	92	42	16	52	5
23	868	33	77	43	15	53	5
24	668	34	63	44	14	54	4
							10,000

15. Marriages of spinsters beyond age 55 years represent only 0.3 percent of the total.

expressed per 10,000 marriages[16] contracted between 15 and 55 years of age is shown in Table 7.4a. It gives Figure 7.5.

This distribution, we must remember, does not apply to any single cohort, but is a summary of nuptiality in 1950–1951. It will help us to identify certain

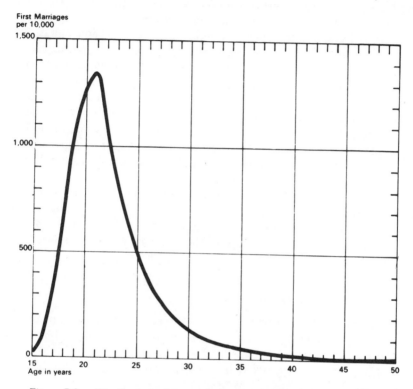

Figure 7.5. Distribution of First Marriages by Age, Based on French Female Nuptiality Table for 1950–51.

simple characteristics applying equally to the distribution of marriages in a cohort. We have in view three parameters of central tendency.

1. *The mean age at marriage.* To obtain this, it is necessary to multiply successively the numbers of marriages at different ages by the ages; thus 25×15, then 118×16, etc. By adding together all these products and then dividing by 10,000, we find the mean, 22.8 years. We must add one-half year to this, since all of the 10,000 marriages do not take place at exact ages x, but are distributed linearly between ages x and $x + 1$, so that they occur, on

16. Let us recall that to express the age distribution of 9,251 marriages in terms of 10,000, it suffices to multiply the number of marriages at each respective age by $10,000/9,251 = 1.08096$ and to round off carefully in order to obtain *exactly* 10,000 in the new total.

the average, at age $x + 0.5$. Thus, the mean age at marriage, with the distribution in Table 7.4a, is 23.3 years.

The mean age so computed differs from other more simply computed mean ages; for example, that obtained by making the computation with the marriage statistics for single females that are given in data for 1950–1951.[17] In these statistics the relative frequency of marriages at different ages depends in effect on the size of the different cohorts, other things being equal.

We may seek to eliminate the direct influence[18] of this inequality of generations by assigning the same total to the different cohorts (1,000, 10,000, 100,000, etc.) and by correcting, in consequence, the corresponding numbers of marriages. Doing this partly eliminates – as in the nuptiality table – the influence of mortality between ages 15 and 55 (if the mean age calculated is limited to that interval of marriages); but, given the different computation procedure, the series of marriages so obtained differs from the series of marriages $m(x, x + 1)$ in the nuptiality table; it follows that the mean ages that result are generally different.

2. *The median age.* This refers to the age at which the 5,000th marriage occurs among the total 10,000 contracted;[19] this is the analogue of the "probable age at death" in the life table. In general, this age is not a round number, and its determination rests on the assumption of a linear distribution of marriages between the rounded ages. Here, there are:

4,917 marriages at 15–22 years, and
6,022 marriages at 15–23 years.

The 1,105 marriages $(6,022 - 4,917 = 1,105)$ of the 22nd year are assumed to be distributed linearly throughout that year of age; according to this hypothesis, the 83rd marriage $(5,000 - 4,917 = 84)$ occurs at 22 years $+ 83/1,105 = 22$ years $+ 0.08$ years $= 22.08$ years, which is the median age at marriage.

3. *The modal age.* This is the age in complete years at which the maximum number of marriages occur (analogue of the modal age at death in the life table). In Table 7.4b the modal age is 21 years.

Some International Findings

In his previously cited paper given at the Congress of the International Union for the Scientific Study of Population at New York in 1961, N. B. Ryder

17. This refers to the mean age of newly married single women of 1950–1951.
18. The indirect effect caused by the inequality of the total numbers in the two sexes persists, evidently, in influencing the values of n_x.
19. Strictly speaking, we ought not to ignore the marriages at ages beyond 55 years in this computation (as in that of the mean age). But the error resulting from our approximation is infinitesimal.

has presented some findings based upon computation of period nuptiality tables for several Western countries. His findings are shown in Table 7.4b.

TABLE 7.4b. *Selected Countries and Years: Percent Ever Marrying and Mean Age at First Marriage, by Sex, Based Upon Nuptiality Tables**

Country	Year for Which Table Computed	Females		Males	
		Percent Ever Marrying	Mean Age at First Marriage	Percent Ever Marrying	Mean Age at First Marriage
New Zealand	1956	97.5	22.38	94.1	25.70
Australia	1954	97.0	22.36	91.3	25.90
Belgium	1947	96.5	23.28	96.0	25.91
Canada	1956	95.5	22.37	93.6	25.25
Netherlands	1947	95.3	24.67	97.2	27.20
Denmark	1955	95.1	22.68	93.4	25.98
England and Wales	1951	93.9	23.07	94.1	25.79
West Germany	1950	93.8	24.36	98.8	26.63
Norway	1950	93.4	24.66	91.3	27.81
Sweden	1950	93.3	24.04	87.9	27.30
Finland	1950	93.1	23.72	93.9	26.71
Austria	1951	91.4	24.41	96.5	27.14
France	1954	91.0	23.65	89.5	26.12
Switzerland	1950	90.7	25.31	89.9	28.06
Scotland	1951	90.6	23.78	92.6	26.14
Portugal	1950	85.2	24.89	89.1	27.68

*For males attaining age 18 years and females attaining age 15 years.

The Study of Divorce and of Remarriage

By exact analogy with nuptiality tables for single persons, we can sometimes construct nuptiality tables for widowed or divorced persons as well as tables showing the dissolution of marriages by divorce. Without denying the practical interest of these tables (in computation of forecasts, for example), we are of the opinion that they do not suffice to analyze the phenomenon studied. The connection with the age of individuals experiencing the phenomenon studied is very close, involving events that apparently depend, above all, on the time elapsed since a prior event.

Thus, a widow's age at remarriage is not the most interesting datum: the remarriage takes place following widowhood, and the time elapsed since the death of the previous spouse is a much more important and essential piece of information. It may also be of interest in combination with other data, such as the age at the time of widowhood.

It seems even more evident that the duration of marriage influences the frequency of divorce. No doubt these durations are related to the age of individuals; for example, long durations of marriage are inconceivable for individuals below some minimal age. But the relationship is quite loose and may vary in time and by countries.

In the study of nuptiality of single persons, the connection with age is justified by the fact that the event prior to marriage can be considered as the attainment of the minimum legal age for marriage (in France, 15 years for girls, 18 years for young men): under these conditions, determining the relationship of marriage to the time elapsed since attaining the legal age, and to the age of single persons at the time of marriage, are two equivalent analytical procedures. This is not the case in the study of terminations of marital unions (by divorce) or of remarriages (after widowhood or divorce): *the duration of the union dissolved or the interval passed since the dissolution of the union must be introduced explicitly.*

TABLE 7.5.   *France: Mean Number of Divorces, per 1,000 Marriages (Cross-Sectional Index)*

Year		Year	
1920	68	1940	90
1925	74	1945	96
1930	79	1950	101
1935	85	1951	102

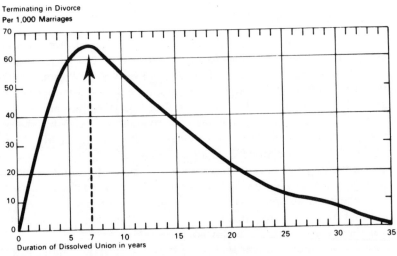

Figure 7.6.   Distribution of Divorces by Duration of the Dissolved Union.

In this way, Louis Henry has arrived at estimates of the mean number of divorces resulting from 1,000 marriages.[20] The results are shown in Table 7.5; they involve period indices that are adjusted on the basis of crude values[21] for the purpose of specifying a trend.

The distribution of 1,000 divorces by duration of marriage is approximately that shown in Figure 7.6. For more details we may refer to Henry's article.

The remarriage of widowed persons was investigated in the same manner in a study that has already been referred to above (see p. 68).

The Study of Widowhood

On the whole this is a question of the study of the mortality of spouses. No reference to duration of the marriage need necessarily be made.

Tables of widowhood by age are justified by practical considerations; thus they may assist in carrying out projections of populations by marital status. However, they do not add anything to our understanding of mortality.

20. L. Henry, "Mésure de la frequence des divorces," *Population*, No. 2 (April–June, 1952).
21. Which reflected very clearly the exceptional postwar conditions.

CHAPTER EIGHT

Natality-Fertility

BY "natality" we understand the demographic phenomena connected with birth; the term is very general. In particular, natality may be considered from the point of view of the individuals who are born or from the point of view of mothers who give birth to a child (or of couples who conceive). When studying the circumstances of human procreation in more detail, we speak of "fertility." A supplementary notion is introduced, that of *fecundity*, or the ability of women to conceive, of which fertility is the manifestation. While infertility may be voluntary, *sterility* (the opposite of fecundity) is physiological (in the same sense, one may speak of the fecundity or sterility of a couple). This last distinction is even more worth making since it may be the origin of some confusion: the French term *fécondité* is translated as "fertility" and *not* as "fecundity"; conversely, *fertilité* is the equivalent of the English "fecundity."

Introductory Remarks

The statistical study of human fertility is particularly complex because of the large number of quantitative factors that can be included a priori to describe it and to analyze its variations. This complexity will be encountered in the text that follows, amplified by the requirement that we dwell on computational techniques.

For this reason, in this general presentation we furnish the reader with an outline that may not be obvious in skimming the pages that follow. The chapter is divided into four parts entitled:

A. Conventional Rates
B. Duration of Marriage
C. Birth Order
D. Statistical Analysis of the Family

The *conventional rates* are, first of all, the crude birth rates and the general fertility rates. The investigation of the former permits us to set up a brief panorama of natality throughout the world; on the other hand, we indicate the limited usage of the second rate.

We then examine the fertility rates by age, essentially the age-specific fertility rates and the marital fertility rates. For a long time these rates were virtually the only analytical tools used by demographers, and so they are still considered by some nonspecialists as being the most refined available for the study of fertility.

We have sought to detail for the reader the spheres in which the different age-specific rates are useful: (1) the age-specific fertility rates (or age group-specific fertility rates) are essentially descriptive and are usually inappropriate for an analysis of fertility, however superficial it may be; (2) the use of marital fertility by age is indicated to the extent that the greatest part of fertility is legitimate, which is the case in the majority of societies.

Nevertheless, since in Malthusian populations it is not the age of the woman that determines the behavior of the married couple, in these populations it is more appropriate to employ marital fertility rates by age (or by age groups) according to the *age (or age group) of the woman at marriage.* Statistical data permitting such computations are quite rare. [The term "Malthusian population" is used here to denote populations characterized by widespread knowledge, acceptance, and practice of family limitation. By contrast, the term "non-Malthusian population" denotes populations characterized by absence of deliberate practice of family limitation. *Trans. note.*]

Finally, it is only in populations not practicing birth control that marital fertility rates by age (or by age group), computed without reference to age at marriage, are of interest.

Combining the rates of each of the preceding series, we obtain synthetic indices of fertility: (1) the *total fertility rate* and *gross reproduction rate* are derived from the sum of the age-specific (or age group-specific) fertility rates. The values of this index are generally highly correlated with those of the crude birth rate; (2) an appropriate combination of the marital fertility rates by age (or by age groups) beginning with, say, 20 years of age in a non-Malthusian population, gives the *mean number of children per marriage* of a woman married at that age. In a Malthusian population, the computation of the mean number of children per marriage requires the use of rates by age and age at marriage.

All the indices we have just considered are usually computed as period, or cross-sectional, indices, primarily because of the nature of the statistics available.

In the parts entitled "Duration of Marriage" and "Birth Order," we present methods of analysis particularly adapted to the study of Malthusian populations. Moreover, these methods assume the treatment of particularly detailed statistical data that are found on a national level only in certain developed countries.

The description of computational techniques has an important place here, for real statistical difficulties are encountered. These sections, aside from their own interest as an introduction to the study of populations in which birth control is practiced, permit the description of fertility in different lights, which should assist the reader in acquiring a sharper and more precise grasp of so complex a phenomenon. Here much attention is paid to cohort analysis, which is of great importance in the study of fertility.

In the last part, the "Statistical Study of the Family," we place fertility within the framework of the couple, a framework that extends beyond the data available in most national statistics. By the same token, some original methods, which we will explain, permit the development of entirely new findings and results that we present for consideration.

These methods, tested on statistical data concerning historical populations, are entirely adaptable to monographic studies based upon the survey questionnaires of a relatively limited number of women, yet they deal only with populations in which contraceptive practices are not widespread.

Finally, we assert that these statistical studies on family composition in the non-Malthusian régime have greatly aided the development of a true biometry of fertility.

A. CONVENTIONAL RATES

Crude Birth Rate

Let us recall that the crude birth rate refers to the relationship between live births in a given calendar year and the mean population of that year (see p. 30). In fact, only a fairly small fraction of the female population is in a position to give birth to children. All other things being equal, the size of the birth rate will depend, then, on the relative size of these groups at fertile ages. Still, the diversity of population composition is demonstrated by the differences in the relative size of adult age groups (which influence natality) being smaller in the more advanced age groups (which influence mortality). Thus, heterogeneity of population composition is a factor not as important in the variability in the crude birth rate as it is in the crude death rate.

But many other factors differentiate crude birth rates: in particular, conditions affecting procreative ability, especially in civilizations in which fertility is basically marital fertility: precocity and intensity of nuptiality; biological factors; the relative prevalence of contraceptive practices; etc.

It is necessary to bear these different factors in mind when comparing birth rates of countries not practicing voluntary limitation of births. In particular, the fact that nuptiality was less precocious and less intense explains, at least partly, why, at the beginning of the statistical era (about 1800), European birth rates were lower without recourse to contraception than the rates of the majority of present-day underdeveloped countries. Thus, while European crude birth rates of the eighteenth century varied between 35 and 40 per 1,000, the present rate in underdeveloped countries typically reaches 40–45 per 1,000. In Western Europe the decline of fertility by voluntary restriction of births lagged behind the decline in mortality by about 100 years, except in France, where the two changes took place almost simultaneously. According to Table 8.1, the beginning of the decline is particularly noticeable in France beginning with 1830, but it had already begun as of the second half of the eighteenth century, while it was not until 1870–1880 that it was plainly apparent in Sweden.

TABLE 8.1. *Trends in Crude Birth Rate (per 1,000) for United States, France, Sweden, and Chile*

Mean Rate	1801–1810	1811–1820	1821–1830	1831–1840	1841–1850	1851–1860	1861–1870
United States	×	×	×	×	×	42.4ᵃ	37.0
France	31.2	31.8	31.0	29.0	27.4	26.3	26.3
Sweden	30.9	33.4	34.6	31.5	31.1	32.8	31.4
Chile*	×	×	×	×	×	47.0	46.6

Mean Rate	1871–1880	1881–1890	1891–1900	1901–1910	1911–1913	1920–1930	1931–1939
United States	35.8	32.8	30.2	27.6	26.8	22.3	17.3
France	25.4	23.9	22.2	20.6	18.8	19.0	15.7
Sweden	30.5	29.1	27.1	29.8	23.5	18.2	14.4
Chile	46.2	47.3	45.4	44.6	44.4	43.0	39.3

*Rates for Chile are for 1850–1859; 1860–1869; 1870–1879; 1880–1889; 1890–1899 ; 1900–1909; 1910–1919; 1920–1929; 1930–1939.
× Not available
ᵃ1855–1860

In Sweden and in several other countries of Western Europe (England and Wales, Belgium, Austria, Norway, Finland) the later decline was much more rapid than in France, and these countries reached the level of France in about 50 years. Certain countries of Western Europe retained a high level of natality later than did the others. Thus, according to recent estimates, the United States experienced very high birth rates until the middle of the nineteenth century, and remained above 30 per 1,000 until the turn of the century. Throughout the period between the two world wars—a period of the lowest natality levels in many countries—Italy, Spain, Portugal, and the Netherlands never had birth rates lower than 20 per 1,000. Another remarkable fact of that period was that Germany and then Austria were the first countries to record a rise in natality as a consequence of governmental measures:[1] in Germany the rate reached 14.7 per 1,000 in 1933 and 18 per 1,000 the following year.

In this period all the birth rates are observed between two extremes: those no longer assuring replacement of successive generations (on the order of 14–15 per 1,000) and those corresponding to a total absence of voluntary birth control and to particularly favorable conditions of nuptiality (rates that could exceed 50 per 1,000). Between the most Malthusian countries of Western Europe, the closely related Anglo-Saxon countries in other parts of the world (the United States, Australia, New Zealand, Canada) and the majority of the countries of Asia, Africa, and South America, which have unrestrained natality, there is interposed a range of countries with intermediate natality. In this category it is appropriate to include especially Japan (with a rate on the order of 30 per 1,000), the majority of countries of Eastern and Southern Europe (rates of 25–30 per 1,000), and the U.S.S.R., where the rate has varied between 30 and 40 per 1,000, according to the years.

In addition to the replenishment of births that follows every war, the close of World War II saw a lasting increase in natality in the countries of Anglo-Saxon settlement abroad (the United States, Canada, Australia, New Zealand) and in France, and a diminishing of natality in the majority of countries of Eastern and Southern Europe and in the U.S.S.R. While natality was maintained at very high levels in nearly all underdeveloped countries, it declined substantially in Japan as a result of official encouragement of contraception and abortion. Similar encouragement was given to contraception in China in 1957, but the propaganda lost its intensity by 1958.

Table 8.2 shows the situation of the principal countries of the world in 1958 and in 1964. We have reproduced only the figures for countries in which the data are most reliable. It is for this reason that the Moslem countries are not shown; for them, we can suggest rates on the order of 45–50 per 1,000 (45 in Algeria, 50 in Egypt and in Iran). Only two African countries have been included; we note that an inquiry conducted in Guinea (then French Guinea) in 1954–1955 gave a rate of 50 per 1,000, which seems similar to the mean value in other African territories (Southern Rhodesia, Ruanda-Urundi). For India a rate of 40–45 per 1,000 is usually assumed.

---

1. Initially this was accomplished especially by relentless suppression of abortion.

TABLE 8.2. *Crude Birth Rates in 1958 and 1964 (per 1,000)*

	1958	*1964*
AFRICA		
Ruanda-Urandi (1957)		
Indigenous Population	49.5	
Union of South Africa		
European Population	25.7	24.0
Colored Population	47.8	46.6
Asiatic Population	29.5	33.3
NORTH AMERICA		
Canada	27.6	23.8
United States	24.3	21.2
Guatemala	48.7	44.4
Jamaica	38.1	39.8
Mexico	44.5	46.7
Panama	39.3	40.1
Puerto Rico	32.7	30.6
El Salvador	47.3	46.8
SOUTH AMERICA		
Argentina	22.7	21.8
Uruguay (1954, 1962)	19.3	22.5
Chile	35.5	32.8
Colombia	43.3	38.6
Ecuador	45.9	46.9
Venezuela	44.7	43.4
ASIA		
Israel	26.7	25.0
Japan	18.0	17.7
Ceylon	35.5	32.6
Mainland China	40.0	
Taiwan	41.7	34.5
Hong Kong	38.8	29.4
Singapore	42.0	33.2
EUROPE		
West Germany	17.0	18.5
Austria	17.1	18.5
Belgium	17.1	17.1
Denmark	16.6	17.6
Finland	18.5	17.6
France	18.2	18.1
Great Britain	16.8	18.8
England and Wales	16.4	18.5
Scotland	19.2	20.0
Northern Ireland	21.6	23.6
Ireland	20.9	22.5

TABLE 8.2 *(continued)*

	1958	1964
Norway	18.1	17.7
Netherlands	21.1	20.7
Sweden	14.2	16.0
Switzerland	17.6	19.2
Spain	21.9	22.2
Greece	19.0	18.0
Italy	17.9	20.0
Portugal	23.7	23.8
Yugoslavia	23.8	20.8
Albania	41.8	37.8
East Germany	15.9	17.2
Bulgaria	17.9	16.1
Hungary	16.1	13.1
Poland	26.2	18.1
Roumania	21.6	15.2
Czechoslovakia	17.4	17.1
U.S.S.R.	25.3	19.6
OCEANIA		
Australia	22.6	20.6
New Zealand	26.6	24.1

Specific Fertility Rates

In the attempt to analyze natality, specific rates of birth are regularly computed, relating to all or part of the female population of child-bearing age. These are called *fertility rates.* In this way the extent to which the natality of a country is attributable to the fertility of women is measured more specifically, while the effects of age composition are eliminated (more or less totally, according to the rates computed). The different rates used and their manner of computation were presented earlier (p. 38). Let us recall that a general fertility rate is computed for the total number of women of child-bearing age (usually 15–49 years of age), and that, for each age or group of ages, fertility rates are related to the number of women at the age in question. Separate computations are made for married women (legitimate, or marital, fertility rates) and for unmarried women (illegitimate fertility rates).

The General Fertility Rate

In the analysis of fertility, the general fertility rate is the first refinement in rates in measuring natality. Computed by relating the births of a given year to the mean total number of women of child-bearing age (see the computation of p. 38), it indicates in part the extent to which the natality of a country is attributable to the age composition of its population. However, the appropriateness of this rate must not be exaggerated. In many circumstances, its computation is not called for, since it makes only an insignificant correction in the birth rate, the relative size of adult (and therefore fertile) categories varying but little from one population to another. Less common than the crude birth rate, it is also less expensive; it has no immediate significance, while the crude birth rate, as related to the crude death rate, permits specifying the natural increase of the population, an important and very concrete datum.

The use of the general fertility rate, then, offers no real interest except when we are concerned with populations having quite dissimilar age compositions. It *is* particularly useful in the case of studies and comparisons of small human groups (small geographic units, for example) of quite variable composition, where, in addition, the computation of more refined indices (like the age-specific fertility rate) is impossible, given the small totals. Certain "child-woman" ratios that are frequently utilized (which will be discussed below) are not fundamentally different from the general fertility rates.

Age-Specific Fertility Rates

Female fertility and age are connected in many ways. In the first place, they are connected by the onset of fecundity at adolescence and its disappearance at varying ages, often near the age of menopause. Moreover, there are social rules fixing sexual customs that are closely associated with age; in the majority of cultures, fertility is primarily legitimate (or marital) fertility, and the customs connected with nuptiality (more or less frequent, and more or less precocious marriages) have a direct impact upon fertility. Finally, in societies in which birth control is practiced, more or less effective voluntary infertility appears after the couple has had the number of children desired, or perhaps before this in the aim of spacing births as they are wanted.

It is thus natural to seek to measure statistically the total incidence of these factors by computing age-specific fertility rates. Fertility rates by age are affected by all the factors enumerated above. In particular, they depend on marriage, the preponderant factor in human fertility, and on the relative incidence of fertility outside marriage.

However, one may want to specify separately the two forms of fertility: marital fertility and illegitimate fertility; accordingly, separate corresponding age-specific rates are computed.

Description of Fertility with the Aid of Age-Specific Rates

We show first of all the most detailed description possible using annual age-specific rates. This example uses cohort rates for France in 1949. Overall age-specific fertility rates as well as marital age-specific fertility rates are shown in Table 8.3.[2] They are shown graphically in Figure 8.1.

The form of the curve of *overall fertility* (marital and illegitimate together) shows principally the effects of nuptiality; it is because of nuptiality that the maximum height of the curve is located at 24–25 years in 1949.

Marital fertility diminishes constantly with age.[3] It is very high at all the young ages, where many marriages are brought about by prenuptial conceptions; because of this and of considerable variations in the total number married from one age to the next, the marital fertility rates at ages 15, 16, and 17 years are not of great importance.

What is of importance is, evidently, the period rate, which demands numerous precautions in interpretation. We shall return to this point.

As we shall indicate later, age-specific fertility rates reflect very much the pattern of nuptiality. Thus, they are of little interest for the analyst. Nevertheless, they are the descriptive indices that can be used to characterize the simplest situations; and, as we shall see below, they are used in the same circumstances for computing projections of births. Finally, it is, in general, these rates that are brought to bear in the computation of the best-known summary index: the gross reproduction rate (see p. 188), and of the related summary index, the total fertility rate.

In the absence of other measures (e.g., in Malthusian populations, the fertility rates by age and age at marriage), age-specific fertility rates ignoring marital status or legitimacy are quite often used. For this reason, it seems useful to indicate the need for caution by showing below (see p. 191), in a particularly complex example, how a situation may become very difficult to analyze using these rates.

The priority attached to the study of marital fertility does not confer as much universal interest on the corresponding age-specific rates. *It is important for distinguishing between groups practicing voluntary birth control and those not practicing birth limitation.*

In France, for example, where such limitation is widely practiced, voluntary infertility occurs among couples having attained the desired or accepted family size. Now, the proportion of such couples rises with the length of the marriage, so that the fertility of Malthusian couples is related to the age of

2. Statistics of illegitimate births by age of mother include 5,992 births (of a total of 60,618) in which age is not given; these births were distributed among the different age groups in the same proportions as among illegitimate births with age of mother given. For a computation of this type, see Table 8.10, p. 208.

3. This remark holds only whenever there is birth control.

the woman mediated by the duration of marriage or, further, if one wishes, by age at marriage.

In computing the age-specific marital fertility rates regardless of age at marriage, the relationship between fertility and duration of marriage is neglected, and the result, in spite of an apparent refinement, is a quite broad description of fertility. This is the case with the rates in Table 8.3 and in Figure 8.1, which is related to them.

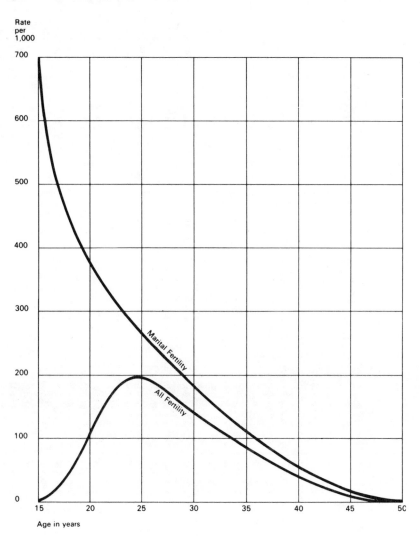

Figure 8.1.   France, 1959: Age-Specific Fertility Rates.

TABLE 8.3. France—Fertility Rates in 1949

	All Fertility		Age Attained by Mother During the year (years)	Legitimate (Marital) Fertility		
All Live Births	Mean Female Population	Fertility Rate (per 1,000)		Legitimate Live Births	Mean Married Female Population	Marital Fertility Rate (per 1,000)
302,363	300	0.992	15	71	103	689
301,704	1,280	4.24	16	626	1,170	535
320,359	4,354	13.6	17	2,778	5,661	491
322,957	10,949	33.9	18	8,064	17,741	455
330,308	21,843	66.1	19	17,786	43,337	410
315,998	32,970	104	20	28,464	72,254	378
321,710	45,956	143	21	41,210	116,960	352
319,911	55,090	172	22	50,477	151,710	333
326,518	61,464	188	23	57,244	184,566	310
326,991	64,633	197	24	60,677	208,602	291
320,731	63,291	197	25	59,833	221,222	270
324,135	61,775	191	26	58,578	235,561	249
326,739	60,447	185	27	57,604	246,667	234
339,839	58,890	173	28	56,223	264,928	212
346,318	56,103	162	29	53,361	275,108	194
208,975	31,459	151	30	29,823	166,209	179
186,911	25,631	137	31	24,209	149,420	162
165,350	21,102	128	32	19,904	132,590	150

			Age			
157,734	18,400	117	33	17,375	126,948	137
196,636	20,289	103	34	19,224	159,365	121
302,120	28,205	93.4	35	26,782	246,390	109
306,002	25,421	83.1	36	24,253	250,560	96.8
310,195	22,472	72.4	37	21,354	254,000	84.1
292,986	18,063	61.7	38	17,157	239,102	71.8
310,944	16,140	51.9	39	15,199	253,056	60.1
310,984	12,873	41.4	40	12,225	252,431	48.4
314,115	10,083	32.1	41	9,497	253,337	37.5
306,096	7,263	23.7	42	6,822	245,765	27.8
310,655	5,193	16.7	43	4,870	247,739	19.7
308,358	3,137	10.2	44	2,948	243,841	12.1
309,479	1,862	6.02	45	1,755	243,043	7.22
307,179	953	3.10	46	895	239,225	3.74
311,839	439	1.41	47	412	240,679	1.71
307,399	176	0.573	48	162	234,678	0.690
296,586	87	0.293	49	85	222,435	0.382
1,577,691	38,726	24.5	15–19	29,325	68,012	431
1,611,128	260,113	161	20–24	238,072	734,092	324
1,657,762	300,506	181	25–29	285,599	1,243,486	230
915,606	116,881	128	30–34	110,535	734,532	150
1,522,247	110,301	72.5	35–39	104,745	1,243,108	84.3
1,550,208	38,549	24.9	40–44	36,362	1,243,113	29.3
1,532,482	3,517	2.29	45–49	3,309	1,180,060	2.80

Conversely, the age-specific or age group-specific legitimate fertility rates are of great interest in Malthusian populations when computed by the woman's age or age group at marriage, assuming that the statistics combine the age of mothers at the birth of their children with their age at marriage.

However, in the absence of voluntary limitation of births, age at marriage does not appear to differentiate marital fertility of women at any given age. Among the studies testing this hypothesis we may cite the one concerning a Norman parish in the seventeenth and eighteenth centuries.[4] The diagrams

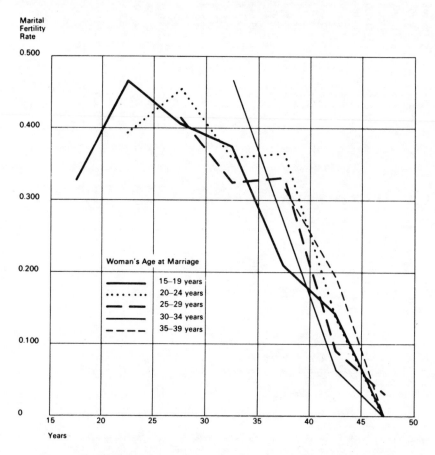

Figure 8.2.   Marital Fertility Rates by Age at Marriage in a Non-Malthusian Population.

4. Louis Henry, *"La population de Crulai, paroisse normande, Étude historique"*. Papers and Documents of the INED., No. 33, 1958.

of Figure 8.2 take account of the random variation of points for a given age group and allow computation of age-specific fertility rates for all ages at marriage combined, describing without ambiguity the fertility of the population studied.

Under these conditions the *age-specific marital fertility rates constitute very good indices of fertility, which permit the differentiation of non-Malthusian populations.*

TABLE 8.4. *Age-Specific Marital Fertility Rates (per 1,000) in Selected Non-Malthusian Populations*

	20–24 years	25–29 years	30–34 years	35–39 years	40–44 years	45–49 years
Crulai[a]						
1674–1742 marriages	419	429	355	292	142	10
French Canada[b]						
1700–1729 marriages	509	496	484	410	231	30
Genevese Bourgeoisie[c]						
Husbands born before 1600	389	362	327	275	123	9
Husbands born 1600–1649	525	485	429	282	141	5
Norway[d]						
1874–1876	396	380	341	289	180	41
Hutterites[e]						
Marriages before 1921	475	451	425	374	205	29
1921–1930 marriages	550	502	447	406	222	61
India[f]						
Bengal (Hindu villages) 1945–1946	323	288	282	212	100	33
Ramanagaram–Mysore District, 1950	314	264	201	146	24	1
Calcutta (Moslems)	276	268	225	143	44	10
French Guinea, 1954–1955[g]	335	310	246	171	69	28

[a]L. Henry, *La population de Crulai,* I.N.E.D. paper No. 33, 1958.

[b]J. Henripin, *La population Canadienne au debut du XVIIIᵉ siècle,* I.N.E.D. paper No. 22, 1954.

[c]L. Henry, *Anciennes familles genevoises,* I.N.E.D. paper No. 26, 1956.

[d]"International Statistics of Population Movements," *Statistique Generale de la France,* Paris, 1907; the rates, which included stillbirths, have been lowered by 4 percent.

[e]J. Eaton and A. J. Mayer. "The Social Biology of Very High Fertility Among the Hutterites. The Demography of a Unique Population." *Human Biology,* Vol. 25, No. 3, Sept., 1953, pp. 206–264.

[f]F. Lorimer, *Culture and Human Fertility,* p. 26.

[g]*Étude demographique par sundage en Guinea* (1954–1955) Final Results, I, Administration Generale des series de la France d'autre-mer, p. 38.

Table 8.4 assembles data concerning historical and contemporary non-Malthusian populations.[5]

The important differences among the separate findings show that marital fertility may vary markedly from one population to the other, even in the absence of voluntary birth control. Variations equally affect a given population in the course of its history (and always in the absence of birth limitation);

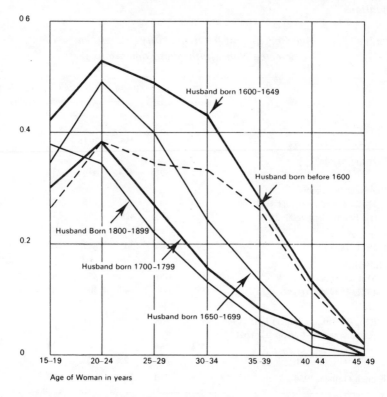

Figure 8.3   Age-Specific Marital Fertility Rates among Genevese Bourgeoisie Women.

this was the case among the former Genevese bourgeoisie and, at the beginning of this century, among the Hutterite Anabaptist sect living currently in the United States and Canada and not practicing birth control (Table 8.1).

In the light of these results, the terms "natural fertility" or "physiological fertility" seem to conceal a quite complex reality that cannot be expressed by

5. In this table we do not show fertility rates at ages 15–19 years, which are computed for some populations; we thus find 320 per 1,000 for Crulai. These rates show, in a general manner, a lower level of fertility, to which we shall return later.

a limited number of indices with a universal validity. We shall return to this point.

Let us indicate, finally, that the change over time in the curve of the age-specific marital fertility rate, in a population that initially does not practice fertility control, may reveal a change in the behavior of such a population. The study of the Genevese bourgeoisie at different dates offers a good example of such a change in the curve of the fertility rates (Figure 8.3). While the earliest curve is convex near the bottom, the more recent curves are concave near the top at the line of the maximum, and thus suggest the appearance in this population of a rising proportion of couples who, beginning at a certain age, become voluntarily infertile.

Computation of Marital Fertility Rates Based on Family Histories

Marital fertility rates have been seen as of particular interest in the study of non-Malthusian populations. In these populations, whether they be contemporary or historical, the data in their limited available detail rest on either small-scale surveys based on samples of women or on reconstructions of family histories on the basis of parish registers. In both cases the statistical documentation is not available in the form that it usually has in developed countries, where births and the corresponding female populations necessary for computation of the rates are almost immediately accessible.

In the estimation of fertility rates in a given age group, for example, 25–29 years, it is appropriate to divide the number of births in this age group by the number of years lived in a state of marriage between the 25th and the 30th birthdays by the total number of women studied. If ages of females are expressed in complete years, a woman married at age 26 will be, on the average, 26.5 years old at marriage; it is from this age that it will be appropriate to count her in the group 25–29 years of age.

The same woman widowed at 29 complete years of age (thus, at 29.5 years of age on the average) should appropriately be included in the observation until the age at which she may still have a legitimate child, that is, nine months or approximately 0.7 years after the death of her husband. Thus, in the present case she will be included in the observation until age $29.5 + 0.7 = 30.2$ years, and will be counted as follows:

$$30.0 - 26.5 = 3.5 \text{ years in the group } 25\text{–}29 \text{ years.}$$
$$30.2 - 30.0 = 0.2 \text{ years in the group } 30\text{–}34 \text{ years.}$$

Thus, we set up an exact count in "woman-years."

This procedure is consistently necessary for the group of women under 20 years of age, in which one includes all females who were married prior to that age.

The Total Fertility Rate and Gross Reproduction Rate

Fertility rates (overall or marital fertility rates) by age or by age group characterize the fertility of a group by a set of fairly abstract indices. By contrast, the *total fertility rate* and the *gross reproduction rate*, which derive from the sum of the age-specific (and age group-specific) fertility rates, permit giving the fertility of a population a unique quantity carrying a concrete meaning.

Fertility rates are generally computed as *period* indices.[6] The better way to present the total fertility and gross reproduction rates is to consider the rates included in their computation as applying to a hypothetical cohort. This is only a convenience in the presentation, and it must be remembered as such in the course of interpretation.

Let us work with the French rates of 1949 (Table 8.3) and, first of all, with annual rates. Let us take, hypothetically, 1,000 girls aged 15 years through all the ages of the fertile life span (from 15 to 50 years of age) without mortality, attributing to them, at each age, the number of births given by the age-specific fertility rates in Table 8.3. The total number of births that would result is obtained simply by adding the 35 rates. Rounding off to the nearest whole number, we find 2,965 children. The mean number of children per woman— 2.965 in this case—denotes the total fertility rate. Retaining only the daughters (100 per 205 births, or 488 per 1,000 births), and expressing the number of daughters per woman, we obtain the gross reproduction rate, R:

$$R = \frac{2,965 \times 0.488}{1,000} = 1.45.$$

If the age specific fertility rates are available only for five-year age groups (for France, in 1949, such rates are the basis for Table 8.3), the computation is somewhat different. Each woman in the hypothetical cohort is considered as remaining in each age group for five years, so that the number of births resulting from the passage of 1,000 women from 15 to 20 years (for example) is then:

$$24.5 \times 5 = 122.5.$$

Similarly, it is necessary to multiply the other quinquennial rates by 5, and, to obtain the total fertility of 1,000 women, it is necessary to add all of the rates so multiplied. More conveniently, the quinquennial rates can be added first of all, here:

$$24.5 + 161 + 181 + 128 + 72.5 + 24.9 + 2.29 = 594.19,$$

6. However, nothing prevents computation of age- or age group-specific fertility rates for a cohort of women, by taking account of married years of life lived by the group in the different age categories and of the births related to it.

a result which is then multiplied by 5:

594.19 × 5 = 2,970.95, rounded off to 2.971 children,

a number slightly different from the preceding one (2,965), since the computation by quinquennial rates is not rigorously and strictly equivalent to the computation by annual rates. The computations of the total fertility rate and the gross reproduction rate are carried out in the same manner.[7]

The gross reproduction rate is an index of fertility; based on the series of age-specific rates, it gives the mean female total fertility, in the absence of mortality, of a group of women who would be subject to these rates. This definition corresponds to the conventional procedure for computation of a gross reproduction rate. Nevertheless, the reference to age-specific birth rates is not obligatory; and it is more important to remember, as a general definition of a gross rate, that it gives the mean female total fertility of a hypothetical cohort of women, given the absence of mortality.[8]

The gross reproduction rate is thus a period (or current) index that seeks to summarize in concrete terms the fertility of a single year or group of years. Therefore, in making this computation, it may be preferable to employ indices judged more appropriate for measuring fertility.

Thus, without going into more technical details, it is conceivable that marital fertility and illegitimate fertility can be separated, by computing how the marriages in a hypothetical cohort of 1,000 girls of 15 years of age would operate and by determining independently the births of the married group and those of the unmarried group.

In proceeding thus, or in a different manner, one can obtain results different from those resulting from the use of age-specific fertility rates; for we see that in certain circumstances it is not the equivalent of using one or another category of indices to measure the fertility of a population.

Finally, we may determine very naturally the analogue of the "gross reproduction rate" for a real cohort by computing the mean number of live-born daughters per woman *surviving* to 50 years of age, called the female completed birth rate. However, an important objection can be made: the fact that the rate is determined for *surviving* women is a selective factor in the cohort, to the extent that there may be a correlation between fertility and mortality. It might, then, be preferable to determine the different fertility

7. With f_x representing the fertility rate at age x and $f_{x; x+4}$ representing the rate for the age group $(x; x+4)$, we have, then, the equations:
$$R = 0.488 (f_{15} + f_{16} + f_{17} + \cdots + f_{49})$$
and
$$R = (0.488) \times S(f_{15; 19} + f_{20; 24} + \cdots + f_{45; 49}).$$

8. We could also compute the cumulative male fertility, but this is not usually done. Still, to stress the distinction, we speak sometimes of male reproduction and of female reproduction.

rates of the cohort by age or by age groups (see note 6 on p. 188) and sub-sequently to compute the gross reproduction rate by the conventional formulas.[9]

Like the period index, in populations with high natality (absence of voluntary birth limitation) the total fertility rate and gross reproduction rate are useful summary indices, for which all computation procedures are nearly equivalent when they are correctly applied; by contrast, in Malthusian populations with irregular compositions and unusual histories, the total fertility rate and gross reproduction rate are not very instructive and are sometimes quite misleading. In either case, it is of considerable interest to complement this index by the analysis of age-specific marital fertility rates.

Mean Number of Children per Marriage

We cannot hope to add the marital fertility rates of the different ages in Table 8.3—which concern a Malthusian population—as was done for the "overall" fertility rates. The outcome would lack any meaning. For this it is necessary that the fertility of a married woman depend only on her age; if so, addition of all of the annual rates, beginning with age 15 years, would lead to the mean number of births (in the absence of mortality) for a woman married at age 15 years; carrying out the same summation beginning with age 21 years, one would obtain the mean number of births (in the absence of mortality) for a woman married since the age of 21 years.

We have already indicated that, in countries generally practicing limitation of births, the marital fertility rate at a given age depends, other things being equal, on the duration of marriage, so that any combination of age-specific fertility rates for all ages at marriage is impossible.[10] To arrive at a synthetic figure for the mean number of children born per marriage it is necessary to use the age-specific rates for different ages or age groups at marriage. By combination of these rates, it is possible to find the different mean numbers of children per marriage corresponding to the different ages at marriage. However, in a population not practicing birth limitation (or practicing it very little), marital fertility at a given age does not depend on age at marriage; consequently, the addition of age-specific legitimate fertility rates beginning with a given age x gives the mean number of children for an aggregate of women in the population who were married at that age, x.

It is thus that adding together the quinquennial rates for French Canadians

9. By this we will not have eliminated entirely the effect of mortality, which prevents us from following completely, from 15 through 50 years, the women dying prior to the latter age.

10. With the legitimate fertility rates of Table 3, we would arrive at the following absurd results: French women married at 15 years of age have, on the average, close to 7 children (exactly 6.73); those married at 21 years of age have close to 4 children (exactly 3.78).

(marriages of 1700–1729; see Table 8.4) and multiplying the result by 5 yields the mean number of births for women married at 20 years of age:

$$(0.509 + 0.496 + 0.484 + 0.410 + 0.231 + 0.030) \times 5 = 10.8 \text{ children.}$$

Limiting the computation to mean number of children of women married at age 20 years, we deduce from the data of Table 8.4 the results shown in Table 8.5.

TABLE 8.5. *Mean Number of Liveborn Children of Women Married at Age 20 Years*

Population and Date	Mean No. of Births
Crulai: 1674–1742 marriages	8.23
French Canada: 1700–1729 marriages	10.80
Genevese Bourgeoisie	
husbands born before 1600	7.42
husbands born 1600–1649	9.36
Norway: 1874–1876	8.13
Hutterites	
marriages before 1921	9.79
1921–1930 marriages	10.94
India	
Bengal (Hindu villages)	6.19
Ramanagavam Mysore District, 1950	4.75
Calcutta (Moslems)	4.83
French Guinea 1954–1955	5.80

Analysis Based on Age-Specific Fertility Rates

In the absence of age-specific legitimate fertility rates by age (or age group) at marriage, analysis of fertility in Malthusian societies is frequently conducted on the basis of age-specific fertility rates. The very broad character of these rates, along with the fact that they refer to period indices, render their interpretation quite problematic. In certain situations it is extremely difficult to undertake an analysis based on their variations. We shall illustrate these difficulties in interpretation in referring to the recent development of French fertility.

Table 8.6a assembles the rates of age-specific fertility rates by quinquennial age groups from 1946–1956 as compared with the situation in 1935–1937. In the last line the gross reproduction rates computed for each year are given. The diagram in Figure 8.4a gives the relative variations among the different rates from 1946–1956, with 1935–1937 as a period of reference (base 100).

TABLE 8.6a. *France: Age-Specific Fertility Rates (per 1,000) and Gross Reproduction Rate*

Age Group	1935–1937	1946	1947	1948	1949	1950	1951	1952	1953	1954	1955	1956
15–19 years	28.0	20.6	23.0	23.7	24.5	24.5	23.4	22.7	22.4	21.7	21.6	22.4
20–24 years	120	139	160	161	161	159	154	153	152	156	156	157
25–29 years	119	186	187	183	181	177	168	166	163	168	169	170
30–34 years	78.8	140	127	126	128	129	121	118	112	110	108	108
35–39 years	44.2	80.6	76.9	75.2	72.5	68.9	63.0	61.9	60.3	63.9	64.1	62.1
40–44 years	15.7	26.1	26.5	26.0	24.9	24.1	22.5	22.2	20.6	20.9	19.3	17.5
45–49 years	1.3	2.2	2.4	2.3	2.3	2.1	2.0	2.0	1.8	1.8	1.7	1.5
Total Fertility Rate	2.03	2.97	3.01	2.99	2.97	2.92	2.77	2.73	2.66	2.71	2.70	2.69
Gross Reproduction Rate	0.99	1.45	1.47	1.46	1.45	1.42	1.35	1.33	1.30	1.32	1.32	1.31

In 1946 all the rates were notably higher than in 1935–1937, except for the rates at ages 15–19 years, which never regained the level of 28.0 per 1,000 characteristic of the 1935–1937 period. This high level derives from the high level of nuptiality of the group in 1935–1937; the 15- to 19-year-old group during that period included the small female generations born during the war in 1914 (World War I); less numerous than the adjacent generations, they were married much earlier. Thus, while the female group aged 19 years at the census of 1946 included 14.5 percent married women, the same age group in the census of 1936 included 19.6 percent married.

With the perspective of time and the aid of other analytical procedures that will be presented later, we can explain the development of the rates of from 20–50 years of age as shown in Figure 8.4a.

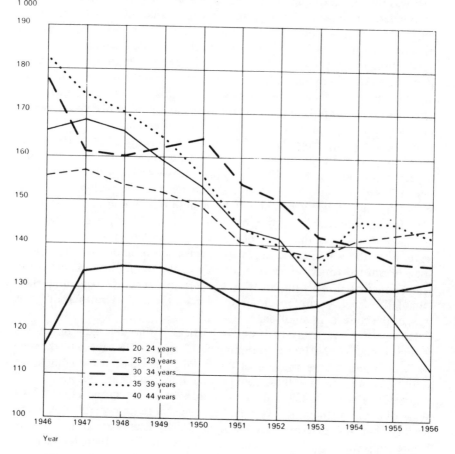

Figure 8.4a. France: Trend of Age-Specific Fertility Rates. (1935 Rate = 100).

All rates are high relative to those of 1935–1937 for two reasons: (a) a change in the behavior of couples, which resulted in a mean final cumulative fertility higher than that before World War II; (b) a recovery of births and of marriages that the war had deferred.

But these two factors have differing effects upon fertility at different ages. The fertility rate at 20–24 years only reaches its maximum around 1947, and its level varies but little after that.

In this age group, where nuptiality is quite high, the fluctuations in numbers of marriages have great implications for fertility. It was necessary to wait until 1946, the first year after World War II, so that certain marriages prevented by the war could be concluded, and, especially, so that the aggregate of the group could benefit from normal nuptiality.

It was the return to nuptiality conditions somewhat closer to normal that preponderantly affected fertility, an effect that was not fully felt until the following year, 1947. Few of the women of this age (in 1946 and after) had already been married before the war; the effect of the recovery of births is very trifling in this group. The effect of the recovery of marriages is no more important. Also, from the start, this group shows fertility almost corresponding to the new behavior of couples in the absence of any appreciable fluctuations of composition and of any significant number of deferred births. We may assert that the rates changed but little after 1947.

In the age group from 25 to 45 years the disturbing effect of the war is most noticeable. In the first place, deferred marriages are very important, especially in the group 25–29 years of age. It is women of this age in 1946 who in 1940 were 19–23 years of age and were in the period of greatest nuptiality, but under very unfavorable conditions that lasted until 1946; also, for an appreciable fraction of them, marriage took place in the years 1946 and after. Thus, the group of women aged 25–29 years during the first years after the war includes a *greater proportion of newly married women* than in normal times: other things being equal, the fertility of this group will be increased. This initial delay for certain women in beginning their cumulative fertility will for a long time inflate the fertility rates at different ages of the cohorts in question.

However, the recovery of births is particularly notable among couples young enough in 1940 (at the beginning of the separations caused by the war) to have begun only a fraction of the number of children (or cumulative fertility) desired. In 1946 these couples were found in the groups aged 25–29 years, 30–34 years, 35–39 years, and, to a lesser degree, in the group 40–44 years of age. For them, recovery had an even more immediate effect upon fertility than did deferred marriages, in which there were certain delays before supplementary births occurred. Also, beginning in 1946, the increase in fertility of the preceding groups was very marked, reaching practically the highest level of the postwar period.

Such compensatory phenomena are particularly marked between the ages of 30 and 40 years. They have a relatively great impact at ages 40–44 years, ages at which fertility is normally low. They are relatively less important at 25–29 years, fertility being normally high at this period of life.

Thus, deferred marriages and the recovery of births exercise a preponderant influence upon the level of the fertility rates as an aftermath of the war. It is necessary to wait until various age groups are reconstituted by sufficiently recent cohorts who have not gone through sustained disturbances in the formation of their cumulative fertility, to reach, through the fertility, what is fundamental couple behavior. The complete replacement of the disturbed cohorts by unscathed ones takes as long as the age of the oldest group: for example, the rate for the group 40–44 years of age will be disturbed as long as the cohorts that were below that age in 1946, and were disturbed by the war, have not as yet left this age group.

However, isolation of the effects of the disturbance with the aid of age-specific fertility rates is not really possible except when these effects are combined with some fundamental behavior that is stable in time; it will still be necessary, in order to set up such a partitioning of factors, to wait the 10 to 15 years necessary for the complete disappearance of the disturbance.

Age-specific fertility rates for the United States in the period 1940–1964 are shown in Table 8.6b and in Figure 8.4b. The trends indicated here have been analyzed and discussed in great detail by American demographers, and, except to note that there is an underlying similarity to the pattern recorded for France in the same period, we shall not enter into this analysis here.

This long reaction of the fertility rates to disturbing causes, and the fact that they do not isolate the marital fertility—the essential component of overall fertility—make them usually unsuitable for a sufficiently detailed analysis of fertility in our quite Malthusian societies.

Such an analysis is inconceivable without a specific investigation of the behavior of the diverse cohorts that are fertile during the period studied.

Analysis by Cohorts

What we have said concerning the interpretation of *period* fertility rates leads naturally to the collection of these indices for *cohorts* in order to show each one's statistical history. This greatly facilitates the interpretation of characteristics of fertility of a given year.

Such historical reconstructions have been made for various populations,

TABLE 8.6b. *Birth Rates by Age of Mother: United States, 1940–1964*

Year	Age of Mother								*Total Fertility Rate*	*Gross Reproduction Rate*
	10–14 years	*15–19 years*	*20–24 years*	*25–29 years*	*30–34 years*	*35–39 years*	*40–44 years*	*45–49* years*		
				Rates per 1,000 women						
Registered births										
1964	0.9	72.9	219.8	178.8	103.5	49.9	13.8	0.8	3.20	1.56
1963	0.9	76.5	231.3	185.4	105.9	51.2	14.2	0.9	3.33	1.62
1962	0.8	81.3	243.8	191.3	108.7	52.6	14.8	0.9	3.78	1.70
1961	0.9	88.0	253.6	197.8	113.3	55.6	15.6	0.9	3.62	1.77
1960	0.8	89.1	258.1	197.4	112.7	56.2	15.5	0.9	3.66	1.78
1959	0.9	89.1	257.5	198.6	114.4	57.3	15.3	0.9	3.67	1.79
Births adjusted for under-registration										
1959	0.9	90.4	260.1	200.5	115.6	58.2	15.5	1.1	3.71	1.81
1958	0.9	91.4	258.2	198.3	116.2	58.3	15.7	0.9	3.65	1.81
1957	1.0	96.3	260.6	199.4	118.9	59.9	16.3	1.1	3.72	1.84

Year										
1956	1.0	94.6	253.7	194.7	117.3	59.3	16.3	1.0	3.63	1.80
1955	0.9	90.5	242.0	190.5	116.2	58.7	16.1	1.0	3.52	1.74
1954	0.9	90.6	236.2	188.4	116.9	57.9	16.2	1.0	3.50	1.73
1953	1.0	88.2	224.6	184.1	113.4	56.6	15.8	1.0	3.38	1.67
1952	0.9	86.1	217.6	182.0	112.6	55.8	15.5	1.3	3.31	1.59
1951	0.9	87.6	211.6	175.3	107.9	54.1	15.4	1.1	3.21	1.59
1950	1.0	81.6	196.6	166.1	103.7	52.9	15.1	1.2	3.03	1.51
1949	1.0	83.4	200.1	165.4	102.1	53.5	15.3	1.3	3.03	1.51
1948	1.0	81.8	200.3	163.4	103.7	54.5	15.7	1.3	3.01	1.51
1947	0.9	79.3	209.7	176.0	111.9	58.9	16.6	1.4	3.16	1.59
1946	0.7	59.3	181.8	161.2	108.9	58.7	16.5	1.5	2.83	1.43
1945	0.8	51.1	138.9	132.2	100.2	56.9	16.6	1.6	2.39	1.22
1944	0.8	54.3	151.8	136.5	98.1	54.6	16.1	1.4	2.47	1.26
1943	0.8	61.7	164.0	147.8	99.5	52.8	15.7	1.5	2.62	1.33
1942	0.7	61.1	165.1	142.7	91.8	47.9	14.7	1.6	2.53	1.28
1941	0.7	56.9	145.4	128.7	85.3	46.1	15.0	1.7	2.31	1.17
1940	0.7	54.1	135.6	122.8	83.4	46.3	15.6	1.9	2.21	1.12

*Rates computed by relating births to mothers aged 45 years and over to women aged 45–49 years.

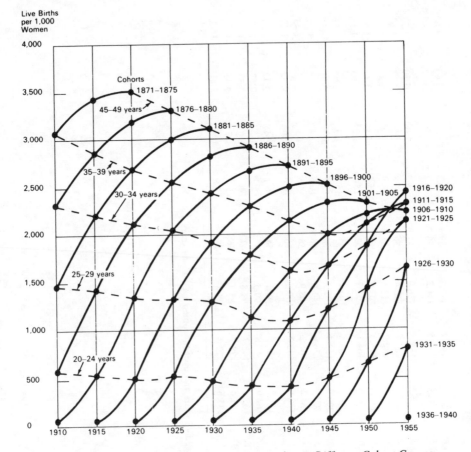

Live Births
per 1,000
Women

Figure 8.4b.   Formation of Cumulative Fertility in Different Cohort Groups.

notably the work of P. K. Whelpton concerning women born in the United
States.[11] Figure 8.4c, taken from the author's *Pratique de la Démographie*,
shows how a revealing graphic representation may be derived from such a form
of organization of data.[12]

B. DURATION OF MARRIAGE

An improvement in the description of the fertility of populations can be
anticipated when the study of cumulative fertility is connected to the event

11. P. K. Whelpton *Cohort Fertility* (Princeton: Princeton University Press, 1952).

12. R. Pressat, *Pratique de la Démographie* (Paris: Dunod, 1967), and, especially, Subject No. 18,
"The Fertility of American Women."

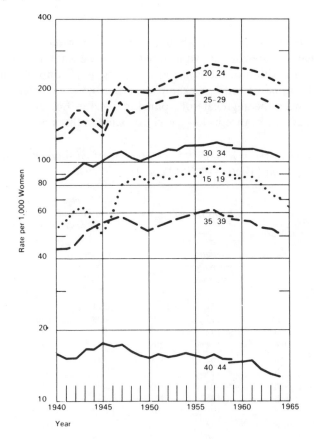

Figure 8.4c. *Birth Rates by Age of Mother. (For 1959–64 based registered live births; for 1940–59, on live births adjusted for underregistration. Semi-logarithmic scale.)*

that most often marks its beginning – marriage. This relationship would appear indicated especially in Malthusian societies where, once the desired family size is attained, the fertility of a couple tends to diminish or disappear entirely. This family size is evidently related to the duration of marriage, so that we might expect greater rigidity in the relationship "fertility-duration of marriage" than in the relationship "fertility-age of the wife."

This manner of viewing the analysis places us directly in a longitudinal perspective; we are concerned with the histories of families, which we seek to reconstruct in a statistical form. We see that period or cross-sectional transpositions are possible. But first it is useful to go into the details of these new forms of description, and, of course, it is best to do this on the basis of real marriage cohorts.

Composition of Cumulative Fertility in a Marriage Cohort

Without going into detail now about treatment of raw data, it is conceivable on the basis of appropriate vital statistics that we can follow from year to year the composition of the *cumulative fertility* of a group of women all married in the same period (for example, during the same calendar year). Table 8.7, showing the aggregate of women married in England and Wales in 1939–1940 and in France in 1943, is constructed in this way.

TABLE 8.7.   *Number of Live Births per 1,000 Married Women (England and Wales, 1939–40 and France, 1943)*

Year of Marriage (n)	Births During nth Year		Total Number of Births from Marriage Until End of nth Year	
	England and Wales 1939–40	*France 1943*	*England and Wales 1939–40*	*France 1943*
1st	211	392	211	392
2nd	217	298	428	690
3rd	193	243	621	933
4th	168	208	789	1,141
5th	162	176	951	1,317
6th	128	156	1,079	1,473
7th	167	139	1,276	1,612
8th	145	117	1,391	1,729
9th	101	99	1,492	1,827
10th	78	86	1,570	1,913
11th	46	74	1,616	1,987
12th	41	64	1,657	2,051
13th	41	56	1,698	2,107
14th	35	48	1,733	2,155

Source: *Études et Statistiques*, Quarterly Supplement to *Monthly Bulletin of Statistics*, No. 4, Oct.–Dec., 1958, p. 15, and U.N. *Recent Trends in Fertility in Industrialized Countries*, N.Y., 1958, Appendix Table J.

Among other things, this table gives the following over-all result: of 1,000 marriages in France in 1943, 2,155 live children were born within 14 years, or, on the average, 2.155 children per marriage, compared to 1.733 per marriage for the 1939–1940 England and Wales cohort. The final cumulative fertility, for all practical purposes, is attained after 25 years of marriage and is very close to being attained after 20 years of marriage.

To be interpreted correctly, these findings require certain qualifications:

1. The data concern the number of children at the moment of their birth; that is, without reference to the mortality that may occur subsequently.

2. The reduction to 1,000 marriages is made by reference to the total number of marriages contracted in 1943 (219,000). So, leaving aside momentarily the influence of possible migratory movements, the fact that certain marriages were broken after this date — by death or divorce — diminishes, all other things being equal, the fertility of this group of married women. If migratory movements did occur, they could have added marriages made outside of France in 1943 and so not registered for the period, but still able to contribute births (in the case of immigration); conversely, migrations could have caused the departures of those married in 1943 and registered in the period, who could then contribute children outside of metropolitan France (in the case of emigration). Actually, the deviations caused by migrations have little importance for France on a national level. They carry more weight at the level of the *département*, for example. Similar considerations hold for the British data.

3. The numbers of Table 8.7 give a statistical estimate of fertility for the aggregate of married women *whatever their age at marriage;* but some of the women, who have passed the age of procreation, carry no weight in this computation. A correction can be added by considering only marriages in which the woman is under 50 years of age at the time of marriage. In what follows we shall always be considering *all* marriages.

The relationship between the different marriage cohorts can be quite instructive, as is, in the case of France, that of the marriage cohorts for 1925, 1938, and 1943 (see Table 8.8a and Figure 8.5). It can be seen that the behavior of families formed in 1943 leads, for whatever the reason, to a mean number of children per marriage that is clearly higher than in families formed in 1925 and in 1938. But the new behavior extends also to families formed just before the war, such as those of 1938; the latter, less fertile in their early years than the older families (those of 1925), eventually catch up (toward the 12th year of marriage) and then clearly overtake the families formed in 1925.[13]

In the United Nations source cited in Table 8.7, similar comparative data are assembled for Australia, Belgium, England and Wales, Finland, New Zealand, Sweden, Switzerland, the Netherlands, and Norway, in addition to those for France.

We cite again (Table 8.8b) data for New Zealand.[14] This time they concern only the final cumulative fertility or "completed birthrate" (estimated

13. A finding the more remarkable since 1938 families were broken up by death and divorce (due to the war) to a larger extent than those of 1925.
14. E. G. Jacoby, "A Fertility Analysis of Marriage Cohorts," *Population Studies,* Vol. XII, No. 1, July, 1958.

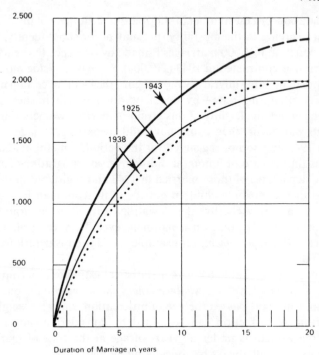

Figure 8.5.   Cumulative Fertility of Different Marriage Cohorts (Numbers of children per 1,000 marriages).

for the most recent marriage cohorts, whose period of reproduction is not yet entirely completed); in addition, corrections have been made to take into account variations in the number of marriages associated with migrations, widowhood, and divorce. Thus, the findings are not exactly comparable to those for France cited in Table 8.8a. Still, the size of the differences proves that the fertility of marriage in New Zealand always stayed a little higher than it was in France for the same cohorts. It may be noted that, in both countries, it is the cohorts married around 1925 that were the least fertile. Finally, to give the reader an idea of the trend in final cumulative fertility of marriage cohorts over an extended period, we show in Table 8.8c the data presented in the *Report of the Royal Commission on Population* for England and Wales.[15] These data, collected sometimes for birth cohorts and sometimes for marriage cohorts, cover practically the entire period of the decline in fertility in England and Wales.

15. Great Britain Royal Commission on Population, *Report Volume, Demographic Papers* (London: HMSO, 1949).

TABLE 8.8a. *France: Formation of Cumulative Fertility in 1925, 1938, and 1943; Marriage Cohorts*

Duration of Marriage years	Cumulative Fertility of Marriages Contracted in			Duration of Marriage years	Cumulative Fertility of Marriages Contracted in		
	1925	1938	1943		1925	1938	1943
1	345	315	392	11	1,675	1,672	1,987
2	610	547	690	12	1,722	1,742	2,051
3	820	725	933	13	1,765	1,800	2,107
4	995	870	1,141	14	1,802	1,847	2,155
5	1,140	1,005	1,317	15	1,835	1,886	2,196
6	1,270	1,123	1,473	16	1,865	1,918	2,231*
7	1,380	1,232	1,612	17	1,890	1,945	2,259*
8	1,475	1,358	1,729	18	1,915	1,966	(2,280)
9	1,550	1,488	1,827	19	1,935	1,982	(2,300)
10	1,620	1,587	1,913	20	1,950	1,994	(2,320)
				Final Cumulative Fertility	1,980	(2,025)	(2,350)

*Estimated
( )Extrapolated

TABLE 8.8b. *Final Cumulative Fertility Among Different Marriage Cohorts in New Zealand*

Marriage Cohort	Final Cumulative Fertility	Marriage Cohort	Final Cumulative Fertility
1913	3.32	1925	2.37
1914	3.34	1926	2.38
1915	3.08	1927	2.41
1916	2.84	1928	2.41
1917	3.04	1929	2.42
1918	3.11	1930	2.45
1919	3.04	1931	2.51
1920	2.63	1932	2.52
1921	2.50	1933	2.58
1922	2.53	1934	2.52
1923	2.41	1935	2.58
1924	2.38	1936	2.56

Source: *Population Studies*, Vol. XII, No. 1, July 1958, p. 24.

TABLE 8.8c. *Final Cumulative Fertility of Women Married in England and Wales* [a]

	Final Cumulative Fertility
Birth Cohorts	
1841–1845	5.71
1846–1850	5.63
1851–1855	5.40
1856–1860	5.08
1861–1865	4.66
Marriage Cohorts	
1900–1909	3.37
1910–1914	2.90
1915–1919	2.53
1920–1924	2.38[b]
1925–1929	2.19[b]

[a]For exact description of the groups for whom final cumulative fertility was computed, see the explanation accompanying Tables XV and XVI (pages 24 and 25) of the *Report* cited.
[b]Extrapolation.

Fertility Rates by Duration of Marriage

Let us now take up the statistical detail and computations that were used in setting up Tables 8.7 and 8.8a–8.8b. For various reasons we will not examine the 1943 cohorts but, rather, the 1946 marriage cohorts.

In the first place, we have an extract of annual statistics of legitimate births by year and by duration of marriage of parents (double classification), referring to the 1946 marriage cohort. The work of reconstruction of the cumulative fertility of those married in 1946, shown in Table 8.9, is in every point analogous to that undertaken previously (see p. 66) in following the deaths in the 1950 male cohort.

Dividing the different number of births in column 3 of the table by the 516,882 marriages in 1946, and then multiplying by 1,000, we arrive at the rates[16] of column 4.

16. These rates, and those we shall deduce from them below are based upon the numbers of legitimate live births (column 3 of Table 8.9) for which duration of parents' marriage is known. To arrive at a more exact measure we should take account of births to parents of unknown durations of marriage, which must assume some previously known distribution of the "unknowns." We have not done this, since our primary purpose here has been to describe the way in which cohort cumulative fertility can be reconstructed on the basis of annual statistics: retaining the uncorrected numbers, the reader can easily recapitulate their origin in the statistics of the French National Statistics Institute, from which they are taken. The underestimate of the fertility rates that results is at the present time, in France, on the order of 7 to 8 percent.

TABLE 8.9. *France: Live Births in the 1946 Marriage Cohort (516,882 Marriages) and Fertility Rates (per 1,000) by Duration of Marriage*

Vital Statistics Used (1)	Duration of Marriage Complete Years (2)	Live Births (3)	Rate per 1,000 Marriages Contracted in 1946 (4)	Rates per 10,000 by Duration			
				In "Calendar year Differences" (5)		In Complete Years (6)	
				Duration	Rate	Duration	Rate
Year 1946	0	58,337	113	0	113		
						0	358
1947	0 before anniversary	126,531	245				
	1 after —	92,518	179	1	424		
						1	328
1948	1 before —	77,122	149				
	2 after —	61,741	119	2	268		
						2	245
1949	2 before —	64,888	126				
	3 after —	52,003	101	3	227		
						3	211
1950	3 before —	56,953	110				
	4 after	44,853	87	4	197		
						4	178
1951	4 before —	46,869	91				
	5 after —	36,502	71	5	162		
						5	148
1952	5 before —	39,645	77				
	6 after —	31,649	61	6	138		
						6	126
1953	6 before —	33,728	65				
	7 after —	26,747	52	7	117		
						7	109
1954	7 before —	29,395	57				
	8 after —	23,346	45	8	102		
						8	93
1955	8 before —	24,586	48				
	9 after —	19,674	38	9	86		
						9	79
1956	9 before —	21,173	41				
	10 after —	17,055	33	10	74		
						10	68
1957	10 before —	18,341	35				
	11 after —	14,715	28	11	63		

These rates may be regrouped in two ways:

1. In column 5 the rates dealing with births in a single calendar year have been added together. These are not, then, rates related to exact durations: we speak of rates by duration of marriage expressed in differences between year of observation and year of marriage ("calendar year" differences), which is the origin of the durations indicated in column 5. These rates are interesting because they are related to well-defined periods (e.g., in the year 1947 for the rate at duration 1; in the year 1951 for the rate at duration 5). This permits circumscribing the fertility in the marriage cohort according to the different years and, eventually, associating it with all the sanitary, social, political, or economic conditions of the corresponding time periods.

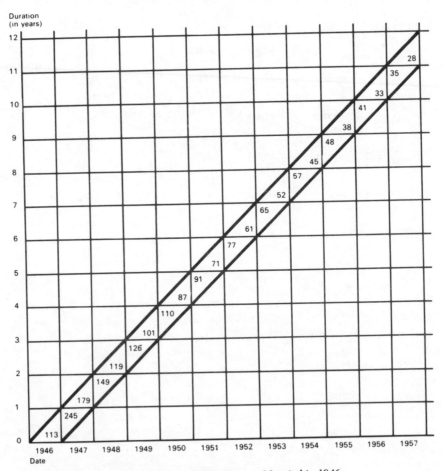

Figure 8.6.   Live Births per 1,000 Women Married in 1946.

2. In column 6 we have added the rates dealing with births that occur during the different durations, expressed in complete years (referring to durations indicated already in column 2): these rates are analogous to those used in Tables 8.7 and 8.8.

In carrying over to Figure 8.6, we can see quite well what distinguishes these two modes of grouping. In both cases there are *rates related to an initial total*, a new notion that will play an essential role in analysis of period marital fertility (in a given year) by time elapsed since marriage. The fact that the rates are calculated in relation to an initial total imposes certain precautions in their interpretation; we have directed attention to this point in the preceding section.

This process of computation derives from the often encountered impossibility of knowing the total number of marriages remaining in each year from each marriage cohort, which prevents computation of rates related to the *current* total number of marriages. By contrast, in the computation of age-specific fertility rates, it was not a question of relating births to the totals of female cohorts aged 15 years (beginning of the fertile period) but rather to the totals remaining each year, the latter being known by annual estimates of population by age and sex (and by marital status).

Period Marital Fertility and Duration of Marriage

Let us return to the period analysis. We shall see the use that can be made of fertility rates by duration of marriage computed for a given year – for example, for the year 1956, in France. These rates include all of the marriage cohorts still making up the population of fertile women in 1956, or, practically speaking, the last 25 marriage cohorts.

The statistics used for computation are, of course, the same as those studied each year in order to follow a given marriage cohort, just as we did in Table 8.9.[17] Nevertheless, this time we shall carry out – as should always be done – the proportional distribution of legitimate births to parents with unknown durations of marriages (4,185 altogether). The previous distribution and the corrected distribution are the subject of Table 8.10, which clarifies this elementary technique for distributing unknown categories.

In Table 8.11 we relate the births (column 2) of the total numbers of marriages (column 1) to which they correspond, with each year of marriage, resulting in two numbers of births according to the principle of double classification. There are precautions to be taken concerning the number of marriages to include. If there have been territorial changes in the country

17. See for the year 1956, *Études statistiques*, No. 4, 1957, Table 22. This table also gives order of birth of children. In contrast to our procedure when following the 1946 cohort, here we use only the data for the total – all birth orders – shown in the third column.

TABLE 8.10. *France: Legitimate Live Births by Year of Marriage and Duration of Marriage, 1956*

Year of Marriage	Duration of Marriage in Completed Years	Legitimate Live Births		
		Known Duration of Marriage	Unknown Duration of Marriage Distributed Proportionally	Total
1956	0	39,219	219	39,438
1955	0	80,299	449	80,748
1955	1	48,532	272	48,804
1954	1	47,852	268	48,120
1954	2	38,721	217	38,938
...	...	...	...	...
1932	24	344	2	346
1931	24	319	2	321
1931 and earlier	25 plus	769	4	773
Total: All Legitimate Live Births		748,033	4,185	752,218

studied, it is necessary to obtain the number of marriages in the territory in which births are registered in the year studied (here, 1956). In the case of France, for instance, the marriages of the period 1940–1945 must be estimated for the present 90 French *départements* and not for the 86 or 87 *départements* in occupied French territory in which there was registration in that period; for the United States, marriages of that period would have to be estimated for the present 50 states and not only for the 48 states of that period.

The resulting rates (column 3) can be regrouped in two ways, according to whether one wishes to obtain a fertility rate for each exact duration of marriage or a rate relative to each marriage cohort for the year 1956 (Fig. 8.7). In the latter case, there is a rate by duration of marriage expressed in calendar year differences. As we have already indicated, the latter index is preferable for analysis of period fertility, because it isolates each marriage cohort for which it gives the fertility during an entire year. The rate for an exact duration rests on the combining of indices from different marriage cohorts; this mongrel character diminishes such a rate's analytical power.

In adding together the fertility rates for all durations of marriage, a synthetic index is obtained, which recalls the index that was the sum of all the fertility rates by year of age in a given calendar year. This time the subject is the mean marital fertility rate for 1,000 new marriages that are taken through all durations of marriage, with the fertility rate observed in France in 1956

TABLE 8.11. France, 1956: Legitimate Births and Fertility Rates, by Duration of Marriage

Year	Marriages Number (1)	Births in 1956 (2)	Rate per 1,000 (3)
1956	293,450	39,438	134
1955	312,703	80,748	258
		48,804	156
1954	314,453	48,120	153
		39,938	124
1953	308,426	40,057	130
		31,802	103
1952	313,892	35,950	114
		27,954	89
1951	319,651	31,604	99
		24,435	76
1950	331,091	28,081	85
		21,870	66
1949	341,091	23,988	79
		18,649	55
1948	370,769	21,162	57
		17,309	47

Year	Marriages Number (1)	Births in 1956 (2)	Rate per 1,000 (3)
1947	427,113	20,262	47
		16,672	39
1946	516,882	21,291	41
		17,150	33
1945	393,000	14,780	38
		9,597	24
1944	205,000	6,870	34
		5,525	27
1943	219,000	5,973	27
		5,337	24
1942	267,000	6,627	25
		5,065	19
1941	226,000	4,873	22
		3,590	16
1940	170,000	2,657	15
		2,445	14
1939	258,429	3,025	12
		2,589	10

Year	Marriages Number (1)	Births in 1956 (2)	Rate per 1,000 (3)
1938	273,917	2,900	11
		2,181	8
1937	274,516	2,185	8
		1,643	6
1936	279,902	1,709	6
		1,267	5
1935	284,895	1,332	5
		923	3
1934	298,482	999	3
		689	2
1933	315,668	721	2
		506	2
1932	314,980	486	2
		346	1
1931 or earlier	about 330,000	1,094	3
		752,218	2,350

applied at each stage. Under these conditions the total number of children born would total 2,350.

The rates applied, being computed relative to the initial total of marriages, take into account the risks of dissolution of marital unions by widowhood or divorce;[18] we do not have, then, a pure index of fertility. Nevertheless, for comparisons over time between comparable dates, the diminishing effect introduced by dissolutions of marital unions is insignificant.

Analysis Based on Fertility Rates by Duration of Marriage

Let us return to the examination of French natality following World War II, this time using for the analysis fertility rates by duration of marriage.

The past history of different marriage cohorts is an important factor in their present fertility, and, in the specification of the present circumstances, it is important to distinguish between this heritage of the past and conditions in each of the years studied. This is why it is important to isolate what current fertility owes to the different marriage cohorts: this requires the use of the fertility rate by duration of marriage in *calendar* year differences. These are the rates that are given in Table 8.12a.

At duration of marriage corresponding to marriages after 1940 (numbers placed above the boldface horizontal bars), the variations in the rate from one year to the next for the same duration of marriage are very small and represent stability of behavior. We may distinguish, as an aggregate movement, only a slight decline in 1951 and a slight rise in 1956. The same development can be seen in the sum of the rates from 0 to 4 years.

Linked with duration of marriage, the fertility of the families formed immediately after the war does not reflect the numerous reports of marriages. Due to the degree of Malthusianism in Western populations, the desired or accepted family size is not such that it demands particularly accelerated family-building after delay of marriage lest the desired size not be attained (for want of a sufficiently long fertile period, or because after a certain age the arrival of children is deemed undesirable). If, in addition, this tendency to shorten the spacing between births is observed among certain couples, it may be compensated for by others who, because of the delay of their marriage and the resulting increase in their ages, are of different psychological dispositions and willingly give up the family size they would otherwise have attained. In any case, delayed marriages make up only a fraction of the postwar marriages and rapidly become negligible.

Finally, the fertility rates by duration of marriage represent an improvement over the age-specific fertility rates; in contrast with the latter, they are

18. Referring not to current risks but, rather, to the various risks encountered in the past by cohorts fertile in 1956.

little influenced by the recoveries of marriages that follow wars and economic crises, and so they permit a more correct perspective of the fundamental behavior of newly married couples during the disturbed periods and immediately afterward. However, as soon as the war ended, the couples formed before the war, many of whom had been separated, recovered all or

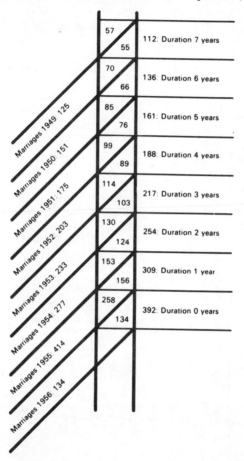

Figure 8.7

part of the births that had been prevented. In these marriage cohorts, the fertility rates after 1945 are higher for any given duration of marriage than they would have been without this separation of some of the couples. This is shown in Table 8.12 below the boldface horizontal bars; for 1946, the duration 6 corresponds to the cohort married in 1940, the duration 7 to the 1939 marriage cohort, etc. The effect of recovery is still more visible in the older cohorts, which are shown in Table 8.12b.

TABLE 8.12a. *France: Fertility Rates (per 1,000 Marriages) by Duration of Marriage*

Duration of Marriage (in Calendar Year Differences)	Year of Observation											
	1946	1947	1948	1949	1950	1951	1952	1953	1954	1955	1956	1957
0	114	124	133	135	134	129	131	129	130	130	134	127
1	412	426	411	411	413	410	405	406	409	409	414	415
2	273	272	270	275	270	269	272	268	274	273	277	287
3	227	226	219	227	224	219	225	228	228	233	233	245
4	200	190	201	197	198	189	192	195	202	200	203	214
0–4 years	1,226	1,238	1,234	1,245	1,239	1,216	1,225	1,226	1,243	1,245	1,261	1,287
5	174	165	177	175	169	162	164	163	170	176	175	183
6	159	143	144	150	152	138	139	137	140	147	151	154
7	155	121	127	127	128	125	119	118	120	120	125	133
8	153	109	104	112	112	106	110	100	103	102	104	110
9	133	108	92	91	96	91	93	92	86	86	86	90
5–9 Years	774	646	644	655	657	622	625	610	619	631	641	670
All durations	2,646	2,465	2,435	2,427	2,399	2,311	2,317	2,292	2,332	2,331	2,350	2,409

Finally, there are random causes for some of the behavior of these rates. The low value of the rate at duration 0 in 1946 (births in 1946 issuing from marriages in 1946) derives from the quite small proportion of illegitimate conceptions; these conceptions result in births at low durations of marriage (less than 9 months), which make up a large part of the rate at duration 0 in calendar year differences. This small proportion can be explained in this way: in the marriages of any year, some (the proportion varies little in normal times) are occasioned by pregnancy; in 1946 the increase in marriages, which was due to postponed marriages or recoveries of delayed marriages, probably included a smaller proportion of marriages occasioned by illegitimate conceptions, and the fertility rate for the aggregate reflects this.

The rates for the marriage cohorts of 1944–1945 are explainable in an analogous way. In 1944 there were few marriages (205,000), and the proportion of those marriages brought about by pregnancies was higher. This

TABLE 8.12b. *France: Fertility Rates (per 1,000 Marriages) by Duration of Marriage*

Duration of Marriage (in Calendar Year Differences)		Year of Observation						
		1946	1947	1948	1949	1950	1951	1952
10 years	Marriage Cohort	1936	1937	1938	1939	1940	1941	1942
	Rate per 1,000	117	96	91	80	81	80	81
15 years	Marriage Cohort	1931	1932	1933	1934	1935	1936	1937
	Rate per 1,000	50	48	45	43	41	38	37

had one lasting consequence, because the prenuptial conceptions are a characteristic of higher fertility social groups, and in this marriage cohort such social groupings are overrepresented, so that the rates at different durations of marriage are higher than in the adjacent marriage cohorts (see Table 8.12a).

An inverse phenomenon, though less marked, occurs in the marriage cohort of 1945. There are numerous marriages recorded that could not have taken place in 1944 (393,000 altogether). To correct these complementary phenomena we may treat the two marriage cohorts (1944–1945) as a single one.

Adding the rates for all durations of marriage for a given year, we obtain the number of live births that would come from 1,000 marriages at all ages contracted during the year. Let us remember that the cumulative fertility thus computed (for example, in 1957, 2,409 children per 1,000 marriages; see Table 8.12a) is affected by dissolution of marriage (death of one spouse or divorce), which diminishes the net period fertility.

Finally, the fluctuation in the fertility rates by duration of marriage is essentially limited to the durations for marriage cohorts in which an appreciable fraction was affected by inhibiting factors caused by events in the course of their marital life. Thus, the disturbances are better identified in these indices than in age-specific fertility rates; however, the number of indices affected is smaller, for the fertile life normally does not extend over more than 20 years of marriage, whereas it concerns at least 30 years of age.

The effect of the disturbance of the war on the sum of fertility rates seems to be almost completely dissipated by 1951. The marriage cohorts still disturbed after this date are in those durations of marriage in which fertility is low, a factor that has only minimal consequences for the total of fertility measured by the mean number of children per marriage. With present conditions, about 2,350 children are born per 1,000 marriages at all ages. Let us recall that, in the prewar situation, the cumulative fertility did not exceed 2,000 children (see Table 8.8 and Figure 8.5).

Age at Marriage and Duration of Marriage

By combining these two data — age at marriage and duration of marriage — age-specific marital fertility rates by age at marriage[19] can be computed. We have seen that this combination is necessary for the study of marital fertility in a situation in which birth control is practiced. However, in the absence of fertility limitation, it adds nothing to our knowledge, since in the different cases in which it can be verified, marital fertility does not depend upon age at marriage.

In French statistics since 1946 the different marriage cohorts are thus classified according to duration of marriage and quinquennial age groups of women at the time of marriage; in addition, live-born children of these marriages are classified by their order of birth (or 'parity'). This last datum permits following the formation of cumulative fertility of the different marriage cohorts in a more detailed fashion, the marriage cohorts being followed as a whole or divided according to the age of the women at marriage.

We will not undertake a detailed examination of these statistics but will limit ourselves to resuming the description of the formation of cumulative fertility in a marriage cohort when the birth orders of the children are identified.

Duration of Marriage and Birth Order

We shall follow exactly the marriage cohort of 1946, citing the computations elaborated by the National Statistics Institute given in the vital statis-

19. However, since classification of women by age at the time or age of marriage is generally done in five-year intervals, the correspondence between duration of marriage and age of women is quite imprecise, and in this case there is no exact equivalence between the two associations.

tics for 1957.[20] The findings are reproduced and presented somewhat differently in Table 8.13.

In the left half of the table are the fertility rates by time elapsed since marriage and by the order of births (parity, limited to the first four birth orders); thus, at duration 7 (in complete years), from the 1,000 marriages contracted in 1946, there were born:

    6 children of first birth order
    25 children of second birth order
    32 children of third birth order
    24 children of fourth birth order

totaling 87 children of first, second, third, or fourth order.

In the final column we give the fertility rates relative to births in all birth orders (the same rates as those in Table 8.9, but this time those with "unknown" duration of marriage are distributed, resulting in slight differences). For the same duration 7 there are, for 1,000 marriages in the 1946 marriage cohort, 110 births in all birth orders, which, when compared with the 87 births of the first four orders, give 23 births in orders higher than 4. The rates concerning births in all orders diverge from the rates concerning the aggregate of births in the first four orders only, beginning with complete duration 3 (the fourth year of marriage).

In the right section of the table, the rates from the left part are cumulated from the time of marriage to the various annual durations. Thus, at the end of the eighth year of marriage (the children of duration 7, in complete years), 1,000 women gave birth to:

    757 first order children
    526 second order children
    266 third order children
    108 fourth order children

which is, all together, 1,657 children of orders one, two, three, or four, to be compared with the 1,711 children of all birth orders.

While Table 8.13 could be continued until duration 25, the last line of the right section shows the cumulative fertility at its final level (final cumulative fertility). Once again it must not be forgotten that this refers to live-born cumulative fertility of marriages contracted in 1946, and represents the issue of 26 years of marriage (and thus is affected also by dissolutions of marriages).

In this sense the results differ from those that would be obtained by classifying women of this marriage cohort still married at this period (and, of course, still living) according to the number of children they have had. This is the procedure used in censuses to obtain family statistics. In addition,

20. See *Études statistiques*, No. 4, October–December, 1958, p. 16.

TABLE 8.13. Number of Liveborn Children per 1,000 Marriages Contracted in 1946

Duration of Marriage	Live Births each Duration						Cumulative Live Births since Marriage					
	1st Order	2nd Order	3rd Order	4th Order	First 4 Birth Orders	All Birth Orders	1st Order	2nd Order	3rd Order	4th Order	First 4 Birth Orders	All Birth Orders
0	343	15	2	0	360	360	343	15	2	0	360	360
1	244	77	7	1	329	329	587	92	9	1	689	689
2	77	143	23	3	246	246	664	235	32	4	935	935
3	40	108	54	8	210	212	704	343	86	12	1,145	1,147
4	23	74	58	20	175	179	727	417	144	32	1,320	1,326
5	14	49	50	27	140	149	741	466	194	59	1,460	1,474
6	10	35	40	25	110	128	751	501	234	84	1,570	1,602
7	6	25	32	24	87	110	757	526	266	108	1,657	1,711
8	5	18	26	21	70	93	762	544	292	129	1,727	1,805
9	4	13	20	17	54	79	766	557	312	146	1,781	1,885
10	3	10	16	15	44	69	769	567	328	161	1,825	1,953

care is not always taken in distinguishing among the annual marriage cohorts; often it suffices to question married women who have just passed the maximum fertility age, most frequently those in the age group 45–49 years of age (or 45–54 years of age, or 50–55 years or 50–59 years, and so on). Sometimes these will include at the same time births from the present marriages and from preceding marriages or prior to marriage. This was the procedure in the census of 1946.

TABLE 8.14.   *France: Live Births per 1,000 Married Women Aged 45–49 Years* at 1946 Census*

	Births of			All Births	
1st Order	*2nd Order*	*3rd Order*	*4th Order*	*First 4 Birth Orders*	*All Birth Orders*
824	569	335	197	1,925	2,234

*Exactly, from 1896–1900 birth cohorts

For these different reasons, the findings that can be obtained in this way are not comparable with those in Table 8.13. However, they are related to them in form, and for this reason we give them in Table 8.14. They assist in estimating how Table 8.13 will end when the marriage cohort of 1946 has become entirely infertile. We will see later what use can be made of these data in a systematic study of fertility by birth order.

Reconstruction of Fertility on the Basis of Family Histories

We have generally followed fertility according to the duration of marriage, using vital statistics. While this procedure has permitted us to go into interesting statistical details and to have a very precise perspective of the phenomenon, it must be recognized that the number of countries in which an analysis of this type is possible is quite limited, usually because the required statistical information is lacking (even in very developed populations).

Moreover, very often the statistical history of families — instead of being followed progressively from year to year with the aid of annual birth statistics — is reconstructed during censuses or by means of special surveys (which can be attached to the census itself). By means of various kinds of data (age of women, age at marriage, date of birth of children), it is possible to reconstruct the various stages in the development of cumulative fertility in different cohorts (groups of marriage cohorts). Even for countries that have annual statistics of fertility by duration of marriage, this source of information is not neglected; for the data obtained are not absolutely equivalent to those obtained on the basis of annual vital statistics. In particular, they can be used to furnish many more details than can be obtained from annual statistics (statistics according to various population groups, the study of spacing between births, etc.). However, it is necessary to note that, too often, interest is focused exclusively on final cumulative fertility.

We have already alluded to possibilities for reconstruction of fertility.[21] Those that depend upon questioning women about the issue of their period of fertility pose the general problem of the relationship between mortality and fertility. If the most fertile women undergo relatively greater risks of mortality (repeated risks of accidents during childbirth), the fact that it is the surviving women who are surveyed operates to bias the results in favor of less fertile women.

However, it may be thought that lower fertility (by physiological ability, or voluntary limitation, or the two combined) is associated with greater physical fragility, and, if the excess maternal mortality is low, then it is certain that the bias operates in the opposite direction.

These general remarks apply to groups of surviving women who are homogeneous in age. If we survey the survivors (at all ages) of a marriage cohort (or group of marriage cohorts), the possible effects of selection we have just indicated are eliminated by a preponderant selective factor. In effect, under these conditions there operates a very clear selection among older surviving families in favor of couples who were married at younger ages: for a given duration of marriage, a marital union faces more chances of being dissolved by mortality if the spouses were older at the time of marriage. Proceeding in this way, we are sure to overestimate the fertility of the aggregate of the marriage cohorts; the remedy lies in distinguishing among surviving couples according to age at marriage.

From this set of general remarks, let us summarize and conclude that varying conditions of statistical observation typically lead to different measures of the same demographic phenomenon: it is important to remember this when making comparisons and interpretations.

C. BIRTH ORDER

It has seemed appropriate to study marital fertility — the main component of fertility in the majority of populations — by relating it to time elapsed since marriage, the event that marks the beginning of this form of fertility. The relationship between fertility and duration of marriage is particularly close among couples practicing contraception, since they seek to become infertile when the desired family size is attained.

But as duration of marriage is only an intervening variable, it is possible to anticipate a more precise description of fertility in Malthusian situations

21. See the preceding section and above, pp. 188 and 190, where we described the computation of total fertility rate and gross reproduction rates for real cohorts or groups of cohorts.

by taking into consideration an essential variable: the number of children already born. Let us give an initial idea of the type of description that is sought by referring to the statistics of the 1946 census, which have been used in constructing Table 8.15a.

Parity Progression Ratios

From the data of Table 8.15a, it is easy to derive Table 8.15b. In the "0 children" column of this table we find, obviously, the total number of women enumerated; in the "1 child" column, the number of women who have had at least 1 child, that is, the total who have had exactly 1 or 2 or 3 . . . or 8 or 9 or more children; in the "2 child" column, the number of women who have had at least 2 children, that is to say, the total of those who have had exactly 2 or 3 or 4 . . . or 8 or 9 or more children; and so on.

From Table 8.15b we obtain for French women born in 1896–1900: (1) by dividing 901,785 by 1,094,294, the proportion of the *total* number of married women who have had *at least* 1 child; (2) by dividing 622,447 by 901,785, the proportion of the total number of married women who have had 1 child, having had (at least) a second child; (3) by dividing 367,129 by 622,447, the proportion of the total number of married women having had (at least) 2 children, who had (at least) a third child; and so on.

Let us summarize as follows: The proportions in France and in the United States among women with

									France	United States
0 children who subsequently had at least 1 child is	a_0	=	0.824	0.814
1	„	„	„	„	„	„	2	„ „ a_1	= 0.690	0.781
2	„	„	„	„	„	„	3	„ „ a_2	= 0.590	0.668
3	„	„	„	„	„	„	4	„ „ a_3	= 0.588	0.654
4	„	„	„	„	„	„	5	„ „ a_4	= 0.605	0.653
5	„	„	„	„	„	„	6	„ „ a_5	= 0.628	0.667 .
6	„	„	„	„	„	„	7	„ „ a_6	= 0.625	0.664
7	„	„	„	„	„	„	8	„ „ a_7	= 0.635	0.673
8	„	„	„	„	„	„	9	„ „ a_8	= 0.628	0.653

The proportion a_1 computed in this way represents, then, the *growth frequencies* of families of different sizes, at the level of the group of women studied. The expression of Louis Henry, who had introduced this notion, is *growth probabilities*;[22] we denote these proportions *parity progression ratios* (the term parity referring to the number of children borne by a woman).

22. Growth in terms of live births, and not necessarily actual growth, to the extent that young children may die. It is clear that these frequencies could have been computed (at least, the first four of them) on the basis of the distribution given in Table 8.14. The first number gives a_0 directly (rounded); dividing 569 by 824 we obtain $0.690 = a_1$; etc.

TABLE 8.15a. Distribution of Married Women[a] Enumerated in Censuses by Total Number of Liveborn Children[b], France, 1946, and United States, White Women, 1960

Country and Census Year	Women's Year of Birth	Number of Women with Exactly Indicated Number of Liveborn Children										Total Number of Married Women
		0	1	2	3	4	5	6	7	8	9	
France, 1946	1896–1900	192,509	279,338	255,318	151,082	85,245	48,617	30,794	18,746	12,145	20,500	1,094,294
U.S., 1960	1896–1900	584,870	559,126	661,860	461,260	302,340	190,119	127,484	82,769	59,017	110,825	3,139,670

TABLE 8.15b. Distribution of Married Women Enumerated in Censuses by Total Number of Liveborn Children, France, 1946, and United States (Whites) 1960

Country and Census	Women's Year of Birth	Number of Women with At Least Indicated Number of Liveborn Children									
		0	1	2	3	4	5	6	7	8	9
France, 1946	1896–1900	1,094,294	901,785	622,447	367,129	216,047	130,802	82,185	51,391	32,645	20,500
U.S., 1960	1896–1900	3,139,670	2,554,800	1,995,674	1,333,814	872,554	570,214	380,095	252,611	169,842	110,825

[a]For U.S.A. ever-married women.

[b]For France includes children born prior to present marriage or prior to first marriage (children born illegitimate). On the other hand, in Table V, p. 102 of Family Statistics of the Census of 1946, from which the data are taken, 69,664 women did not give the number of liveborn children. Given the manner in which the questionnaire was administered, we might suppose that the "unknowns" all comprise women who had not had any children; accordingly we have added them to the 122,845 women declaring that they had had no liveborn children.

With the aid of these parity progression ratios it is easy to compute the manner in which different family sizes are distributed[23] (for a total of 1,000 women, for example).

Knowing that for French women $a_0 = 0.824$ indicates that of 1,000 women, 824 had had at least 1 child and (by subtracting from 1,000) 176 never had a child.

Knowing that $a_1 = 0.690$ indicates that among the 824 women who had had at least 1 child, $824 \times 0.690 = 569$ had at least 2 children, while (subtracting from 824) 255 had *exactly* 1 child.

Knowing that $a_2 = 0.590$ indicates that among the 569 women who had had at least 2 children, $569 \times 0.590^{24} = 335$ had at least 3 children, while (subtracting from 569) 234 had exactly 2 children, etc.

At this point in the breakdown we know, then, that for every 1,000 French women:

176 had 0 children
255 had 1 child
234 had 2 children
335 had 3 children or more.

For every 1,000 white women in the United States:

186 had 0 children
178 had 1 child
211 had 2 children
425 had 3 children or more.

The computation can be carried out in a systematic fashion, so that it follows:

Among 1,000 married French women:

1,000	1,000 had at least 0 children
$1,000 \times 0.824$	824 had at least 1 child
$1,000 \times 0.824 \times 0.690$	569 had at least 2 children
$1,000 \times 0.824 \times 0.690 \times 0.590$	335 had at least 3 children
$1,000 \times 0.824 \times 0.690 \times 0.590 \times 0.588$	197 had at least 4 children
$1,000 \times 0.824 \times 0.690 \times 0.590$ $\times 0.588 \times 0.605$	119 had at least 5 children

23. It is entirely clear that in the present case the recourse to parity progression ratios is unnecessary, since these results are obtainable directly with the data of Table 8.15: in effect, it suffices to divide each of the numbers of this table by 1,094,294, the total number of women considered. But in certain instances, the parity progression ratios do not yield data analogous to those of Table 8.15 (for example, in computation of period parity progression ratios). The computation scheme we present here is then very useful.

24. Exactly $824 \times 0.690 \times 0.590$. Because of rounding 569 in a value in excess of 824×0.690, it follows that $569 \times 0.590 = 336$, while $824 \times 0.690 \times 0.590 = 335$; evidently, it is 335 that should be adopted.

$1,000 \times 0.824 \times 0.690 \times 0.590$
  $\times 0.588 \times 0.605 \times 0.628$ 75 had at least 6 children
$1,000 \times 0.824 \times 0.690 \times 0.590 \times 0.588$
  $\times 0.605 \times 0.628 \times 0.625$ 47 had at least 7 children
$1,000 \times 0.824 \times 0.690 \times 0.590$
  $\times 0.588 \times 0.605 \times 0.628$
  $\times 0.625 \times 0.635$ 30 had at least 8 children
$1,000 \times 0.824 \times 0.690 \times 0.590$
  $\times 0.588 \times 0.605 \times 0.628$
  $\times 0.625 \times 0.635 \times 0.628$ 19 had at least 9 children.

By successive subtractions, among the same 1,000 women it also follows:

$1,000 - 824 = 176$ had 0 children
$824 - 569 = 255$ had 1 child
$569 - 335 = 234$ had 2 children
$335 - 197 = 138$ had 3 children
$197 - 119 = 78$ had 4 children
$119 - 75 = 44$ had 5 children
$75 - 47 = 28$ had 6 children
$47 - 30 = 17$ had 7 children
$30 - 19 = 11$ had 8 children
19 had 9 or more children.

Finally, there were born to these 1,000 women:

824 first-order children
569 second-order children
335 third-order children
197 fourth-order children
119 fifth-order children
75 sixth-order children
47 seventh-order children
30 eighth-order children

which gives, for the 1,000 women, 2,196 children first to eighth in order of birth. Let us assume that the 19 women who had 9 or more children had, on the average, 10 children; in this case these 19 women had $19 \times 10 = 190$ children, of which $19 \times 8 = 152$ who have already been counted among the children of the first eight birth orders. To the preceding total we must add $190 - 152 = 38$ children, to have the total number of children born to 1,000 women of the 1896–1900 generations who had married in 1946. We obtain:

$$2,196 + 38 = 2,234 \text{ children.}[25]$$

25. This is also the mean number of Table 8.14; the latter was computed in absolute numbers, also on the assumption that the women having 9 or more children had 10 children on the average.

Parity Progression Ratios and Description of Marital Fertility

As we have seen, knowledge of parity progression ratios permits a quite expressive and natural description of the fertility of a group of women. This description is integrated in the explanatory scheme we have presented several times. In this scheme, a birth of a given order, say, the third birth order, is the demographic event subsequent to a birth of the preceding order, here, the second. The complete statistical description of the movement from one event to a succeeding event requires knowing these points:

1. Among women who have borne their second live child, what is the proportion who have a third live child?

2. How are the lengths of the intervals separating the birth of the third child from that of the second child distributed?

It is clear that the response to the first question is given by the parity progression ratios. In the example we have treated, $a_2 = 0.590$: 59 percent of the women having given birth to a second live-born child had also had a third live-born child.

With only the statistics of Table 8.15a we are not able to reply to point 2. Furthermore, statistics permitting the study of the spacing between births of different orders are rare. L. Henry has been able to study this spacing[26] on the basis of prewar vital statistics for Czechoslovakia and statistics of families in the French census of 1906 (that part devoted to the 1907 survey concerning government workers and employees). For example, he was able to establish, on the basis of the French statistics, that of 100 third-order births (that is, subsequent to second-order births):

2 took place at duration[27]	0 years
16 took place at duration	1 year
33 took place at duration	2 years
19 took place at duration	3 years
11 took place at duration	4 years
7 took place at duration	5 years
4 took place at duration	6 years
3 took place at duration	7 years
2 took place at duration	8 years
2 took place at duration	9 years
1 took place at duration	10 years.

Let us observe that we have presented parity progression ratios in cohort analysis, which is always the most natural manner of introducing an analyti-

26. Louis Henry, "Étude statistique de l'espacement des naissances," *Population,* 1951, No. 3.

27. Referring to durations in calendar year differences, this distribution is extracted from Table IX, p. 127, of *Fécondité des marriages, Nouvelle méthode de mésure,* by Louis Henry, a table that is reproduced in the Appendix.

cal procedure. But here, too, transpositions into period analysis are permitted and are often of great interest.

Before going into the details of these transpositions, let us present some supplementary notes concerning definitions and modes of computation of parity progression ratios for marriage cohorts.

Choice of Marriage Cohorts for the Computation of Parity Progression Ratios

There are many ways of choosing the groups of women for whom parity progression ratios for marriage cohorts are to be computed. In the presentation we have just given, the French group was composed of all the women of the cohorts born in 1896–1900 who were married at the time of the 1946 census: it was, then, a "marriage cohort" composed of all married women of a group of birth cohorts still living. If we had made the year-by-year count of children in different birth orders born to *all* the women of the birth cohort who had been married prior to 1946, we would have obtained different results,[28] but the composition of the marriage cohort would not have been essentially different: it would simply have been enlarged by a certain number of women whom the first observation procedure eliminated.

As was done in the study of fertility by duration of marriage, we can put together cohorts of women married during the same calendar year (or group of calendar years).[29] There again it is possible to follow them in time or to study — on the basis of a census — only the survivors at a given date (chosen to assure that all the women will have passed the age limit of procreation).

Finally, it is possible to compose a marriage cohort for the computation of each parity progression ratio. One might, for example: (1) take the 1930 marriage cohort for computation of a_0 in that cohort; (2) take the cohort of married women who had their *first child* in 1930, for computation of a_1 in this cohort; (3) take the cohort of married women who had their *second child* in 1930, for the computation of a_2 in this cohort; and so on.

Alternatively, the marriage cohorts may be observed from year to year after their formation, on the basis of adequate annual statistics, or studied a posteriori, on the basis only of survivors who can be reached at the time of a census.

Before showing the actual computations, let us illustrate the type of find-

28. For the women dying or separated from their husbands (by widowhood or divorce) prior to reaching 50 years of age will be included in the computation. Naturally, when making such continuous observations, caution should be taken to include such women only during the time in which they belong to the computation.

29. In this case, we can limit the observation only to women married prior to the age limit of procreation.

ings that can be obtained for a marriage cohort (and based on cumulative annual observations), citing once more the Jacoby study already used.[30] The findings are given in Table 8.15c.

TABLE 8.15c. *Parity Progression Ratio for Different Marriage Cohorts in New Zealand (per 1,000)*

Marriage Cohort	a_0	a_1	a_2	a_3	a_4	a_5	a_6
1913	890	825	816	680	637	613	616
1914	898	857	782	668	639	600	597
1915	879	843	744	641	630	593	578
1916	862	780	747	625	628	603	546
1917	914	807	704	653	627	550	632
1918	918	817	736	636	588	595	596
1919	909	846	693	635	598	582	595
1920	849	767	698	612	584	582	575
1921	818	782	679	596	560	551	587
1922	840	754	677	593	593	565	564
1923	800	763	682	589	555	578	537
1924	810	742	670	589	562	547	594
1925	793	759	660	594	598	533	604
1926	807	743	688	571	576	526	583
1927	818	760	645	601	574	536	561
1928	808	765	649	583	588	567	542
1929	811	769	673	520	638	558	601
1930	820	770	660	569	584	565	540
1931	830	765	668	603	580	532	541
1932	801	786	705	599	557	600	500
1933	828	789	693	596	590	535	527
1934	800	801	704	591	562	580	490
1935	824	803	704	590	527	537	550
1936	802	805	723	618	509	513	496

The Frequency of First Births in a Marriage Cohort

We shall illustrate these general considerations by a type of computation recalling that of Table 8.9; it involves the study of the birth of the first child in the marriage cohort of 1946 on the basis of annual vital statistics. Table 8.16 does not differ from Table 8.9 except that it contains only first-order births.

The absence of continuity in the statistics used is indicated in the note;

30. E. G. Jacoby, *op. cit.*

it clearly reduces the quality of the findings that can be derived, since they are restricted to only those births for which duration of marriage of parents and birth order are reported.

TABLE 8.16. *France: First Order Live Births Among 516,882 Marriages Contracted in 1946**

| Vital Statistics Used | First Order Births | | First Order Fertility Rates (per 1,000 Marriages) |
	Duration of Marriage (in completed years)	Number of Births	
1946	0	57,641	112
1947	0	125,244	242
	1	79,916	155
1948	1	50,711	98
	2	20,739	40
1949	2	17,808	34
	3	10,009	19
1950	3	9,576	19
	4	5,820	11
1951	4	5,286	10
	5	3,360	6.5
1952	5	3,431	6.6
	6	2,262	4.4
1953	6	2,382	4.6
	7	1,557	3.0
1954	7	1,645	3.2
	8	1,145	2.2
1955	8	1,204	2.3
	9	853	1.7
1956	9	1,013	2.0
	10	798	1.5
1957	10	758	1.5
	11	574	1.1
First Order Births in the 1946 Marriage Cohort, to 1957, inclusive		403,732	780.6

*Source: Provisional Statistics of population movements appearing in the Quarterly Supplement of the *Monthly Bulletin* of the I.N.S.E.E. statistics of births by birth order shown in this publication differ from those shown in the final statistics of population

On a base of 1,000 marriages, these numbers of first births give what we have called the first-order fertility rate (related to an initial total of marriages). Added, these rates give (rounded to the nearest whole number) the number of first births in 1,000 marriages by the end of 12 calendar years (1946 to 1957 inclusive), which is 780.6 (resulting from the division of 403,732 first births by 516, 882 marriages).

But at the end of these 12 years not all first births have yet occurred, and eventually the number of first births of 1946 marriages will be greater than 780.6 per 1,000 marriages; nevertheless, the correction applied to this number is small, for first births after long durations of marriage are quite exceptional. At durations of marriage beyond 12 years (in calendar year differences), they represent barely 1 percent of the total. It is for this reason that the probable final number of first births will turn out to be about 785 per 1,000 marriages; in the 1946 marriage cohort, a_0, the *parity progression ratio* of newly married couples is about 0.785. Consequently, in this marriage cohort, 21.5 percent of the couples will never have had children. Let us recall again that broken marital unions (by death or divorce), reduce the fertility rates of couples still married at the end of the fertile ages.

Working successively with births of the different orders, as we have done with births of the first order, we can compute the various parity progression ratios a_1, a_2, ..., relative to a *single given marriage cohort*.[31]

In order to be able to compute parity progression ratios a_1, a_2, ..., a_n for marriage cohorts of women who have had, respectively, their first, second, ..., nth child during the same year, births by birth order of a given year must be classified according to the year of birth of the preceding child. This has been done in France since 1959.

---

movements in 1946 to 1950. Because of a mistaken interpretation of questions shown in the registration form for births, some persons imputed a birth order to the newborn child taking into account births *prior* to the present marriage as well. Until 1950, the I.N.S.E.E. made corrections in the provisional statistics (those which we are using), while the new data are given in the final statistics of population movements.

On the other hand, the definition of order of a live birth is not the same for all years. Until 1954, it refers to order of confinement, whether previous births were live births or stillbirths. Since 1955, the order is defined in terms of live births only. In both cases, it refers to order of birth in the *present marriage*. Finally, in this table, no account was taken of birth order where the parents' year of marriage was unknown; such births represent just under 1 percent of the total number of legitimate births each year. As we have already said elsewhere, because we constructed our Table in this manner, the reader is able to locate numbers of births in the annual statistical tables from which they are taken.

31. Of course, if one wishes to obtain only the parity progression ratio, it is not necessary to set up a table analogous to Table 8.16; it suffices to divide the total number of births of a given order by the total number of births of the preceding order.

Frequency of Legitimate First Births as a Period Index

The computation of a_0 as a period index — applying, for example, to the year 1956 in France — is based on the computation and then the addition of first-order fertility rates in 1956 for different marriage cohorts still fertile in that year. The procedure is exactly the same as that which permitted computation of a synthetic mean number of children per marriage for a given calendar year on the basis of fertility rates by duration of marriage (see p. 181, Table 8.11).

While the addition of fertility rates by duration of marriage (in Table 8.11) gives the mean number of children for 1,000 married women, the addition of first-order fertility rates in Table 8.17 gives a mean number of first-order children (to be precise, of live births) for 1,000 married women, that is, the period or cross-sectional parity progression ratio, a_0.[32]

The addition of first-order fertility rates leads to the parity progression ratio $a_0 = 826$ per 1,000, reflecting the fertility conditions of 1956.[33]

Computation of Period Parity Progression Ratios Other Than a_0

The preceding method applies also to the derivation of higher-order parity progression ratios. But in this case it requires *annual birth order statistics according to time elapsed since the preceding birth*. These statistics are not generally available.[34] We shall present an approximate method that depends only upon annual statistics of births by birth order, data that are available frequently.

The method employed is that of the weighted mean, a technique used fairly often in demography in carrying out a period analysis. To explain it, let us reconsider the computation of a_0 (for France, 1956) performed with the data in Table 8.17.

The 257,855 legitimate first-order births that enter into the computation are classified according to the year of the parents' marriage, each number of births being divided by the corresponding number of marriages.

32. Statistics of births by duration of marriage and birth order include various "not reported" categories (see *Études statistiques*, No. 9, October–December, 1957, p. 16, Table 22), which must be distributed. In the present case, the appropriate distributions are available with a maximum of detail. The numbers of births shown in Table 8.17 take account of these distributions; we present the reader with the results of the computations, but urge him to follow us in the computations until he has proved his mastery of this elementary, but indispensable, technique.

33. We could have computed a_0 on the basis of the first-order fertility rate related only to marriages in which brides were under 50 years of age (those in which the brides were still exposed to the possibility of having children), and we would then have had a more refined measure of fertility, with values of a_0 apparently being slightly higher.

34. As indicated earlier, such statistics are available in France since 1959.

Thus:

$$a_0 = \frac{38,864}{293,450} + \frac{119,695}{312,703} + \frac{42,632}{314,453} + \frac{19,204}{308,426} + \cdots$$

If the number of marriages were equal for all years, it would suffice to divide the total of 257,855 first-order births by this constant number. The weighted mean method consists in dividing the total number of births of the order in question (here, first order), which is generally the only datum available, by the mean number of marriages appropriately worked out.

In the example of the computation of a_0, on the basis of what we know, this mean number M should be such that:

$$\frac{257,855}{M} = 0.826.$$

In other words:

$$M = \frac{257,855}{0.826} = 312,173 \text{ marriages.}$$

But for practical purposes the problem will be posed in an exactly inverse manner: the value of a_0 must be derived from the prior determination of M.[35] It is possible that, in the direct determination of M, the numbers of marriages in the different marriage cohorts must be brought in with a weight that – all other things being equal – is in proportion to their contributions to first-order births during the calendar year considered.

It seems there is a vicious circle, since it is this contribution that we ignore for lack of appropriate statistics. Yet the contribution of each marriage cohort depends, all other things being equal, on the time interval elapsed since marriage; in other words, it is related to the distribution of first births by the time elapsed since marriage.

But we do know (and we shall return to this point), on the basis of certain particularly detailed statistics, some types of spacing between marriages and first births and between births of different orders. From these we can choose those that, from all appearances, best apply to the population studied. Without going into premature details, let us consider as acceptable the distribution given in Table 8.18 of intervals between marriage and first births.

This distribution leads to the inclusion of these figures in the computation of the denominator M (number of marriages to which to relate the 257,855

---

35 At least this is the case when first-order births are not classified by parents' year of marriage, which renders impossible the computation of first-order fertility rates as done in Table 8.17.

TABLE 8.17. *First Order Legitimate Births by Duration of Marriage and First Order Fertility Rates per 1,000 Marriages*

Marriages Year	Number	1st Order Births	Rate per 1,000 Marriages
1956	293,450	38,864	132
1955	312,703	79,476 / 40,219	254 / 129
1954	314,453	28,900 / 13,732	92 / 44
1953	308,426	11,998 / 7,206	39 / 23
1952	313,892	7,177 / 4,490	23 / 14
1951	319,651	4,643 / 3,109	15 / 9.7
1950	331,091	3,187 / 2,183	9.6 / 6.6
1949	341,091	2,085 / 1,431	6.1 / 4.2
1948	370,769	1,496 / 1,104	4.0 / 3.0
1947	427,113	1,227 / 935	2.9 / 2.2
1946	516,882	1,023 / 805	2.0 / 1.6
1945	393,000	601 / 372	1.5 / 0.9
1944	205,000	197 / 147	1.0 / 0.7
1943	219,000	133 / 125	0.6 / 0.6
1942	267,000	149 / 100	0.6 / 0.4
1941	226,000	91 / 64	0.4 / 0.3
1940	177,000	52 / 54	0.3 / 0.3
1939 and before	About 275,000	480	1.7
TOTAL		257,855	826.2

TABLE 8.18. *Distribution of First Births by Duration Elapsed (in Calendar Year Differences) Since Marriage (per 100 Total First Births)*

Duration (in calendar year differences)	0	1	2	3	4	5	6	7	8	9	All Durations
Births	16	47	17	8	4	3	2	1	1	1	100

first-order births of the year 1956):

the marriages of 1956 by 16 percent of their number
the marriages of 1955 by 47 percent of their number
... etc.
the marriages of 1947 by 1 percent of their number.

In this way a *weighted mean* is constructed, for which the computation includes the different numbers of marriages with their different weights (here the coefficients 0.16, 0.47, 0.17, etc).[36] The result is:

$$M = 293,450 \times 0.16 + 312,702 \times 0.47 + 314,453 \times 0.17 +$$
$$308,426 \times 0.08 + 313,892 \times 0.04 + 319,651 \times 0.03 +$$
$$331,091 \times 0.02 + 341,091 \times 0.01 + 370,769 \times 0.01 +$$
$$427,113 \times 0.01$$
$$= 312,210$$

very close to 312,173 and leading to the same value for a_0.

In fact, the method of weighted means is used each time the computation of the fertility rate by birth order is impossible, that is, essentially for the computation of parity progression ratios other than a_0.

The available distributions of intervals between birth orders derive, as indicated earlier, from prewar Czech statistics and from a 1907 survey of French government employees and workers. Thus, we have five sets of spacings.

These sets obviously do not have universal applicability.[37] During a computation of parity progression ratios by the method of weighted means, it is appropriate to choose the type of spacing best matching the type of

36. Whereas the arithmetic mean would include them all with equal weight.

37. This is particularly the case for distributions of protogenetic intervals (marriage to first birth), the variable importance of prenuptial conceptions playing an important role; thus, in the Appendix we have not proposed any model distribution for this first interval; furthermore, computation of a first-order fertility rate is quite often possible on the basis of a weighted mean of marriages, and renders the computation of a_0 unnecessary. The distribution of Table 8.18 was computed on the basis of Table 8.17, and it is presented only to permit our explanatory computation.

fertility being studied. Thus, the spacings taken from Sub-Carpathian Russia or from Slovakia around 1930 are appropriate for determining parity progression ratios for prewar Italy, then not very Malthusian. By contrast, the French series of 1907 or that taken about 1930 in Bohemia is more appropriate for present-day Italy.

In all cases the rule of spacing adopted will always deviate from reality in some measure, and the determination of a_1 will never be definitive. But the variations resulting from the use of quite different weights or weighting coefficients (that is, different types of spacing) will never be very large.

The use of these coefficients, however, works uniquely to counteract to a great extent the effect of the inequality of the numbers of marriages and of different order births on the figures for births in a given year, so that period fertility conditions can be reached successfully. Expression of these period conditions rests precisely upon a modification of the intervals between births in certain marriage cohorts, so that the elimination of the compositional effects would never be complete, and the situation of a given year will always be evaluated relative to a norm more or less representative of the mean level of the fertility studied.

The computation procedure is the same whatever the order of the parity progression ratio. In the case, for example, of the computation of a_2, it is necessary to ascertain a weighted mean of second-order births that can be related to a third-order birth. Table 8.19 concerns Italy after World War II (the years 1950–1955); the coefficients used are those of Bohemia, which assume, among other things, that for all practical purposes all third-order births occur during the 11 years following the preceding second-order births. Table 8.19 suggests a convenient manner of presentation for the work sheet.

Period Parity Progression Ratios Larger Than Unity

What is inconceivable for parity progression ratios of cohorts, where it is impossible to record, for example, more second-order births than first-order births, sometimes occurs in period parity progression ratios: the computations based on birth order fertility rates, like those based on weighted means, lead, under certain exceptional conditions, to values of a_1 that are greater than unity.

This formal absurdity merits explanation. Attention was first directed to it by P. K. Whelpton, following computation of period parity progression ratios for white American female cohorts.[38] We shall make such an explana-

---

38. P. K. Whelpton, "Reproduction Rates Adjusted for Age, Parity, Fecundity, and Marriage," *Journal of the American Statistical Association*, Vol. 236, December, 1946.

TABLE 8.19. *Computation of a_2 by Weighted Mean Method (Weighting Coefficients for Bohemia: 2, 21, 28, 17, 11, 7, 4, 4, 2, 2, 1, 1)*

Second Order Births

Year	Number (in thousands)	1950	1951	1952	1953	1954	1955
1955	222.1						4.4
1954	222.3					4.4	46.7
1953	215.0				4.3	45.2	60.2
1952	213.8			4.3	44.9	59.9	36.3
1951	214.0		4.3	44.9	59.9	36.4	23.5
1950	227.2	4.5	47.7	63.6	38.6	25.0	15.9
1949	223.1	46.9	62.5	37.9	24.5	15.6	8.9
1948	219.2	61.4	37.3	24.1	15.3	8.8	8.8
1947	219.4	37.3	24.1	15.4	8.8	8.8	4.4
1946	251.2	27.6	17.6	10.0	10.0	5.0	5.0
1945	171.6	12.0	6.9	6.9	3.4	3.4	1.7
1944	169.0	6.8	6.8	3.4	3.4	1.7	1.7
1943	174.9	7.0	3.5	3.5	1.7	1.7	
1942	194.8	3.9	3.9	1.9	1.9		
1941	199.0	4.0	2.0	2.0			
1940	227.6	2.3	2.3				
1939	217.9	2.2					
Weighted Means of							
Second Order Births		215.9	218.9	217.9	216.7	215.9	217.5
Third Order Births		127.3	123.0	124.0	123.6	128.3	127.0
a_2		0.590	0.562	0.569	0.570	0.594	0.584

tion in order to establish the ideas with respect to a_0. The example given will be entirely artificial.

Let us imagine that in a perfectly stable population (in the sense used by A. J. Lotka, in particular, see p. 318), first-order births are distributed according to duration of marriage in a cohort of 1,000 marriages as shown in Figure 8.8a, with no first-order birth occurring beyond the seventh triangle in the *Lexis* diagram. Thus, a_0 is equal to 900 per 1,000.

Let us envisage now the occurrence of some disturbance (war, for example) entailing a decline of fertility in the Years I, II, III (Figure 8.8b). Year IV, then, can be marked by recoveries; in the triangles of the *Lexis* diagram of the same number (and hence of the same duration) the fertility will be higher in Figure 8.8b than in Figure 8.8a. With the fertility records adopted in Figure 8.8b, $a_0 = 1,250$ per 1,000.

In certain periods, following previous postponements, there is a sort of

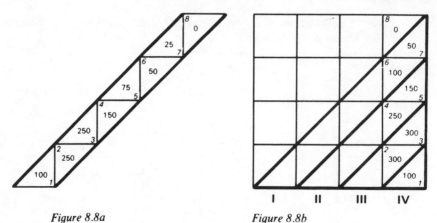

Figure 8.8a   Figure 8.8b

overlapping of different marriage cohorts in the development of their cumulative fertility. Though unsatisfactory from a formal point of view, it offers certain advantages for analysis. A value of a_1 greater than 1 will be a certain index of a recovery of births (whether or not accompanied by a durable rise in fertility). Moreover, the chances of passing unity are the greater if the ratio in question is closer to 1 in its stable state. Also, it is essentially a_0, and still more, a_1 that are subject to these values above unity,[39] (thus in France in 1946; see Table 8.20).

Evidently, there can be a recovery or rise in fertility without any a_1 surpassing unity, but then it is difficult to decide whether or not such a recovery has actually taken place. The reference to a stable state, if it exists, would permit deciding this, just as it could indicate a decline. Thus, in our artificial example, any a_0 greater than 900 per 1,000 is a sign of growth (at least temporary) of fertility and any a_0 smaller than 900 per 1,000 indicates a decline.

Parity Progression Ratios as an Analytical Instrument

Using the French example (Table 20 and Figures 8.9a and 8.9b),[40] we shall examine briefly the kind of analysis to which the use of period parity progression ratios leads. For statistical reasons, the ratios are related to

39. However, we could compute period a_i's, which cannot surpass unity by using probabilities of fertility by parity. For the different probabilities, a_0, q_1, q_2, ... relative to parity, i, we have the equation:

$$a_i = 1 - (1 - q_0)(1 - q_1)...(1 - q_i)....$$

It is generally impossible to compute or estimate these probabilities, a fact that leads to derivation of the period a_i as suggested in the text.

40. This table and figure are taken from the article by L. Henry, "Mise au point sur la natalité francaise," *Population*, No. 2, April June, 1954.

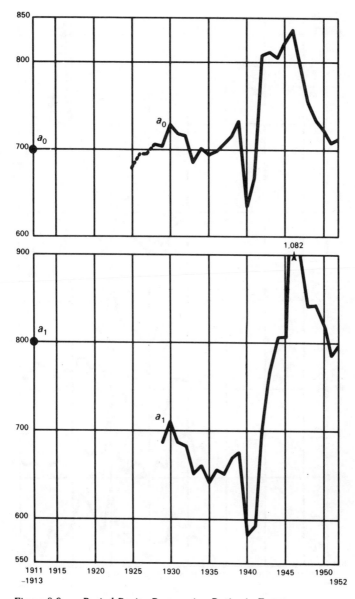

Figure 8.9a. Period Parity Progression Ratios in France.

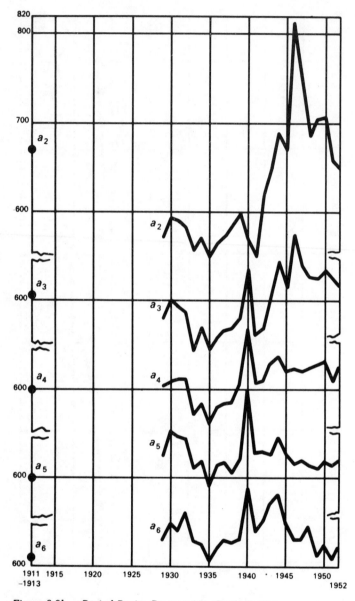

Figure 8.9b. Period Parity Progressions Ratios in France.

birth order defined by the number of children already born to the same mother.[41]

Let us ignore for the moment the points indicating the situation in 1911–1913. Instead, let us note first the traits common to the different curves: these are those resulting from great economic and political events that have affected the country.

1. A little after 1930 there is a general decline of parity progression ratios followed by certain recovery until 1939: the effects of the economic depression, followed by a mild recuperation.

2. In 1940 (and sometimes in 1941), there is a sizable decline in fertility among families with 0, 1, and 2 children; conversely, an increase in fertility in larger family sizes. It is necessary to impute this phenomenon to the war and to the legislative arrangements concerning recruitment: fathers of 6 or more children were not mobilized and, at the end of 1939, fathers of 4 and 5 children were returned to their households. This situation encouraged supplementary births in families of 5, 4, and 3 children, and the increase, in 1940, of a_3, a_4, a_5 (and even a_6).

3. The end of the war (1945) brought about a recovery of births (1946) particularly noticeable at family sizes 1, 2, and 3.

On the other hand, each ratio has its own characteristic development:

1. In France, a_0 is fundamentally stable (if one excludes the disturbed periods). Thus, before World War II, this ratio was at the same mean level as in 1911–1913; and around 1950, after the recovery of the immediate postwar period, it regained approximately the old level. Just as the complement of a_0 measures the proportion of women (or of couples, in accordance with the type of statistics) who never had a child, the stability of a_0 takes into account the stability over time of the proportion of women or of couples totally infertile (because of sterility or voluntary infertility). In particular, this stability seems to show that measures of family compensation taken in France after 1940 did not cut into the infertility of couples most effectively practicing contraception.[42]

2. After 1950, a_1, a_2, and a_3 recovered their 1911–1913 levels and are clearly above their immediate prewar level, especially in the case of a_1; the probable effect on natality of current family legislation would affect only families of sizes 1, 2, and 3, which would more often continue to grow larger.

3. Apart from the wars and economic crises, a_4, a_5 and a_6 have been more or less stable since the beginning of the century. Thus, until 1952, the policy

41. The interruption of the curves for 1913 through 1929 is caused by the absence of birth order statistics in the periods 1914–1919 and 1919–1924.

42. To have full confirmation of this, it will be necessary to consult family statistics relating to very recent data.

of aid to the family did not increase the fertility of already large families.[43]

To this quite expressive description of family fertility, the parity progression ratios add the no less remarkable advantage of recording fluctuations in fertility quite sensitively and of being influenced by disturbing factors over very short time intervals. These indices are particularly useful in the studies of period fertility, which normally are made difficult by the persistent past histories of the different fertile marriage cohorts.

TABLE 8.20. *France: Parity Progression Ratios, a_i (Birth Order Defined by Number, i, of Children Previously Born to the same Mother)*

Year	a_0 (per 1,000)	a_1 (per 1,000)	a_2 (per 1,000)	a_3 (per 1,000)	a_4 (per 1,000)	a_5 (per 1,000)	a_6 (per 1,000)
1911–1913	700	800	670	605	600	600	610
1925	679						
1926	694						
1927	695						
1928	705						
1929	703	685	572	581	604	625	630
1930	726	708	593	601	609	651	648
1931	718	687	590	594	611	646	641
1932	715	683	582	586	612	643	661
1933	687	652	558	544	573	612	628
1934	701	661	569	568	584	619	624
1935	695	641	552	545	563	592	607
1936	698	656	564	557	580	615	620
1937	706	652	572	565	584	618	629
1938	715	669	585	569	585	606	627
1939	731	677	598	581	605	621	630
1940	634	583	568	636	666	702	690
1941	665	593	552	561	606	628	639
1942	808	702	618	569	609	628	650
1943	812	768	652	606	628	626	671
1944	806	806	688	645	637	645	681
1945	823	807	672	619	621	626	648
1946	836	(1,082)	812	675	622	616	629
1947	794	902	745	640	620	619	630
1948	755	842	688	626	622	614	645
1949	734	842	704	624	627	611	614
1950	721	823	706	634	630	618	625
1951	707	785	658	624	609	614	609
1952	711	797	648	614	626	619	624

43. However, we must observe that to the extent that a larger proportion of women attain parity 4 (due to increase of a_1, a_2 and a_3), despite the stability of a_4, a_5, and a_6, there is an increase in the number of families having at least 5, 6, and 7 or more children (among the same 1,000, for example).

The explanation of this sensitivity rests in the fact that the a_1 are connected to the fertility of marriages by order of children born. Should there occur disturbance with a negative impact upon fertility, it may be reacted to differentially by couples according to the size of family already reached. A reaction that could be recorded in a diffuse fashion by indices dependent upon ages of women or their duration of marriage could indicate much more profoundly the fertility of families of certain sizes: this cleavage by existing family size is, in effect, greatest in a largely Malthusian society, where current fertility is affected at the same time by the number of children already born and by the family size desired or, at least, the size that is accepted a priori.

The disturbance is more quickly obliterated in the a_i than in any other index. This is because the delay introduced by a disturbance is usually translated by a deferred birth, less frequently by two. As soon as this birth is accomplished, usually within only a few years, the couples are in a psychological situation quite close to the one they would have known without the disturbance.

Mean Number of Children per Marriage Based on Period Parity Progression Ratios

To illustrate the ideas, we will suppose that the a_i have been computed on the basis of statistics in which the order of birth is defined *in the course of the present marriage*. We have seen that under these conditions (see p. 221): a_0 represents the proportion of marriages producing at least 1 child; $a_0 \times a_1$ represents the proportion of marriages producing at least 2 children; $a_0 \times a_1 \times a_2$ represents the proportion of marriages producing at least 3 children, etc.

Finally, $a_0 + a_0 \times a_1 + a_0 \times a_1 \times a_2 + \cdots$ gives the *mean number of children per marriage* according to the current fertility conditions, which are measured by the sequence of a_i.

This synthetic index of fertility assumes a concrete sense and is extremely sensitive, due to two factors:

1. The sensitivity of the a_i themselves, which we have already seen.

2. The same mode of combination of the a_i to arrive at the mean number of children. Thus, in this combination are included the factors $a_0 \times a_1 \times a_2$; if each one of the a_i diminishes by 10 percent in a given year, relative to the preceding year:

$$a_0 \text{ becomes } 0.9\, a_0$$
$$a_1 \text{ becomes } 0.9\, a_1$$
$$a_2 \text{ becomes } 0.9\, a_2$$

and $a_0 \times a_1 \times a_2$ becomes $0.9 \times 0.9 \times 0.9\, a_0 \times a_1 \times a_2 = 0.729\, a_0 \times a_1 \times a_2$.

The value of this factor is thus about 30 percent lower than that of the pre-ceding year.

More responsive than the mean number calculated on the basis of fertility rates by duration of marriage, the mean number of children computed on the basis of the a_i reports almost instantaneously what will be the final cumulative fertility to which changes in cohort behavior (temporary or not) are leading. In this regard, the comparison of values of two indices in Italy, for 1935–1951, shown in Figure 8.10, is very suggestive:[44] the influence of the war in Ethiopia (1936) and the recovery that followed, the collapse due to World War II, the recovery of 1946, and, finally, the depression in 1951 are clearly more marked on one curve than on the other.

We have seen in the presentation of parity progression ratios that the knowledge of the a_i in a cohort permits distribution of the members of the cohort according to the number of live births (see p. 223).

The same arithmetic treatment with period parity progression ratios permits associating a distribution of marriages according to number of live births with the synthetic mean number of children per marriage.

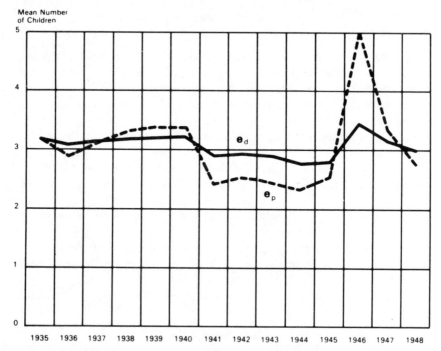

Figure 8.10.   Italy: Mean Number of Liveborn Children per Marriage.

44. e_d is the mean number computed on the basis of fertility rates by duration of marriage, and e_p is the mean number computed on the basis of parity progression ratios.

Let us recall the manner of computation:

a_0 gives the proportion of marriages yielding at least 1 live birth;

$a_0 \times a_1$ gives the proportion of marriages yielding at least 2 live births;

$a_0 \times a_1 \times a_2$ gives the proportion of marriages yielding at least 3 live births;

$a_0 \times a_1 \times a_2 \times a_3$ gives the proportion of marriages yielding at least 4 live births; and so on.

By successive subtractions:

$1 - a_0$ represents the proportion of marriages yielding exactly 0 children;

$a_0 - a_0 \times a_1$ represents the proportion of marriages yielding exactly 1 child;

$a_0 \times a_1 - a_0 \times a_1 \times a_2$ represents the proportion of marriages yielding exactly 2 children; and so forth.

With the sequence of parity progression ratios given in Table 8.21, where the birth order is defined in accordance with the number of children born in the present marriage,[45] we find that 1,000 marriages, under the conditions of the year 1952, yield:

$1,000 - 755 = 245$ families without live births.

$1,000(0.755 - 0.855 \times 0.733) = 202$ families with exactly 1 live birth.

$1,000(0.755 \times 0.733 - 0.755 \times 0.733 \times 0.652) = 192$ families with exactly 2 live births.

Comparison of the distribution of family size, calculated for different time periods, leads to interesting analyses. Table 8.22 gives these distributions for France at three dates: 1910, 1935, and 1952. Figure 8.11, which illustrates this table, shows clearly the return to larger (3 or greater) families after the concentration of single-child families in 1935.

TABLE 8.21. *France, 1952: Period Parity Progression Ratios (per 1,000) (Birth Order Defined by Number of Children Born in Present Marriage)*

a_0	a_1	a_2	a_3	a_4	a_5	a_6	a_7
755	733	652	620	629	625	621	597

Parity Progression Ratios for Female Birth Cohorts

Nothing prevents defining and computing parity progression ratios for female birth cohorts. Though in principle it is preferable to make such com-

45. A sequence that, accordingly, differs from that of Table 8.20.

TABLE 8.22.   *France: Distribution of 1,000 Marriages by Number of Live Births, on the Basis of Period Parity Progression Ratios*

Date	Number of Live Births								Mean Number
	0	1	2	3	4	5	6	7 and above	
1910	255	175	190	150	95	55	30	50	2,240
1935	210	350	190	105	65	30	20	35	1,855
1952	245	202	192	137	83	53	33	55	2,232

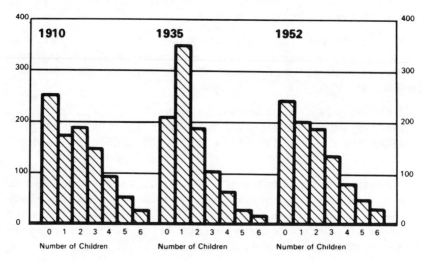

Figure 8.11.   *France: Distribution of 1,000 Marriages by Number of Liveborn Children.*

putations for marriage cohorts, the nature of available statistics may oblige us to consider birth cohorts. We may also be led to compute period parity progression ratios for birth cohorts.

Such findings are available for the United States, where the analysis of the fertility of marriage cohorts is generally not possible. N. B. Ryder has presented a long series of birth cohort and period parity progression ratios, deducing the former from the latter ratios.[46]

46. See N. B. Ryder, "An Appraisal of Fertility Trends in the United States," in *Thirty Years of Research in Human Fertility: Retrospect and Prospect* (New York: Milbank Memorial Fund, 1959).

D. STATISTICAL ANALYSIS OF THE FAMILY

Some Conventions of Terminology

The family is taken here in a very limited and very specific sense: it consists of the father, the mother, and the live-born children (eventually, stillborn children will be included as well). The definition adopted is the one that is most useful for the study of legitimate fertility. It is to this definition that we have had recourse more or less implicitly until now, each time we have been interested in the cumulative fertility of various cohorts.

It is important to establish firmly a distinction between this idea and the one habitually understood as "family" in the sense of "the family statistics" in censuses. There, the reference is often to the number of *surviving* children *not yet having attained some given age* (14, 16, 18, or 21 years) of a couple, of a widowed man or woman, or of divorced persons.

Finally, it is useful to reserve a term for families in which the group (parents and live-born children) resulting from a marital union does not dissolve before the woman has reached the age limit of procreation, which, in practice, is 50 years (a limit of 45 years sometimes suffices). We call these *complete families.*

This would call "incomplete" a family or the union of a man and woman that is interrupted (by widowhood or divorce) before the woman reaches 50 years of age. We must consider "statistically incomplete" a family that cannot be followed by a survey until the woman reaches 50 years of age, either because she has not yet attained that age at the time of the survey or because she has been excluded from observation before reaching that age (in the case of historical reconstruction of the family on the basis of vital records). This does not imply in either case that this family could not have become complete.

The Family as a Complex Statistical Unit

We have already studied the family statistically in the sense that we are using now. The point of view remains quite broad. Usually it involves following the number of live-born children in a marriage cohort from year to year (see, for example, Table 8.8a); sometimes the composition of cumulative fertility is studied by birth order of the children (see, for example, Table 8.13). This investigation was carried out generally on the basis of annual vital statistics. The description given always includes incomplete families (due to widowhood or divorce) that are mixed with families still in the course of formation; it is at the end of the observation, after about 25 years of marriage, that the heterogeneity is greatest.

When still-married women are questioned (in a census, for example)

concerning the children born in the fertile period of their life, the answers
give the total number of complete families in the cohort considered. The
information requested rarely permits obtaining anything other than classification according to size of family attained (see, for example, Table 8.14).
In both cases the reference to the family (in the statistical sense that we understand here) is above all a support for the description of fertility; conversely,
the family as a complex statistical unit is not the subject of a systematic
study.

This statistical unit is defined by the birth dates of the spouses, their date
of marriage, and the dates of birth of the children.[47] From this aggregate of
information and data there comes, in particular, a knowledge of family
size (defined by the number of births), of intervals between marriage and the
first birth, and of intervals between successive births.

With this type of data a group of new problems is posed; at the same time,
original and highly interesting results are established. *It is a remarkable
fact that here demographic analysis is able to respond to outstanding questions
concerning the biometry of human fertility, which seemed — and which still
seems to many — the exclusive province of the biologist.*[48]

Statistical Materials

Nothing would prevent the study of intervals between births on the basis
of appropriate vital statistics; this is what was done by L. Henry on the basis
of prewar Czechoslovakian statistics. However, the necessary information
that must be assembled becomes quite cumbersome, and it is practically
impossible to separate incomplete families and families still in the course of
formation.

The census is better adapted to the statistical description of the histories
of complete families. However, at the period of the census, the investigation
of the national aggregate of families in which the woman had completed the
fertile period can be a task too great, too costly, and too difficult to handle
under the best conditions. In a country the size of France, for instance, the
number of women to be questioned would surpass a million (to obtain, for
example, five age groups). Under these conditions it is preferable to interview
a limited sample of women (50,000 in the French census of 1954); one can
anticipate a sufficient representation and hope to receive information of
better quality.

47. Live-born and sometimes stillborn; it might be interesting to add the date of mortality of
very young children to these data.

48. The methods of analysis and findings to which we allude derive essentially from three studies
of historical populations appearing in the Papers and Documents of the INED:

  Jacques Henripin, *La population Canadienne au debut du XVIIIe siècle*, No. 22;
  Louis Henry, *Anciennes familles genevoises*, No. 26;
  Etienne Gautier and L. Henry, *La population de Crulai, paroisse normande*, No. 33.

Of course, nothing requires that such inquiries be made at the time of the census. They can be undertaken as well in areas where an actual census is impossible, for example, in certain underdeveloped countries. The limits of such inquiries derive, naturally, from the difficulty that those investigated have in responding precisely and completely to demands for particularly detailed information.

One particular form of retrospective inquiry is that based on the reconstruction of family histories on the basis of vital registration, such as those made in France on the basis of the registration of baptisms, marriages, and burials in the parish registers under the Ancien Régime. The scope of the work required by such reconstructions, as well as the narrow framework in which they operate (most often the parish), limits the size of the sample studied and imposes certain statistical precautions in the treatment of data. However, the quality of these data is generally very good, in precision as well as in completeness and richness of detail.

Populations Studied

The infrequency of family information in developed countries, and its relative abundance in currently underdeveloped populations and especially in historical populations, have operated so that the studies carried out heretofore have concentrated on the historical information. The same circumstances have caused the statistical studies of the family that have been undertaken chiefly to clarify various aspects of pre-Malthusian fertility and sometimes to bring out details of the earliest manifestations of voluntary birth control. It is primarily with reference to recently undertaken studies of historical populations that we shall present the main types of analysis and the principle findings acquired.

The Protogenetic Interval

The interval between marriage and first birth is called the protogenic interval. This subject has a particularly privileged place, for its study permits ascertaining certain biological characteristics of fertility. Let us note that, in obtaining the total number of births at less than 8 months of marriage (in complete durations), the relative number of prenuptial conceptions in the populations studied can be evaluated. This remark holds whatever the fertility régime: with voluntary limitation or without limitation of births. However, the time limit is imprecise, and the division at 8 months leads to the classification of "prenuptial" for some postnuptial conceptions that end in premature deliveries, just as it rejects as prenuptial certain conceptions occurring just before marriage.

To be conducted correctly, the study of the interval between marriage and the first birth must be carried out for an aggregate of women who are all observed for a long enough time to allow all lengths of intervals the chance to appear. A too short period of observation (for example, two or three years) would operate to bias the findings in favor of short durations, with long durations being inadequately represented. There is general agreement that a period of at least five years is necessary.[49]

We confine ourselves to the investigation of women for whom it can be assumed that they have virtually all conceived during marriage (delivery at a duration of marriage equal to or above 8 months in complete durations). To separate certain details to which we shall return, let us imagine that our observations are carried out on a group of young married women between 20 and 30 years of age. Certain of these young married women are sterile[50] and consequently will never have children. We eliminate these by retaining only those having at least a first-order child[51] (which is another reason for the necessity of observing women for a long enough time).

Because of variations in the durations of pregnancies, there is no strict equivalence between the distribution of conceptions by duration elapsed since marriage and that of first births by duration elapsed since marriage minus 9 months. Nevertheless, we will make the best of this approximation.

Next, we transform our statistics of first births by time elapsed since marriage into statistics of conceptions in a group of fecund women, classified by time elapsed since marriage.

Fecundability

For couples not practicing contraception, the relative number of conceptions following the first ovulation — hence the conceptions that occur during the first menstrual cycle — [52] depend on physiological possibilities.

They surely also depend upon the greater or lesser frequency of sexual relations[53] apart from any contention that more frequent sexual relations favor conception; but since it is impossible to isolate the role of this behavioral factor, it is included in association with a genuine physiological factor in all

---

49. It will be very much longer with Malthusian populations, in which the number of first births is still statistically appreciable after ten years of marriage (see Table 8.13, p. 216).

50. Or at least are part of sterile couples, the sterility being that of the husband, of the wife, or of the two jointly.

51. It is obvious that we have in mind here only couples not practicing contraception; if not, it would be impossible statistically to distinguish voluntary infertility from sterility. Since we are evaluating the possibility of conception, this could as well be a stillbirth.

52. On the average, during the first 28 days of marriage.

53. Even without the desire to control them in order to prevent conception.

the calculations that can be made of the fertility of couples not practicing contraception.

Among these couples, the beginning of normal sexual relations does not bring with it the certainty that the woman will be fertile at the next ovulation. Statistically, among couples not practicing contraception, only a small proportion of the women are fertile at the end of each ovulation. This proportion, which is the statistical measure of the probability that a woman in a given group will conceive during each menstrual cycle, has been given the name *fecundability*.

This definition implies the manner of computing fecundability: it consists of relating the total number of women fertile at the completion of a single menstrual cycle (the period during which an ovulation necessarily occurs) to the total number of married women not yet fertile at the beginning of the period.

TABLE 8.23. *First Conceptions in the Absence of Contraception among a Group of Fecund Young Married Women*

	Duration in Completed Months							
	0	1	2	3	4	5	6	7
Conceptions at Durations Indicated	1,343	1,053	756	580	448	348	272	218
Women Not Yet Conceiving at the Beginning of the Interval	6,552	5,209	4,156	3,400	2,820	2,372	2,024	1,752
	Duration in Completed Months							
	8	9	10	11	12	13	14	15
Conceptions at Duration Indicated	188	161	128	108	105	97	87	66
Women Not Yet Conceiving at the Beginning of the Interval	1,534	1,346	1,185	1,057	949	844	747	660

The lengths of the cycle vary among women; the most frequent length, 28 days, does not fit well with statistics by duration, which are most often set up by months. Practically, the conceptions for one month will be related to the total number of married women not yet fertile at the beginning of the month. These approximations introduce certain inaccuracies in the measure of fecundability.

With the data of Table 8.23 from P. Vincent, who took them from the list of families that are candidates for the Prix Cognacq (that is, families in which the mothers have all given birth to at least 9 surviving children), the fecundability measured for conceptions of the first month following marriage is equal to

$$f_1 = \frac{1,343}{6,552} = 20.5 \text{ percent.}$$

Thus, about one-fifth of the women were fertile at the first ovulation.

Let us repeat the computation for the rest of the women. At the end of the second ovulation we find:

$$f_2 = 1,053/5,209 = 20.2 \text{ percent fertile women,}$$

a result very like the first one. Then:

f_3 = 18.2 percent	f_8 = 12.4 percent	f_{13} = 11.1 percent
f_4 = 17.1 percent	f_9 = 12.3 percent	f_{14} = 11.5 percent
f_5 = 15.9 percent	f_{10} = 12.9 percent	f_{15} = 11.6 percent
f_6 = 14.7 percent	f_{11} = 10.8 percent	f_{16} = 10.0 percent.
f_7 = 13.4 percent	f_{12} = 10.2 percent	

According to this series, there is a progressive decline of fecundability among the remaining women; it reaches no more than 10 percent by the end of the 15th month. In fact, this decline is attributable to the heterogeneity of individual fecundability; as women with the greatest fecundability are most exposed to conceiving and so leaving the field of observation, a progressive selection operates in favor of those less fertile. This is easily seen in a quite elementary scheme.

TABLE 8.24.   *First Conceptions among a Group of Women*

Duration in Completed Months	Group 1 (f_1 = 0.30)		Group 2 (f_2 = 0.10)		Total		Value of Mean Fecundability
	Women Not Conceiving*	Con- ceptions	Women Not Conceiving*	Con- ceptions	Women Not Conceiving*	Con- ceptions	
0	500	150	500	50	1,000	200	0.20
1	350	105	450	45	800	150	0.188
2	245	74	405	41	650	115	0.177
3	171	51	364	36	535	87	0.163

*Women not yet having conceived at the beginning of the interval.

Let us imagine a group of 1,000 newly married women, of whom 500 have fecundability $f_1 = 0.30$ and 500 have fecundability $f_2 = 0.10$. Table 8.24 shows the conceptions. Due to the operation of selection, the fecundability of the group drops from 20 percent to 16.3 percent three months later.

We have distinguished degrees of natural fertility among women; the fecundabilities measuring them must vary ordinarily at least from 10 percent to 30 percent. The case of sterile women clearly corresponds to zero fecundability.

Valuable as it is, this finding is somewhat tentative. It can be obtained only in non-Malthusian populations and only on the basis of the study of first-order births. With this last restriction, it is not possible to study how fecundability varies with age.

Fertility of Very Young Women

The study of protogenetic intervals yields proof of the lower fertility of the youngest women. This lower fertility appears sometimes in the investigation of fertility rates for women 15–19 years of age or "under 20 years of age." But in this group, which includes all of the entries of young married women observed, a neutral period of 9 months is included for each of them (at least for those not having conceived before marriage), which, all other things being equal, diminishes the fertility of the group relative to that of older groups.[54]

It is by comparing the protogenetic intervals for women married at differ-

TABLE 8.25. *Protogenetic Interval, by Age at Marriage*

Protogenetic Interval	Genevese Bourgeoisie			Crulai		
	Age at Marriage			Age at Marriage		
	Under 17 Years	*17–18 Years*	*19–24 Years*	*16–17 Years*	*18–19 Years*	*20–29 Years*
Under 12 months	4	10	51	0	4	32
12 months or more	26	24	58	6	7	42
Total	30	34	109	6	11	74

54. The same phenomenon is observed in other age groups, e.g., 20–24 years, for women newly married at that age; but its relative frequency is lower, for these observed newly married women coexist with women married in the preceding age interval, for whom the phenomenon is nonexistent. Finally, in the group of newly married women, the 9-month neutral period has relatively little weight, the mean length of time in the 20–24 year group being greater than that passed by the newly married at ages 15–19 in this group.

ent ages that we may bring conclusive evidence of this lower level of fertility.[55] In addition, the method is applicable even with a quite limited number of observations. In Table 8.25 we assemble observations grouped by age at marriage and classified according to whether the first birth (providing it was a legitimate conception) took place more or less than 12 months after marriage.

The differences are nearly all significant[56] in the sense that there is a lower fertility among all of the younger women, a phenomenon recognized under the name "adolescent sterility."[57]

Intergenetic Intervals

Intergenetic intervals are the intervals between successive births or between successive confinements. In non-Malthusian populations, particularly those historical populations for which we possess exact observations, the intergenetic intervals are clearly longer than the protogenetic interval.

The figures for French Canadians at the beginning of the eighteenth century indicate the orders of magnitude: while the mean protogenetic interval is equal to 17.3 months, the mean intergenetic intervals vary between 21.1 months and 26.0 months, depending on the birth order. A comparison limited to the intervals from marriage to first confinement, and from first confinement to second confinement, was made for a group of 81 women living at Crulai (a parish in Normandy), also in the eighteenth century. All had married at 20–29 years of age and had had at least two confinements. It was found (1) for the first interval: 16.2 months; (2) for the second interval: 26.5 months.

A recurring phenomenon is present: while the mean protogenetic interval varies from 15–17 months, the mean intergenetic intervals always surpass 20 months. Of the explanations proposed to account for these differences, that citing temporary sterility related to nursing is the most plausible. It is thus that a higher mean intergenetic interval is reported when the preceding child has survived, and hence has been nursed.[58] For example, among

55. We could try to undertake fecundability computations, but the relative number of women married quite young is small; also, the observable effects are of quite small magnitudes.

56. To decide – given the small absolute numbers involved – we must apply statistical tests, the theory of which is the province of mathematical statistics.

57. However, we might ask if this is due to the sterility of an appreciable fraction of the young women or, rather, from lower fecundability.

58. In fact, this relationship between weaning and conception must be discussed. We may, for example, reverse the causal chain and hypothesize that a conception while nursing increases the risk of death of the child.

The sexual taboos during nursing, observed in certain populations, can be a factor only if the delay in resumption of sexual relationships after confinement goes beyond the delay in the reappearance of ovulation. Finally, this factor does not appear seriously to differentiate the fertility of different populations.

French Canadians the mean intergenetic interval is 25.0 months if the child born at the beginning of the interval lived one year or more, 23.5 months if the child born at the beginning of the interval lived from 7–12 months, and 18.8 months if the child born at the beginning of the interval lived for only 0–6 months.

It is the existence of this temporary sterility that prevents the measurement by menstrual cycle (fecundability) of women's ability to conceive after successive confinements.

Comparison of Intergenetic Intervals

If the computations, even summary ones, suffice to differentiate between intergenetic and protogenetic intervals, the comparisons among intergenetic intervals are much more difficult to establish.

To identify concretely the nature of these difficulties and the kinds of errors possible, it seems best to work from a model that is undoubtedly very schematic, but sets forth certain essential mechanisms very well. Let us imagine a group of 100 married women, fecund and not practicing contraception, among whom fecundability appears to be constant and equal at 15 percent throughout the fertile period. The duration of this period has been taken as the same for all women (230 months), and we assume that each conception is followed by a fixed period of sterility of 21 months.[59]

With this scheme, the conceptions have a random character, and conceivably one can "construct" families on the basis of "drawing lots" appropriately to conform to the hypotheses advanced and reproduce the observable results in the actual cases in which these hypotheses are verified.

We have, then, 100 women with similar capabilities (the same fecundability), not practicing contraception, and remaining fertile throughout the same time interval.

The results are:

> 4 families with 7 children,
> 19 families with 8 children,
> 57 families with 9 children,
> 20 families with 10 children.

Naturally, a different sequence of "drawings" might give a different distribution.

It is essential to note that the perfectly identical aptitudes (the same fecundability, $f = 0.15$) and the absence of contraception do not necessarily

---

59. Exactly, the first ovulation occurs 21 months after the last conception; consequently, in this period of sterility there are 9 months of pregnancy and 12 months of nursing. Thus we assume implicitly that there is no infant death before that age. We note, finally, that for reasons of convenience the first ovulation was assumed to take place at the time of marriage.

lead all the women to the same family sizes. This occurs because the delay between two conceptions is a sort of lottery: certain women accumulate long intervals simply by chance, which, considering the finite duration of the fertile period,[60] prevent them from having as many children as others who accumulate shorter intervals between conceptions. It is thus that, in our fictitious sample, we have two extreme sequences as follows:

Interval	Duration in Months	
Between marriage and 1st birth	23	13
Between 1st birth and 2nd birth	26	22
Between 2nd birth and 3rd birth	43	21
Between 3rd birth and 4th birth	45	21
Between 4th birth and 5th birth	21	23
Between 5th birth and 6th birth	39	41
Between 6th birth and 7th birth	34	21
Between 7th birth and 8th birth		21
Between 8th birth and 9th birth		21
Between 9th birth and 10th birth		21
Between marriage and the last birth	231	225

This difference between findings attained can bring about errors of interpretation.

Let us imagine that to compare the different intergenetic intervals we compute the means for the *group* of intervals observed at the different birth orders (the total for the first intervals, for the second intervals, etc.). We find:

1st interval (between 1st and 2nd birth)	27.1 months
2nd interval	26.2 months
3rd interval	26.6 months
4th interval	26.5 months
5th interval	27.5 months
6th interval	27.0 months
7th interval	27.0 months
8th interval	25.2 months
9th interval	23.8 months

Thus, while from the 1st to the 7th interval the variations are small and at random, the decline at the 8th and 9th orders is quite clear.

For the group of the first 6 intervals (until the birth of the 7th child, since we are considering only intergenetic intervals), we find a mean intergenetic interval of 26.8 months.

60. 230 months, which forces the sum of all intervals between births not to exceed 239 months (the last possible birth is located 9 months after the last possible conception).

Only the 96 women (of a total of 100) who had had at least 8 children are included in computing the 7th interval; only those 77 women who had had at least 9 children are included for the 8th interval; and, finally, only those 20 women having had 10 children (no women in the constructed sample had had more than 10 children) are entered in computing the 9th interval.

This progressive restriction of the total number of women for whom the intervals of higher order are computed works in favor of the women who have had the greatest number of children, hence a smaller mean intergenetic interval (since the total time span in which all conceptions occur is the same for all the women, here, 239 months). Thus, by the operation of this selection, the mean intergenetic interval computed for all the women represented diminishes to the extent that the birth order increases. More precisely, this decline is reflected only beginning with certain birth orders in which certain women (those having had the fewest children) are no longer represented.[61]

In this way a computation of mean intervals carried out without precautions leads to the conclusion that the last intervals are of clearly shorter duration, and that fertility rises with rising birth order. It must be seen clearly that a mean interval computed for the total of families results from the means observed in each category (the category of complete families of 7 children, that of families of 8 children, etc.). For the total number of intervals for which all categories are represented, there are no variations or differences (except

TABLE 8.26. *Mean Intergenetic Intervals (in months) by Size of Families*

	Seven Children Families (4 Families)	Eight Children Families (19 Families)	Nine Children Families (57 Families)	Ten Children Families (20 Families)	Total All Families (100 Families)
1st Interval	30.2	28.9	27.1	24.9	27.1
2nd Interval	35.0	28.4	25.7	23.8	26.2
3rd Interval	33.0	30.5	25.8	23.7	26.6
4th Interval	26.8	29.3	25.8	25.9	26.5
5th Interval	37.5	28.5	27.5	24.5	27.5
6th Interval	30.8	32.2	25.8	24.5	27.0
7th Interval		30.5	26.6	25.2	27.0
8th Interval			25.6	23.9	25.2
9th Interval				23.8	23.8
Mean Interval	32.2	29.7	26.2	24.5	26.6

61. Yet, here the exclusion of 4 women having had only 7 children has no effect upon the mean value of the 7th interval, the relative importance of the selection taking place here being quite little.

random ones) between the different birth orders[62]; but, to the extent that the smaller categories are successively excluded from the calculations, the intervals clearly diminish in length.

These considerations are clarified by examination of Table 8.26, in which the means are recorded for different categories of families. Within any given category, the only differences between intervals are random ones.[63] When considering the mean interval of a certain birth order for the total number of families, one takes the mean of the figures on the same line of Table 8.26, weighted by the relative number of families in each category.

Thus, the general mean of 26.5 months for the 4th interval derives from:

$$26.8 \times 0.04 + 29.3 + 0.19 + 25.8 \times 0.57 + 25.9 \times 0.20 = 26.5.$$

The general mean of 25.2 months for the 8th interval derives from:

$$\frac{25.6 \times 57 + 23.9 \times 20}{77} = 25.2^{64}.$$

It follows from the preceding analysis that to evaluate correctly the influence of birth order on the length of the intervals it is necessary to study this influence for *each* complete family size. However, when the study is carried out within a group of families of different sizes, the weighting introduced for each type of family in determining mean intervals is the same to the degree that it involves intervals for which all the families studied are represented. This is what happens in our model of Table 8.26 up until the 6th intergenetic interval.

This observation dictates a practical procedure to be followed when the number of complete families observable is so small that a study of each family size turns out to be impossible. We may then observe the first intergenetic intervals, say, the first three, in the total of families that have attained a sufficient size; in our example this minimal size must be at least 4. However, given the specifications characteristic of the last and sometimes of the next-to-last interval, there is considerable interest in studying them as they are. Therefore, an investigation of the first three intervals, for example, should be conducted for all the families with 6 children, so that in each category of families, one of the three first intervals will not be the last or the next-to-last. At the same time we can carry out a valid comparison between the first three intergenetic intervals and a study of the two final intervals.

62. At least in the hypotheses of our model, where fecundability is the same for all the women.

63. See note 62 above.

64. This remark assumes a prior datum, when we have mean values of a given intergenetic interval (say, the 4th) for each of the different family sizes, we shall obtain the mean interval for the total of the families by taking a mean *weighted* by the totals of each family size.

Final Intervals

Usually, in the absence of birth control, the variations by birth order in the mean intergenetic interval for a category of families of given size are relatively small and, in any case, not significant except as far as the last or next-to-last interval is concerned.

This constancy of the mean interval is a sign of the constancy of fertility (in the absence of contraception) in the corresponding categories of families during the major part of the procreative period. Under the same conditions a progressive increase in the mean interval between successive confinements would be a sign of diminishing fertility. Louis Henry has observed such an increase in the historical population of Crulai, a parish in Normandy. The corresponding decline in fertility can be attributed a priori to either a decline of fecundability by age or a progressive lengthening of periods of temporary sterility following confinements, or to the influence of the two factors. Other analyses suggest that only the second factor matters.

The marked lengthening of the last interval in relation to the preceding ones seems to be a universal fact in populations not practicing fertility limitation. Most often the increased length of the interval is noticeable beginning with the penultimate interval.

Table 8.27a shows the comparisons that can be carried out – following the suggestions of the preceding paragraph – for the total of complete families in Crulai that had had at least 6 children.[65]

TABLE 8.27a. *Crulai—Mean Intergenetic Intervals in Families Having Had at Least Six Children (in months and tenths of months)*

1st Interval	2nd Interval	3rd Interval	4th Interval	Penultimate Interval	Final Interval
24.1	26.9	27.7	31.3	31.9	39.7

TABLE 8.27b. *Geneva—Mean Intergenetic Intervals in Families Having Had at Least Six Children (in months and tenths of months)*

1st Interval	2nd Interval	3rd Interval	4th Interval	Penultimate Interval	Final Interval
23.6	24.1	23.9	25.2	30.0	37.5

65. We have, then, studied the final and penultimate intervals in computing the means of these intervals for the total of the families, regardless of size.

With the data on historical families of Geneva (marriages of men born before 1650), Louis Henry has found the intervals shown in Table 8.27b.

In the first example, the growth indicated from interval to interval is especially marked for the final one; in the second example, the first intervals do not differ significantly, and the increase is quite noticeable for the next-to-last and then for the last interval.

These findings indicate that the appearance of final sterility is preceded by a period of diminishing fertility due to the probable increase, at the approach of menopause, of the frequency of non-ovular cycles.

Fecund Couples and Fertile Couples

In Malthusian societies infertility is no proof of sterility. By contrast, in populations not practicing birth control, a fecund couple, given sufficient time, must have children. The study of these populations should, then, permit the measurement of human fecundity.

Nevertheless, a fecund couple, when the woman is a given age, can remain subsequently infertile because the time when the couple will become finally sterile is quite close and the random character of fertilization would not permit procreation in the short interval of time in which it might yet occur. The risk of remaining infertile is all the greater – in equal available time periods – the lower the fecundability.

In a group, the number of fecund couples at a certain age is never identical to the number of fertile couples in the group after that age, the first always being larger than (and eventually equal to) that of the second. Yet the difference is even smaller than is the case at an age further from the period in which an appreciable fraction of couples become sterile. In what follows we add the fecund couples at a given age x to the fertile couples after age x (couples subsequently fertile). Let us notice that the overall statistics for the different age groups of couples subsequently fertile assume, in their construction, that the statistical history of each family has been reconstructed.

We begin at a given age for the woman, for example, 30 years. Let S be the percentage of sterile couples at that age: $(100 - S)$ is, then, the percentage of fecund couples. What is conventionally measured at that age is the fertility rate, which is

$$f_{30} = \frac{b}{100}$$

b being the mean number of births per 100 women in the group.

The fertility rate for only the women in fecund couples is

$$f'_{30} = \frac{b}{100 - S}$$

The same mean number of births is related only to the women of the initial group of 100 who belong to fecund couples.

In working out:

$$\frac{f_{30}}{f'_{30}} = \frac{b}{100} \times \frac{100-S}{b} = \frac{100-S}{100}$$

we find the proportion of fecund couples in which the woman is 30 years of age.

In fact, if the elements b and S are known, the computation of f_{30} and f'_{30} is an intervening computation useless for finding $100-S/100$. But in practice things occur differently. We generally work on age groups. For a group, say, 30–34 years of age, we would calculate (1) a fertility rate according to an eventual count in woman-years, if certain women are not observed throughout the five years of the group; (2) a fertility rate for women subsequently fertile, the computation of which will involve, in the denominator, the women who have had children in an age group following the one studied (here 35–39 years of age); and, in the numerator, the births in the group of women between 30–35 years of age.

Thus, given the conditions of statistical observation, we do not arrive directly at the equivalent of the quantities b and S of which we have spoken; what is computed directly is the equivalent of f_{30} and f'_{30}, since we are working on quinquennial groups and considering not fecund women but women subsequently fertile.

We assume that these transpositions do not change the legitimacy of the

TABLE 8.28. *French Canadians at Beginning of 18th Century: Estimated Proportion Fecund among Couples, by Age of Wife*

	Age of Women					
	Under 20 Years	20–24 Years	25–29 Years	30–34 Years	35–39 Years	40–44 Years
Fertility Rates (Fecund and Sterile Couples, per 1,000)	493	509	496	484	410	231
Fertility Rates of Couples Ultimately Fertile (per 1,000)	512	522	522	512	495	328
Ratio	0.963	0.975	0.950	0.969	0.828	0.704

computation, which has necessarily been rigorously carried out only under quite constraining assumptions.[66]

Table 8.28 shows the findings obtained for the Canadian population.

Taking the complement of the ratios obtained, we obtain the estimated proportion of couples definitely sterile in the groups at the ages indicated. Interpolations can be made to estimate the percentage of sterile couples at rounded ages of the woman (25 years, 30 years, etc.).

These percentages are reproduced in Table 8.29, together with those obtained for two other historical populations.

TABLE 8.29. *Estimated Percentage Finally Sterile among Couples by Age of Wife, in Three Historical Populations*

	25 Years	30 Years	35 Years	40 Years
	percent	percent	percent	percent
Canada	3	5	9	21
Crulai	3	7	15	36
Geneva	7	12	19	39

The computations for 20 and 45 years are much less stable; accordingly we have not reproduced the results. As they are, these findings give some indications, according to the wife's age, of the progression of final sterility.

Concluding Remarks

We have tried only to present certain of the types of analysis by which statistical study of the family is conducted; in particular we are virtually exclusively limited to the study of populations not practicing birth control.

The methods are quite different from those employed in conventional analysis carried out on the basis of the usual census statistics or vital statistics. However, the particular character of the data assembled permits response to numerous questions left unresolved by the national statistics, which remain quite broad.

It is hoped that these forms of analysis will be developed by extension of the appropriate inquiries (carried out in both developed countries and demographically primitive underdeveloped countries) and of the more and more expanded exploitation of historical vital registers (parish registers).

66. In fact, retaining the subsequently fertile women, we introduce two types of bias which, however, are not marked when we work with quinquennial age groups (they occur in opposite directions). They would be marked around the usual onset of the menopause working with single years of age.

Part III

POPULATION SIZE AND STRUCTURE

CHAPTER NINE

Population Composition

THE WORD "population" has a rather general meaning in what follows. Heretofore, we were content to indicate by this word the total number of human beings living in a given geographic area, usually the territory of a nation or state. This restrictive sense was sufficient for us to obtain the indispensable (statistical) base to which are associated the vital events (mortality, nuptiality, natality) we have undertaken to study in the preceding chapters.

But in the course of this study we have already seen that we may be led to consider human populations not circumscribed by a geographic area. In particular, the study of certain differential phenomena, such as mortality or fertility, leads to consideration of populations defined by religious, social, economic, or professional membership. Thus, we might speak of the Catholic population of a country, of its agricultural population, etc.

With these categorizations, we still see all the usual vital events. This is no longer the case when we are concerned, for example, with the population of retired persons in an old people's home, in which only mortality plays a part. Considering the population of pupils in an educational institution, we may even say that while mortality is low, this population is, practically speaking, not subject to any of the vital phenomena that have been the concern of the preceding chapters.

Nevertheless, despite their particular character, there is sometimes great interest in studying human aggregates of this type.[1] Attention is then drawn more to certain structural features of these populations than to the vital phenomena that take place within them.

In addition, in the study of these particular populations, the usual ideas of

1. Let us give as other examples the population of skilled workers in an automobile factory, the population of mathematics teachers in French secondary education, etc.

natality and mortality must be transposed. No doubt, there is mortality in every human aggregate, and its demographic role remains; nevertheless, its importance is sometimes negligible—as we have seen in a preceding example—and may be overshadowed relative to other ways of *exit* from the group studied, e.g., in the case of a professional corps: dismissal, resignation, promotion into another corps and, especially, retirement. As for natality, which in these populations no longer intervenes directly as a phenomenon modifying composition,[2] it finds its analogue in the different ways of *entrance* into the population studied. These may include hiring, promotion, admittance, etc., according to the type of population considered.

Attributes of the Structure of a Population

Interesting information concerning a population (understood in the quite broad sense that we have just indicated) can be obtained only after certain structural characteristics are established. The study of the *age structure* is of particular interest. This structure largely determines the development of populations, since the two phenomena that determine change—fertility and mortality—are closely related to the age of individuals.[3]

The distinction among individuals by sex, a quite simple characteristic and more inclusive than age, is rarely made alone; it is usually combined with the study of structure by age. The representation known as the *age pyramid* derives from the composition of a population by sex and by age.

In fact, a considerable group of attributes, each of which concerns a particular phenomenon, can be attached to each individual. Thus;

1. relative to *marital status*, we distinguish individuals according to whether they are *single, married, widowed,* or *divorced*;[4]
2. relative to *economic activity*, we distinguish *economically active* and *economically inactive*; or, *in the labor force* and *not in the labor force*;
3. pursuing the analysis further, we can work out distinctions within the category of *active* persons; for example, keeping to a simple mode of analysis, we will distinguish among individuals employed in the *primary* sector, those employed in the *secondary* sector, and, finally, those employed in the *tertiary* sector;
4. referring to *school attendance*, we can classify individuals as to whether they attend or do not attend some educational institution. We can similarly

2. It can operate indirectly in bringing about the skipping of professional activity by mothers; it would then entail *exit* from the group studied.

3. More generally, this is also the case for factors of entering and leaving the particular populations, in which natality and mortality play a secondary role.

4. Possibly, in the case of polygamy, we could distinguish those married monogamously, bigamously, etc., among married men.

classify pupils according to the type of school attended; for example, retaining only the broadest categories, we may distribute them according to whether they are in *primary* education, *secondary* education, or *technical* education;

5. similarly, we may distribute the working population of an industrial establishment according to degree of skill: *skilled workers, semiskilled workers, unskilled workers*; etc.

We may *associate* several structural characteristics and work out classifications corresponding to the populations studied; for instance, we have seen that it has been common to associate sex and age. It can be said that there are few studies of population structure in which no account is taken of the age of individuals, so much do the characteristic attributes of individuals depend, all other things being equal, upon their age. For example, the study of school attendance has meaning only when carried out by age of individuals.

We turn our attention first to the study of composition of a population by sex and by age.

Population Composition by Sex and by Age

The data used for this study are of the type contained in Table 9.1. In this table, the United States population of July 1, 1967, is classified by sex and by age in complete years at that date (and, consequently, by exact age attained in the course of the year July 1, 1966 to June 30, 1967); the total of persons of each sex aged 85 years or above has been grouped.

Let us specify that the statistics in Table 9.1 result from estimates. A census of population is needed to know the grand total and the totals for each age; the choice of the date of a census depends on considerations of convenience (accessibility of the population, period of fewest geographic migrations) and never falls on a January 1st. It is by using annual statistics of births, deaths, and migrations by age that estimates of the population by age and sex for successive midyear dates are obtained; thus, the figures in Table 9.1 are based on data of the census of April 1, 1960.[5]

The statistical information contained in Table 9.1 is difficult to grasp in its totality; on the other hand, the graphic representation, called an age pyramid, yields a total picture of a population by age and sex.

The Age Pyramid

In this graphic representation (see Figure 9.1), ages are located on a vertical axis, and the totals at each of the different ages or age groups (or

5. Still, the annual estimates sometimes remain approximate. In the case of France, for example, this is due to the low quality of migration data.

generations, in the event that estimates are for January 1st and the two coincide) are shown on a horizontal axis. The left part is reserved for males and the right for females.

For each sex, at each age, there is a rectangle whose length measured on the horizontal axis is equal to the total; thus, the group of females aged 43 complete years, who total 1,283,000, is associated with the rectangle in Figure 9.2a. In the same manner, the different ages are represented by rectangles whose areas are proportional to the totals.

TABLE 9.1.   *Estimated Population of the United States, July 1, 1967, by Sex and Age (Numbers in thousands; Ages in completed years)*

Age	Both Sexes	Males	Females
Total—All Ages	199,118	97,945	101,173
0– 4 years	19,191	9,795	9,397
0	3,539	1,806	1,733
1	3,649	1,861	1,788
2	3,857	1,966	1,892
3	4,039	2,065	1,974
4	4,107	2,097	2,010
5– 9 years	20,910	10,642	10,268
5	4,184	2,136	2,049
6	4,281	2,184	2,097
7	4,150	2,109	2,041
8	4,153	2,108	2,045
9	4,142	2,105	2,037
10–14 years	19,885	10,101	9,784
10	4,128	2,097	2,031
11	4,023	2,045	1,978
12	4,001	2,035	1,966
13	3,903	1,980	1,923
14	3,829	1,944	1,885
15–19 years	17,868	9,082	8,786
15	3,691	1,877	1,814
16	3,600	1,830	1,770
17	3,504	1,782	1,722
18	3,533	1,794	1,739
19	3,540	1,798	1,741
20–24 years	15,197	7,665	7,531
20	3,761	1,907	1,854
21	2,799	1,413	1,386
22	2,823	1,424	1,399
23	2,819	1,418	1,401
24	2,995	1,503	1,491

Age	Both Sexes	Males	Females
25–29 years	12,118	6,035	6,083
25	2,672	1,341	1,332
26	2,467	1,233	1,234
27	2,350	1,167	1,182
28	2,329	1,154	1,175
29	2,300	1,140	1,160
30–34 years	10,975	5,437	5,538
30	2,229	1,106	1,123
31	2,206	1,096	1,110
32	2,205	1,092	1,113
33	2,145	1,060	1,084
34	2,190	1,083	1,107
35–39 years	11,610	5,713	5,897
35	2,245	1,109	1,136
36	2,285	1,126	1,158
37	2,317	1,140	1,177
38	2,361	1,160	1,201
39	2,403	1,179	1,224
40–44 years	12,374	6,034	6,341
40	2,436	1,193	1,243
41	2,459	1,201	1,258
42	2,479	1,209	1,270
43	2,498	1,216	1,283
44	2,501	1,215	1,286
45–49 years	11,841	5,745	6,097
45	2,476	1,202	1,274
46	2,427	1,178	1,249
47	2,372	1,151	1,221
48	2,311	1,121	1,190
49	2,255	1,094	1,162
50–54 years	10,780	5,224	5,556
50	2,216	1,075	1,141
51	2,189	1,062	1,127
52	2,160	1,047	1,113
53	2,127	1,031	1,097
54	2,088	1,010	1,078
55–59 years	9,526	4,574	4,952
55	2,035	982	1,052
56	1,971	949	1,022
57	1,906	915	991
58	1,839	880	959
59	1,775	847	928

Age	Both Sexes	Males	Females
60–64 years	8,048	3,798	4,250
60	1,717	816	901
61	1,664	788	876
62	1,610	760	850
63	1,557	732	825
64	1,500	701	798
65–69 years	6,501	2,958	3,543
65	1,436	667	769
66	1,369	630	739
67	1,300	592	709
68	1,230	553	677
69	1,166	517	649
70–74 years	5,177	2,236	2,941
70	1,115	489	626
71	1,075	467	608
72	1,036	447	589
73	998	427	571
74	953	406	547
75–79 years	3,785	1,587	2,198
75	895	379	516
76	825	347	478
77	756	316	439
78	688	287	401
79	621	257	363
80–84 years	2,160	874	1,286
80	555	228	327
81	491	200	291
82	429	173	256
83	370	148	222
84	314	124	190
85 years and over	1,174	446	727

Source: U.S. Bureau of the Census, *Current Population Reports.* Series P-25, No. 385, Feb. 14, 1968, Table 1.

In fact, it is fairly unusual for the representation to be made by single years of age; one works most often with quinquennial age groups and sometimes with decennial age groups. Sometimes it happens that the pyramid is designed by year of age for the younger ages and by quinquennial (or decennial) groups afterwards.

In this last case, an error awaits the novice. We shall give warning by an example: How may the group of females 40–44 years of age be represented

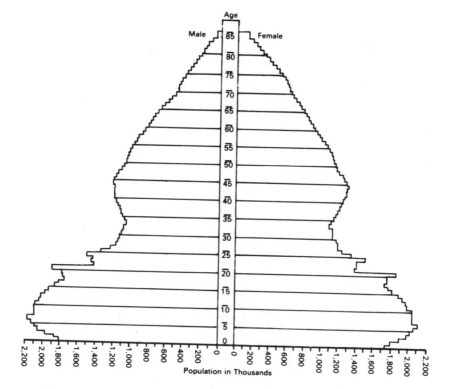

Figure 9.1

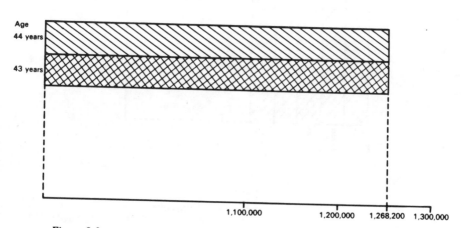

Figure 9.2a

as a group with the horizontal scale measuring the total of each age?[6] (See Figure 9.2b.) This group has a total of 6,341,000; the rectangle associated with this total, the small side of which goes on the vertical axis of 40–45 years of age, should have a length measured on the horizontal axis equal to:

$$\frac{6,341,000}{5} = 1,268,200$$

and not 6,341,000.

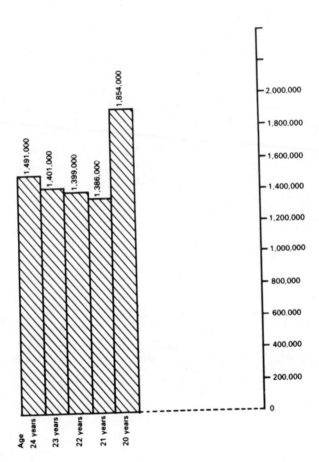

Figure 9.2b

6. This problem occurs when one wishes to sketch the pyramid more rapidly (a diagram by single years of age is quite laborious) or simply because the distribution of the population by single years of age, or by some single-year ages, is not available.

This procedure operates to associate with each of the age groups (40 years, 41 years, 42 years, 43 years, 44 years) the same mean number, equal to one-fifth of the total of the five-year group, 40–44 years of age. In this manner, the rectangle for the group 40–44 years of age has the same area as that of the sum of the five rectangles representing, respectively, the totals of the groups 40, 41, 42, 43, and 44 years of age.

Naturally, in representing together the group 40–44 years of age, the pyramid loses in precision; but at least the general format of the group remains correct.

The substitution of five equal mean rectangles for the real rectangles is an approximation that becomes more crude as the variations are greater in the totals for the different single years of age. In the example in Figure 9.2a, the class 20 years of age has a total notably greater than that of the four other single-year age classes 21, 22, 23, and 24 years; this important inequality disappears in the representation by quinquennial groups.

A final difficulty in the construction of a pyramid derives from the existence of an open-ended age group – the oldest persons, e.g., in Table 9.1, the male and female groups "85 years and over." There is, evidently, no rigorous way to estimate the number for each single year of age on the basis of this information about the group. We may, for example, determine how, in a stationary population (see Chapter 10) with a life table[7] similar to that of the population to be represented, persons aged 85 and over are distributed by single years of age; or, in addition, we may have recourse to an appropriate stable population model (see p. 318). But these are refinements allowing us to reach a reasonable representation, but no more.

For those very much concerned with aesthetic considerations, one may always sketch the end of the pyramid by successive diminutions, making the area of the surface enclosed equal (on the scale adopted) to the population "90 years old and over" that it is intended to represent. This is the way we have proceeded in Figure 9.1. It is very clear that in so doing we have no purpose other than to achieve a continuous pattern, agreeable to the eye, and that this procedure is perfectly justified, given the small totals involved.

In other cases, the decision may be more difficult to make. In effect, the greater the last open-ended group, the greater the imprecision. Let us imagine that we know the French female population as of January 1, 1959, by quinquennial age groups to 65 years of age and by totals only for the years

---

7. Compare P. Vincent, "La mortalité des vieillards," *Population,* No. 2 (April–June, 1951). Nevertheless, it must be remembered that the relative number of survivors at different ages does not depend only upon past attrition by death, but also on the relative size of generations at birth (and, to some extent, upon migrations). So estimating the internal composition of an age group by using a life table is justified only if the population in question has but little growth and, strictly, only if it is stationary (see p. 307). But, in the present case, the weight of mortality is such that the other factors have little influence.

following (see Table 9.2, where at ages beyond 60 years the only numbers known are the totals 1,276,000 and 3,260,000).

TABLE 9.2.   *French Population, January 1, 1959*

Year of Birth	Age Group	Number (in thousands)
...	...	...
1898–1894	60–64	1,276
1893–1889	65–69	1,098
1888–1884	70–74	919
1883–1879	75–79	661
1878–1874	80–84	390
1873–1869	85–89	152
1868 and before	90 plus	40

(1,098 through 40 grouped together: 3,260)

A first important comment must be made: in such a case, one is not required to locate the class totals by year of age on the horizontal axis, since with the statistics available it is necessary to work with at least five-year age groupings. The five-year totals can be placed directly on the horizontal axis. It is useful to proceed in this way, for reading the pyramid becomes easier, but, at the same time, it is necessary to indicate explicitly the notations of the scale adopted (see Figure 9.3).

If it is appropriate to consider as negligible the totals beyond 95 years of age, it is possible to distribute the 3,260,000 women 65 years of age and over

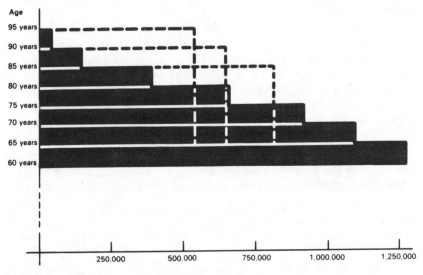

Figure 9.3

in six equal quinquennial groups, with about 543,000 women per quinquennial group. But, in the end, the cutoff at 95 years is quite arbitrary, with the size of the neglected totals beyond this point being judged chiefly by their *relative* size in relation to the total of the open-ended group. Thus, by placing the cutoff at 90 years, we neglect 40,000 women who are distributed incorrectly in the group 65–89 years of age; doing so, we exaggerate the total size of the group 65–89 years of age by a little more than 1 percent, and we understate the number of women in the group 90 years of age and over. There may be good reason to prefer the method of design that fills a surface coming nearer to that outlined by the exact contour of the pyramid (see Figure 9.3). It seems that even a cutoff point at 85 years would be acceptable (an error of 5 percent) and would dissociate even less the end of the pyramid that remains. But, as in practice we cannot know the relative size of the neglected classes (for which the totals below the cutoff point are recorded), the decision is even more difficult to make.

It is, then, not possible to fix precise rules; when decisions must be taken in each particular case, it must be remembered that it is worth neglecting certain of the oldest age classes in order to give the rectangle representing the last open-ended class a form sufficiently approximating the exact pyramid. It would be a mistake to force the rectangle to "continue" to 100 years (or more!) on the pretext that the population studied includes individuals of that age.

Good readability of the pyramid requires judicious choice of the height-width relationship. We may take as desirable a "height" (age axis) equal to two-thirds of the total width (sum of the two semi-axes of the totals).

When one wants to compare the structures of different populations, it is not necessary to adopt uniform scales for all the pyramids, for the different totals, represented by a common height for all the pyramids, would then correspond to very variable widths (they will vary nearly like the population totals). Under these conditions, usually, the rule of two-thirds would not be observed; for this would diminish the legibility and render comparisons considerably more difficult.

To mitigate this inconvenience, it is necessary to reduce the various populations being studied to a common grand total. Thus, if we wish to compare, for July 1, 1961, the pyramid of the total Canadian population (17,769,000 inhabitants) with the pyramid of the population of Prince Edward Island (105,000 inhabitants), it is necessary to bring the two populations to a single common total expressed in a round number—10,000, for example. In this case, we should multiply each of the age groups by

$$\frac{10,000}{17,769,000} = 0.005628 \text{ for Canada,}$$

and by

$$\frac{10,000}{105,000} = 0.952381 \text{ for Prince Edward Island.}[8]$$

We would then construct the two pyramids with identical horizontal and vertical scales.

The horizontal scales of different pyramids can also be appropriately used in taking account of the populations in the preceding example; this approach led to adopting a scale for Prince Edward Island 169 times as large as that for Canada:

$$169 = \frac{17,769,000}{105,000}.$$

But this procedure is not always applicable. It happens sometimes, in certain cases, that one is satisfied with a choice of scales made by guessing, as was done below for age pyramids for different categories of teachers.

The Study of a Pyramid

The rectangle representing an age class or a group of ages has a length that depends on three factors: (1) the total at birth of the corresponding cohort or group of cohorts; (2) the amount of reduction by mortality; (3) the amount of migration.

All other things being equal, the reduction by mortality is of greater importance the older the cohorts are; besides, mortality always ends by having a predominant role, since in the long run it leads to the disappearance of all the cohorts. It is because of this preponderant role that the age pyramids of populations always take on the noticeably triangular form[9] from which their name is derived.

Let us illustrate the manner of reading a pyramid, using the example of the population of France on January 1, 1959 (Figure 9.4). We see that the classic generally triangular form appears, but with numerous deviations, projections, and notches, signs of the intervention of a multitude of factors in the past. Let us begin with the study of the pyramid at its summit.

8. Let us note that in proceeding in this way we are not assured of having exactly the same size pyramid in the two cases, as the size is measured by the horizontal distance between the points at the extreme right and the extreme left. This method is no less effective when we are concerned with comparing population compositions, since it leads to obtaining the same *total surfaces* of pyramids for populations of different total sizes, which permits taking account of differences in the patterns of these surfaces by age.

9. This observation is correct only when we consider a population in the most common sense; it is false in the case of certain particular populations (for example, the total number of children in school).

At the most advanced ages, the numbers of each sex are very unequal. Thus, at around 65 years of age, the totals for females surpassed the number of males by 50 per cent; by 75 years of age, they surpassed the number of males by 75 percent; and by 85 years of age, by 100 percent.[10] This fact is virtually universal, like the phenomenon that is its cause: the excess male mortality that occurs at all ages of life, soon bringing the observed excess of males at early ages (at birth there are about 105 boys per 100 girls) to an excess of females.[11] However, in the case of France, to this "civilian" excess mortality must be added the excess mortality due to World War I (1914–1918); the latter affects only the generation engaged in this war, chiefly the youngest, those born in the last two decades of the previous century. The imbalance between the totals for each sex is clearly less severe beginning with the 1896 generation; beginning with the 1899 generation, it is, for practical purposes, imputable only to the natural excess mortality of the male. The particularly great contraction of the male part of the pyramid beginning with 63 years of age is explained in this way.

Below this age, the pyramid is noticeably symmetric, with a slight feminine excess after 35 years of age taking the place of a slight masculine excess prior to this age. The deep symmetrical niche affecting the 1915–1919 generation is due to the deficit of births caused by World War I. The years 1920–1921 mark a recovery.

The second niche, which is less deep but wider, is centered on the 1940 generation; it is due simultaneously to the lowering of fertility (especially before 1940) when the groups born in 1915–1919, themselves small, arrived at the age of procreation, and to separations due to World War II.

The large and lasting increase in natality beginning with 1946, due partly to recovery and essentially to the change in behavior, gives a quite wide base to the French pyramid.

For the youngest birth cohort (1958 cohort, who as a group had not yet sustained, as of January 1, 1959, all the damage of infant mortality) it is true that more boys than girls are born.

Forms of Pyramids

The three factors that determine the form of a pyramid (natality, mortality, migration) may vary within broad limits. This results in population pyramids that may take very different forms.

10. We examine here, very succinctly, how the sex ratio varies by age. Let us note that the study of the sex ratios by age allows correction of certain errors in censuses. On this subject, see L. Henry, "La masculinité par âge dans les recensements," *Population*, No. 1 (January–March, 1948).

11. Moreover, there is an excess of females in the total population.

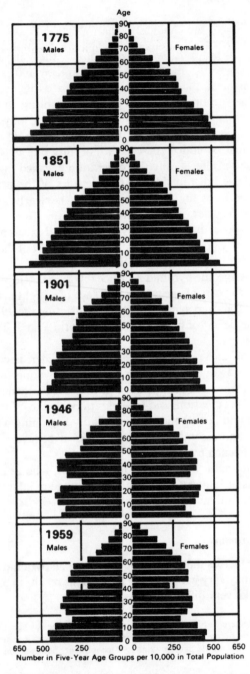

Figure 9.4. Pyramids of French Population in Various Periods.

Examination of the changes in the French pyramid since the eighteenth century (Figure 9.4) allows us to obtain a good sample of the most frequent forms of age pyramids. In addition, it is possible to describe in this way an historic development similar to that of many developed populations.

The pyramid of 1775 is that of a population characterized by high natality and high mortality: a broad base and a rapid narrowing. In such a population, natality and mortality are not far from being in balance, so that the total population varies little, as does the annual number of births. In other words, all the generations have nearly the same total at birth, and the base of the pyramid, in a system of unvarying stages, is nearly always the same relative size. Mortality appears, then, at first as the primary cause of the successive narrowing of the rectangles in the pyramid. However, it is not possible to distinguish between the respective roles of natality and mortality in determining the form of the age pyramids; and in the previous example the role of mortality is only apparently predominant. In fact, without the high fertility that balances the toll taken by mortality the annual number of births would continue to decline, and, in this case, the pyramid would be completely modified. By contrast, with high fertility[12] and low mortality, there is still a rapid narrowing or contraction of the age pyramid; this is because, in such a case, the annual number of births is growing rapidly, so that even in an age pyramid constructed to represent cohorts constantly by their totals *at birth*, the rectangles of successive groups of cohorts would be substantially diminished.[13] No matter how low it may be, mortality can only accentuate the phenomenon that is explained essentially by high natality. It may then be said that there is no pyramid with a broad base and rapid narrowing without high natality. This form of pyramid is, besides, characteristic of a young population, that is, of a population in which the proportion of young elements is relatively high. In France in 1775, for each 100 persons there were:

> 42.8 between 0 and 20 years of age;
> 49.9 between 20 and 60 years of age; and
> 7.3 above 60 years of age.

The pyramid of 1851 has a narrower base than the one for 1775 (with the same horizontal scale for the same total population brought to 10,000, for

12. We speak here without distinction between natality and fertility, although natality (measured in births per 1,000 population) is the outcome of a given fertility (measured in the mean number of live births per woman) upon population composition; in fact, with the usual types of composition, the relative size of fertile age classes varies but little, and, consequently, for a given level of fertility the corresponding natality levels vary but little.

13. For instance, let us imagine a population with a crude birth rate of 40 per 1,000 and a crude death rate of 10 per 1,000; the population, as well as the number of births, grows accordingly by 3 percent annually. In this case, the numbers *at birth* or quinquennial groups of successive generations grow by 16 percent.

example), and the general form is more bulging. The population has aged, in the sense that the young elements are in smaller proportion than in 1775, and, correlatively, the aged persons have accrued a relatively greater weight. For every 100 persons in the total, there were:

> 38.5 between 0 and 20 years of age;
> 51.3 between 20 and 60 years of age; and
> 10.2 above 60 years of age.

While the pyramid of 1775 results from a demographic situation virtually immovable in time (a case of a primitive demographic régime characterized by high fertility and a relatively low mean length of life), the pyramid of 1851 results from a demographic situation in full development: mortality and natality diminishing during numerous decades. This development is to continue throughout another century.

The pyramid of 1901 is even somewhat more narrow at the base and more swollen than the preceding one; some young cohorts are declining relative to the older cohorts (e.g., those of the groups of ages 5–9 years in relationship to the group 10–14 years). The aging of the population is accentuated. Among 100 persons in the total, there were:

> 34.3 between 0 and 20 years;
> 52.7 between 20 and 60 years;
> 13.0 above 60 years of age.

The year 1946 marks an extreme point in the development of the French population. At this date, the younger cohorts are in a declining movement; the pyramid rests on a quite narrow base over which older cohorts jut out; the total for the group aged 0–4 years is smaller than the totals of numerous quinquennial age groups (both sexes together), including that for 45–49 years. Finally, the pyramid has lost its regular form, because of World War I, which severely cut into some male cohorts and caused a large deficit of births. For each 100 persons in the total, there were:

> 25.9 between 0 and 20 years of age;
> 54.5 between 20 and 60 years of age;
> 16.0 above 60 years of age.

The pyramid of 1959, about which we have already commented in detail, is characterized by a broad base that gives the younger persons an increased relative size. Typical of a population in the course of rejuvenation caused by the recovery of natality, this pyramid is summarized by the following structure: for every 100 persons, there are:

> 31.8 between 0 and 20 years of age;
> 51.6 between 20 and 60 years of age;
> 16.6 above 60 years of age.

The Ageing of a Population

Let us compare the preceding distributions of the French population by broad age groups at different dates (see Table 9.3). The change over time of the age composition is characterized by the continuing decline (at least until 1946) of the relative number of young persons (under 20 years of age) and of the continuing increase (until 1959) of the relative number of elderly persons (60 years of age or over); conversely, the relative number of adults (20 to 59 years of age) has remained virtually the same (see Figure 9.5).

TABLE 9.3. *Percentage Distribution of French Population by Three Large Age Groups*

Age in Completed Years	1775	1851	1901	1946	1959
0–19	42.8	38.5	34.3	29.5	31.8
20–59	49.9	51.3	52.7	54.5	51.6
60 plus	7.3	10.2	13.0	16.0	16.6
All ages	100.0	100.0	100.0	100.0	100.0

To take account of this progressive accumulation of the population in the advanced age groups, we say that there is *demographic ageing*, or, alternatively, *ageing of the population* (the expression used in the preceding section). The notion of ageing results, then, from statistical evidence. The economic and social consequences of such a development need hardly be emphasized. As for the causes of this phenomenon, some additional materials are required for them to be clarified.

The first idea that comes to mind is to explain this increased relative number of aged persons by the decline in mortality: such a decline permits an increased proportion of newborn children to reach advanced ages, say, ages beyond 60 years; and the percentage of sexagenarians in the population will accordingly be increased.

In so reasoning, we implicitly compare the population considered to a stationary population.[14] In fact, in such populations, the lower the level of mortality, the higher the proportion of aged persons, which can be seen directly upon examination of survival curves.

But this comparison is generally inadmissible. If, prior to each decline of mortality, we can consider that real populations were close to theoretical

14. The study of stationary populations will be the subject of a later chapter. It suffices now to know that, in such a population, the total size is constant (as are, in consequence, the annual numbers of births and deaths), that the life table is invariable over time, and that the age pyramid of the population is identical to the survivors column (with the annual number of births in the population as radix).

stationary populations,[15] from the time that mortality begins to diminish, the approximate equilibrium between natality and mortality is disturbed, and populations begin to deviate quite considerably from the stationary state. The stationary state is obviously regained when natality in turn begins to diminish, and there is a new approximate equilibrium between mortality and natality, a new equilibrium that will be established at lower levels. Certain of the present-day Western populations are not far from this state.

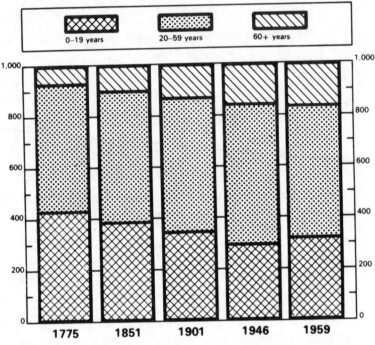

Figure 9.5. Relative Size of Three Large Age Groups in the French Population.

Comparing these populations with present-day underdeveloped populations, in which the situation is close to that of historical Western populations,[16] we may again be tempted to establish a parallel between their age structure and their mortality levels and to affirm once more that ageing of the population is linked with the increase in the mean length of human life. This is to forget that, between the two categories of populations, the differences rest not only on the levels of mortality but also upon levels of natality;

15. Besides, this referred more to populations stationary "on the average," for the balance between natality and mortality is realized only on the average.

16. This was the case especially some years ago, before mortality had declined. It is exactly in this period that we place ourselves.

it is, as we shall see, because there was a decline in natality that there has been an ageing, while the decline of mortality has not had any appreciable effect on the structure of the population.

It can already be observed that when mortality diminishes there are gains in human lives at all ages. In particular, if we recall the relative magnitude of the infant mortality rate and of the mortality rates of young children when the general level of mortality is high, we can measure the volume of progress possible and the important gains in the young elements that may result from a decline of mortality. Also, it does not seem certain that this decline entails demographic ageing, since the gains in the young and in the elderly may compensate for each other to the point of leaving unchanged the proportions of one or the other in the total population.

Our purely qualitative reasoning does not permit any decision in the matter; it is in referring us to either the experience furnished by certain developments of real populations or the results deriving from theoretical calculations that this point can be decided precisely. From such calculations, an attempt has been made to sketch the future development of certain under-developed populations under certain hypotheses.[17] From the aggregate of the results obtained, we abstract the results given in Table 9.4.

In the two types of development indicated, mortality diminishes regularly at a rate that recalls that of European countries in the nineteenth and

TABLE 9.4. *Change in Population Composition with Declining Mortality*

Age Group	Initial Population Composition and Mean Length of Life	Population Composition and Life Expectation After Change (Duration of Change: 100 years)	
		Declining Mortality and Constant Fertility	Declining Mortality and Declining Fertility
	CBR: 50 per 1,000 CDR: 30 per 1,000	CBR: 46 per 1,000 CDR: 7 per 1,000	CBR: 17 per 1,000 CDR: 13 per 1,000
0–19	55.6	58.6	31.4
20–59	41.5	37.5	53.6
60 plus	2.9	3.9	15.0
All ages	100.0	100.0	100.0
Mean Length of Life	33 years	66 years	

CBR = Crude Birth Rate
CDR = Crude Death Rate

17. See *Le Tiers Monde*, INED Document No. 27.

twentieth centuries, with the mean length of life changing in 100 years from 33 to 66 years.

1. *With fertility remaining unchanged* (at a high level of 7 children per woman, on the average), the composition varies very little: a slight increase in the percentage of young persons (58.6 instead of 55.6) and of older persons (3.9 instead of 2.9) and a slight decrease for adults (37.5 in place of 41.5).

Let us observe, in passing, that this change in the composition has brought about a slight decline in natality (46 per 1,000 instead of 50 per 1,000 previously), although fertility does not vary.

2. *With fertility diminishing rapidly* (by the end of the development the successive cohorts assure only their exact replacement), the composition is very profoundly modified: a steep decline in the percentage of young persons (31.4 instead of 55.6), a considerable increase in the percentage of older persons (15.0 instead of 2.9), and an appreciable increase in that of adults (53.6 instead of 41.5).

Although the intrinsic level of mortality is the same as in the first computation, the crude death rate is about twice as high because of the ageing of the population (13 per 1,000 instead of 7 per 1,000).

It is well established that ageing of population has resulted exclusively from the decline of fertility. Ageing appears to be an inevitable development in the composition of human populations. As soon as there is a decline of mortality in a population, there results, in a transitional period, a considerable demographic expansion; a decline in fertility intervenes sooner or later as an indispensable corrective: it is this decline that engenders the ageing of the population.

In France, the two movements were almost simultaneous, so that the population increases in the nineteenth century were much smaller than in other European countries, and so the ageing took place earlier; it is already very visible in the pyramid for 1851, while, at that date, it is not at all pronounced in neighboring countries. This early date of the change in France caused the present degree of ageing in the French population (despite the recent rejuvenation at the base)[18] to be one of the most accentuated in the world.

At the present time, among all of the underdeveloped countries, only mortality has declined, so that these populations have retained a youthful structure. In order to specify the orders of magnitudes, we may indicate that, in the present populations, the proportion of "under 20 years of age" varies from 30 to 50 percent, while, at the same time, the proportion of "60 years of age or older" varies from 17 to 4 percent. It follows that the proportion of

18. An expression the opposite of "aging at the base," which is explained below. Let us observe that this rejuvenation did not go so far as to halt the growth of the relative size of the elderly groups, but only slowed it (see Table 9.3).

adults (the group 20 to 59 years of age) varies within fairly narrow limits, between about 45 and 55 percent. In ageing, the population of a country seems to replace its young elements by the elderly elements, effecting a periodic movement around the adult population, whose relative size is fairly stable.

The ageing of populations is far from being at its end, even among those countries most advanced in this development. If, for example, the population of the world becomes stabilized in the stationary state corresponding to an expectation of life at birth of around 80 years, there will be about:

> 25 percent under 20 years of age;
> 50 percent at 20 to 59 years;
> 25 percent at 60 years of age and older.

Naturally, in the case of a declining population, the relative size of the aged population could be even greater.[19] But, in any case, as long as the decline of mortality is translated into a decline of risks at all ages, it will not be a factor in ageing;[20] it is thus when improvements in sanitation and health bring about a decline only in exogenous causes of death. Ageing, then, results from a decline of natality.[21] One may say that there is an *ageing at the base* (meaning at the base of the pyramid): the relative weight of elderly persons is augmented by the relative decline in the number of young persons.

In the most advanced countries, only slight improvements remain to be achieved in order to wipe out exogenous deaths completely. Thus, at the present time, Norway is not far from attaining the biological limit of mortality. Beyond this, the progress will come from an effective battle against endogenous deaths, that is, essentially against the deaths due to ageing: on the basis of the limited life table, which includes only endogenous causes, there occur only 12 deaths prior to age 20 years per 1,000 newborn children. A decline in mortality would spare chiefly the lives of aged persons: under these conditions, the decline of mortality would become a factor in the ageing of the population. It would become the *ageing at the summit* (again, meaning the summit of the pyramid).

Heretofore, we have examined only the effects of natality and of mortality on the degree of ageing of a population. It is quite evident that migratory movements, by the removals or the additions (depending on the direction of

19. See Table 10.6, p. 330.

20. To the extent, naturally, that the benefits in human lives that result from it are distributed appropriately among the different ages so that they do not cause changes in the age composition. In fact, this is clearly what has taken place thus far.

21. Thus, in our last example, the fact that the population becomes stationary with an expectation of life of 80 years has required that natality diminish as mortality has; we can as well see an indirect cause of ageing in the decline of mortality if, for various reasons, a change in mortality necessitates an appropriate adjustment in natality.

movement) that they cause, are capable of modifying the age composition of populations. In reality, the migrants are usually young people (young workers, sometimes accompanied by children). Migrations also bring about an ageing of the population of the country of origin and a rejuvenation of the population of the country of destination. If the country that receives migrants is undergoing, because of internal demographic conditions, an accelerated ageing process, the contribution of migrants may hold back this ageing. Without the migratory increase of the last 20 years, France would have, at the present time, a measurably older population. Let us indicate that the occupational migration of farmers and the rural exodus that often results from it are factors in the ageing of the French countryside.

General Remarks on the Study of Age Composition

There is no human aggregate for which a study of composition by age would be of no interest. We have studied the usual case of national populations considered in their totality; certain extensions are possible in two directions:

1. The study of age structure and the construction of a pyramid retain their importance and their interest for small populations. Thus, while we avoid computing the rates for micro-populations because of considerable random variations in the appearance of vital events within small groups, the study of composition, and especially of age composition, always retains an intrinsic significance. We shall see presently (Part III, Chapter 11), that in the evaluation of the demographic situation of a population – particularly in the case of a small population – the study of the age composition furnishes the decisive elements in the response.

2. The question may arise of populations in the broad sense, that is, of human aggregates whose members are not necessarily distinguished by geographic association: e.g., the total number of employees in a given commercial enterprise. In both cases, the notion of ageing has its place.

In the study of age composition, the formation of age groups is determined in a general way by the nature of the problems studied. For instance, if one wishes to study the age composition of the economically active population in a country, one could – along with a study of traditional quinquennial age groups[22] – work out a cutoff point around a central age, marking approximately the middle of the period of the economically active life of individuals, e.g., 40 or 45 years. The two groups would then be 14–39 years, and 40 years and over; or perhaps 14–44 years, and 45 years and over. According to an

22. In France, labor force participation cannot legally begin before age 14. We could deal with a group 14–19 years, then 20–24 years, 25–29 years, etc.

estimate of the economically active population as of January 1, 1956, and the projections of that date for January 1, 1960 and 1965,[23] the change shown in Table 9.5a is anticipated.

TABLE 9.5a.   *Trend in Size and Composition of French Economically Active Population (numbers in thousands)*

	Jan. 1, 1956 (Estimate)		Jan. 1, 1960 (Projection)		Jan. 1, 1965 (Projection)	
Age	Number	Percent	Number	Percent	Number	Percent
14–44 years	11,766	60.2	11,712	59.7	12,901	64.1
45 years and over	7,765	39.8	7,907	40.3	7,241	35.9
All ages	19,531	100.0	19,619	100.0	20,142	100.0

Ageing reaches its maximum in 1960; 1965 marks the arrival of the first large group born in 1946 and after at the economically active age, which leads to a rejuvenation. However, in working out a cutoff point in the economically active population at 40 years of age, we would have a different image of the development of the age structure of this population; Table 9.5b shows the percentages in the two categories at the three dates.

TABLE 9.5b

Age	Jan. 1, 1956	Jan. 1, 1960	Jan. 1, 1965
14–39 years	50.4	53.1	52.5
40 years and over	49.6	46.9	47.5
All ages	100.0	100.0	100.0

The reader will be able to study the reasons for this apparent disagreement. The fact that we have considered only two age classes causes an automatic diminution of the relative size of the older age group when the relative size of the younger age group increases, and vice versa. Previously, to evaluate the degree of ageing in the *total* population, we considered *three* age classes, and the extreme groups could both vary in the same direction to the detriment (sometimes to the advantage, but this eventuality is more uncommon) of the central adult class, so that there could be simultaneous ageing (by increase in the percentage of the elderly) and rejuvenation (by increase in the percentage of young persons).

In the study of the structure of the economically active population, nothing prevents the similar consideration of three age groups in order to show smaller differences. However, in so doing, it is not necessary to try to establish a parallel with the classification of the *total* of the population in

23. See *Études et conjoncture.*

three groups; by this classification, we try to clarify the relative size of well-defined categories — youths, adults, and elderly — who assume different roles and have clearly different needs in society. The greater homogeneity of the economically active population does not permit such absolute distinction.

Sometimes the study of the population composition is translated into relationships between carefully chosen age groups, which permits us to see how the replacement of certain generations takes place and to make forecasts about the future of the population studied. Let us show this by an example.

The economically active agricultural population is recruited almost exclusively from among children of farmers; the occupational activity begins quite early, and the population is quite diminished by occupational migration. The replacement of this population requires, upon reaching maturity, that the groups of the youngest cohorts be at least as numerous as the groups of the oldest cohorts whom they must replace. In this respect, the comparison of the two groups 15–34 years and 35–54 years, which together cover the main part of the economically active population, is very instructive. Let us carry out this comparison for the economically active male agricultural population of four French *départements* (Table 9.6).

TABLE 9.6. *France: Economically Active Male Agricultural Population, May 10, 1954 Census (5 percent Sample Results)*

Age on Jan. 1, 1955	Maine-et-Loire	Aisne	Moselle	Pyrénées-Orientales
15–34 years	28,560	18,840	7,200	8,220
35–54 years	20,580	14,050	8,140	10,050
Ratio: Number Aged 15–34 per 100 Aged 35–54 years	139	134	89	74

In the first two *départements*, the replacement is largely assured (taking account only of mortality, which must in 20 years reduce the total group 15–34 years of age by about 6 to 7 percent). In the other two *départements*, there will be (unless there is a quite improbable migration of workers to agriculture) a considerable deficit in any contingency.

An Example: The Professional Population

After having considered populations in the usual sense of the term, we have just looked at more specific human aggregates, for which the study of age composition still retains its interest.

To be complete and sufficiently inclusive, this study, like those of conventional populations, requires the sketching of the age pyramid. As these particular populations are subject not only to strictly demographic events (natality, mortality), but also to other factors of entrance and exit, their composition reflects some unusual aspects rather far from the regular form of present-day age pyramids. The pyramid remains no less the result of past demographic history (in the broad sense) of the population in question, but a correct interpretation supposes a sufficient knowledge of the rules of recruitment that are in effect in the social group considered.

We shall illustrate these generalities by considering the age pyramid of a professional group, that of teachers in French secondary education. The study will be restricted to teachers considered "certified" in the categories "Literature" (*Lettres*), "Physics," and "Natural Sciences"; the situation is that of March 11, 1957, with classification of ages as of January 1, 1957.[24]

All these pyramids (Figure 9.6, a, b, and c) relate to the age interval 20–65 years.[25] The age at entrance into the group depends on the success in a competitive examination; the great dispersion in the ages of candidates admitted gives the base of the pyramid a very tapered form. Retirement, obligatory at 65 years of age and possible between 60 and 65 years of age, according to the wishes of the persons concerned, leads to a very sharp decline at 60 years of age and a termination at 65 years. Tapered at the extreme ages, inflated at the medium ages—these are the gross characteristics of the three pyramids, which, nevertheless, display large differences among themselves.

The "literature pyramid" is the one that conforms most to the general scheme. The narrowing, beginning at age 40 years, derives from two causes: (1) mortality and other factors of attrition (essentially, the promotion into other groups); (2) the expansion of the teaching corps due to the general expansion of French instruction at the secondary level, which is expressed in an increasingly greater recruitment from year to year. As this expansion continues, the conditions of admission into the profession become more flexible (by cancellation of the competitive examinations, for example), and the age classes of 30–34 and 25–29 years of age will, in the future, be able to see their numbers considerably inflated, becoming the largest groups in the pyramid.

The total numbers of males and of females are almost equal; however, in the youngest groups (25–29 years and 30–34 years), the females are more

24. Cf. Répartition par âge des professeurs de l'enseignement du second degré d'après le tableau du 11 Mars, 1957. (Ministère de l'Éducation Nationale, Direction de l'Enseignement du Second Degré. 5ᵉ Bureau, Section des Études statistiques.)

25. To be exact, there was no teacher younger than 22 years of age (23 years in the physical sciences).

numerous than the males; this may result from the men's relative dissatisfaction with the teaching career, as compared with the women's continued
interest.[26]

Certain characteristics of the composition of the total population can be
found in human aggregates that are subcategories of it. For example, the
deficit of births due to World War I, which affects the generations of 1915–
1919, is reflected also in the deficit of teachers in the same generation; to
see this, it is necessary to go into the details of each generation; this is what
is done in Figure 9.6a for women only.[27]

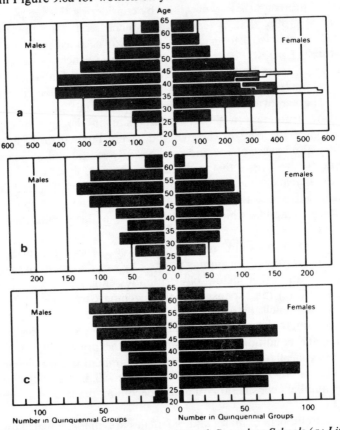

*Figure 9.6.   Pyramids of Teachers in French Secondary Schools (a: Literature;
b: Physics; c: Natural Sciences).*

26. And also to the influence of military service in the group 25 29 years.

27. To that for the horizontal scale relating to the totals of *quinquennial* groups, it was necessary
to multiply by 5 the totals for each year of age (the opposite of what is done when the scale is
annual and one wishes to represent a group of 5 years). This must be taken into account in reading
the pyramid.

The "physics pyramid" does not have the regularity and symmetry observed for the "literature pyramid." There is a great predominance of men beyond the age of 45 years and an equality of men and women (when there is not a slight predominance of females) before this age. There is also, as in the case of "literature," a tendency towards "feminization" of the group, for lack of male candidates. This tendency is even more remarkable because, formerly, there was a substantial majority of males.[28] Recognizing that the growth in the need for teachers is related to the growth in the number of pupils, it may be affirmed that this pyramid does not meet our needs, as the recruitment in the groups that must become the largest (from 35–45 years) has not been sufficient. Even if the relative number of women has increased in the younger generations, the recruitment cannot have been sufficiently large to meet the overall needs.

The "natural science pyramid" (Figure 9.6,c) confronts the same anomalies – but even more clearly – than the "physics pyramid" does. The dissatisfaction of young male generations is quite clear; the best-supplied age class is between 55 and 60 years! But this time the female candidacies are apparently sufficient to make up for the male deficit; from this it follows that the total number of females is 44 percent larger than the total number of males (466 as compared with 323).

Other Types of Composition

The study of age composition is often completed by studying each age or age group in the classification of the population by certain criteria. Thus, (1) by marital status: single, married, widowed, divorced; (2) by occupational activity and its categories; and (3) by school attendance and its categories.

Age Composition and Marital Status

The very high nuptiality at the beginning of adult ages operates to make the majority of each generation pass quickly from the single category into the married category. Then, with advancement in age, and, consequently, in duration of marriage, numerous marital unions are terminated either by widowhood or by divorce. In the general scheme, the differences are recorded according to sex and period:

1. Male mortality being higher than female mortality, and, in addition, the age of married men being on the average higher than that of their wives, we observe (among persons who have been married) a larger proportion of widows than of widowers at the same age.

28. This observation is justified only if there are no admissions at more advanced ages (say, beyond age 45) to the corps in question, for then more substantial numbers in the groups of elderly male generations derive from earlier recruitment. This is indeed the case here.

2. The decline of mortality has noticeably reduced, at each age, the proportion of widowed persons; the continuing increase in divorce has, in contrast, increased the proportion of divorced persons.

The figures in Table 9.7, as well as Figure 9.7, which illustrates them, take account of the volume of this phenomenon for France and its differential aspects according to sex and period. Table 9.7b provides an illustration for the United States.

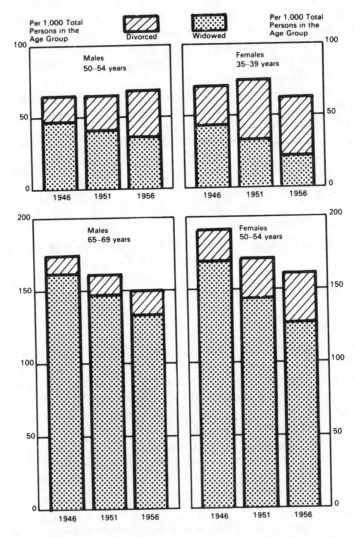

Figure 9.7

TABLE 9.7a. *France, Selected Age Groups by Sex: Percentage Distribution by Marital Status (Single [S], Married [M], Widowed [W], Divorced [D]) for Selected Dates*

	Jan. 1, 1946					Jan. 1, 1951					Jan. 1, 1956				
	Total	S	M	W	D	Total	S	M	W	D	Total	S	M	W	D
Males															
20–24	100.0	77.2	22.6	0.1	0.1	100.0	77.3	22.6	—	0.1	100.0	78.7	21.2	—	0.1
35–39	100.0	16.1	80.2	1.4	2.3	100.0	15.5	80.7	0.8	3.0	100.0	12.7	84.2	0.6	2.5
50–54	100.0	8.1	85.4	4.7	1.8	100.0	8.9	84.6	4.1	2.4	100.0	9.4	83.8	3.6	3.2
65–69	100.0	7.1	75.5	16.2	1.2	100.0	6.7	77.2	14.7	1.4	100.0	6.3	78.7	13.3	1.7
Females															
20–24	100.0	53.3	45.8	0.4	0.5	100.0	49.8	49.7	0.2	0.3	100.0	51.1	48.5	0.1	0.3
35–39	100.0	12.3	80.7	4.4	2.6	100.0	10.5	82.1	3.3	4.1	100.0	10.2	83.6	2.2	4.0
50–54	100.0	12.2	68.7	17.0	2.1	100.0	11.2	71.7	14.4	2.7	100.0	10.2	73.7	12.7	3.4
65–69	100.0	10.3	41.5	46.7	1.5	100.0	10.2	41.9	46.1	1.8	100.0	11.1	43.0	43.9	2.0

TABLE 9.7b. United States: Percent Distribution by Marital Status, Males and Females, Selected Age Groups and Selected Dates

Sex and Age Group	1930				1940				1950				1965			
	S	M	W	D	S	M	W	D	S	M	W	D	S	M	W	D
Males																
20–24	70.8	28.1	0.3	0.4	72.2	27.4	0.1	0.3	59.1	39.9	0.2	0.9	52.9	46.3	0.1	0.7
35–39	15.4	81.0	2.0	1.5	15.3	81.6	1.3	1.8	10.1	86.8	0.7	2.4				
50–54	10.9	81.0	6.3	1.6	11.0	81.9	5.1	2.0	8.3	85.0	3.7	3.0				
65–69	9.3	71.5	17.8	1.3	10.3	71.9	16.2	1.6	8.7	74.0	15.0	2.3				
Females																
20–24	46.0	51.6	1.0	1.1	47.2	51.3	0.6	0.9	32.3	65.6	0.4	1.7	32.5	65.6	0.3	1.6
35–39	10.4	82.3	5.3	1.9	11.2	81.5	4.6	2.8	8.4	85.5	2.7	3.5				
50–54	9.2	72.3	16.9	1.5	8.7	73.3	15.9	2.0	7.7	75.0	13.9	3.3				
65–69	8.4	46.6	44.1	0.8	9.4	46.5	43.1	1.0	8.4	48.9	41.1	1.5				

At 50–54 years of age among men, and at 35–39 years among women, the effects of the decline in widowhood and those of the increase in divorce almost compensate for one another. Beyond that, the gain in continued unions is quite clear.

At 65–69 years of age, three-quarters of the men are still married (to be exact, between 75.5 percent and 78.7 percent, according to the date) as compared with about 40 percent of the women at the same age (to be exact, between 41.5 percent and 43.9 percent).

Economic Activity and School Attendance

The divisions at each age between economically active and economically inactive, or the number in the labor force and the number not in the labor force, and between persons attending school and those not attending school, are made explicit by means of rates:

1. The *labor force participation rate* at a given age (or age group) is the ratio between the number of persons economically active or in the labor force and the number of the total population of the same age. The classification into economically active and economically inactive is made according to rules that are to a certain extent arbitrary. Certain economic activities are not recognized as such (for example, the mother in a household); conversely, a person who, in a census or survey, declares himself to be carrying out some economic activity is classified as economically active even if he is engaged in quite restricted activity (this is the case of elderly farmers).[29] Finally, certain activities that should be declared are concealed (activities of certain retired persons, for example) in order to avoid any tax deductions from remuneration, and the person in question is not recorded as being "active" or in the labor force during censuses or surveys.[30]

2. The *school attendance rate* for a given age (less frequently for an age group) is the ratio between the number of children in instruction or attending school and the total number of the population of the same age.

Some examples of the computations are shown in Tables 9.8a, 9.8b, and 9.8c.

While the statistics of the economically active population derive generally from the census or survey, statistics of the school population, while they can also be obtained from censuses, are often given by the administrations that

29. Let us specify again that the conventions concerning soldiers in national service can vary according to the country. In France these soldiers are generally not classified as economically active. However, professional soldiers are considered in the labor force. Finally, persons usually in the labor force, but seeking employment at the time of the census or survey, are included among the economically active population.

30. An unnecessary sham, since the information given in censuses and surveys is kept secret by law.

TABLE 9.8a.   _France, May 10, 1954 Census_

Age and Sex on Jan. 1, 1955	Economically Active Population (in thousands)	Total Population (in thousands)	Labor Force Participation Rate (per 1,000)
Males:			
35–39 years	866.6	886.9	977
Females:			
35–39 years	354.8	904.5	392

Source: _Études et conjuncture_, No. 1–2, Jan.–Feb., 1956, and _Recensement général la population de Mai 1954_. Resultats du sondage an 1/20 e. Menages, Logements, France entiére.

organize and control all or part of the educational system (in France, the Ministry of National Education). This is the case in France, where for several years statistics of pupils by age and by type of instruction have been given at each reopening of the schools. It is possible, then, to compute – along with the rates by age for the total – the school attendance rates by type of school; thus, the 64,800 boys of 17 years of age who were in school during the school year 1957–1958 (see Table 9.6b) can be classified (Table 9.9) as to whether they are in primary instruction, in secondary instruction, in technical instruction, or in post-secondary instruction.

Such a division is equally possible for the economically active population (for example, in making the distinction of the active population according

TABLE 9.8b.   _France, School Attendance in 1957–1958_

Sex and Age on Jan. 1, 1958	Population Attending an Educational Institution (in thousands)	Total Population (in thousands)	School Attendance Rate (per 1,000)
Males			
3–5 years	1,189	740.6	623
...	...	...	...
17 years	263	64.8	246
Females			
3–5 years	1,142	737.9	646
...	...	...	...
17 years	254	66.8	263

Bureau Universitaire de Statistique. Feuille documentaire No. 817. Nov.–Dec., 1958.

to sector, in the sense of C. Clark), but it is not generally practiced. Participation rates for the labor force are calculated in appropriately defined subpopulations, such as the agricultural population[31] and the nonagricultural population. Finally, whether the question is of economic activity or of school attendance, there may be interest in making computations by age for administrative or geographic subdivisions.

The conditions under which economic activity or school attendance is

TABLE 9.8c. *United States: School Enrollment by Age and Sex, 1950 and 1965*

Sex, Age and Year	Total Population	Number Enrolled in School	Percent Enrolled in School
1950			
Males			
5 years	1,390,000	717,000	51.6
6 years	1,390,000	1,336,000	96.1
7– 9 years	4,012,000	3,963,000	98.8
10–13 years	4,565,000	4,506,000	98.7
14–17 years	4,200,000	3,54Γ,000	84.3
Females			
5 years	1,336,000	693,000	51.9
6 years	1,341,000	1,313,000	97.9
7– 9 years	3,879,000	3,840,000	99.0
10–13 years	4,417,000	4,346,000	98.4
14–17 years	4,151,000	3,412,000	82.2
1965			
Males			
5 years	2,118,000	1,488,000	70.3
6 years	2,096,000	2,067,000	98.6
7– 9 years	6,221,000	6,180,000	99.3
10–13 years	7,808,000	7,752,000	99.3
14–17 years	7,068,000	6,613,000	93.6
Females			
5 years	2,044,000	1,430,000	70.0
6 years	2,033,000	2,010,000	98.9
7– 9 years	6,027,000	5,984,000	99.3
10–13 years	7,573,000	7,534,000	99.5
14–17 years	6,916,000	6,420,000	92.8

31. Population of households whose head is a farmer or a person employed in agriculture. Although there are some mixed households (in which the head is engaged in farming but some members do not work in agriculture, or in which the head is not engaged in agriculture but other members are), the main part of activity in the agricultural sector is carried out by members of the agricultural population so defined.

measured usually are such that the rates that can be calculated cannot be related to precise ages or age groups. For instance, the rates of economic activity shown in Table 9.8 concern groups somewhat younger than those indicated in the first column, where the age given is that of the January 1st following the census. This holds as long as a classification is made in the census by cohort or by groups of cohorts, and this classification coincides only with that by age or age groups as of January 1st (which is practically never the date of the census). The deviations are unimportant for the age periods at which economic activity varies but little with age; this is not true for quite young ages or advanced ages, at which the variations are fairly considerable: we are, therefore, led to making graphic interpolations in order to estimate the rates of labor force participation at exact ages or age groups.[32]

TABLE 9.9. *France, School Attendance, by Type of School, 1957–1958 (Boys) (Numbers of Population and Pupils in Thousands; School Attendance Rate per 1,000)*

| | Age on Jan. 1, 1958: 17 years Total Population: 263 | |
	No. of Pupils	Rate of Attendance
First Level	0.1	1
Second Level	30.1	114
Technical	32.0	112
Higher Education	2.3	9
Total	64.8	246

Source: Cf. Table 9.8b

The preceding observation holds for the school attendance rates with the specification that, since the rates are computed on the basis of administrative information (furnished in France by the Ministry of National Education), the situation they describe is usually a little later than the reopening of the schools, which takes place about the 1st of October—for example, the situation at the beginning of November, which results from administrative arrangements set up once the reopening is completely effected. Provided

32. By exact age we mean here the age (or class of ages) in completed years common to all the persons in the group in question. For example, when we say, further on, that the labor force participation rate of boys at 14 years is 250 per 1,000, it means that of a total of *all* the boys aged 14 complete years at a given date (who are between 14 and 15 years old at that date), a quarter are in the labor force.

that the variations in the total numbers in the course of the school year are fairly small,[33] there is no inconvenience in constructing the groups according to age or age groups of the pupils in complete years of age as of the January 1st (sometimes the December 31st, which is equivalent) following the re-opening of the school year.

Figure 9.8 shows the orders of magnitude and the variation by sex and age of the labor force participation rates in a developed country, as they occurred in France in 1954 (census of May 10).

The rates correspond to the ages or age groups at the date of the census; as indicated, they result from interpolation on the curve of the rates relative to ages or age groups as of January 1, 1955.

Economic activity begins at 14 years of age (before that age, school attendance is compulsory in France). The rates rise very rapidly with age, reaching a steady maximum between 25 and 45 years of age among men (about 97 percent in the labor force), and a maximum at 19 years among women (about 64 percent in the labor force), followed by a sharp decline and then by another rise, which reaches a second maximum (relative) between 45 and 50 years of age that is considerably lower than the first (about 47 percent in the labor force).

Beyond 75 years of age, economic activity is very much reduced, and usually the statistical measurement exaggerates the real extent of this phenomenon (by the classification among the economically active population — according to their declarations — of persons having only very reduced activity, notably in agriculture).

At all ages, the male labor force participation rates exceed those of the females. The sharp decline of the female rate after 19 years of age corresponds to marriage and the coming of children, which keep an appreciable fraction of women tied to their households. There is a recovery after 35 years of age, when the presence of women in the home is less indispensable (with children partially grown).

The phenomenon of school attendance is dominated by the existence of a period of obligatory school attendance, which varies according to the country. In France, school attendance is obligatory between the 6th and the 14th birthdays; before 6 years of age and after 14 years of age, only a fraction of the cohorts are in school voluntarily.

At the reopening of the school year in 1957, the situation for the total of both sexes was that shown in Table 9.10a; school attendance has been studied only until 18 years of age.

From the ages of 6–13 complete years, the rates of school attendance are

---

33. And it may be presumed that this is generally the case, except at ages marking the beginning (6 years, in France) and the end (14 years) of compulsory school attendance, where fairly large-scale entries and exits can take place.

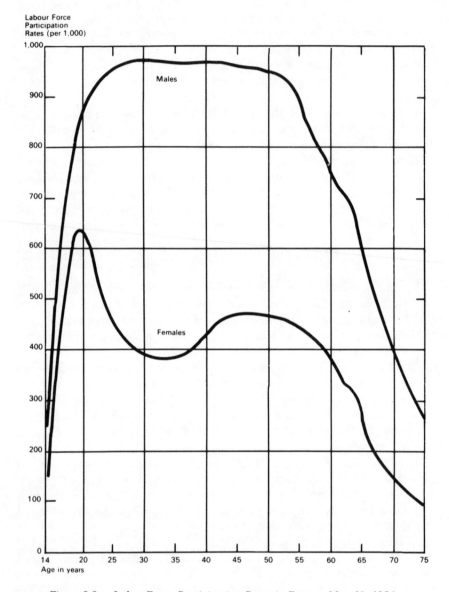

Labour Force
Participation
Rates (per 1,000)

Males

Females

Age in years

Figure 9.8. Labor Force Participation Rates in France, May 10, 1954.

TABLE 9.10a. *School Attendance in France (Both Sexes) During the School Year 1957–1958*

Age on Dec. 31, 1957 (years)	School Attendance Rate (per 1,000)	Age on Dec. 31, 1957 (years)	School Attendance Rate (per 1,000)
3–5	634	12	984
6	993	13	981
7	994	14	660
8	992	15	496
9	992	16	414
10	991	17	255
11	987	18	148

Cf. Table 9.8b

quite close to 1,000.[34] Beginning at the age of 14 complete years,[35] the rates measure the numbers in voluntary school attendance. The accelerated progress of such school attendance is one of the notable social factors of the present period in developed countries. Table 9.10b permits us to realize the importance of this development in France from the reopening of school in 1953 until school opened in 1957.

TABLE 9.10b. *France, School Attendance Rate (per 100)*

Age in Completed years on Dec. 31 Following School Reopening	School Reopening	
	1953	1957
14 years	56	66
15 years	39	49.5
16 years	30	41.5
17 years	19	25.5

34. The rest comprise essentially children who are prevented from attending school by illness or infirmity.

35. Let us observe that the group that is 14 complete years of age on December 31, 1957, as it is formed in Table 9.10a, includes children still under compulsory school attendance: those not reaching their 14th birthday until October, November, and December. More exactly, if the situation described in Table 9.10a corresponds to an inquiry carried out around the 1st of November, only children whose birthdays occur in November and December are included as a whole in the statistics of pupils in school at 14 complete years; the corresponding rates do not, in including them, measure voluntary school attendance exactly. We could make corresponding observations for the group of 6-year-olds. But it will be agreed that the inaccuracy thus introduced is truly minimal and ought to be left the same order as the imprecision of the data, in particular, the inaccuracy resulting from the vagueness that accompanies the enforcement of a law that is never strictly obeyed.

But these national means obscure considerable regional differences; here, for the beginning of the school year in 1955, the situations in two extreme *départements* are shown (rates per 1,000).[36]

Age	Seine	Loir-et-Cher
14 years	962	333
15 years	751	171
16 years	569	124
17 years	344	71

A final remark: it may be tempting to relate the labor force participation rate and the school attendance rate at a given age by assuming that economic activity and school attendance are mutually exclusive. It may seem that if there were no unemployed the labor force participation rate and the school attendance rate at the same age should be complementary, and the knowledge of one ought to permit determination of the other.

In fact, the connection is quite loose. Other than the fact that certain partial economic activities are accompanied by a certain amount of school attendance (most often of a technical nature), very often between the end of school attendance and the beginning of economically active life, there is an intervening period of inactivity of greater or lesser length. This is especially notable among the girls, of whom an appreciable fraction remain at home, for varying amounts of time, at the end of school attendance. So, at a given age, the sum of the labor force participation rate and of the school attendance rate is smaller than unity; and a knowledge of the variations in time of one of the rates—for example, the school attendance rate—does not permit deduction of the corresponding variations in the other rate (here, the labor force participation rate).[37]

Other Compositional Characteristics

The types of composition we have studied result from the examination of individual characteristics and of the formation of subpopulations in which all individuals possess the same characteristics or the same set of associated characteristics; for example, the composition according to membership in different age groups; the composition by triple membership in one of the

36. INSEE, *Coût et développement de l'enseignement en France* (Paris, 1958).

37. This observation is valid because it is generally possible to follow the school attendance rate from year to year; the labor force participation rate is known only at the time of censuses or surveys. It is thus tempting to deduce the latter rate from the former; in fact, this method is almost never practicable.

two sexes, in one of the various age groups, and in one of the various marital statuses; etc.

The characteristics discussed are not exclusively demographic; certain concern the economic sphere (labor force participation or nonparticipation) or the social sphere (school attendance); one could consider, similarly, geographic characteristics in relation, for example, to certain types of habitation (urban, rural), etc. In other types of population description, the individual no longer plays an essential role; he does not appear except as a member of certain groupings—*families* and *households*—which receive special attention.

By *family* is usually understood the restricted nucleus comprising the father, the mother, and the children. But many difficulties arise with this definition.

It may be appropriate to consider as a *family* a couple without children (who either never had any children or who have none because the children have died), such a family being terminated by the death of one of the two spouses. Conversely, the nuclear family with children continues to be a family if deprived of either the father or the mother by virtue of death or divorce; in the latter case, it is necessary to agree that the family is formed around the spouse who has, or has had (if the children are grown), the care of the children.

But how should unmarried mothers be considered? It may seem natural to admit that they form a family with their children, even aside from a possible future spouse. Here it can be seen how juridicial questions are mixed with factual situations, since at one time we reject what is not consecrated by an official union (the concubine), while considering that a certain nuclear family results from one or many illegitimate births.

But, principally, the notion of family thus adopted does not lend itself to a precise coverage of the entire population. On one hand, it neglects the unattached individuals, that is, those without immediate ancestors or immediate descendants still living, or without a spouse. On the other hand, in the statistics of families as defined, an individual can be included at the same time in a familial nucleus in which he is considered as a child (because of the survival of at least one of his parents) and in the familial nucleus in which he is the father or the mother. One can question the interest there is in considering as a family unit those parent-child associations that are not concretized by a mode of life in common.

In fact, the data concerning families that are obtained in censuses are of two sorts:

1. Family statistics, according to the number of *surviving* children. To indicate the interest in such statistics, it is necessary to relate them to other characteristics: marital status, age and social-occupational group of the

family head, age of children. The statistics so assembled are of economic and social significance; they allow the measurement of family dependence in the different categories of population. Again, it is appropriate for this purpose to arrange statistics according to the number of children under some given age as of the date of the census (for example, 14 years of age, then 16 years, 18 years, and 21 years, as was done in the French census of 1946).[38]

2. Statistics of families according to number of *live-born children*. These are no longer clearly statistics of population structure. We reconstruct, in a fashion, the past history of families with the essential purpose of studying fertility; this point has been explored in the chapter on natality. In accord with the purpose of these statistics, the age of the head of the family is not taken, but rather that of the wife, who is the much more decisive factor in the fertility of couples; special interest is attached to statistics of live-born children in completed families, that is, in those in which the wife has already passed the age limit of fecundity (practically, about 45–50 years).

By *household* we understand the aggregate of persons living in the same dwelling whether or not they belong to the same family (in the narrow sense of the preceding section or in a broader sense). Some among them can be boarders, tenants, live-in servants, etc. These dwelling places can be furnished rooms in hotels or furnished houses, for persons who have no place of residence other than a hotel.[39]

Thus defined, the number of households is identified with the number of individual dwelling places,[40] so that the composition of households results not only from the operation of sociological or demographic factors, but depends also on the relative size of the land inheritance and of the manner in which it is placed at the disposition of the population. It may even be tempting to consider this latter factor as playing a preponderant, indeed exclusive, role especially when living in a period of housing shortages. But it is necessary to have simultaneously a serious housing shortage, the absence of any new construction, and some growth in the population for the desire of any group of persons to set up a household to be entirely frustrated because of the unavailability of a dwelling. In fact, demographic trends, like behavior, have always had an influence on the number of households, with

38. Let us specify that, at this census, the statistics of families according to number of surviving children is limited to legitimate couples, including couples dissolved by the death of one spouse or by divorce. In addition, to avoid double counting, we have kept out the declarations (about number of children) of divorced men (these children are recovered, in effect, in the declarations of divorced woman); however, in doing so we neglect the families in which the woman is divorced and the husband dead or remarried.

39. Persons living more or less in institutions (members of religious communities, elderly in homes for the aged, personnel of hospitals, educational institutions, etc.) all belong to the category of *collective* or *institutional households*.

40. The number of vacant dwelling units generally being negligible.

TABLE 9.11. *France, Census of March 10, 1946. Distribution of Families* by Number of Surviving Children Under 21 Years of Age*

Age of Head of Family (years)	Total	Number of Families with Indicated Number of Surviving Children under 21 Years of Age							
		0	*1*	*2*	*3*	*4*	*5*	*6+*	*Unknown*
Under 25	1,235	444	456	84	16	3	—	1	231
25-34	10,881	2,733	3,912	1,828	689	227	91	57	1,344
35-44	33,678	6,506	10,517	6,700	3,359	1,730	830	866	3,170
45-54	46,328	19,014	11,669	5,859	2,736	1,313	669	647	4,421
55-64	51,392	37,112	6,078	1,968	708	296	130	100	5,000
65 plus	44,013	38,661	969	188	65	22	10	14	4,084
Unknown	53	26	5	7	1	—	1	—	13
Total	187,580	104,496	33,606	16,634	7,574	3,591	1,731	1,685	18,263

*Families with head a widower belonging to the "Employees, Workers, and Laborers Category."

the real-estate situations always adjusting somewhat — in a manner more or less satisfactory — to the expressed needs.

Statistics for households constitute the true statistics of the structure of the population, which include the total number of inhabitants of a territory (with the extension that includes institutional households). They are often organized around the head of the household, who is the person declared as such in the census. In practice, we do not encounter heads of households among married women; however, all other categories may yield heads of households (with variable frequencies, according to sex, age, and marital status).

The tables that can be set up usually combine the size of the household, the age, the marital status, and the social-occupational category of the head of the household, and the number of children in the household not yet having attained some given age (16 years, for example).

The household is a sociological and economic unit. In particular, there are scarcely any types of consumption that are not affected by the grouping of individuals in households: in the first place, the dwelling and all that goes into its equipment, but also numerous types of consumption that are individual in nature (food consumption, for example).

CHAPTER TEN

Population Models

AT THIS point in the work, the exact effects of patterns of fertility and mortality on development of the size and composition of the population cannot easily be analysed. The difficulty we experience in grasping the connection between these two orders of phenomena is obvious enough in the preceding chapter, where we tried to show by what mechanism the ageing of populations takes place.

In this chapter, we shall study two theoretical models of population in which the link between the patterns of fertility and mortality, on the one hand, and the structure of the population, on the other, is made completely explicit. Obviously, this involves these quite simple models, far-removed from real populations that react to changing demographic patterns and whose compositions are generally very complex; however, these models are useful to the demographer in that they often support demographic thought.

Age Pyramid Associated with a Survival Curve

The manner in which birth cohorts progressively disappear under the impact of mortality leads us to a first theoretical population model. Let us specify how this extention of cohorts we are to consider takes place; for this, let us choose a life table, that of Duvillard, which is considered to be representative of average French mortality in the eighteenth century ($e_0 = 28.8$ years).

The figures in Table 10.1 are illustrated by the survival curve in Figure 10.1. By inverting the coordinates (this time locating the total sizes on the horizontal axis and the ages on the vertical axis), we obtain Figure 10.2a, the form of which recalls the age pyramid (more precisely, a "demi"-pyramid). We shall show how one can produce a population whose pyramid is precisely that given by Figure 10.2a.

For this, let us see the details and direct our attention to the first 5 years of age (Figure 10.2b).

TABLE 10.1. *Duvillard's Survival Table*

Age	Survivors	Age	Survivors
x	l_x	x	l_x
0	10,000	40	3,694
1	7,675	45	3,341
2	6,718	50	2,297
3	6,246	55	2,572
4	5,987	60	2,136
5	5,831	65	1,664
		70	1,177
10	5,510	75	717
15	5,290	80	347
20	5,022	85	119
25	4,714	90	38
30	4,382	95	11
35	4,040	100	2

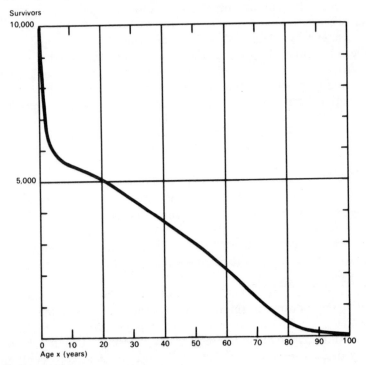

Figure 10.1

Whatever the manner in which the axes of ages and of numbers are arranged, the survival curve represents the number of survivors of a given number of newborn children (here 10,000) at different *exact* ages: 1 year, 2 years, 3 years, 4 years, 5 years, 10 years, 15 years, ⋯, 100 years. Graphic interpolation, such as that carried out in Figure 10.2b, can give an estimate of the survivors at exact ages that are not expressed in a whole number of years.

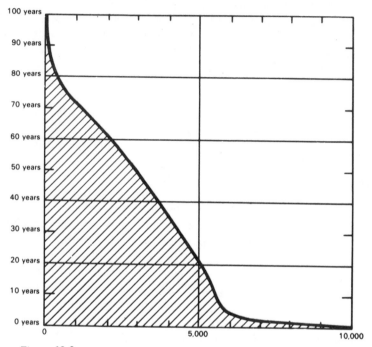

Figure 10.2a

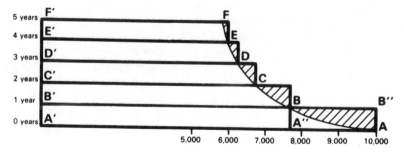

Figure 10.2b

Let us consider the 10,000 newborn in the Duvillard table as being new-born of a certain year A. Let us begin at January 1st $(A+1)$:

If all the newborn of the year A were born on the 31st December, their survival rate (per 10,000) would, in practice, be read at A.

If all the newborn of the year A were born on the 1st of January, their survival rate (per 10,000) would be read at B.

If the births are equally distributed throughout the year, then the survival rate of the different newborn is read along the line AB.

Let us now agree to establish an equivalence between the total of 10,000 persons surviving at a given moment and the surface of a rectangle having, in the same system of axes as in Figure 10.2b, a length of 10,000 on the horizontal axis and a width of 1 year along the vertical axis.

Let us consider again the 10,000 newborn of the year A and place ourselves at January 1st $(A+1)$.

If all the newborn of the year A were born on December 31st, the surface representing them would be the rectangle $AA'B''B'$.

If all the newborn of the year A were born on January 1st, the surface representing them would be the rectangle $A''A'B B'$.

When the births are equally distributed throughout year A, it can be easily assumed that the surface representing them is the trapezoid $AA'BB'$.[1]

Retaining the assumption of 10,000 births linearly distributed in the course of the year A, it is easily seen as well that the number of survivors on January 1st $(A+2)$, is represented by the trapezoid $BB'CC'$, the number of survivors as of January 1st $(A+3)$ by the area $CC'DD'$, etc.

Thus, the area of Figure 10.2a can be considered as a sum of "stacked-up" areas, as the decomposition in Figure 10.2b suggests, these areas representing the number of survivors of the 10,000 newborn of a year, respectively, as of January 1st $(A+1)$, $(A+2)$, $\cdots$, $(A+100)$, that is, the number of survivors of these 10,000 newborn at ages (in completed years) 0 years, 1 year, $\cdots$, 99 years.

This succession of areas gives an account of the passage of 10,000 new-born of a given year to being survivors on successive January 1sts; referring again to the *Lexis* diagram (Figure 10.3), to the left and using the letters on that diagram, it involves passages $A \to (A+1)$, $A \to (A+2)$, $A \to (A+3)$, etc.

Now, if we consider a population in which *mortality does not vary and there are consequently 10,000 births each year*, these passages are equivalent, respectively, to those noted in Figure 10.3 (to the right) with the letters: $(A-1) \to A$, $(A-2) \to A$, $(A-3) \to A$, etc., which occur in this population.

Consequently, the pyramid in Figure 10.2a (which is read with the convention adopted for Figure 10.2b) represents the structure of a population

---

1. The rigorous proof of this involves the use of integral calculus.

on January 1st (of, say, the year A), in which there occur each year 10,000 births and in which mortality is constant over time and is defined by the Duvillard life table (the survival table shown in Table 10.1).

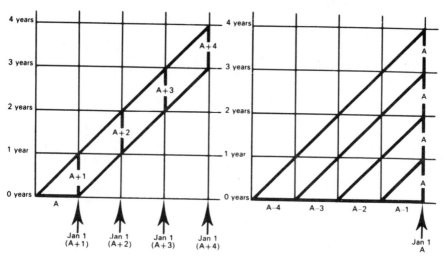

Figure 10.3

Construction of a Stationary Population

From now on, we shall use the term *stationary population* for the theoretical population that is deduced from a life table according to the procedure just described. We shall later justify the reason for this name.

As a preliminary, we shall learn to construct such a population on the basis of a given life table, for example, the Duvillard life table. The procedure employed rests on the determination of passages $(A-1) \rightarrow A$, $(A-2) \rightarrow A$, etc., according to the notation of the right section of Figure 10.3. It involves the determination of how one moves from the groups of newborn in the years $(A-1)$, $(A-2)$, $(A-3)$, etc., into the groups of survivors at age 0 years, 1 year, 2 years, etc., as of January 1st of the year A.

The life table (here, that of Duvillard) gives the numbers reaching *exactly* 0 years, 1 year, 2 years *in the course* of the year $(A-1)$ and *in the course* of the year A (see Figure 10.4). It is clear that on January 1st, A, the number of persons aged 0 complete years of age, 1 complete year, 2 complete years, etc., is intermediate between those whose birthdays are circumscribed by the same generations. For instance, the total group with 2 complete years on January 1st, A, numbers between 6,718 and 6,246.

For determining the population as of January 1st, A, we assume that the deaths in the whole birth cohort are equally distributed in time between the two successive birthdays; in other words, we shall assume that there is an equal number of deaths in the two triangles of a *Lexis* parallelogram. This hypothesis leads us to adopt as the population, L_2 at the age of 2 complete years as of January 1st, A:

$$L_2 = \frac{l_2 + l_3}{2}$$

which is

$$L_2 = \frac{6,718 + 6,246}{2} = 6,482.$$

The question is one of a generally acceptable approximation;[2] it is for determining the population L_0 that it is most open to criticism, the deaths in the first *Lexis* triangle being, on the average, twice as numerous as in the second.[3]

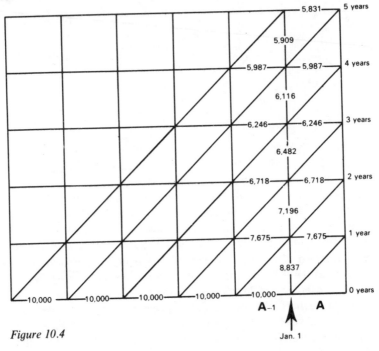

Figure 10.4

2. It traces the pyramid of Figure 10.2a by joining A and B with a straight line, then B and C, etc.

3. This suggests a refinement in the computation. Thus, there are $10,000 - 7675 = 2,325$ deaths between 0 and 1 years of age, of which we assume that 2/3 or $(2,323 \times 2)/3 = 1,550$ occur in the first triangle of the *Lexis* diagram, under this hypothesis, L_0 is equal to $10,000 - 1,550 = 8,450$, instead of 8,837 obtained under the hypothesis of equal or linear distribution of the deaths.

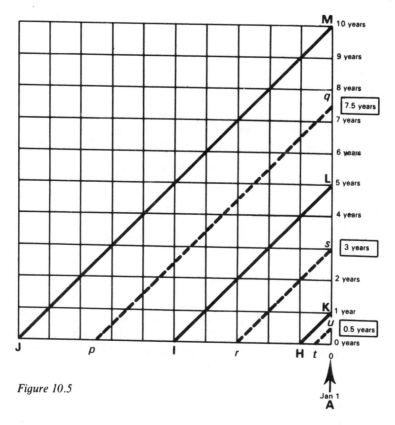

Figure 10.5

To compute a stationary population according to the principles just presented assumes a computation of about 100 arithmetic means of survivors. This computation can be unduly long for the degree of accuracy that we need to obtain. Moreover, we might have access only to an abridged life table giving survivors over 5-year periods only, on the basis of which, nevertheless, we expect to deduce the associated stationary population. It is then appropriate to set up the problem slightly differently; we shall explain what makes up the new treatment of the series of $[l_x]$, reduced to values of x multiples of 5 by taking the example of the determination of L_5 the stationary population aged 5–9 complete years, (denoted $_5L_5$), on the basis of l_5 and l_{10}.

Let us consider Figure 10.5. Those who are 5–9 years of age on January 1st, A, were born in JI, which represents an interval of 5 years and a total of $5 \times 10,000 = 50,000$ births. The approximation consists here in grouping the total of the life lines of the 50,000 newborn to 50,000 life lines centered at pq, which constitute, in some fashion, the mean life line for all the cohorts considered. With this approximation, the ageing from IJ (exact age 0 years) to LM (population in the group 5–9 years of age) is compared or associated with the movement from l_0 (point p) to $l_{7.5}$ (point q); as a supplementary approximation, we may assume that:

$$l_{7.5} = \frac{l_5 + l_{10}}{2} = \frac{5,831 + 5,510}{2} = 5,670^4.$$

Thus, we assume that, on the average, there remain alive in the group 5–9 years of age the 5,670/10,000 of the total newborn from IJ, whence

$$_5L_5 = \frac{50,000 \times 5,670}{10,000} = 28,350.$$

Treating similarly the aggregate of births at OI, we arrive at

$$l_{2.5} = \frac{l_0 + l_5}{2} = \frac{10,000 + 5,831}{2} = 7,915.$$

$$L_0 = 50,000 \times \frac{7,915}{10,000} = 39,575.$$

These last two approximations may be judged a little crude, infant mortality having had such a preponderantly great influence in the aggregate of mortality from 0–5 years of age. It may then be preferable to compute the groups L_0 and $_4L_1$ separately as of January 1st, A.

$$l_{0.5} = \frac{l_0 + l_1}{2} = \frac{10,000 + 7,675}{2} = 8,837.$$

$$L_0 = 10,000 \times \frac{8,837}{10,000} = 8,837.$$

$$l_3 = \frac{l_1 + l_5}{2} = \frac{7,675 + 5,831}{2} = 6,753.$$

$$_4L_1 = 40,000 \times \frac{6,753}{10,000} = 27,012.$$

Thus, we find for the total $_5L_0 = L_0 + {_4L_1}$

$$8,837 + 27,012 = 35,849$$

instead of 39,575.

4. If we possess a complete life table giving survivors at each year of age, we can then take the mean $(l_7 + l_8)/2$ as an approximation for $l_{7.5}$, obtaining here:

$$l_{7.5} = \frac{5,658 + 5,602}{2} = 5,630.$$

Table 10.2 shows the computation of the aggregate of the stationary population which is associated with a given life table and in which 10,000 births occur annually. Two examples are treated in this table, one example taken from the Duvillard life table ($e_0 = 28.8$ years) and one example taken from the Norwegian (1951–1955) female life table ($e_0 = 74.7$ years), which corresponds to the lowest mortality currently observed within a national population.

The total populations $\sum_{l=1}^{\omega} L_i$ (289,139 and 746,698) differ considerably,[5] which is easily explained by differences in mortality: with the Norwegian mortality rate, the same annual total of 10,000 newborn is reduced from year to year in much lower proportions than with those of the Duvillard table, and so at all ages there remain more survivors in the first case than in the second. We may note, in addition, that the totals are clearly identified with the expectations of life at birth, when the decimal point is moved (289,139 and 28.9 years on one hand, and 746,698 and 74.7 years on the other); this indicates a strict property of stationary populations to which we will return.

Let us shift our attention now to the age structures, and let us bring the two populations to the same total (100,000, for example). This permits drawing the two pyramids of Figure 10.6. We can summarize the characteristics of age composition, considering only the three large age groups (Table 10.3).

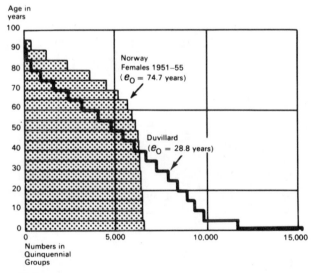

Figure 10.6

5. We equate ω with 100 years, the number of persons living beyond that age being absolutely negligible.

TABLE 10.2. Computation of Stationary Populations[a] (to a Base of 10,000 Births Annually)

	Duvillard Life Table (e_0 = 28.8 years)				Age Groups (in completed years)	Norwegian Female Life Table (1951–1955) (e_0 = 74.7 years)				
	l_x	l_x+l_{x+k}	$\frac{l_x+l_{x+k}}{2}$	$k \times \frac{l_x+l_{x+k}}{2}$		$k \times \frac{l_x+l_{x+k}}{2}$	$\frac{l_x+l_{x+k}}{2}$	l_x+l_{x+k}	l_x	
l_0	10,000	17,675	8,837	8,837	L_0	9,900	9,900	19,801	10,000	l_0
l_1	7,675	13,506	6,753	27,012	$_4L_1$	39,108	9,777	19,555	9,801	l_1
l_5	5,831	11,341	5,670	28,350	$_5L_5$	48,715	9,743	19,486	9,754	l_5
l_{10}	5,510	10,800	5,400	27,000	$_5L_{10}$	48,724	9,724	19,448	9,732	l_{10}
l_{15}	5,290	10,312	5,156	25,780	$_5L_{15}$	48,525	9,705	19,410	9,716	l_{15}
l_{10}	5,022	9,736	4,868	24,340	$_5L_{20}$	48,405	9,681	19,362	9,694	l_{20}
l_{25}	4,714	9,096	4,548	22,740	$_5L_{25}$	48,245	9,649	19,298	9,668	l_{25}
l_{30}	4,382	8,422	4,211	21,055	$_5L_{30}$	48,035	9,607	19,214	9,630	l_{30}
l_{35}	4,040	7,734	3,867	19,335	$_5L_{35}$	47,760	9,552	19,104	9,584	l_{35}
l_{40}	3,694	7,035	3,517	17,585	$_5L_{40}$	47,375	9,475	18,951	9,520	l_4^0
l_{45}	3,341	6,312	3,156	15,780	$_5L_{45}$	46,815	9,363	18,726	9,431	l_{45}
l_{50}	2,971	5,543	2,771	13,855	$_5L_{50}$	45,960	9,192	18,384	9,295	l_{50}
l_{55}	2,572	4,708	2,354	11,770	$_5L_{55}$	44,645	8,929	17,859	9,089	l_{55}
l_{60}	2,136	3,800	1,900	9,500	$_5L_{60}$	42,635	8,527	17,054	8,770	l_{60}

l_x					$_5L_x$					l_x
l_{65}	1,664	2,841	1,420	7,100	$_5L_{65}$	39,505	7,901	15,802	8,284	l_{65}
l_{70}	1,177	1,894	947	4,735	$_5L_{70}$	34,540	6,908	13,816	7,518	l_{70}
l_{75}	717	1,064	532	2,660	$_5L_{75}$	27,230	5,446	10,892	6,298	l_{75}
l_{80}	347	466	233	1,165	$_5L_{80}$	18,075	3,615	7,230	4,594	l_{80}
l_{85}	119	157	78	390	$_5L_{85}$	9,195	1,839	3,678	2,636	l_{85}
l_{90}	38	49	24	120	$_5L_{90}$	2,995	599	1,198	1,042	l_{90}
l_{95}	11	13	6	30	$_5L_{95}$	415	83	166	156[a]	l_{95}
l_{100}	2								10[b]	l_{100}
				289,139	$\sum\limits_{i=0}^{\omega} L_i$	746,698				

[a] We explain the notation at the heads of the columns: l_x denotes the number of survivors attaining exact age x. K is generally equal to 5, so that $l_x + l_{x+k}$ represents, for example, $l_{50} + l_{55}$, or $l_{75} + l_{70}$; however in the first line $k = 1$ and in the second line $k = 4$. To obtain numbers of population (the L_0, $_4L_1$, $_4L_5$, etc.) it is necessary to take account of the number of generations included; this number is exactly k, which leads to the formula

$$k \times \frac{l_x + l_{x+k}}{2}.$$

[b] The numbers are not given in the Norwegian table. We have derived them from the life table for elderly persons of P. Vincent (Population, April–June, 1951) on the basis of the last known l_x, here $l_{90} = 1,042$. According to Vincent's table, for $l_{90} = 1,000$, $l_{95} = 150$, $l_{100} = 10$. We can take this information and use it "to close" theoretical populations including life tables ending somewhat early. This is, of course, only an approximation that concerns only quite small numbers for which it suffices to deal with an admissible order of magnitude.

TABLE 10.3.   *Age Composition of Stationary Populations*

Age Groups	$e_0 = 28.8$ years	$e_0 = 74.7$ years
0–19 years	40.5	26.1
20–59 years	50.6	50.5
60 plus	8.9	23.4
All ages	100.0	100.0

The population is very young in the first case; in the second case, the population is very old, older than all (national) populations observed thus far (in France, there is currently slightly less than 17 percent aged 60 years and over). We have seen in the preceding chapter that, in the presence of such population models, it is tempting to associate low mortality and quite pronounced ageing. We shall see, again, when we have established the characteristics and properties of the stationary population, why this association is misleading.

Some Properties of Stationary Populations

We have introduced the stationary populations as theoretical populations characterized by the invariance of the annual number of births and the invariance of mortality defined by a table. On the basis of this definition we shall establish various properties of stationary populations. We shall consider these populations as determined by the construction procedure in Figure 10.4 (and not by the abridged procedure of Figure 10.5).

In Figure 10.4, we see clearly that the *number L* of this population, as well as the annual number of deaths (*D*), is constant, since from one year to the next the same number of survivors are found at the same ages, and the same losses by deaths are found in the same *Lexis* triangles; thus, the *age composition* is therefore *invariable*. We know, however, that by definition the *annual number of births* (*B*) is similarly constant (equal here to $l_0 = 10,000$). The constancy of the total of this closed population implies that

$$B - D = 0, \text{ or, } B = D = 10,000.$$

And the crude rates are themselves constant, since

$$n = \frac{B}{L} = d = \frac{D}{L}. \quad \text{[6]}$$

---

6. Let us observe that here the constancy of the population size over time frees us from all the precautions concerning the choice of a base population for use in the denominator.

Here, for the Duvillard stationary population, $b = d = 10,000/289,139 = 34.6$ per 1,000, and for that associated with the Norwegian table, $b = d = 10,000/746,698 = 13.4$ per 1,000.

According to our procedure in construction of the population,

$$L = (l_0+l_1)/2+(l_1+l_2)/2+(l_2+l_3)/3+\cdots+(l_{99}+l_{100})/2+(l_{100}+l_{\omega+1})/2 \text{ }^7$$

which can be written:

$$L = l_0/2+l_1+l_2+l_3+\cdots+l_{100}.$$

We see again in this formula the expression of the sum of the years lived by the l_0 newborn in the life table defined by the sequence $[l_x]$.

It is by dividing this sum by the l_0 newborn that one finds e_0.

$$e_0 = \frac{(l_0/2)+l_1+l_2+\cdots l_{100}}{l_0} = \frac{L}{l_0}. \tag{I}$$

Here, by inverting the numerator and denominator, we find the rates of natality and mortality:

$$b = d = \frac{l_0}{(l_0/2)+l_1+l_2+\cdots+l_{100}} = \frac{l_0}{L}.$$

Thus, in a stationary population,

$$\frac{b}{A} = \frac{d}{A} = \frac{1}{e_0}. \text{ }^8$$

Let us remark that in equation (I), the numerator, that is, the total number of L of the stationary population associated with the sequence $[l_x]$ is divided by $l_0 = 10,000$; it is for this reason that we have observed previously that the numbers of the total populations in Table 10.2, with the decimal point moved (and taking account of the degree of approximation of computation), are associated with the expectations of life at birth. We may say, conversely, that a stationary population in which there are each year $l_0 = 10,000$ births and in which the expectation of life is $e_0 = 74.7$ years (for example) has a total of

$$L = l_0 \times e_0 = 10,000 \times 74.7 = 747,000,$$

a 3.5 year gain in the mean duration of life would bring e_0 to its maximum biological limit for the female (J. Bourgeois-Pichat; see p. 129). The associated stationary population (on a base of 10,000 annual births) would yield a number L' larger than L by

$$10,000 \times 3.5 = 35,000.$$

7. Let us recall that for convenience of presentation we adopt $\omega = 100$ years ($l_{\omega+1} = l'_{\omega+2} = \cdots = 0$).

8. Accordingly, in our two examples, $1/28.8 = 34.7$ per 1,000 (instead of 34.6 in the first computation) and $1/74.7 = 13.4$ per 1,000.

In conclusion, a stationary population is characterized by these properties:

1. The total number of the population is constant.
2. The annual number of births (and, consequently, the annual number of deaths) is constant.
3. The total number in each age group and, consequently, the age composition, is invariable.
4. The crude death rate, which is equal to the crude birth rate, is equal to the inverse of the expectation of life at birth.

Thus, in case of a stationary model, all the imaginable characteristics of the population are fixed in time, which justifies the name given.[9]

Theoretical Stationary Populations and Real Populations

The simplicity of the model we have just presented raises questions about its benefit when facing the always complex reality of human populations. It is certain that there is never a real population strictly conforming to the stationary model, but one can think that certain human aggregates have developed, at certain periods in their history, in an obviously stationary manner. For example:

1. Before the demographic revolution, when the total human population lived in a primitive demographic régime caused by high mortality and high natality, the natural growth was virtually null, as witnessed by the small total reached by world population at the beginning of the nineteenth century (considering the long period since the appearance of the first human being). A constant level of mortality and of natality, and the equilibrium between these two components of natural increase being nearly attained (at least on the average during a period of several decades), the various human populations must never have deviated very noticeably from the stationary state.[10]

2. At the present time in some highly developed countries, the natality rate has declined to the point of meeting the mortality rate, which is braked in its fall by the ageing of populations. We again find the establishment of conditions that must lead populations progressively to a stationary state (see note 10).

In fact, the hypothesis of a lasting stability of the fertility and mortality levels is virtually never fulfilled:

1. In the primitive demographic régime the very moderate mean rates of

9. This is the case because, in a stationary population, cohort and period analyses are equivalent.

10. Here we make use implicitly of the following result established by Lotka (of which we shall speak again): whatever the initial structure of a population, the continuous maintaining of fixed fertility and mortality régimes brings the population toward a stable structure. The stationary structure is a special case of the stable structure; it corresponds to the constant maintaining of fertility and mortality schedules *that balance exactly.*

population growth hide the quite violent sprints and starts in the development. In the absence of epidemics, famine, wars, the mortality rate barely exceeded 30 per 1,000, while the natality rate usually exceeded 40 per 1,000; the population thus grew quite distinctly until severe excess deaths made it regress, wiping out, at least partially, the growth of many years. In such a scheme, we are quite far-removed from conditions that ought to be fulfilled to obtain a strict stationary state. It is not certain, in particular, that the severe losses undergone by these populations could have avoided disturbing the composition rather near a stationary composition that might have resulted from natality moderately exceeding mortality;

2. In presently developed countries, characterized by only a slight natural increase of the population, the approximate equilibrium between births and deaths has been realized only in the past few decades and is accompanied by a simultaneous decrease in the two corresponding rates. Finally, almost all these countries have an age composition disturbed by accidental events (for instance, the deficits in births due to the wars). But while the correspondence of real populations to stationary populations is never entirely rigorous, in certain cases, when this correspondence is possible, it does give certain useful indications.

We have already indicated that the continuation of a mean duration of life lower than 20 years (computed for a period long enough to encompass the years of high excess mortality) in demographically primitive populations would have been unthinkable, since the crude death rate in a stationary population with an expectation of life of 20 years is fixed at

$$1/20 = 50 \text{ per } 1,000.$$

A population that had permanently (or on the average over a long period) a crude death rate higher than 50 per 1,000 would be destined for rapid disappearance, since natality cannot usually be established at so high a level.

In the present state of medicine and therapy, human populations can reach a mean length of life in the neighborhood of 80 years (77.2 years for the total of both sexes, according to the biological-bound life table of Bourgeois-Pichat). Moreover, demographic growth need not continue indefinitely. So the stationary state, defined by a mean duration of life in the neighborhood of 80 years, can well constitute a point of stabilization (at least provisionally) for populations—a state not so far distant from certain populations that are currently the most developed. In this state we would have, obviously:[11]

> 25 percent 0–19 years of age
> 50 percent 20–59 years of age
> 25 percent 60 or more years of age.

11. It suffices to round the numbers in the distribution of Table 10.3 ($e_0 = 74.7$ years) a little more in the direction of ageing.

Thus, populations seem bound to a considerable ageing, which will, more-over, be still more accentuated if future medical progress permits an effective battle against the diseases of ageing.

In the stationary state defined by $e_0 = 80$ years,

$$b = d = 1/80 = 12.5 \text{ per } 1,000.$$

In stationary populations, ageing is often the more marked the higher the expectation of life (compare, for example, the data of Table 10.3). It is this implicit correspondence of real populations with stationary populations that sometimes leads – incorrectly – to the association of the phenomenon of ageing with that of prolongation of human life.

It should not be forgotten that, in the stationary population of Duvillard, mortality is higher than in the Norwegian stationary population (see Table 10.3), and natality, which is equal to mortality, is also higher (34.7 per 1,000 instead of 13.4 per 1,000). It is this second factor that is the decisive one, as the reference to the stable population model will permit us to show.

The Stable Population

The model of the *stationary* population resulted from the action of a life table upon a fixed annual number of births. The *stable* population model results from the operation of a life table upon an annual number of births that varies from year to year at a constant rate.

While in the stationary model all the birth cohorts that made up the population at a given date derived from the same total at birth (10,000, for example), in the stable model the totals at birth of two consecutive genera-tions have a fixed relationship. We denote this relationship by $(1+r)$.[12] In this way, if the cohort aged 99 complete years as of a given January 1st (let us say, as previously, in the year A) comprises 10,000 newborn,

the cohort aged 98 years comprises $10,000\,(1+r)$ newborn
the cohort aged 97 years comprises $10,000\,(1+r)^2$ newborn
the cohort aged 96 years comprises $10,000\,(1+r)^3$ newborn
....
the cohort aged 2 years comprises $10,000\,(1+r)^{97}$ newborn
the cohort aged 1 year comprises $10,000\,(1+r)^{98}$ newborn
the cohort aged 0 years comprises $10,000\,(1+r)^{99}$ newborn.

12. It would be simpler to denote it k. Thus, 10,000 births in a year would be followed in the next year by $10,000\,k$ births, then by $10,000\,k^2$ births, etc. But, noting the relationship $1+r$, we produce the rate of increase r (at least if r is positive; if r is negative, we have a decrease). In effect (sup-posing r positive, for the sake of the argument), if the 10,000 births of one year are augmented at a rate of r the following year, this increase is written $10,000 \times r$, and the *total* number of births is $10,000 + 10,000 \times r = 10,000\,(1+r)$. We see, similarly, that these $10,000\,(1+r)$ annual births, which have increased by the following year to $10,000\,(1+r)r$, became *in all*, that year, $10,000\,(1+r) + 10,000\,(1+r)r$, or $10,000\,(1+r)\,(1+r) = 10,000\,(1+r)^2$, etc.

Taking account of the meaning of *r* (we shall later enlarge on the restricted sense that we have given it for the time being), this rate of annual variation in births is usually positive and in practice almost never surpasses 3 to 4 percent.

To follow this presentation of the stable population in a concrete manner, we fix this rate at 1 percent, for example, and place ourselves at January 1st of the year *A*. Let us again adopt 10,000 as the number at births of the oldest cohort,[13] the one aged 99 years on this date.

Under these conditions:

the cohort aged 98 years comprises $10{,}000\,(1.01)$ newborn
the cohort aged 97 years comprises $10{,}000\,(1.01)^2$ newborn
....
the cohort aged 2 years comprises $10{,}000\,(1.01)^{97}$ newborn
the cohort aged 1 year comprises $10{,}000\,(1.01)^{98}$ newborn
the cohort aged 0 years comprises $10{,}000\,(1.01)^{99}$ newborn.

If we had made the hypothesis that 10,000 was the total number of newborn of the youngest cohort (the cohort [*A*-1], which was 0 years of age on January 1st, *A*), then

the cohort aged 1 year comprises $10{,}000\,(1.01)^{-1}$ newborn[14]
the cohort aged 2 years comprises $10{,}000\,(1.01)^{-2}$ newborn
the cohort aged 3 years comprises $10{,}000\,(1.01)^{-3}$ newborn
etc.

This presentation, which adheres strictly to the hypotheses set forth, reduces the writing and computations when only the youngest generations are being considered.

Let us determine what remains of these generations on January 1st, *A*, with the mortality still being that of Duvillard. For this, it suffices to take again the computations of Figure 10.4, introducing correction factors that would take account of the inequality of the totals among the successive generations at birth. This is what is done in Figure 10.7; the same correction factors are found on the vertical line as of January 1st, *A*.

13. As previously, we neglect the rare persons who live beyond 100 years of age.

14. Let us recall that $(1.01)^{-1}$ is the conventional way of writing $1/(1.01)$; $(1.01)^{-2}$ is the conventional way of writing $1/(1.01)^2$, etc.; and that these negative exponents have all the properties of ordinary positive exponents. From this we can readily see that

$$10{,}000 : 10{,}000\,(1.01)^{-1} = 10{,}000\,(1.01)^{99} : 10{,}000\,(1.01)^{98}$$

(the relationships, under the two hypothesized systems, between the total number at birth in cohorts $(A-1)$ and $(A-2)$.

Thus, under the hypothesis for two populations subject to the Duvillard life table – the one stationary, in which each year there are 10,000 newborn; the other stable, in which the annual number of births increases by 1 percent annually, the number of births of the year $(A-1)$ being 10,000 – we have the following situation as of the 1st of January of the year A (Table 10.4).

The computation by year of age is even more laborious here than in the derivation of a stationary model; the question of a more rapid construction

TABLE 10.4.   *Stationary and Stable Populations*

Age at Jan. 1, A	Stationary Population	Stable population		
0 year	8,837	8,837		= 8,837
1 year	7,196	7,196 $(1.01)^{-1}$	=	7,125
2 years	6,482	6,482 $(1.01)^{-2}$	=	6,354
3 years	6,116	6,116 $(1.01)^{-3}$	=	5,936
4 years	5,909	5,909 $(1.01)^{-4}$	=	5,678
..	..	..		

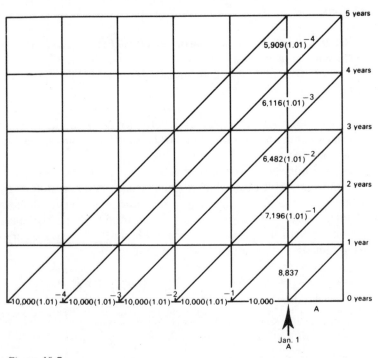

Figure 10.7

of stable population models is equally relevant; this suggests, also, the need to obtain such models on the basis of more abbreviated survival tables.

Figure 10.8 explains how the computation can be carried out when we have access to a series of survivors, limited to multiples of 5 (with the additional knowledge of l_1); this figure is a transposition of Figure 10.5, which resolved an identical problem in the case of the stationary model.

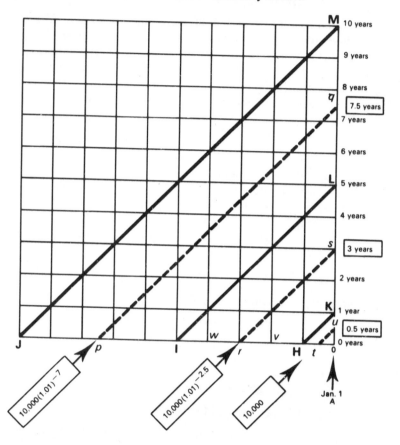

Figure 10.8

The total at birth of the youngest generation being taken as equal to 10,000 (meaning the births between *0* and *H*), we compare the group of lifelines of these 10,000 newborn with 10,000 lines centered at *tu*, considered the "mean" lifeline of the cohort. The survival rate to be applied is that leading from *t* to *u*, that is, the survival rate to 0.5 years.

It is the aggregate of newborns between *H* and *I* that is the source of the survivors of the group 1–4 years old on January 1st, A. These newborn are numbered:

$$10,000 \, (1.01)^{-1} \text{ for the youngest cohort } (Hv)$$
$$10,000 \, (1.01)^{-2} \text{ for the following cohort } (vr)$$
$$10,000 \, (1.01)^{-3} \text{ for the following cohort } (rw)$$
$$10,000 \, (1.01)^{-4} \text{ for the following cohort } (wI).$$

We again compare the aggregate of lifelines of these newborn with a similar number of lines all concentrated at rs, considered as the "mean" lifeline for the group of four cohorts. The survival rate to be applied is that leading from r to s, which is the survival rate to three years. But to achieve a still greater saving in computations, the approximation does not stop there; it equally concerns the estimation of the number of births for the four cohorts in question. The computation of

$$10,000 \, (1.01)^{-1} + 10,000 \, (1.01)^{-2} + 10,000 \, (1.01)^{-3} + 10,000 \, (1.01)^{-4} \quad (S)$$

and those analogous to it that occur in what follows are actually quite laborious. To dispense with this computation, we shall assume that the *mean* of the total numbers at birth in the four generations is equal to the total at birth of one cohort, of which the mean point would be r.[15] Having, on the average, 2.5 years more than the cohort OH, this cohort has, then, a total of:

$$10,000 \, (1.01)^{-2.5}$$

and, consequently, we obtain the sum (S) by

$$4 \times 10,000 \, (1.01)^{-2.5} = 40,000 \, (1.01)^{-2.5}.$$

By virtue of the same approximations, the total born in IJ will be taken as equal to

$$5 \times 10,000 \, (1.01)^{-7} = 50,000 \, (1.01)^{-7}.$$

The other groups of five cohorts will have totals at birth of

$$50,000 \, (1.01)^{-12}, 50,000 \, (1.01)^{-17}, \ldots, 50,000 \, (1.01)^{-97}$$

A stable model is then constructed on the basis of the stationary model, having the same mortality table and applying to the total of the age groups the series of 20 correction factors $(1.01)^{-2.5}, (1.01)^{-7}, (1.01)^{-12}, \ldots, (1.01)^{-97}$.[16]

15. The aggregate of points representing these newborn will be, then, a segment centered at r and 1 year in length; this will refer in fact to two half-generations, one belonging to wr and the second to rv.

16. Note that the number of the first age group (0 years) is not changed, the total being taken as equal to 10,000 at birth.

TABLE 10.5. *Computation of Stable Populations (to a Base of 10,000 Newborn in the Youngest Generation)*

	Stable Populations with r = +1 per 100					Stable Populations with r = −1 per 100		
	Duvillard Table		Norwegian Female Table (1951–1955)		Age Group in Completed Years		Duvillard Table	Norwegian Female Table (1951–1955)
Multipliers	$k\frac{l_x+l_{x+k}}{2}$ *	Stable Population	$k\frac{l_x+l_{x+k}}{2}$ *	Stable Population		Multipliers		
1	8,837	8,837	9,900	9,900	0	1	8,837	9,900
$(1.01)^{-2.5}$ = 0.9754	27,012	26,348	39,108	38,146	1– 4	$(0.99)^{-2.5}$ = 1.0254	27,698	40,101
$(1.01)^{-7}$ = 0.9327	28,350	26,442	48,715	45,436	5– 9	$(0.99)^{-7}$ = 1.0729	30,417	52,266
$(1.01)^{-12}$ = 0.8875	27,000	23,963	48,620	43,150	10–14	$(0.99)^{-12}$ = 1.1282	30,461	54,853
$(1.01)^{-17}$ = 0.8444	25,780	21,769	48,525	40,975	15–19	$(0.99)^{-17}$ = 1.1863	30,583	57,565
$(1.01)^{-22}$ = 0.8034	24,340	19,555	48,405	38,889	20–24	$(0.99)^{-22}$ = 1.2475	30,364	60,385
$(1.01)^{-27}$ = 0.7644	22,740	17,382	48,245	36,878	25–29	$(0.99)^{-27}$ = 1.3117	29,828	63,283
$(1.01)^{-32}$ = 0.7273	21,055	15,313	48,035	34,936	30–34	$(0.99)^{-32}$ = 1.3793	29,041	66,255
$(1.01)^{-37}$ = 0.6920	19,335	13,380	47,760	33,050	35–39	$(0.99)^{-37}$ = 1.4504	28,043	69,271
$(1.01)^{-42}$ = 0.6584	17,585	11,578	47,375	31,192	40–44	$(0.99)^{-42}$ = 1.5252	26,821	72,256
$(1.01)^{-47}$ = 0.6265	15,780	9,886	46,815	29,330	45–49	$(0.99)^{-47}$ = 1.6038	25,308	75,082
$(1.01)^{-52}$ = 0.5961	13,855	8,259	45,960	27,397	50–54	$(0.99)^{-52}$ = 1.6864	23,365	77,507
$(1.01)^{-57}$ = 0.5671	11,770	6,675	44,645	25,318	55–59	$(0.99)^{-57}$ = 1.7733	20,872	79,169
$(1.01)^{-62}$ = 0.5396	9,500	5,126	42,635	23,006	60–64	$(0.99)^{-62}$ = 1.8647	17,715	79,501
$(1.01)^{-67}$ = 0.5134	7,100	3,645	39,505	20,282	65–69	$(0.99)^{-67}$ = 1.9608	13,922	77,461
$(1.01)^{-72}$ = 0.4885	4,735	2,313	34,540	16,873	70–74	$(0.99)^{-72}$ = 2.0619	9,763	71,218
$(1.01)^{-77}$ = 0.4648	2,660	1,236	27,230	12,657	75–79	$(0.99)^{-77}$ = 2.1682	5,767	59,040
$(1.01)^{-82}$ = 0.4422	1,165	515	18,075	7,993	80–84	$(0.99)^{-82}$ = 2.2799	2,656	41,209
$(1.01)^{-87}$ = 0.4208	390	164	9,195	3,869	85–89	$(0.99)^{-87}$ = 2.3974	935	22,044
$(1.01)^{-92}$ = 0.4003	120	48	2,995	1,199	90–94	$(0.99)^{-92}$ = 2.5209	303	7,550
$(1.01)^{-97}$ = 0.3809	30	11	415	158	95–99	$(0.99)^{-97}$ = 2.6509	80	1,100
		222,445		520,634	Total		392,779	1,137,016

*Cf. Table 10.2: refers to numbers in age groups of the stationary population associated with the life table used.

This is what was done in Table 10.5, in which correction factors called *multipliers* are shown in two columns:

In a first column is a series of negative powers of 1.01 $(1.01)^{-2.5}$, $(1.01)^{-7}$, etc.; applying this series successively to stationary populations deduced from the Duvillard table and from the Norwegian table, we obtain corresponding stable populations in which the annual rate of increase in the number of births is 1 percent.

In a second column, there is a series of negative powers of 0.99 $((0.99)^{-2.5}$, $(0.99)^{-7}$, etc.); it corresponds to the variation in the annual number of births, from −1 percent in populations that are deduced from it. In other words, this involves populations in which, from year to year, the annual number of births diminishes by 1 percent; in the expression $1+r$ of the relationship introduced at the beginning of this paragraph, $r = -0.01$, and consequently the relationship is evaluated at $1-0.01 = 0.99$. Applying this new series of multipliers to the same stationary populations as before, we obtained two new stable populations characterized by their mortality tables and by an annual rate of increase in the number of births equal to −1 percent.[17]

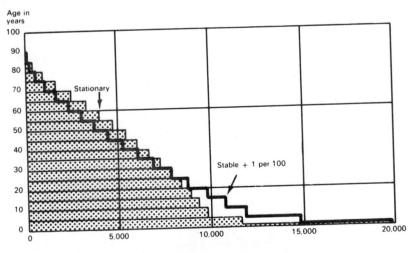

Figure 10.9a

To make useful comparisons among populations computed in this way, it is convenient to bring them to a common total (100,000, for example). The pyramids of Figures 10.9 and 10.10 can then be drawn. In these drawings, we have superimposed in gray the pyramids of the stationary populations constructed previously.

17. The word "increase," found in the expression "natural increase," does not imply that it must necessarily be a case of an increase in the usual sense of the term, i.e., a *positive* variation; the increase we understand here can equally be found to be *negative*.

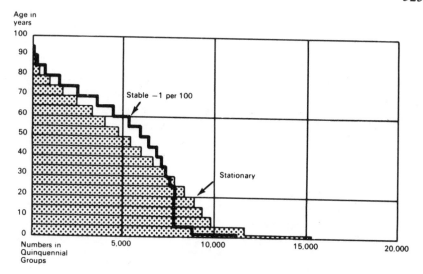

Figure 10.9b

In Figures 10.9a and 10.10a, the increasing stable populations[18] ($r = +1$ percent > 0) are compared with stationary populations having the same life tables; in Figures 10.9b and 10.10b, decreasing stable populations ($r = -1$ percent < 0) are compared with the same stationary populations.

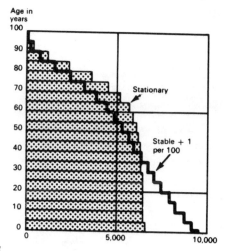

Figure 10.10a

18. The real justification of the term will be given in what follows.

The group of six pyramids furnishes us with a large range of population structures, from the quite young population of Duvillard (a growing or increasing stable population with [$r = +1$ percent]), (Figure 10.9a) to the quite aged population with a pyramid of a somewhat unlikely form (decreasing stable population [$r = -1$ percent]) according to the Norwegian female table (Figure 10.10b). The systematic study of these population structures and associated demographic characteristics will be undertaken after we have established the properties of stable populations.

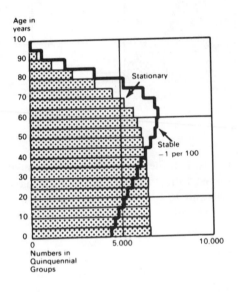

Figure 10.10b

Some Properties of Stable Populations

We shall establish these properties by studying Figure 10.11, which is simply a recapitulation of Figure 10.7 detailing the movement of a stable population (defined by the Duvillard life table and with $r = +1$ percent) from one January 1st to the following January 1st.

Observing that the correction factors ([1.01]$^{-1}$, [1.01]$^{-2}$, etc.) attached to each cohort affect successive age groups one year apart from a January 1st, ([$A - 1$] for example) to the following January 1st, (January 1st, A), it is seen that between these two dates the total at any given age is multiplied by 1.01. Thus for 2 years, at January 1st, ($A - 1$), the total would be 6,482 (1.01)$^{-3}$; for 2 years, at January 1st, A, the total would be 6,482 (1.01)$^{-2}$ and

$(1.01)^{-2} = (1.01)^{-3} \times 1.01;^{19}$ between the dates, there has been a multiplication by 1.01.

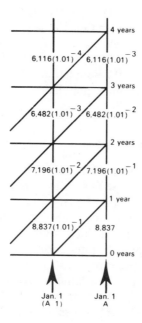

Figure 10.11

As this multiplication takes place at all ages, the total population is found to be multiplied by 1.01 from one January 1st to the following January 1st. This annual rate of (natural) increase is then 1 percent. In a general way, *in a stable population in which the rate of variation of the annual number of live births is r, the annual rate of (natural) increase is also r*.

The rate of variation in births and that of the population being the same, the relationship births/population is invariable. Thus, in a stable population, *the crude rate of birth (b) is constant*.

As the rate of natural increase is also constant (and is equal to *r*),

$$n = b - d = r \text{ and } d = n - r,$$

and the crude death rate is constant.

Finally, the relationship of the totals of different age groups to the total

19.
$$(1.01)^{-2} = \frac{1}{(1.01)^2}; (1.01)^{-3} = \frac{1}{(1.01)^3};$$

and we have

$$\frac{1}{(1.01)^2} = \frac{1}{(1.01)^3} \times (1.01).$$

population is likewise constant.[20] In other words, *the age composition of a stable population is invariable.* In conclusion, in a stable population:

1. The total size of the population varies by a constant rate (r).

2. The crude rates of births and of deaths are constant (considering the first property, this implies that the annual numbers of births and of deaths vary at a constant rate r).

3. The age composition of the population is fixed.

Let us observe that a stationary population is a special case of the stable population, one in which $r = 0$.

Some Examples of Stable Populations

Table 10.5 summarizes four examples of stable populations. We can summarize the composition of these populations by computing the relative size of the three large age groups (0–19 years, 20–59 years, 60 years and over). It is useful, finally, to compute the rates of natality and mortality. Let us work on the stable population deduced from the Duvillard table, in which $r = +1$ percent, and compute the rates during the year $(A - 1)$.[21] During this year, there were 10,000 births. It remains to determine the mean population, as the mean of the populations on January 1st $(A - 1)$ and January 1st (A); or, again, as the population in the midpoint of the year $(A - 1)$. Since on January 1st $(A - 1)$ the total was 1 percent smaller than it was on January 1st (A), it can be assumed that on July 1 $(A - 1)$ it was 0.5 percent smaller than it was on January 1st (A). Toward the middle of $(A - 1)$ the total population increased to:

$$222,445 \times 0.995 = 221,333$$

from which comes the crude birth rate:

$$b = \frac{10,000}{221,333} = 45.2 \text{ per } 1,000$$

but

$$b - d = r = 10.0 \text{ per } 1,000$$

---

20. Thus, let us compare (Figure 10.11) the relationship of the population aged 3 complete years to the total population at the two dates, January 1st $(A - 1)$, and January 1st (A). Let P be the total at the first date; at the second date the total becomes $P \times 1.01$. These two relationships are written:

$$\frac{6.116(1.01)^{-4}}{P} \quad \text{and} \quad \frac{6.116(1.01)^{-3}}{P \times 1.01}$$

and thus are equal.

21. The choice of year is of little importance since the rates are constant.

then
$$d = 45.2 - 10.0 = 35.2 \text{ per } 1,000.$$

In addition to the four populations in Table 10.5 and the two stationary populations in Table 10.2, we have assembled in Table 10.6 the stable populations derived from the Norwegian life table, with rates of increase of 2 and 3 percent, and the stable populations derived from the Duvillard life table, with rates of increase of -2 and $+2$ percent. Similarly included are the five stable populations derived from the Swedish male life table of 1891–1900 (with $e_0 = 50.9$ years) and six stable populations derived from the Swedish male mortality table of 1816–1840 (with $e_0 = 39.5$ years). We thus possess a large range of population models that will permit us to show the relationships existing between certain characteristics of these populations.

We see that for the aggregate of the populations derived from a given life table and hence for the aggregate of populations in which the *mortality risk* is the same, the degree of ageing can be quite variable. Thus, following the data of Table 10.6, we find associated:

a mean duration of life of 28.8 years, and percentages of "60 years and over" varying from 3.8 percent to 18.4 percent;

a mean duration of life of 39.5 years, and percentages of "60 years and over" varying from 2.8 to 20.0 percent;

a mean duration of life of 50.9, and percentages of "60 years and over" varying from 4.6 to 22.0 percent;

a mean duration of life of 74.7 years and percentages of "60 years and over" varying from 7.3 to 31.6 percent.

The extreme values we have obtained do not necessarily correspond to rigid limits; we have simply limited ourselves to construction of populations in which natality and mortality take admissible values. It is for this reason that certain columns of Table 10.6 remain empty: the populations that might be located there would have quite exceptional rates of natality.[22]

These variable degrees of aging have implications for the crude death rates, which, in populations in which expectation of life is the same, may sometimes vary from 1 to 4 (from 4.3 per thousand to 18.8 per thousand in the populations derived from the Norwegian tables (see Figure 10.12).

22. Thus, in constructing the stable population for the rate of increase -2 percent in the Norwegian table — we would have a model in which there would be 40.7 percent aged "60 years or older" and in which the crude death rate and crude birth rate would be 25.4 per 1,000 and 5.4 per 1,000, respectively. To exist, a real population resembling this would have to reduce its fertility to a completely unprecedented level. By contrast, in the case of populations based on the Duvillard table, a fairly high crude birth rate must be reached to neutralize a high crude death rate and yield a marked rate of increase, r. We see already that if $r = 2$ percent, we require that $b = 56.8$ per 1,000, which is not far from the physiological maximum. To attain $r = 3$ percent, b must surpass 60 per 1,000; we reach unrealizable values. Although we cannot define a precise upper limit, we see that in this case all the population models are unimaginable, some of them assuming the attainment of fertility levels that are not possible in the human species.

TABLE 10.6. Examples of Stable Populations

	Rate of National Increase					
	3 per 100	2 per 100	1 per 100	0	−1 per 100	−2 per 100
Norwegian Female Life Table (1951–55) (e$_0$ = 74.7 years)						
0–19 years	50.4	42.4	34.1	26.1	18.9	
20–59 years	42.3	46.4	49.4	50.5	49.5	
60 plus years	7.3	11.2	16.5	23.4	31.6	
All Ages	100.0	100.0	100.0	100.0	100.0	
Crude Birth Rate (per 1,000)	34.3	26.3	19.3	13.4	8.8	
Crude Death Rate (per 1,000)	4.3	6.3	9.3	13.4	18.8	
Swedish Male Life Table (1816–40) (e$_0$ = 39.5 years)						
0–19 years	58.7	51.8	44.4	36.7	29.1	22.1
20–59 years	38.5	43.8	48.8	53.2	56.4	57.9
60 plus years	2.8	4.4	6.8	10.1	14.5	20.0
All Ages	100.0	100.0	100.0	100.0	100.0	100.0
Crude Birth Rate (per 1,000)	53.0	42.9	33.6	25.2	18.2	12.4
Crude Death Rate (per 1,000)	23.0	22.9	23.6	25.2	28.2	32.4

	Rate of National Increase					
	3 per 100	2 per 100	1 per 100	0	−1 per 100	−2 per 100
Swedish Male Table (1891–1900) (e$_0$ = 50.9 years)						
0–19 years	55.6	48.1	40.2	32.1	24.5	
20–59 years	39.8	44.7	49.0	52.1	53.5	
60 plus years	4.6	7.2	10.8	15.8	22.0	
All Ages	100.0	100.0	100.0	100.0	100.0	
Crude Birth Rate (per 1,000)	44.7	35.4	27.0	19.6	13.5	
Crude Death Rate (per 1,000)	14.7	15.4	17.0	19.6	23.5	
Duvillard Life Table (e$_0$ = 28.8 years)						
0–19 years		55.6	48.2	40.5	32.6	25.1
20–59 years		40.6	45.9	50.6	54.4	56.5
60 plus years		3.8	5.9	8.9	13.0	18.4
All Ages		100.0	100.0	100.0	100.0	100.0
Crude Birth Rate (per 1,000)		56.8	45.2	34.7	25.3	17.7
Crude Death Rate (per 1,000)		36.8	35.2	34.7	35.3	37.7

It is appropriate to note that when expectation of life is low and the population is young (due, as we have seen, to high natality), an increase in the relative number of aged persons brings about only a relatively small increase in the crude death rate, and sometimes even a decrease (see in Figure 10.12 the curve showing $e_0 = 28.8$ years). In the latter case, the explanation is the relative weight of the mortality of young persons (we may recall, for example, on the basis of the Duvillard table, that about half of the newborn died prior to age 20 years). Under these conditions, a greater youthfulness of the population can increase the relative numbers of deaths. In addition, when the process of ageing is underway, the loss in young persons is translated first of all by an increase in the relative number of adults, whose mortality is lower than that of aged persons. This can be verified in the models derived from the Duvillard table, in which $r = 2$ percent, then 1 percent (see Table 10.6).

With constant *mortality risk* (measured by a given life table) the variation in the degree of ageing in different stable populations can be imputed only to concomitant changes in fertility. In effect, it is enough that fertility varies

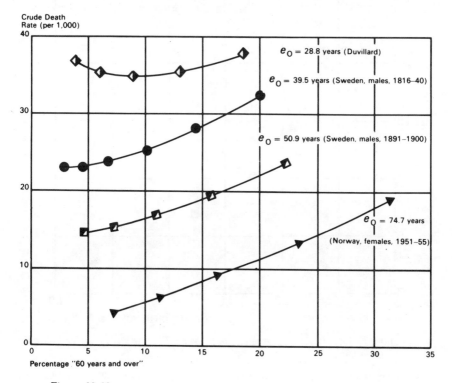

Crude Death Rate (per 1,000)

$e_0 = 28.8$ years (Duvillard)

$e_0 = 39.5$ years (Sweden, males, 1816–40)

$e_0 = 50.9$ years (Sweden, males, 1891–1900)

$e_0 = 74.7$ years

(Norway, females, 1951–55)

Percentage "60 years and over"

Figure 10.12

from one population to the next to bring birth rates[23] to desired values, making apparent the growth rates *r* (chosen before construction of the model).

Figure 10.13 shows the close relationship that exists in stable populations between the crude birth rate and the extent of ageing (measured by the percentage at "60 years of age or older"), *no matter what the level of mortality* (measured intrinsically by a life table; and in the case of Figure 10.13, the range of the tables used is as wide as possible, ranging from $e_0 = 28.8$ years

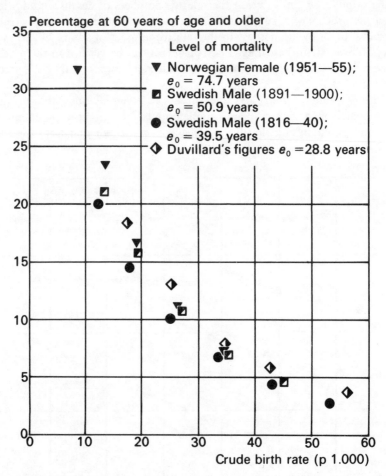

Figure 10.13. Extent of Ageing and Crude Birth Rate in Diverse Stable Populations.

23. And indirectly the crude death rate, by the degree of ageing that, as we shall see, implies a given level of the crude birth rate.

to $e_0 = 74.7$ years). Thus, we find, in the case of our population models, the general connection, properly detailed (and even quantified), that was found in the preceding chapter between natality and degree of ageing in a population.

Theoretical Stable Populations and Real Populations

Stable populations are richer and more variable models that stationary populations, since a given life table can be associated with an infinite number of stable populations, each one individualized by the given rate of natural increases.

If there are reasons to think that real populations have retained the same life table as well as the same rate of natural increase for a long period of time, we may seek to compare them to corresponding stable populations.

An apparent gap remains in our presentation of stable populations as in that of stationary populations (which are only special cases of stable populations): the fertility patterns are not always explicitly included. In fact, we know how to relate the rate of natural increase of a stable population to its gross reproduction rate R. However, it is established that a population subject to a given life table and following an invariable fertility régime defined by *a series of age-specific fertility rates* is a stable population.

Beginning with this, if we wish to construct a stable population defined by a life table and a series of age-specific fertility rates, we will summarize these rates by the gross reproduction rate R and compute the rate of natural increase that corresponds to the stable state. This leads to constructing a stable model defined by a life table and a rate of natural increase. This problem will be reviewed and explained in the next chapter.

On the other hand, the following interesting property has been established by A. J. Lotka (an American demographer, 1880–1949): in a population of *any age composition*, subject to invariable fertility (defined by age-specific rates) and of mortality (defined by a life table), the annual number of births is *characterized by fluctuations that diminish little by little, until eventually they end by varying from one year to the next at a constant rate.*

But we know that a population in which the mortality régime is invariable and in which the annual number of births varies by a constant rate is a stable population (besides, it is thus that we have introduced this theoretical model). Consequently, the preceding result is apparently equivalent to the following: *a population of any given age composition, subject to an invariable pattern of fertility and mortality, tends progressively toward a stable state associated with this régime.*

In particular, upheavals can be caused in real populations by the effects of wars or epidemics, which create serious disturbances in the age distribution. The Lotka result assures us that the continuation of a constant régime of mortality and fertility will eventually correct such disturbances in the age pyramid, which will tend progressively toward the theoretical model.

This property leads to the association of a real population with the rate of natural increase that it would have as the result of continued maintenance of its present fertility and mortality régime, i.e., when the limiting stable state was attained. An intrinsic rate of growth is thus defined, independent of disturbing influences on the present structure of the population studied, an inheritance from past history that masks the current growth capacity of the population. This rate is called the *intrinsic rate of natural increase* or the *Lotka rate*. We shall return to this index and to the manner of computing it in the following chapter; similarly, as we have said above, we shall study the construction of the stable population to which we have already referred, that is, the stable population deriving from given patterns of mortality (defined by a life table) and of fertility (defined by a series of age-specific fertility rates).

Let us observe, finally, that the theoretical models we have presented are all population models for a single sex. In fact, the theory of stable populations leaves aside the factor of nuptiality. It is always possible—but the construction is purely formal—to construct a stable population with two sexes. To do so, it is appropriate to choose a life table for each sex (the relationship between the two tables must be appropriate, that is, must retain the plausible differences between male and female mortality in the same period), and to take into account the relationship of masculinity at birth (105 boys to every 100 girls born). It remains to apply the series of correction factors corresponding to the rates of natural increase chosen to the two stationary populations deriving from the preceding data (see the "multipliers" of Table 10.5).

CHAPTER ELEVEN

Replacement

BECAUSE of births and deaths, every population is subject to a continuous process of renewal to which is given the name *replacement*. Two ideas are associated with this process: (1) the idea of natural increase of a population; (2) the idea of replacement of generations.

The annual rate of natural increase is a global index, very much influenced by the effects of age compositions. When the balance of births and deaths is positive, it gives the impression that the replacement of generations is assured, although sometimes this is not the case.

The measurement of replacement of generations is carried out with the aid of the net reproduction rate, which, in essence, is an index of cohort analysis. But, usually, this net rate is calculated as a period index. Thus, we are trying to reach the fundamental characteristics of a period, uninfluenced by the effects of age composition; under these conditions, the net reproduction rate is often interpreted in a predictive sense that is not without its dangers. The same care in eliminating the influence of current age composition sometimes leads to the computation of the intrinsic rates of natural increase defined by Lotka.

But there remain numerous cases in which it is more important to highlight the consequences of current composition for short-run demographic change than to try to determine what the operation of certain basic conditions brings about in long-term development: it is thus when the present population compositions largely condition these populations' immediate future.

Natural Increase

The most elementary way of following the development of a population is to compute the annual increase[1] in its total number. To be able to make comparisons between populations of quite different absolute sizes, an annual rate of increase is computed, which is given as the quotient

$$\frac{\Delta P}{P_m}$$

multiplied by 100 or by 1,000; ΔP is the population increase during the year in question (that is, between two successive January 1sts) and P_m is the mean total number in the population during the same year (the total at about the middle of the year or the arithmetic mean of the totals on the two successive January 1sts.

Usually, attention is directed particularly to the *natural movement of populations*, that is, to the variations resulting from births and from deaths, but excluding migrations. The natural increase ΔP_1, which we will show here, represents, then, the balance of births (B) and of deaths (D); in this case:

$$\Delta P_1 = B - D$$

and the annual rate

$$n = \frac{\Delta P_1}{P_m} = \frac{B - D}{P_m} = b - d \qquad (A)$$

is equal to the difference between the crude birth rate and the crude death rate, these different rates being generally given per 1,000 (which would lead to modification of formula (A), in consequence).

Let us treat a numerical example, that of the United States in 1965:

Estimated population on January 1, 1966:   195,382,000.
Estimated population on January 1, 1965:   193,034,000.
Increase ΔP: 2,348,000.

During this year, 1965, there were in the United States:

Births (B):   3,806,000.
Deaths (D):   1,828,000.
Natural increase (ΔP_1):   1,978,000.

Thus, part of the increase ΔP results from the positive migratory balance: $\Delta P - \Delta P_1 = 2,348,000 - 1,978,000 = 370,000$[2]. The mean population P_m is equal to

$$P_m = \frac{193,034,000 + 195,382,000}{2} = 194,208,000$$

1. As in the previous chapter, the word "increase" need not necessarily imply *augmentation*; the term is used in its algebraic sense and is synonymous (more or less) with variation.

2. Even though in developed countries natural increase is known very exactly (just as the numbers of births and deaths are known), the numbers concerning migration are very approximate.

and the rate of natural increase is

$$n = \frac{1,978,000}{194,208,000} = 10.1 \text{ per } 1,000.$$

It is equal to

$$b - d = 19.5 - 9.4 = 10.1 \text{ per } 1,000.[3]$$

It is lower than the rate of increase $\Delta P / P_m$, which includes the migratory balance (which is positive) in its numerator; we have

$$\frac{\Delta P}{P_m} = \frac{2,348,000}{194,208,000} = 12.1 \text{ per } 1,000.$$

The Rate of Natural Increase: Variations in Time and Space

On a world-wide level, it is clearly only natural increase that determines the development of the total size of the population. For the great majority of countries, it is also natural increase that represents the essential part of population growth. However, at certain times in their histories, countries have seen their demographic development dominated by migration. Restricting ourselves to mentioning recent movements, let us remember the importance of immigration in the growth of the population in the United States in the nineteenth century and the beginning of the twentieth century, and correlatively the "brake" that was applied to natural increase in certain European countries by migrations from these countries to the United States and to the New World in general. In France, between 1920 and 1930, the arrival of two million aliens obscured the demographic weakening of the indigenous population. Finally, later in time, there has been the massive movement of refugees (from former German territories annexed to Poland, Czechoslovakia, to East Germany), which each year have brought hundreds of thousands of persons to West Germany (close to 4.5 million in the 10 years from 1946 to 1956).[4]

Migratory movements within a given country are generally much more frequent and of much greater magnitude than movements between a country and other countries. Also, in the framework of small territorial units (in the *départements* of France, for example), internal migrations are often of much greater magnitude than is natural increase of the population.

Given what we know about fluctuations in mortality before progress was made in medicine, hygiene, and the economy, we see that under those conditions natural increase of populations must have been subject to very substantial fluctuations; natality being, in effect, but little variable, the fluctuations in the mortality rates must have been reflected almost exactly in the

3. See our computation on p. 30.

4. Leaving aside numerous arrivals during or immediately after the end of the war.

rates of natural increase. Aside from periods of war, epidemics, and famines, natality exceeded mortality slightly, and the annual excess of population must have reached a few units per 1,000, with a limit of the order of 10 per 1,000 or 1 percent. If a mean rate, intermediate between 5 per 1,000 and 10 per 1,000, had been maintained over a long period, it would have doubled the population in about a century. With a more probable mean rate of 4 to 5 per 1,000, the doubling of the population would have occurred only after about two centuries. But catastrophes came unexpectedly, reversing the balance of births and deaths and devouring the demographic increase of many years.

It is because there was a decline in mortality before the decline in natality that the rate of natural increase remained positive in the countries of Western Europe during virtually all of the years of the nineteenth century. In France, where natality had begun to decline in the second half of the eighteenth century, the natural increase of the population was considerably less than in the neighboring countries. We observe:

a mean annual rate of 5.3 per 1,000 during the period 1801–1825;
a mean annual rate of 4.3 per 1,000 during the period 1826–1850;
a mean annual rate of 2.1 per 1,000 during the period 1851–1875;[5]
a mean annual rate of 1.8 per 1,000 during the period 1876–1900.[5]

Beside these quite low rates, let us cite those of Sweden, a country representative of all Western Europe:

the mean annual rate is 8.1 per 1,000 during the period 1801–1850;
the mean annual rate is 11.5 per 1,000 during the period 1851–1900.

After 1850, the trend of declining natality was extended little by little to the various countries of Europe and to the countries of Anglo-Saxon settlement overseas. So the natural increase of population in these countries continued to diminish, to the point where certain of them finally had only an infinitesimal rate of natural increase (2 to 4 per 1,000); in France, where the economic crisis and an unfavorable age composition added their effects to the decline of fertility, the rate became negative beginning with 1935. The acceleration of the decline of mortality at the end of World War II, along with an increase in natality in the case of France and certain other countries (including the United States), led to an increase in the rate of natural increase, which, in general, currently exceeds 5 per 1,000 in these countries.[6]

But at the present time, the most obvious fact is the rapid and sizable decline in the last 15 years in mortality in the underdeveloped countries, in the face of a continuation of the high level of natality; there follows a

5. The balance of births and deaths was negative only in 1854, 1855, 1870, 1871, 1890, 1891, 1892, and 1895.

6. In the United States the rate of natural increase is at present about 1 percent annually.

considerable rise in the rate of increase, which sometimes takes values never before attained. An annual increase of more than 20 per 1,000 (2 percent) obtains in these countries; many of them have attained 30 per 1,000 (3 percent), and certain countries come close to 40 per 1,000 (4 percent).

Figure 11.1 shows recent trends in the crude rate of natural increase for

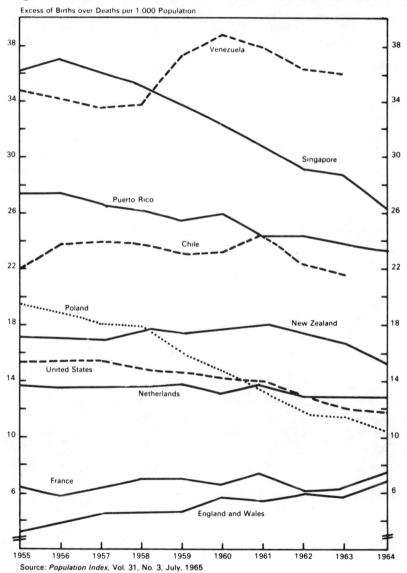

Excess of Births over Deaths per 1,000 Population

Venezuela

Singapore

Puerto Rico

Chile

Poland

New Zealand

United States

Netherlands

France

England and Wales

1955 1956 1957 1958 1959 1960 1961 1962 1963 1964

Source: *Population Index*, Vol. 31, No. 3, July, 1965

Figure 11.1

TABLE 11.1.   *Rates of Natural Increase in 1958 (per 1,000)*

	1958	1965
AFRICA		
Union of South Africa		
European Population	17.1	
Colored Population	30.8	
Asiatic Population	21.3	
NORTH AMERICA		
Canada	19.7	13.9
United States	14.8	10.0
Guatemala	27.4	26.7
Jamaica	29.3	31.5
Mexico	32.0	35.8
Panama	30.6	
Puerto Rico	25.8	23.6
El Salvador	33.8	36.0
SOUTH AMERICA		
Argentina (1964)	14.6	13.5
Chile (1964)	23.4	21.6
Colombia	30.5	
Ecuador	30.7	
Venezuela	35.3	
ASIA		
Israel (1964)	20.8	16.2
Japan	10.5	11.5
Ceylon	25.3	
Mainland China	27.0	
Taiwan	34.1	27.2
Hong Kong	31.3	22.3
Singapore	35.0	22
EUROPE		
West Germany	6.2	6.7
Austria	4.9	4.9
Belgium	5.9	4.3
Denmark	7.4	7.9
Finland	9.6	7.3
France	7.0	6.5
Great Britain	5.1	6.9
England and Wales	4.7	6.6
Scotland	8.4	7.3
Northern Ireland	9.6	12.5
Ireland	8.9	10.7
Norway	9.2	8.4
Netherlands	13.6	11.9
Sweden	4.6	5.8

	1958	*1965*
Switzerland	8.1	9.4
Spain	13.2	12.6
Greece	11.9	
Italy	8.5	9.2
Portugal	13.5	12.5
Yugoslavia	14.6	12.2
Albania (1964)	32.5	29.1
East Germany (1963)	3.4	4.9
Bulgaria	10.0	7.4
Hungary	6.2	2.4
Poland	17.8	9.9
Rumania	12.9	6.0
Czechoslovakia	8.1	6.4
U.S.S.R.	18.1	11.2
OCEANIA		
Australia	14.2	10.8
New Zealand	17.7	14.1

selected countries. The figures in the table are obtained by subtraction of crude death rates from crude birth rates; their value, then, depends upon those of the rates from which they are obtained.[7] Let us add that, for the total population of the world, the annual rate of increase is estimated presently at 1.7 percent, or 17 per 1,000.

But the rate of increase, despite its appearance, remains a somewhat abstract index. The exclusive use of this rate does not allow appropriate ranking of the actual increases in populations; in particular, it leads to minimizing, unconsciously, the increases of populations in which rates are the highest.

The computations of population change by a constant rate of natural increase permit us better to take account of the different rhythms of growth that are associated with the various annual rates of increase.

Change in Populations with a Constant Rate of Natural Increase

We denote by P_0 the total of a certain population on January 1st of the year of origin (we may call it A) in our models of change, and we shall determine what will be the total population in the years that follow, according to the value of the rate of natural increase n (positive or negative), which we assume to be constant in time.

7. However, underestimation (per 1,000) equal to the crude death and crude birth rates, respectively, leads to correct estimation of the rate of natural increase.

In the year A, that is, between January 1st (A) and January 1st ($A+1$), the population has changed by $P_0 \times n$; by January 1st ($A+1$) it has then reached a total of $P_0 \times n + P_0$, or $P_0(1+n)$. Between the two January 1sts, the population has then been multiplied by $(1+n)$. Thus:
(1) if $n = 15$ per $1,000 = 1.5$ percent, or 0.015, then $1+n = 1.015$, which is the multiplying factor;
(2) If $n = -5$ per $1,000 = -0.5$ percent or -0.005, then $1+n = 0.995$, which is the multiplying factor.

If the rate does not vary in time, it is then very clear that the annual multiplying factor is also invariable. Consequently, with a total equal to P_0 on January 1st (A) and a constant annual rate of natural increase equal to n, we have the following change:

$$
\begin{aligned}
\text{January 1st } (A) \quad &: \quad P_0 \\
\text{January 1st } (A+1)&: \quad P_0(1+n) \\
\text{January 1st } (A+2)&: \quad P_0(1+n)^2 \\
\text{January 1st } (A+3)&: \quad P_0(1+n)^3 \\
&\ldots \text{ etc.} \\
\text{January 1st } (A+k)&: \quad P_0(1+n)^k \\
&\ldots \text{ etc.}
\end{aligned}
$$

At the close of k years, the initial total P_0 is multiplied by $(1+n)^k$: the population increases in a *geometric progression*.

Let us illustrate this in solving two kinds of problems. To make the effects of a continuation of a constant annual rate of increase more tangible, we often determine the time period necessary for the population to double;[8] in other words, we seek the duration x necessary for the quantity $(1+n)^x$ to be equal to 2. The solution to the equation $(1+n)^x = 2$ is obtained by going to logarithms:

$$x \log(1+n) = \log 2 = 0.30103 \text{ and, consequently,}$$

$$x = \frac{0.30103}{\log(1+n)}.$$

With $n = 0.5$ percent $= 0.005$, $1+n = 1.005$,

$\log(1+n) = \log 1.005 = 0.00217$, and $x = 0.30103/0.00213 = 139$ years.

With $n = 4$ percent $= 0.04$, $1+n = 1.04$, $\log(1+n) = \log 1.04 = 0.01703$

$$x = \frac{0.30103}{0.01703} = 17.7 \text{ years.}$$

8. This problem evidently has meaning only if n is positive, which is generally the case. With a negative value of n, we can seek the time period required for a decline of one half.

Table 11.2 gives the time periods required for doubling of the population corresponding to different values of the annual rate of increase.

TABLE 11.2. *Time Period Required for Population to Double at Selected Constant Annual Rates of Increase*

Annual Rate of Increase	5 per 1,000	10 per 1,000	15 per 1,000	20 per 1,000	25 per 1,000	30 per 1,000	35 per 1,000	40 per 1,000
	Years	Years	Years	Years	Years	Years	Years	Years
Time Required for Doubling of Population	139	69.7	46.5	35.0	28.1	23.4	20.1	17.7

We can also compute the growth of the population at the end of a given period of time, for example, 100 years. In this case, at the end of this period there is a multiplication by $(1+n)^{100}$, which is our unknown. Going again to logarithms:

$$\log (1+n)^{100} = 100 \log (1+n).$$

Following the calculation, reading the table of logarithms yields the value of $(1+n)^{100}$

With $n = 5$ percent, $\log (1+n)^{100} = 100 \times \log 1.005 = 0.217$ and $(1+n)^{100} = 165$.

With $n = 4$ percent, $\log (1+n)^{100} = 100 \times \log 1.04 = 1.703$ and $(1+n)^{100} = 50.5$.

There is, then, in the first case, multiplication by 1.65 (65 percent increase); in the second case multiplication by 50.5 (4,950 percent increase!). Table 11.3 gives the percentage increase in the population over 100 years of change at a constant rate associated with some various values of n.

TABLE 11.3. *Percentage Increase in Population at the End of 100 Years of Constant Increases at Selected Annual Rates*

Annual Rate of Increase	5 per 1,000	10 per 1,000	15 per 1,000	20 per 1,000	25 per 1,000	30 per 1,000	35 per 1,000	40 per 1,000
	%	%	%	%	%	%	%	%
Percentage Increase in Population over 100 years	65	170	344	624	1,080	1,820	3,020	4,950

The Over-All Character of the Rate of Natural Increase

The only refinement that the annual rate of natural increase brings to the balance of births and deaths is that it neutralizes what the balance owes to the *total number* of the population, by virtue of relating it to a standard total, usually equal to 1,000. By contrast, the influence of *age composition* upon the rate of increase remains. In populations of different age composition it is possible to observe similar levels of fertility and of mortality being expressed[9] by quite different rates of increase.

Without doubt, a population always ends by having the age composition its fertility determines, if the latter remains constant over a sufficiently long period of time:[10] but, in periods of fluctuating or disturbed fertility, calculations will be based on an age structure inherited from the past, leading to a natality rate that poorly reflects the current intrinsic conditions; it follows that the same lag affects the rate of natural increase.

To illustrate, let us take France as an example. Although since 1890 current conditions of fertility and mortality have been insufficient to assure the integral replacement of generations, the annual rate of natural increase remained positive until 1934 (except during some few isolated years and, naturally, during World War I). The French population benefited from an age composition more favorable than that warranted by the fertility and mortality of that period, and it gave the impression of the continuation of its expansion, while the intrinsic conditions for such continuation were no longer realized.

Let us consider another example, this one artificial, but demonstrating well to what erroneous impressions certain demographic structures may lead. Let us imagine a population of persons newly married in a year: very few deaths take place in this young population, but an appreciable number of births occur, even though each couple has, on the average, only a single child. The conditions of integral replacement of generations are far from being realized, and yet the balance of births and deaths, like the rates of increase, is largely positive during several years. We are then confronted with the following problem: to assess the capacity of increase of a population that is based upon the intrinsic conditions of its current fertility and its mortality, and abstracted from the facts of its age composition.

The Net Reproduction Rate

To assess the extent to which a given generation assures its replacement, it is appropriate to follow this generation from the instant of its birth until

9. By means of the crude birth and death rates.

10. We do not speak of its mortality since, as we have already seen, the level of the latter has practically no influence upon the age composition (at least in the absence of reversal of mortality due to ageing, which at this point has not yet occurred).

it has brought all of its descendants into the world. There is integral replacement if 1,000 persons of a cohort, taken from their birth, bring 1,000 newborn children (live born) into the world. This is true a fortiori if there are more than 1,000 live births, in which case there may even be an excess.

The manner in which couples are established makes it difficult to isolate the fertility of the marriages of the *aggregate* of newborn (men and women) of a generation. Also, in general, we are interested in only the female part of cohorts, for whom the age limits of the period of procreation are most circumscribed and for whom, especially, the imputation of maternity does not, in general, create any difficulty; we study, therefore, female replacement, which is the cumulative fertility of a certain number of females at birth, in terms of the number of newborn daughters.

It is thus that in observing 100 girls chosen at random among the newborn baby girls of the French female cohort of 1831–1835, a mean of 97 female births was observed. Expressing this result in terms of a single daughter (based on the group of cohorts for whom cumulative fertility was studied), we obtain what is called the *net reproduction rate*. In our example, it is then equal to 0.94. In a general manner, we will designate this index by the notation R_0.

If the net reproduction rate is less than 1, the integral replacement is not assured (it is short by $1 - R_0$); it is assured if R_0 is equal to 1 and is even more certain if R_0 is greater than 1; in the latter instance an excess is produced (which is measured by the quantity $R_0 - 1$). With a net rate of 0.94, a further increase of 6 live births would be necessary in the total of 100 daughters (considered from their births) to assure integral replacement. By contrast, with R_0 equal to 1.34, for example, there is a 34 percent excess of births over the number necessary to assure strict replacement.

The conditions of statistical observation are poorly adapted to the direct determination of net reproduction rates as we have defined them; the only quantity we can attain conveniently is the mean number of daughters (live-born) brought into the world by the survivors of different female generations that are observed at a census. We have seen above (see p. 189) that the mean numbers of daughters borne by women past 50 years of age do yield acceptable estimates of gross reproduction rates for the various cohorts involved. To move from these gross rates to the corresponding net rates, it is necessary to include in the computation the mean numbers of daughters born to women of the various cohorts: (1) the number of live-born daughters of women dying before the census; and (2) the total number of women of the cohort dying before the census.

The net reproduction rate we have just defined is a cohort rate. Like the majority of cohort indices, it is defined in a quite understandable manner, and it suggests a quite concrete meaning; so it represents the best introduction to the index considered. Nevertheless, it is more common (though often more questionable), to compute the period net reproduction rates.

The Period Net Reproduction Rates

The construction of a period index rests on the composition of a hypothetical cohort, which is subjected to the demographic phenomena being considered with the same intensity as exists in various real cohorts observed during the period studied. We have just seen that the cohort net reproduction rate involves the fertility of women and their mortality until 50 years of age (the age limit of procreation). As a period index, this rate will be computed, then, by subjecting a theoretical cohort of 1,000 daughters at birth (for example) to the life table of the period studied (until 50 years of age), and then applying to the survivors the indices of fertility (usually age-specific fertility rates) observed during the same period.

Let us explain the practical operations by computing the net reproduction rate for France in 1949. We have already computed the age-specific fertility rates for that year (see p. 182). However, we do not have a life table; we shall adopt the 1946–1949 life table computed by the National Statistics Institute,[11] which is closely representative of mortality in 1949.

The elements used in the computation are assembled in columns 1 and 2 of Table 11.4. The product 1 × 2 has a clear meaning: it gives, for each age, the number of births that would occur in a cohort of 1,000 daughters at birth, experiencing the French female mortality of 1946–1949 and having the age-specific fertility rates of French women in 1949.

Let us observe that the fertility rates used are cohort rates (see Table 8.3 and the corresponding explanations in the text); thus, the rate of 34 per 1,000 at 18 years is the rate for women who reach 18 years of age during the year, hence the rate of a group 18 years old *on the average*. It is, then, appropriate to reduce the number of births indicated (34) by the survival rates to exactly 18 years (0.925), to arrive at 31 births.[12] Conversely, if the rate at 18 years of age was the conventional rate relating to women all the same age in complete years (and thus computed as the relationship between births to women 18–19 years of age during the year 1949 and the mean total number of women at the same age in the same year), it would refer to births to women averaging 18.5 years of age. It would then be necessary to use the survival rate to that age, which is generally taken as being equal to the arithmetic mean of the rates of survival to the adjacent ages in completed years:

$$\frac{0.925 + 0.923}{2} = 0.924.$$

11. See, for example, *Bulletin mensuel de Statistique* (May, 1952).

12. In fact, instead of carrying out 34 × 0.925, following the instructions at the top of the columns in Table 11.4, we carry out 925 × 0.034, which is clearly equivalent.

According to the French fertility and mortality conditions of 1949, 1,000 women, studied from birth on, would have 2,686 children, or 2.686 per woman. Retaining only female births (100 out of 205 births, or 0.488 of the total), we have

$$R_0 = 2.686 \times 0.488 = 1.31.$$

This computation can be made more rapidly by working with quinquennial groups (see Table 11.4a). The procedure is the same. The survival rates to be used are those to 17, 22, 27, 32, 37, 42, and 47 years (this can be verified by using a *Lexis* diagram).[13] In addition, a quinquennial fertility rate is a mean fertility rate *valid for five years*. It is assumed that during the five years they spend in the age group 20–24 years, 1,000 women will bring, on the average, 161 children into the world each year; but, according to the life table, only 918 women of the 1,000 at birth will have children while in this age group; consequently, it is necessary to correct the number of births that will occur (161 × 0.918); we thus have 148 births. But as the women remain five years in each quinquennial age group, it is necessary to multiply these 148 births by 5, which gives 740 births.

Continuing in this way for all the age groups, and adding the results, we find 2,695 children, or 2.695 per woman (from birth). Retaining only the female births, we may deduce

$$R_0 = 2.695 \times 0.488 = 1.32.$$

The small deviation from the first result derives from the groupings by five years of age. In the preceding computations, each of the age-specific (or age group-specific) fertility rates was multiplied by the corresponding survival rates. A more rapid but sufficiently precise procedure, even though approximate, consists in adding together the various rates[14] and then multiplying the *sum* of the rates by the rate of survival to the mean age of mothers at confinement, and, finally, in multiplying the result by the proportion of females among births (0.488).

In fact, the mean age we use is that which would characterize mothers if they were not subject to mortality, or, in other words, the mean age that could be calculated on the basis of the series of numbers in column 2 of Table 11.4a.

Naturally, we do not undertake this computation, for with it the work would not be lighter, but heavier. As the mean ages vary but little from one

13. If the quinquennial groups 15–19, 20–24, etc., were age groups in completed years (which is often the case), the survival rates to be used would be those at 17.5 years, 22.5 years, etc.

14. Taking the precaution of multiplying the sum of the *quinquennial* rates by 5, we may recall that we obtain the total fertility of 1,000 women passing through all the ages of life without mortality (see p. 189). Multiplying this total fertility rate (per individual woman) by the inverse of the sex ratio (0.488), we find the gross reproduction rate (*R*).

population to another (a deviation of some five years at maximum), a mean value is chosen — 28 years, for example — from which the real value certainly cannot deviate by more than 2 or 3 years. At 28 years of age, the survival rate is equal to 0.907. Consequently, with this method, (1) on the basis of the data in Table 11.4a, we find $2,964 \times 0.907 = 2,688$ instead of 2,686; and (2) on the basis of the data in Table 11.4a, we find $594 \times 5 \times 0.907 = 2,694$ instead of 2,695.

The multiplication of the mean number of births per daughter (2.688 or 2.694, according to the computation) by the proportion of females (0.488) leads in both cases to $R_0 = 1.32$.

If, to effect these successive multiplications, the order of multiplication chosen is 0.488 and then 0.907 (instead of 0.907 and then 0.488), we would obtain, after the first multiplication, the gross reproduction rate, R (see note

TABLE 11.4a.   *France, 1949: Computation of Net Reproduction Rate*

Age*	Survivors ($l_0 = 1,000$) (1)	Fertility Rate (per 1,000) (2)	$(1) \times (2)$	Age*	Survivors ($l_0 = 1,000$) (1)	Fertility Rate (per 1,000) (2)	$(1) \times (2)$
15	928	1	1	35	892	93	83
16	927	4	4	36	889	83	74
17	926	14	13	37	887	72	64
18	925	34	31	38	884	62	55
19	923	66	61	39	882	52	46
20	922	104	96	40	879	41	36
21	920	143	132	41	876	32	28
22	918	172	158	42	873	24	21
23	917	188	172	43	870	17	15
24	915	197	180	44	867	10	9
25	913	197	180	45	864	6	5
26	911	191	174	46	860	3	3
27	909	185	168	47	856	1	1
28	907	173	157	48	852	1	1
29	905	162	147	49	848	—	—
30	903	151	136				
31	901	137	123				
32	898	128	115			2,964	2,686
33	896	117	105				
34	894	103	92		$R_0 = 2.686 \times 0.488 = 1.31$		

*Refers to exact ages of survivors and to ages reached during 1949 (or ages in calendar year differences) with respect to fertility rates.

TABLE 11.4b. *France, 1949. Computation of Net Reproduction Rate*

Age Group*	Survivors $(l_0 = 1,000)$ (1)	Fertility Rate (per 1,000) (2)	(3) $=$ $(1) \times (2)$	$(3) \times 5$
15–19	926	24.5	23	115
20–24	918	161	148	740
25–29	909	181	165	825
30–34	898	128	115	575
35–39	887	72.5	64	320
40–44	873	25	22	110
45–49	856	2	2	10
			594	2,695

$$R_0 = 2.695 \times 0.488 = 1.32$$

*Age Group refers to ages reached during 1949. The numbers of survivors are, as explained in the text, related to 17 years, 22 years, 27 years, 32 years, 37 years, 42 years, 47 years respectively.

14, p. 347). Consequently, we arrive at the following approximate formula:

$$R_0 = R \times l_{28 \, years} \qquad \text{(F)}$$

with $l_{28 \, years}$ indicating the female survival rate to 28 years; more precisely, we may recall, it refers to what would be the mean age of mothers at confinement if they were not subject to mortality, a mean age that has been taken here as equal to 28 years.

All the computations just presented in this paragraph, as well as formula (F), could have been applied to a real birth cohort, for whom one could have followed the mortality and fertility over time. This also would be the most satisfactory procedure of computation of the net rates in cohorts for whom it is not possible to follow all the members individually; and this is virtually always the case.

Gross Rates and Net Rates

The relationship between gross and net rates is shown by the approximate formula (F). R being an index of pure fertility, this formula, because of the mediating factor $l_{28 \, years}$, specifies the influence of mortality upon the replacement of generations.

It was always apparent a priori that, in the sense understood here, this replacement does not depend on the level of female mortality after 50 years of age. Formula (F) shows how, *in practice*, mortality is a factor only until the young adult ages. R defines the conditions of replacement if there is no mortality. At the level of the biological minimum of mortality, $l_{28\ years} = 0.987$, and R_0 is very close to R. With the mortality calculated by Duvillard ($e_0 = 28.8$ years), $l_{28\ years} = 0.452$ and R_0 is less than half of R.

High fertility—for example, $R = 3.5$ (on the average, 7 children per woman)—associated with high mortality—for example: $e_0 = 28.8$ years ($l_{28\ years} = 0.452$)—gives a net rate, R_0, equal to 1.58. The same fertility associated with minimum mortality for women ($e_0 = 78.2$ years and $l_{28\ years} = 0.987$) gives $R_0 = 3.45$.

Net Reproduction Rate and Lotka's Theoretical Results

On one hand, the intrinsic conditions of mortality and natality in a population lead to definition of the net reproduction rate, R_0, which determines to what extent the replacement of generations is assured. When referring to a period rate, R_0 indicates to what extent the generations will replace themselves in the population in question if the current mortality and fertility are maintained in the future.[15]

On the other hand, it is known, following Lotka, that a population subject to fixed conditions of mortality and fertility tends toward a stable state that does not depend upon the initial age composition, but only upon the mortality and fertility. We are thus led to associate with given levels of mortality and fertility the rate of natural increase, ρ, that would result in the limiting stable state, with ρ called the *intrinsic rate of natural increase* or the *Lotka rate.*

R_0 and ρ are two intrinsic indices independent of the age composition of the population for which they are computed. Since they fulfill the same function, it is not surprising that they are linked by a given relationship. Lotka established the following approximate functional relationship:

$$(1+\rho)^x = R_0, \tag{L}$$

x being the mean age of mothers at confinement, which can be taken again as equal to 28 years.[16]

According to formula (L), the net reproduction rate in the stable state represents the multiplying factor of the population during the mean interval separating two generations, the word here being understood as designating,

15. Also, before making prognoses about the future of the population studied, it is appropriate to see whether or not the prevailing conditions have any chance of continuing. We shall return to this point.

16. Strictly speaking, the reference is to the mean age of mothers having the age-specific fertility considered and belonging to the stationary population defined by the life table considered. This mean age is different from that defined in the presentation of equation (P), but the values are quite close, and it is not inappropriate to take x as also equal to 28 years.

on one hand, the generation of mothers (in the usual demographic sense) and on the other, the aggregate of daughters who are their children.

One obtains from formula (L),

$$(1+\rho) = \sqrt[x]{R_0}$$

and, consequently,

$$\rho = \sqrt[x]{R_0} - 1. \qquad (L')$$

We are then able to associate with given levels of mortality and fertility: (1) the net reproduction rate R_0; (2) the intrinsic rate of natural increase ρ, which is derived from knowledge of R_0 by means of formula (L').

Following this, we can verify that if $R_0 = 1$, then $\rho = 0$: the population evidently ends by becoming stationary, whatever the initial composition by age, if the generations can assure only their exact replacement.

TABLE 11.5. *Computation of the Intrinsic Rate of Natural Increase on the Basis of the Gross-Reproduction Rate*

$R_0 = 1.58$	$R_0 = 3.45$
$28 \log (1+\rho) = \log 1.58$	$28 \log (1+\rho) = \log 3.45$
$\log (1+\rho) = \dfrac{0.19,866}{28}$	$\log(1+\rho) = \dfrac{0.54,158}{28}$
$= 0.0070950$	$= 0.0193421$
$1+\rho = 1.017$	$1+\rho = 1.046$
$\rho = 17$ per 1,000	$\rho = 46$ per 1,000

We present in Table 11.5 two computations of ρ based on given values of R_0, deriving from the relationships:

high fertility ($R = 3.5$)
high mortality ($e_0 = 28.8$ years) $\Big\}$ $R_0 = 1.58$
high fertility ($R = 3.5$)
very low mortality ($e_0 = 78.2$ years $\Big\}$ $R_0 = 3.45$

In the first case, the highest observable crude birth rates are reached (on the order of 50 per 1,000); a life expectancy of 28.8 years corresponds to the level of mortality[17] of a population living in a primitive demographic régime, granting a crude death rate of at least 30 per 1,000. With these references to the observed situations, we find a rate of natural increase (50 per

17. Aside from catastrophes (wars, epidemics, famines).

1,000 − 30 per 1,000 = 20 per 1,000) on the order of magnitude of the rate computed in Table 11.5.

If, however, high fertility (b = 50 per 1,000) is associated with a life table with a very high expectation of life, the crude death rate will be very low, as the population is very young (because of the high level of natality) and subject to a minimum risk of mortality; the crude death rate will reach only a few points (per 1,000), and the rate of natural increase will be close to the crude birth rate, hence, close to 50 per 1,000. The computation of the Lotka rate gives 46 per 1,000.

The relationship between R_0 and ρ furnishes a procedure for construction of stable populations defined by the combination (the life table and the gross reproduction rate). With these data, we move in effect from R to R_0 by formula (F), and then from R_0 to ρ by formula (L′); we thus come to the construction of stable populations determined by the combination of life table and rate of natural increase, a problem we have learned to resolve in the preceding chapter. Thus we have (1) the French female life table for 1957, in which $l_{28} = 0.952$; and (2) the gross reproduction rate for the same year, $R = 1.32$.

It follows from these that $R_0 = 1.32 \times 0.952 = 1.26$; and by a computation of the same type as those carried out in Table 11.5, we find that $\rho = 8.3$ per 1,000. Thus, we are enabled to construct a stable population with the French female life table for 1957 and the annual rate of natural increase of $\rho = 8.3$ per 1,000.

However, the gross reproduction rate is a summary index of fertility, and different sets of age-specific fertility rates can correspond to identical gross reproduction rates. Our procedure assumes that, whatever the age-specific fertility rates, they are involved in the derivation of corresponding stable populations only through their sum R.[18] In fact, this is not always the case, but the variations in fertility by age for a given aggregate level (and defined by R), are not considerable, and we could assume that, in the construction of a stable population corresponding to a series of given age-specific fertility rates, it suffices to use the corresponding gross reproduction rate.

Limitations of the Net Reproduction Rate

The net reproduction rate is a very expressive index. The great popularity still enjoyed by this index originated in the fact that the period rate had predicted − between the two world wars − that the majority of Western countries were faced with approaching depopulation[19] (in France, since 1890, this rate has, in effect, been below unity), while the balance of births

18. Where their sum is multiplied by 5 if quinquennial rates are involved.
19. This depopulation occurred in France from 1935 to 1944.

and deaths remained positive. By succeeding in eliminating certain effects of age composition to reveal the full consequences of the continuation of given intrinsic conditions of fertility and mortality, the net reproduction rate appears in the eyes of certain persons as an excellent criterion of the demographic situation of a population.

In fact, a net reproduction rate must always be interpreted with caution and must always be only one of the indicators concerning the situation of a population.

1. It is as a cohort index that the net rate seems most incontestable inasmuch as in this case its definition appears natural and its computation free of theoretical difficulties.

For a given cohort, this rate has been defined as being equal to the mean number of daughters born (living) to a woman of the cohort in question, *taken from birth.* We effect, in short, the ratio between the number of girls at exact age 0 and the number of girls in the mothers' generation also at exact age 0. For a given girl, belonging to the generation for which we are studying the replacement conditions (a point represented by M in Figure 11.2), we associate the eventual number of her live born daughters (points represented by F_1, F_2, F_3 in Figure 11.2, where three live births are assumed).

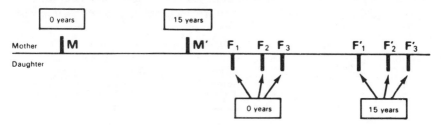

Figure 11.2

Now, it is also entirely legitimate to retain in the mothers' generation only the number reaching 15 years of age, the beginning of the period of procreation, and to count the daughters born when they, too, attain 15 years of age. This is what results in Figure 11.2 when the number of points representing daughters aged 15 years (at $F'_1 F'_2 F'_3$ in the case of a given mother) are related to the number of points representing eventual mothers also aged 15 years (M'). At the level of an entire generation of women, this results in substituting the mortality to which the daughters are subject in their childhood for the mortality to which their mothers were subject during their childhood. In a period of declining mortality this substitution is not a matter of indifference, since it results in replacing the conditions of mortality of a given period by the conditions obtaining 25 or 30 years later, and this for juvenile mortality, which is the most sensitive to variations.

Indeed, in France for the cohorts born in the nineteenth century, the difference between the two methods of computation is marked; it is particularly large for cohorts born in the second half of the century. Whereas the first computation suggests an absence of integral replacement since 1825, the second computation indicates a notable deficit beginning only from 1865.

2. The period net reproduction rate, for its part, requires certain precautions.

For this computation, it is necessary to draw upon period measures of mortality and of fertility. We have seen that one can better separate the conditions of period mortality when there is reason to suppose that the mortality level of a given year does not, for all practical purposes, reflect the level of previous years, and that, in addition, the period life table gives a correct measure of this mortality. Not so the case of fertility, where the level in a given year depends not only on the conditions of that year but also (and sometimes preponderantly) on the past history of the various cohorts involved in natality during the year studied. In addition, we have no measure that would permit properly separating that part of fertility due to past conditions, on the one hand, or to current conditions, on the other. Thus, age-specific fertility rates are currently used, and these are employed as we have already seen in the computation of R_0; the critical comments we have already made on the subject (see p. 190) are relevant again in connection with

TABLE 11.6. *Cohort Net Reproduction Rates*

Cohort	Rates at Birth	Rates at Age 15 years
1826–1830	0.95	0.98
1831–1835	0.95	0.98
1836–1840	0.97	0.99
1841–1845	0.98	1.00
1846–1850	0.97	1.01
1851–1855	0.95	1.00
1856–1860	0.93	1.00
1861–1865	0.91	0.98
1866–1870	0.87	0.95
1871–1875	0.82	0.92
1876–1880	0.83	0.92
1881–1885	0.78	0.86
1886–1890	0.74	0.83
1891–1895	0.70	0.79
1896–1900	0.69	0.77
1901–1905	0.76	0.84

Source: P. Depoid, *Reproduction nette en Europe depuis l'origine des statistiques de l'état civil.* Paris, 1941.

the values associated with the net rate. We have likewise indicated, in a sequence of comparable ideas (see p. 189), that the gross reproduction rate, defined and computed by reference to the age-specific fertility rates, in fact recapitulates a broader notion, and that alternative methods of computation of R, and therefore of R_0, can be conceived, leading to different values. Thus, in France in about 1950, the net rate was fixed at somewhat above 1.30 in a computation based on the age-specific rates and at about 1.20 in the computations based on parity progression ratios. In Belgium in about 1953, R_0 was greater than 1.03, or less than 0.95, depending on the computation procedure, which led to these disparate conclusions.

Thus, the period net rate, which is determined unambiguously and is a faithful reflection of the cohort net rate when demographic conditions are stable,[20] is an index that is uncertain and difficult to interpret in a period of change; it can be particularly misleading and difficult to determine in a disturbed period and can lead to erroneous conclusions.

Finally, it should not be forgotten that any prediction of the future of a population based on consideration of the net reproduction rate is based on the results of Lotka, according to whom the continuation of fixed conditions of fertility and mortality leads the population in question toward a corresponding stable state, at the end of an infinite amount of time; that is, the time in which the value of the annual rate of natural increase will reach accord with the net reproduction rate. Without doubt, the "infinite" delay is theoretical, and in practice, the necessary delay can be quite short. But often interest may be directed to this transitional period; this is notably the case in populations characterized by great increase, in which one may hope or plan that behavior vis-à-vis natality will change more or less rapidly.

Growth Potential of a Population

With the net reproduction rate (and Lotka intrinsic rate of natural increase) the demographers have sought to eliminate the undermining effects of age composition, in order to measure the consequences of the continuation of given intrinsic conditions of fertility and mortality on the growth of populations. Populations that were the subjects of such computations before World War II were most often those in Western countries, many of which were, in that period, on the brink of decline (let us recall that after 1935 France actually experienced depopulation). The net reproduction rate appeared as a predictive indicator that fixed the inevitable *long-term development*.

Present-day conditions direct us toward an inverse problem: after being freed from the effects of age composition that concealed the actual fate of

20. In the ordinary sense of the word.

Western Malthusian populations, demographers rediscovered the importance of such compositions in the study of populations of underdeveloped
countries. Such a population, which currently grows at an annual rate of
3 percent, could reduce its fertility instantaneously to the point of no longer
assuring the strict replacement of generations, but would still be assured
of substantial short-term increases.

Projective computations for underdeveloped populations with a rapid,
large-scale decline of fertility have been carried out,[21] and these have shown
clearly the importance of the inertia of demographic composition in short-
term change. For by its age composition, a population in a way hides a
potential for growth that the net reproduction rate, by its very construction,
does not take into account. So, with underdeveloped populations, we live
in the fear of an overly long continuation of present demographic conditions,
which constitute one of the obstacles to development. Here, the viewpoint
is the reverse of that which the demographers had before World War II
with respect to the Western countries. We are assured that in every instance —
that is, even if fertility were to diminish very markedly and instantaneously —
the underdeveloped populations would continue to grow in an appreciable
manner. One of the objects of demographic analysis can be precisely to
measure this growth potential that a given population owes to its composition,
and to attach to the population an index that, along with the net reproduction
rate, would show the two sets of factors governing its future.

We content ourselves here with referring to P. Vincent's classic study,[22]
which can furnish an index complementing the theory of Lotka, by separating
what the future development of a population, under the hypotheses of fixed
fertility and mortality, owes only to the initial age composition. For India,
with its age composition of 1921, this gives the index 1.44, which indicates
that if mortality and fertility of this country were to be stabilized suddenly
at a level leading the population to a stationary state,[23] there would nevertheless result, before this state was attained, a *transitional* population growth
of 44 percent. The French population, with an index of 1.03 in 1945, had only
a very slight growth potential, given its age composition, dulled by a century
and a half of declining natality.

The Case of Small Population Groups

The demographer must often study small aggregates, sometimes including

---

21. See, for example, the population projections presented in *Le Tiers Monde*, INED. Document
No. 27.
22. P. Vincent, "Potentiel d'accroissement d'une population," *Journal de la Societé de Statistique
de Paris*, Nos. 1–2, January–February 1945.
23. More exactly, this concerns a stationary structure of reference adopted by the author as a
base for computing his index.

only a few hundred individuals; this problem is generally posed for small geographic units, for example, the commune in France and the county in the United States and Great Britain.

A first difficulty arises when one wants to compute the most elementary demographic indices — the crude rates, for example — for these small groups. Wishing to measure the vital events (natality, mortality) whose frequency is low (on the order of 25 per 1,000 at maximum in France), we encounter random variations, sometimes considerable, from one year to the next and from one group to another. A crude birth rate or crude death rate computed for one year on populations of a few hundred or even of a few thousand inhabitants has but little meaning. A fortiori there would be no question of constructing age-specific rates or the summary indices that are derived from them. In the study of micro-populations we often find ourselves deprived of the use of indices habitually employed in demographic analysis.

However, until now in this chapter we have been particularly interested in intrinsic conditions of mortality and of natality to emphasize the intrinsic development capacities of populations. We have nevertheless recognized the importance of age compositions in short-term change; in particular, the rate of natural increase is reflected in these age compositions essentially by means of the crude death rate.

Now, in small groups the variation in composition can be very great, much greater than in national populations. This is due to the influence of the migratory factor, which, this time, plays a preponderant role in the movement of population and differentiates age compositions more than could be done by possible variations in the level of fertility. Also, in micropopulations generally, the future change by natural increase will be dominated for a long time by the initial age structure.

Besides, to the extent that the computation of crude rates in small groups is possible, these rates are most often the reflection of age composition rather than a genuine measure of fertility or of mortality; this is particularly true of the crude death rate, which, as we know, is more influenced by age composition of the population than is the crude birth rate. Because of this, when the population suffices (5 to 10,000 inhabitants at least), when computing a death rate we are in fact determining more an index of ageing than a genuine index of mortality. Figure 11.3 shows this; it relates to 90 French *départements*, each point concerning one of them and showing the relationship existing between the percentage "65 years and over" and the crude death rate: a clear correlation appears between these two indices, even while differences in real mortality are fairly great (to an extreme difference of more than five years in expectation of life), greater, no doubt, than those that can be observed within a group of small aggregates (for example, the rural communes of a *département*).

Consequently, not only are crude rates difficult to compute in small populations, they also have limited significance. We are led to give up their use in assessing the demographic situation of micropopulations (as we did the use of different rates by age or age groups, and of crude and net reproduction rates); only a careful examination of age composition remains.

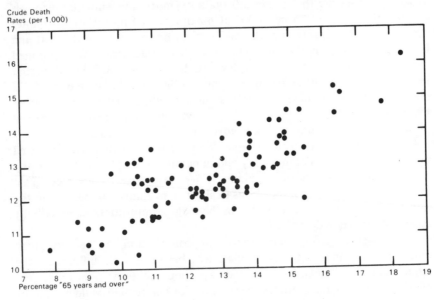

Figure 11.3

These age compositions result from vital events (natality, mortality) and from migrations that have occurred during the last 100 years; in fact, the oldest groups (over 80 years of age) have but little importance, and it is the history of the last seven or eight decades that almost completely determines the age pyramid.

Among the possible indices of age composition, some are already familiar; e.g., the index measuring the degree of ageing, which can be the percentage "60 years and over" or "65 years and over."

As an indicator of the overall level of fertility, we cannot hope to use the measure of relative size of the youngest age groups in the *entire* population. In the computation of the relationship

$$\frac{\text{children}}{\text{total population}}$$

the denominator is, in effect, weighted down by the aged population. Instead it is necessary to relate the children (let us say infants between birth and 5 years of age) to only the population in the reproductive ages; these groups are well defined only for the female population. To be certain of including practically all, it is necessary to take the age limits of 15 and 50 years; but fertility is very low after 40–45 years of age, and few mothers of children aged 0–4 years at a given time are then less than 20 years of age. Finally, it seems appropriate to take, as an index of fertility, the ratio

$$\frac{P_{0-4}}{F_{20-44}} \qquad \text{(F)}$$

P_{0-4} being the number of children aged 0 to 4 years in completed years at the date considered, and F_{20-44} being the number of women aged 20 to 44 years. We thus obtain a fairly sensitive indicator that accumulates the effects of marital fertility, illegitimate fertility, nuptiality, and the quasi-sum of infant mortality (and partially that of mortality between 1 and 5 years of age).

The use of "child-woman" ratios is not limited to micropopulations; they can usefully be employed in populations with deficient vital statistics and where *correct* censuses[24] can be carried out; moreover, after appropriate surveys,[25] they may refer to populations that are both small in size and without vital statistics, such as those that can be expected in underdeveloped countries.

Finally, the study of the age composition of adult age classes offers interesting indications about the demographic future of a population, notably when it is a question of a small group. These age classes include essentially economically active persons, and comparison of judiciously chosen groups can indicate in detail the condition of renewal of the labor force. The study of this latter point seems to us far removed from considerations of pure demography. This is slightly true if we consider national populations in which a short-lived decline of the potentially economically active population may not have important implications for general demographic conditions; but this is not the case in small human groupings located in delimited geographic areas and forming fairly complete economic units, for whom a decline (which is sometimes very great) of the labor force is often the beginning of a general demographic decline, leading sometimes to the complete disappearance of the population group.

24. In particular, it is important for us that young children be correctly registered, but in underdeveloped countries the gaps in this area are frequent.

25. We establish theoretically that the ratio (F) (or a similar ratio in which the age limits of the female population can be slightly different, for example 15 and 50 years), divided by the corresponding ratio (F′) in the stationary population associated with the life table of the population studied, provides a good approximation to R_0, the net reproduction rate: this is the *replacement index* proposed by the American demographer W. S. Thompson in 1920.

As a purely descriptive measure, let us indicate the use that there may be in forming the ratio

$$\frac{P_{15-39}}{P_{40-64}},$$

P designating the population of both sexes within the age limits (in complete years) indicated by the indices. When this relationship is below unity, the prognosis is poor, since in the population studied the renewal of the adult population (essentially, the economically active) is going poorly, the 25 youngest generations being less numerous than the 25 oldest generations that they must replace – after undergoing considerable mortality.

Part IV
POPULATION PROJECTIONS

CHAPTER TWELVE

Introduction to Projections

IT IS readily seen that we may apply some observed fertility and mortality patterns to a population whose present structure is known, and that this would permit determination of the new structure of the population for each of the years to come. Naturally, the closer the patterns chosen to represent the trend of fertility and mortality are to the actual trends, the closer the results of such computations to the real future situations.

But, under certain circumstances, such projective computations seek less to forecast than to evaluate the effects in the structure of a population, in 10 years or 20 years, or more, of certain demographic characteristics chosen for particular reasons. Thus, A. Sauvy calculated that if French fertility progressively attained the level observed in 1928 in the *département* of Seine, then the population of the country would diminish from 40,700,000 inhabitants in 1930 to 29,000,000 in 1980. Fearing the effects of the decline in natality, the author wished to show what the French population would become if fertility declined in the country as a whole to the level already reached in the Seine. Quite recently, in a somewhat different point of view, projective computations have shown that with an immediate and rapid decline of fertility the population of India would, nevertheless, increase by 40 percent in the next 20 years.[1]

Projections and Predictions

It is thus that certain projective computations have no predictive pretensions; they simply illustrate the effect on a population (on its total or its age and sex composition) of the operation of certain fertility and mortality

1. See *Le Tiers Monde*, INED Document No. 27. Projections of populations in the underdeveloped countries.

conditions,[2] chosen for specific purposes—whether they be hypotheses whose realization is doubtful or hypotheses singled out because they represent extreme situations between which the real situations seem certain to take place.

It is, moreover, in this manner that projective computations were introduced in demography only a few decades ago; we have just referred to Sauvy's computations for France, which illustrate a *conditional* forecast generally called a *projection*. But with the progress of demographic analysis, and in response to the needs of certain users, projective computations are now often conducted to furnish predictions about the future size and structure of the population.[3]

If the research goals are different, the operations present the same characteristics whether for a conditional forecast or for a restricted forecast.[4] It is necessary always (1) to make hypotheses about future levels of fertility and of mortality (and sometimes of nuptiality) and to choose indices of measurement correctly translating these hypotheses; (2) to proceed to the projective computations.

To have a clearer awareness of the concrete problems that are posed in this way, it is best to examine now the form in which a demographic projection is presented.

Presentation of Demographic Projections

Some projective computations that would be carried out on the total of a population can only be managed on the basis of indices of gross measurement (for example, the annual rate of natural increase), and would not permit arriving at actual forecasts, if these are felt to be necessary. In addition, the interest in projective computations (whatever their nature) rests especially on the details they give regarding the future distribution of the population by sex and age. Also, population projections are spoken of correctly only with respect to computations that go into these details. It is thus that projections carried out based on the estimate of the French male population by age as of January 1, 1956, are presented as shown in Table 12.1.

The situations being those of successive January 1sts, there is a cohort corresponding to each year of age. To follow a given cohort from year to year, it must be read on the diagonal, the passage from one January 1st to the following January 1st being marked by one year of ageing. It is

2. We can also try to make use of laws of migration. But our objective here is to study projections of changes in the population entailed by natural increase.

3. In some respects the restricted forecast remains conditional: we exclude wars, major crises, etc.

4. In what follows we shall usually use the word "projection," which refers to a conditional forecast or a restricted forecast.

thus that the 1955 male cohort, which was 0 years old on January 1, 1956, and totaled 398,600, was 1 year old on January 1, 1957, and totaled 394,100; it was 2 years old on January 1, 1958, and totaled 393,200; and so on. To carry out projective computations consists precisely in reducing the total of each of the cohorts from year to year according to an appropriate pattern of mortality, beginning with the number estimated for the initial date of the projection (here, January 1, 1956).

TABLE 12.1a. *France, Projections of the Male Population made as of January 1, 1956 (numbers in thousands on January 1)*

Age (in completed years)	1956		1957		1958	
	Birth Cohort	Number	Birth Cohort	Number	Birth Cohort	Number
0	1955	398.6	1956	390.1	1957	385.6
1	1954	394.5	1955	394.1	1956	386.0
2	1953	389.3	1954	393.6	1955	393.2
3	1952	400.5	1953	388.9	1954	393.2
4	1951	393.8	1952	400.2	1953	388.6
...	...	...	...	...	...	...
85	1870	20.0	1871	17.7	1872	21.6
86	1869	15.4	1870	15.7	1871	14.0
87	1868	9.5	1869	12.1	1870	12.1
88	1867	6.8	1868	7.6	1869	9.8
89	1866	5.7	1867	5.4	1868	6.1
...	...	...	...	...	...	...
All ages	1955 and earlier	20,948.0	1956 and earlier	21,073.1	1957 and earlier	21,194.7

A different problem is presented concerning cohorts that are not yet born at the initial date of the projection; that is, in this case, the 1956, 1957, 1958, etc., birth cohorts. It is necessary to estimate, on the one hand, their total number at birth and, on the other, their numbers surviving to successive January 1sts. Only these last numbers are shown in Table 12.1a, below the horizontal separation lines.

All this is read in a more meaningful way in a *Lexis* diagram (Figure 12.1a). The losses by mortality experienced by each cohort from one January 1st to the following January 1st are shown in the series of corresponding parallelograms. The newborn males of one year (400,000 in 1956, 395,000 in 1957) furnish the survivors at age 0 (in complete years) on the following January 1st; thus the 400,000 newborn of 1956 furnish 390,100 survivors on January 1, 1957, the mortality experienced resulting in the corresponding movement in Figure 12.1a; after which, the ageing from year to year occurs just as for cohorts already present at the beginning of the projection. The projections as we have presented them go into a maximum of details. To be carried out, they assume a perfect knowledge of the initial structure of the population; they find their usefulness in economic and social spheres of life, which require quite detailed attention to demographic developments (for example, when studying school or educational needs).

Sometimes, it suffices to carry out slightly more gross computations, either because at the beginning there is no access to the population by year of age (for example, if the quality of censuses is poor) or because the projective computations are to be utilized for studies not requiring very detailed demographic projections. In either case, we proceed generally to computation by quinquennial age groups, giving the situation for five-year intervals. The results are presented in Table 12.1a.

It must be observed that in working with quinquennial age groups, we are virtually obliged to make the projections only for five-year intervals.[5] It is, in effect, only at the end of a period of five years (or a multiple of five years) that a conventional quinquennial age group (5 to 9 years, for example) reappears in a conventional form (10 to 14 years at the end of five years, 15 to 19 years at the end of ten years, etc.). Doubtless, we could follow the groups from year to year first constituted, and study, for example, the group 5 to 9 years of age in 1956, which becomes the group 6 to 10 years in 1957, 7 to 11 years in 1958, 8 to 12 years in 1959, etc. But interest is directed more to the variations in the total age group fixed in time (the group 5 to 9 years old in 1956, 1957, 1958 …) than to the manner in which a given group of cohorts is reduced by mortality.

Naturally, with a given time period for projections, the material work is considerably lightened if it is carried out for quinquennial groups, the number of operations necessary being divided by $5 \times 5 = 25$.

The data of Table 12.1b are shown in the *Lexis* diagram in Figure 12.1b. In this diagram are shown the 1,947,000 male births of the period 1956–1960 and the 1,813,000 births of the period 1961–1965.

Decomposition of a Projective Computation

Following the analysis we have just carried out, we see that a projective computation results from an integrated succession of three operations: (1) to compute the survivors on each January 1st of the persons present at the beginning of the projection (computation of survivors); (2) to compute

─────────────

5. Similarly, working with decennial groups, the projections are carried out for 10-year intervals.

TABLE 12.1b. *France, Projection of the Male Population Made as of January 1, 1956 (Numbers in thousands on January 1)*

Age (in Completed Years)	1956		1961		1966	
	Cohorts	Number	Cohorts	Number	Cohorts	Number
0– 4	1955–1951	1,976.7	1960–1956	1,883.7	1965–1961	1,765.5
5– 9	1950–1946	2,070.7	1955–1951	1,965.9	1960–1956	1,876.7
10–14	1945–1941	1,409.0	1950–1946	2,066.5	1955–1951	1,963.7
85–89	1870–1866	57.4	1875–1871	66.9	1880–1876	66.0
All Ages	1955 and earlier	20,948.0	1960 and earlier	21,527.9	1965 and earlier	21,974.7

the births in each year by reference to women of child-bearing ages (pro-jections of births); (3) to compute the survivors, on each January 1, of the newborn computed in (2) (computation of survivors).

The various methods that permit carrying out the operations indicated in (1) and in (3) (computation of survivors) differ little from each other. By contrast, operation (2) (projection of births) can be carried out with very diverse procedures; in particular, although the different techniques used all involve—at least implicitly—the total number of women in the reproductive ages, certain of these methods lead to calculating separately the projections of legitimate births and the projections of illegitimate births; in such cases, it is necessary first to compute some projections of marriages, which will intervene in the computation of the projection of legitimate births.

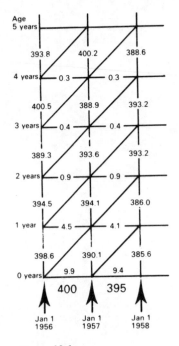 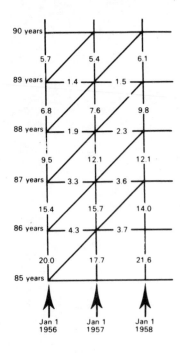

Figure 12.1a

Other Types of Projections

The projective computations that we now present furnish descriptions of the population by age and sex. These are surely the most important charac-teristics of population structure, and projections based upon these distinc-tions and classifications may be used for many purposes. But many other

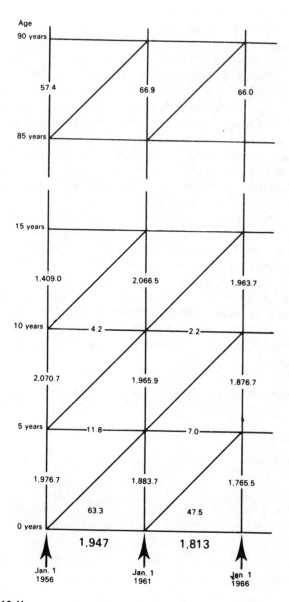

Figure 12.1b

types of composition may be conceived according to which we might wish to carry out projective computations. Let us cite, for example, a projective computation that would be carried out in distinguishing, at the same time, sex, age, and marital status. On the other hand, we may seek to carry out computations in which the individual would not be a basic unit. The unit might be the family (the father, the mother – to the extent that they survive – and the surviving children below a certain age), or the household (the group of persons living in the same dwelling unit). Clearly it would be desirable to attach to different individuals certain interesting characteristics, and, most important, age. We might thus imagine projections of households by the age of the head of the household and by the size of the household. The attempts in this sphere are very few, and the methodology is still uncertain. We shall not examine here the problems thus raised and the solutions – partial – that have been proposed.

Finally, population projections may concern geographic areas in which migratory movements have a decisive influence upon demographic development.[6] This is the case in urban areas, and any projection of the population of the city that would be a forecast cannot hope to free itself of hypotheses concerning migration. As has already been stated, we leave aside these projections involving migrations and content ourselves with examining how projections of natural increase and resulting population change are set up. Moreover, the latter always constitute an indispensable step in any projective computation that wishes to take account of physical movements of individuals.

6. This is always the case to some extent; however, at the level of the small interior area of a national territory, the migratory movements generally have a much greater relative importance than on the level of the total country.

CHAPTER THIRTEEN

Computation of Survivors

ALL population projections require the computations of survivors. Sometimes, moreover, the entire projection is reduced to this computation, because the cohorts that are of interest are all already born at the base date of the projections. This is the case in short-term projections of the school-age population and in fairly long-term projections (say, 15 years) of the population in economically active age groups.

This is a sure and straightforward procedure, for the rather strong stability of mortality patterns precludes the possibility of large errors, and the measurement indices used are simple and always meaningful. At ages at which mortality is quite low (from 5 to 35 years of age, for example), the risks of errors become insignificant, there being very little human attrition due to mortality.[1]

Introduction to the Chapter

After having presented the projective mortality probability, which is the specific index involved in all computations of survivors, we shall consider in a general manner the problem of determining the level of mortality in a projective computation.

In practice, the projective mortality probabilities to be applied will usually derive from the conversion of data given in a life table and the extrapolation of the values obtained; we give details on how these conversions and these extrapolations are carried out. Finally, we examine the model life tables of the United Nations in their form adapted for computation of survivors.

1. At least in France.

The Projective Mortality Probability

It is the projective mortality probability that is involved (more or less explicitly according to the circumstances) in all computations of survivors. We have defined it on p. 146. Let us take again the examples of Tables 12.1a and 12.1b on pp. 365 and 367, limiting ourselves to examining the changes in the totals taking place among the youngest cohorts respectively in 1956 and during the period 1956–1960 (Figures 13.1a and 13.1b).

According to Figure 13.1a, the totals at ages 1 year and 2 years (in complete years) on January 1, 1957, are derivable from the totals at ages 0 years and 1 year as of January 1, 1956, by subtracting, respectively, 4,500 and 900

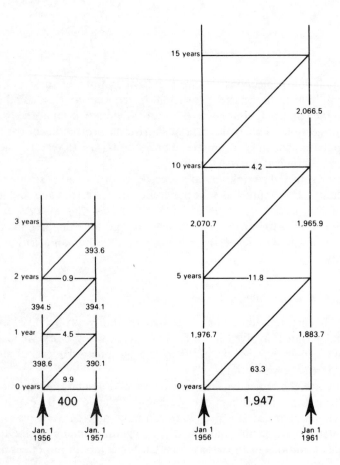

Figure 13.1a.   *Figure 13.1b.*

individuals. That is to say, then, that:

$$\frac{4,500}{398,600} = 113 \text{ per } 10,000 \text{ individuals aged 1 complete year on January 1,}$$

1956 and

$$\frac{900}{394,500} = 23 \text{ per } 10,000 \text{ individuals aged 1 complete year on January 1, 1956}$$

disappear in the course of 1956.

It is the *previous choice of probabilities* (which are precisely the projective probabilities)[2] that permits, by an inverse process, estimating the 4,500 and 900 deaths in the two generations considered and obtaining by subtraction the survivors on January 1, 1957.

Similarly, following Figure 13.1b, the previous choice of quinquennial projective probabilities (see note 2)

$$60 \text{ per } 10,000 = \frac{11,800}{1,976,700}$$

and

$$20 \text{ per } 10,000 = \frac{4,200}{2,070,700}$$

permits the estimation of 11,800 and 4,200 deaths between January 1, 1956, and January 1, 1961, in the cohort groups of 1951–1955 and 1946–1950.[3]

Similarly (Figure 13.1), among the 400,000 newborn anticipated for 1956, there were 9,900/400,000 = 247 per 10,000 deaths prior to January 1, 1957, and among the 1,947,000 newborn anticipated for the period 1956–1960, there were 63,300/1,947,000 = 325 per 10,000 deaths prior to January 1, 1961.

It may still be convenient to call these two latter quotients projective probabilities of mortality, observing, however, that in the present case the definition is different, since it refers to indices permitting the movement — of a given cohort or group of cohorts — from the total number at birth to a total number of survivors.

The projective probability, then, constitutes the type of index that allows the application of a given mortality in a population, in order to determine

2. Therefore, we define here *annual* projective probabilities. We could as well define probabilities covering several years, e.g., quinquennial probabilities, for date D, giving the number per 10,000 persons of a cohort or group of cohorts dying before the date $D + 5$. In the section that follows we use quinquennial projective probabilities for five-cohort groups.

3. In computing the projective probabilities of surviving from 85 years to 86 years, from 86 to 87 years, etc., with the data of Table 12.1a (and Figure 12.1a), we will record theoretically impossible variations. In fact, these recorded anomalies are slight and result from approximations (from rounding, for example) carried out in the computation of survivors.

the deaths in the different cohorts or groups of cohorts and, by subtraction, to deduce the survivors at projected dates. If we do not make the computation of deaths explicit, it constitutes a useless intermediate stage. Knowing the projective mortality probability that applies to a given cohort, we may, in effect, apply the complement of this probability to the total of the cohort and thus directly obtain the number of survivors. For example, knowing that the total of the group aged 1 year on January 1, 1956, is 394,500 and that it is necessarily subject to the annual projective mortality probability of 23 per 10,000, we deduce that the proportion surviving will be

$$1 - 23 \text{ per } 10,000 = 9,977 \text{ per } 10,000$$

or, for the total of the cohort,

$$394,500 \times 0.9977 = 393,593 \text{ survivors}$$

(rounded to 393,600) on January 1, 1957 (aged 2 complete years).

The determination of projective probabilities that can be properly applied to a given population to "age" that population is only a matter of computation technique; first of all, it is necessary to choose the mortality pattern that will be used, and its future change.

Present Level and Future Change of Mortality

Fairly often the current level[4] of mortality in the population to be projected is known in sufficient detail from a recent life table or from the sequence of age-specific rates for recent years. But rather frequently it happens that there is no access to any detailed data permitting definite determination of the present pattern of mortality in the population studied.

For example, we may have reliable information about the mortality of a given human group without being able to say anything—in the absence of appropriate measures—about the mortality of subpopulations deriving from this group. This is the case in the French *départements*, where the different levels of mortality are measured in a rather summary manner and for periods quite distant from one another.

On the other hand, there are serious difficulties in measuring mortality in groups with small totals, which may happen to be the subject of projective computations, and we will often be led to impute to them plausible levels of mortality suggested by comparisons with other, better-studied, groups. This position will be taken when it is a question of having to "age" populations in which mortality has not been measured for a long time, or has been poorly measured, or, indeed, has never been measured, as is the case in the majority of underdeveloped populations.

4. That is, the initial date for computing the projections.

It is not possible to give, in a general form, the procedures for arriving at a reasonable choice of initial mortality in similar cases. It will be necessary to be guided by historical, sociological, economic, and cultural analogies to obtain an acceptable indication of the level of mortality appropriate in the absence of a fully satisfactory estimate.

Another more fundamental and entirely general uncertainty presents itself: what will be the future development of mortality for a given population?

As we have already shown, all projective computations are not forecasts, and hypotheses about future mortality need not necessarily constitute actual predictions. For example, it is possible to make use, of hypotheses representing a future stability of mortality that, contrasted with the current trend toward a world-wide decline, certainly constitutes an extreme hypothesis of the future that, all other things being equal, underestimates, the actual future growth of populations:[5] we can see the importance of minimal projections of this nature.

But every time that the demographer is obliged to make *predictions*, there is a question about the *most probable* future development of mortality. In this case, the hypothesis of stability does not retain its previous weight; the determination with which mortality is universally fought and the success of the methods used against it lead to the study of the pace of future declines and, eventually, to the determination of how much can be achieved.

For the mortality (by age) of a population, it is customary to take the continuation of a previously observed rate of decline as the possible pace of the decline. When the past trend is not easy to specify, we generally make use of the experience of a neighboring country in which mortality conditions are comparable, but which is somewhat advanced. Thus, for French forecasts made in 1954 with mortality data up to 1952, the experience of the Netherlands (from 1947 to 1952) was useful for carrying out extrapolations; these extrapolations were carried out graphically in Figure 13.2. The use of semi-logarithmic paper is particularly appropriate, for on such paper a constant annual percentage decline of a rate or probability is expressed by a straight line of the representative points; but real changes are frequently changes with an obviously constant *relative* decline, so that in this case the extrapolation is reduced to the extension of a trend line. Let us observe that in Figure 13.2 the aggregate of all points of the same age group, whether for France or for the Netherlands, are well fitted to the same straight line.

It is tempting to criticize this method of forecasting mortality, as it is based on somewhat synthetic analyses and employs a quite global extrapolation procedure. Besides, whatever the care that is taken in measuring

---

5. We exaggerate the declines in cases in which there would be depopulation in any case.

recent trends, is there not a risk of possible sudden future acceleration in progress, associated with unforeseeable changes in the state of science?[6] Might not there be, during the coming decades, some major scientific discovery to upset the mortality conditions; and is it not possible to go so far as to issue a prognosis of the mortality of the most backward countries, since these countries, benefitting from exterior technical resources and aids, are probably on the way to progressing (or indeed have already done so) at a more rapid pace than did the Western countries previously?

These questions are pertinent, and the demographer has no answer for certain questions that arise when it is necessary to choose appropriate hypotheses that will permit making projections of survivors. However, let us not overestimate the importance of the objections that can be made. No doubt, the demographer must ignore the unforeseeable, for example, the possible cure for cancer; but is it necessary to resolve to reject every projective computation that may fail to anticipate some unusual contingencies, whose outcome no one is able to foresee?

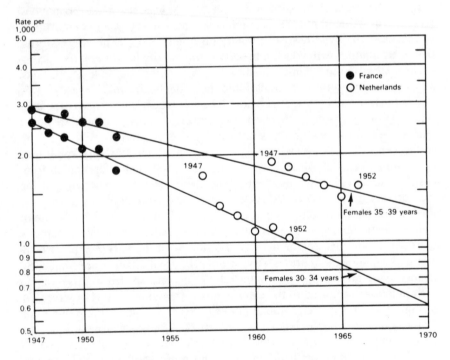

Figure 13.2.   Trend of Mortality.

6. And we do not speak of possible and brutal changes in economic and, especially, political conditions (wars, for example).

Rather than being resigned to ignoring entirely the future of a population, is it not preferable to propose approximate computations making use of somewhat uncertain mortality patterns? Moreover, the margin of uncertainty is often much less than some people suppose, since in certain populations the risk of mortality has become quite low for large intervals of life.

Projective Probabilities and the Life Table

Projective probabilities, not being part of the usual stock of descriptive indices of mortality, are never included in the detailed data contained in statistical collections. So, when one wants to undertake the computation of survivors, it is necessary — in the most favorable cases[7] — to compute probabilities for the most recent years, in order to decide which values to retain for the initial computations and which future trends to adopt.

This may involve a direct computation, which is carried out on the basis of appropriate death statistics in accordance with data given previously (see p. 144), or an indirect computation, requiring the conversion of available detailed data into sequences of equivalent projective probabilities. This problem of conversion typically concerns life table probabilities; generally it is posed as follows: how should a mortality level given by a life table be used in the computation of survivors?

We shall base all our explanations on the data of the 1952–1956 French life table, which may be adopted to guide the beginning of projective computations concerning France as of 1955 or even 1960.[8] In what follows, we shall be concerned only with females.

According to this table, we know the frequencies of deaths from each birthday to the following birthday (mortality probabilities). Let us concern ourselves with two periods of life: the very earliest years, and the end of the adult ages, around 50 to 55 years. The corresponding extracts of the table are reproduced in Table 13.1a; they are limited to probabilities and survivors.

These probabilities, rounded off and expressed per 10,000, are shown in Figures 13.3a and 13.3b; by definition, they measure the frequency of deaths along the life lines plotted by these figures. Now they must be used for the aggregate of life lines going, for example, from *AB* to *A'B'* (Figure 13.3a).

The simplest idea is to assume that the overall mortality risk during

---

7. These are those in which a current and sufficiently refined measure of mortality is possible. In the other cases we are reduced to a more or less crude estimate on the basis of which projective probabilities are determined.

8. With the possible reservation, in this last case, that some improvements may occur in infant mortality, where annual fluctuations are fairly sizable.

TABLE 13.1a. *Life Table for France (Females) 1952–1956*

Age x	Mortality Probability q_x (per 1,000)	Survivors l_x	Age x	Mortality Probability q_x (per 1,000)	Survivors l_x
0	31.41	100,000	50	5.72	89,412
1	4.00	96,859	51	6.15	88,901
2	1.50	96,472	52	6.60	88,354
3	0.91	96,327	53	7.10	87,771
4	0.69	96,239	54	7.60	87,148
5	0.54	96,173	55	8.20	86,486
6	0.45	96,121	56	8.90	85,777
...	...	...	...	...	...

one year of age for the total number of persons – who are, initially, for example, between 0 and 1 year of age – is equal to the arithmetic mean of the probabilities q_0 and q_1, which measure rigorously the risks run by persons who are initially exactly 0 years of age (at the instant of their births) and who are 1 year of age (Figure 13.3a: the movement from A to A' and from B to B); this involves the risks run by the youngest and the oldest persons in the group. We thus adopt as a projective probability for the group aged 0 years.

$$q_0' = \frac{q_0 + q_1}{2}$$

and similarly,

$$q_1' = \frac{q_0 + q_1}{2}$$

$$q_{50}' = \frac{q_{50} + q_{51}}{2}.$$

In this way, one goes from the data in Figure 13.3, taken from the life table, to those in Figure 13.4, which will permit the computation of survivors.[9]

From this approximation it is possible to give the following interpretation. It is assumed that everything occurs as if the progress of the cohort 50 years old on January 1, A for example, shown in the parallelogram

9. Note that the projective probability for the aggregate of individuals aged x (in complete years) is denoted q_x'; consequently, we assume that

$$q_x' = \frac{q_x + q_{x-1}}{2}$$

PP'QQ' (Figure 13.3b) were statistically equivalent to the progress along the line *uu'* (equidistant from the upper and lower diagonal bounds of the parallelogram), which represents the life line of persons *exactly* 50.5 years of age on January 1, *A*. We assume also that the mortality probability of these persons from one January 1st to the next is the arithmetic mean of the conventional probabilities at the neighboring rounded ages.

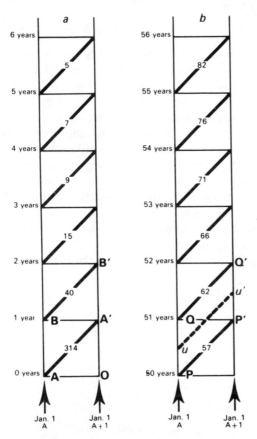

Figure 13.3

In this way, a total of 385,877 girls of the group aged 0 years on January 1, A^{10} will be reduced by mortality as of January 1 $(A+1)$ by:

$$385,877 \times \frac{177}{10,000} = 6,830 \text{ units.}$$

10. Meaning the estimated number of girls in France aged 0 years on January 1, 1957.

Accordingly, the number of survivors at the latter date will be

$$385,877 - 6,830 = 379,057 \text{ girls.}$$

As we have already observed, if we are not explicitly interested in the number of deaths, it is possible to work directly with the complement of the projective probabilities $(1 - 177 \text{ per } 10,000 = 0.9823)$, to obtain the total number of survivors:

$$385,877 \times 0.9823 = 379,057.$$

We thus derive the projective mortality probabilities by linear interpolation of the bounding regular mortality probabilities. In fact, the projective probability depends, at the same time, on the age composition of the group considered and on mortality variations by age. Thus, if the group aged 0 years includes a majority of persons closer to the date of their first birthday than to their birth (because of irregularities in the distribution in time of the corresponding births), all other things being equal, the mortality of the group will be lower. The variations that introduce such disequilibria will be accentuated by the nonlinear variations in mortality by age. Accordingly, we feel that the estimates of projective probabilities we have just derived are only approximate.

We might seek to interpolate not on the probabilities but on the survivors. In this case, we would treat each age category as belonging to a stationary population, the one defined by the life table used. Thus (Figure 13.3a):

the total at AB is taken equal to

$$\frac{l_0 + l_1}{2} = L_0,$$

and the total at $A'B'$ is taken as equal to

$$\frac{l_1 + l_2}{2} = L_2.$$

In the present case

$$L_0 = \frac{l_0 + l_1}{2} = \frac{100,000 + 96,859}{2} = 98,430.$$

$$L_1 = \frac{l_1 + l_2}{2} = \frac{96,859 + 96,472}{2} = 96,666.$$

Hence the probability of survival from age 0 complete years to age 1 complete year is

$$\frac{96,666}{98,430} = \frac{L_1}{L_0} = 0.9821.$$

More generally, using the entries of the life table stationary population, L_x, it is possible to estimate the probability of survival from age x complete years to age $x+k$ complete years by the ratio:

$$\frac{L_{x+k}}{L_x}.$$

The loss by mortality is estimated at

$$98,430 - 96,666 = 1,764.$$

This gives, as an estimate of the projective probability,

$$q'_0 = \frac{1,764}{98,430} = 179 \text{ per } 10,000,$$

instead of 177 per 10,000 in the first computation.

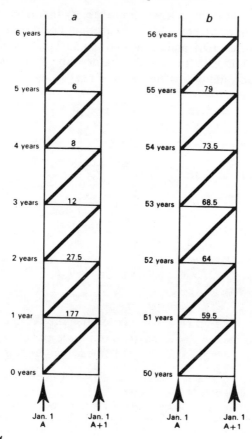

Figure 13.4

But usually the two methods give the same result (at least when limited to expressing the probabilities per 10,000); it is necessary to reach the highest ages (more than 80 years) to record deviations, which are very small even then. Accordingly, we shall content ourselves with the computation by interpolation on conventional mortality probabilities.

There remains one problem to resolve: how to move from the number of newborn of one year (at AO in Figure 13.3a) to the total number of survivors on the following January 1st (at OA'). We may again seek to take the arithmetic mean of the probability, q_0, which describes the losses by mortality in the course of the movement from A to A', and of the probability (equal to zero) that corresponds to that obtaining at 0 years; and we then find

$$q'_B = \frac{314}{2} = 157 \text{ per } 10,000,$$

the index recalling that this refers to a probability that is applied beginning with birth.[11] In short, we obviously can partition the mortality risks equally between the triangles AOA' and ABA', but we know that the risks are higher the younger the child is.[12] It would then be desirable to arrive at a partition of q_0 that takes account of this inequality of risks by age.

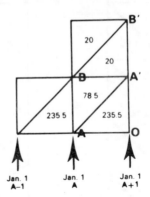

Figure 13.5

We can again bring up what was said on this subject in connection with the study of the measure of infant mortality (see p. 56) and assume that 2/3 or 3/4 of infant deaths occur at AOA' (the actual proportion is generally

11. Since we pass from the newborn to the group aged 0 complete years, the notation adopted is not completely consistent with the preceding one.

12. In a general way, there are always age variations in mortality (and variations in the totals) so that every equal distribution of deaths between two contiguous triangles of a *Lexis* diagram is erroneous. But it is between ages 0 and 1 years that the error so introduced is the greatest, to the extent that such an approximation is inadmissible.

located between these two extremes). Adopting the fraction 3/4, we arrive at the distribution of Figure 13.5.[13] We see that the values of q'_B and q'_0 are modified:

$q'_B = 235.5$ per 10,000.
$q'_0 = 78.5$ per $10,000 + 20$ per $10,000 = 98.5$ per 10,000.

The preceding computations rest on the knowledge of a complete life table; they assume, among other things, that the computations of survivors are being carried out by single years of age.

But frequently it is necessary to carry out computations for age groups (usually quinquennial); in such a case, it is no longer absolutely necessary to use a complete life table.[14] The problem then becomes making use of the data of an abridged table in calculating survivors by age groups. We shall illustrate the method to follow in Table 13.1b, using the abridged table deduced from the complete female French life table for 1952–1956.

The data shown in the diagrams of Figures 13.6a and 13.6b are the probabilities $_5q_x$ of Table 13.1a expressed in round numbers per 10,000. The analogy with Figures 13.3a and 13.3b is complete, so that the same type of approximations can be carried out. We can thus adopt as a projective probability $_5q'_0$, measuring mortality among 10,000 (or 1,000 or 100,000)

TABLE 13.1b. *Abridged Life Table for France (Females) 1952–1956*

Age x	Mortality Probability $_5q_x$ *(per 1,000)*	Survivors l_x	Age x	Mortality Probability $_5q_x$ *(per 1,000)*	Survivors l_x
0	38.27	100,000	50	32.72	89,412
5	2.05	96,173	55	47.37	86,486
10	1.76	95,976	60	71.10	82,389
15	2.85	95,807	65	113.59	76,531
20	4.19	95,534	70	189.13	67,838
...	...	...	...	...	...

13. In this diagram we are implicitly assuming that mortality has been constant from one year to the next. If this has not been the case, it will be appropriate to change the numbers accordingly. On the other hand, 78.5 per 1,000 does not represent the probability of going from AB to BA', but, rather, the probability related to 10,000 newborn. But here the distinction between these two very close quantities is superfluous.

14. When the initial population is known only by five-year age groups, it can be said that the detail of the year-by-year table constitutes an embarrassing datum that, in any case, is best condensed.

persons in the age group 0–4 years (in complete years) until this group be-comes the age group 5–9 years (in complete years),[15] the arithmetic mean

$$_5q'_0 = \frac{_5q_0 + _5q_5}{2},$$

and similarly,

$$_5q'_5 = \frac{_5q_5 + _5q_{10}}{2}$$

$$\dots\dots\dots\dots$$

$$_5q'_{50} = \frac{_5q_{50} + _5q_{55}}{2}.$$

It is in this way that the projective probabilities shown in Figures 13.7a and 13.7b have been obtained. From there we deduce that the total of 1,910,822 girls in the group 0–4 years old on January 1, A,[16] will be reduced by mortality, by January 1 $(A + 5)$, by

$$1,910,822 \times \frac{202}{10,000} = 38,599 \text{ units.}$$

At the latter date, the number of survivors will be:

$$1,910,822 - 38,599 = 1,872,223 \text{ girls.}$$

If we are interested only in the number of survivors, it suffices to multiply:

$$1,910,822 \times \left(1 - \frac{202}{10,000}\right)$$

We can also seek to carry out the interpolation on the number of survivors and not on the probabilities, treating each age group as belonging to a stationary population — the one defined by the life table used. In this way the population aged 0–4 years $(_5L_0)$ is taken equal to

$$_5L_0 = \frac{l_0 + l_5}{2} \times 5$$

15. Let us observe that it is thus a *quinquennial* probability (with respect to the time period covered). It is the index 5, placed at the bottom left side, that indicates that reference is to a five-year period of observation (a notation analogous to that used with conventional mortality probabilities and life table functions).

16. Referring, in our numerical example, to the estimated number of girls in France aged 0–4 years on January 1, 1957.

and similarly,

$$_5L_5 = \frac{l_5 + l_{10}}{2} \times 5.^{17}$$

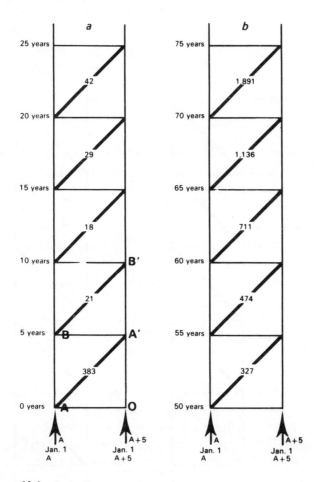

Figure 13.6

17. If we have the complete series $[l_x]$, we may obtain a better approximation by the formulas:

$$_5L_0 = \frac{l_0}{2} + l_1 + l_2 + l_3 + l_4 + \frac{l_5}{2};$$

$$_5L_5 = \frac{l_5}{2} + l_6 + l_7 + l_8 + l_9 + \frac{l_{10}}{2}.$$

In this way

$$_5L_0 = 490,430; \quad _5L_5 = 480,375.$$

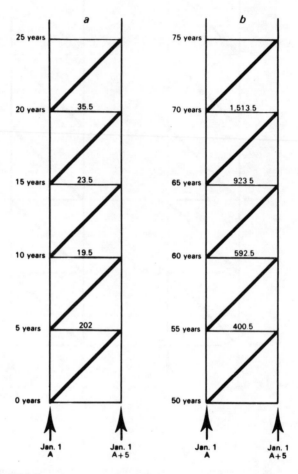

Figure 13.7

This corresponds to

$$_5q_0' = 1 - \frac{480{,}375}{490{,}430} = 209 \text{ per } 10{,}000 = 1 - \frac{_5L_5}{_5L_0}$$

instead of 202 per 10,000 as given by the other method.

The deviation this time is more noticeable; it occurs for all ages. However, it still remains negligible from 5 to about 60 years of age; but between 70–74 and 75–79 years (for example) the difference is 21 per 10,000 (1,513 per 10,000 in one computation and 1,491 in the other).

Neither of the two methods is satisfactory for describing the passage from AB to $A'B'$ and, even less, that from AO to OA' (see Figure 13.6); the rapid drop in mortality makes the preceding methods of interpolation (which held for probabilities or for survivors) considerably overestimate, in general,[18] the mortality that the group 0–4 years of age must experience. Correspondingly, they underestimate the mortality of the group of newborn in a quinquennial period during this period. Any more correct estimation procedure must be based on a separation of mortality between 0 and 10 years of age. Since the mortality table by year of age is not always available, it is sometimes necessary to estimate the elements that are absent.

Isolating infant mortality from the total mortality for 0 to 5 years (whether the table being used permits this distinction or whether various methods are necessary to carry out the separation), considerable improvement of the results is obtained. Let us carry out, for example, a linear interpolation involving l_0, l_1, l_5, l_{10} (Figure 13.8). According to the French female life table for 1952–1956,

$$l_0 = 10{,}000, \ l_1 = 96{,}859, \ l_5 = 96{,}173, \ l_{10} = 95{,}976.$$

With the datum for l_1, the estimation of $_5L_0$ in the stationary population is much more precise;

$$_5L_0 = \frac{l_0 + l_1}{2} + \frac{l_1 + l_5}{2} \times 4 = L_0 + {_4L_1}.$$

Here this equals:

$$\frac{100{,}000 + 96{,}859}{2} + \frac{96{,}859 + 96{,}173}{2} \times 4 = 484{,}494.$$

$_5L_5$ does not change:

$$_5L_5 = \frac{l_5 + l_{10}}{2} \times 5 = \frac{96{,}173 + 95{,}976}{2} \times 5 = 480{,}373.$$

---

18. So that there will be only a slight overestimate, or even no overestimate, the annual number of births must be in a rapid decline.

We derive from this:

$$_5q'_B = \frac{15,506}{500,000} = 310 \text{ per } 10,000.^{19}$$

$$_5q'_0 = \frac{4,121}{484,494} = 85 \text{ per } 10,000 \text{ (instead of 202!)}.$$

We present in Table 13.2 a projection of the French female population for January 1, 1962, based on the number by age groups as of January 1, 1957.

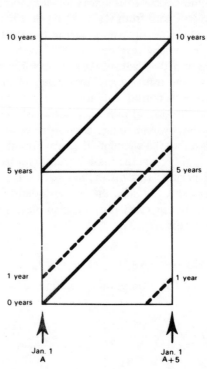

Figure 13.8

The mortality applied is that of 1952–1956, which has been used to present the methods for computing projective probabilities; the latter probabilities were computed by interpolation on regular mortality probabilities (see the computations of Table 13.1a), except for $_5q'_B$ and $_5q'_0$, which were determined

19. The probability $_5q'_B$ thus defines the passage of newborn through the group aged 0–4 complete years; consequently, the notation adopted here is not entirely consistent with the preceding one.

as we have shown above. The number of female births for the period 1957 to 1962 was taken as equal to 1,980,000, without our having explained, for the time being, the manner in which this estimate was obtained.

To understand Table 13.2 completely, it is necessary to remember that the figures in the last column (January 1, 1962) are dropped down one line relative to the figures in the two other columns, from which they are derived.

Future Change of Projective Probabilities

We have already presented, from a general point of view, the problem of determining the future development of mortality that is to be used in a projective computation. It is important to detail this further, with concrete examples.

TABLE 13.2. *France, Projected Female Population*

Age Group	Population, Jan. 1, 1957 (thousands)	Projective Mortality Probability (per 10,000)	Deaths, Jan. 1, 1957– Jan. 1, 1962 (in thousands)	Projected Population, Jan. 1, 1962 (in thousands)
Births[a]	1,980.0	*310*	61.4	
0–4	1,910.8	*85*	16.2	1,918.6
5–9	1,996.1	*19*	3.8	1,894.6
10–14	1,510.3	*24*	3.6	1,992.3
15–19	1,339.3	*35*	4.7	1,506.7
20–24	1,497.2	*50*	7.5	1,334.6
25–29	1,573.6	*67*	10.5	1,489.7
30–34	1,592.0	*92*	14.6	1,563.1
35–39	1,233.8	*128*	15.8	1,577.4
40–44	1,246.8	*202*	25.2	1,218.0
45–49	1,495.4	*290*	43.4	1,221.6
50–54	1,488.1	*401*	59.7	1,452.0
55–59	1,385.4	*592*	82.0	1,428.4
60–64	1,250.4	*924*	115.5	1,303.4
65–69	1,077.6	*1,513*	163.0	1,134.9
70–74	899.1	*2,514*	226.0	914.6
75–79	635.6	*3,945*	250.7	673.1
80–84	371.7	*5,699*	211.8	384.9
85–89	130.0	*7,530*	97.9	159.9
90–94	33.6	*8,974*	30.2	32.1
95–99	5.2[b]		5.2	3.4
All ages	22,672.0		1,387.3	23,203.3

[a]Births in the 1957–1961 period and deaths to newborn of this group during the same period ($_5q'_n = 310$ per 10,000).
[b]All persons are assumed to die before reaching 100 years.

The usual procedure of extrapolation of recent trends was shown on p. 375 for the most appropriate hypothesis, that in which projective mortality probabilities can be computed at different ages for the last years preceding the projections. We have seen that this extrapolation can be guided by the experience of other populations, in which mortality is lower (see Figure 13.2).

But quite often the projective probabilities will be determined indirectly, generally, as we have explained, by treatment of the conventional mortality probabilities in a recent life table. In this case, it is rare for the study of the last available mortality tables to allow definition of a trend, for the periodicity of these tables is rarely less than five years and most often equal to ten years or even more. These benchmarks in time are too widely spaced, especially for a period in which sharp accelerations occur in the decline of mortality.

It is thus more valuable to follow the change from year to year with the aid of conventional rates by age or by age groups and to adopt probable future trends as derived, in order to specify the change of projective probabilities at the corresponding ages or age groups. Figures 13.9a and 13.9b illustrate this mode of procedure.

The projective probability $_5q'_B$ is closely related to infant mortality; it is thus reasonable to anticipate a parallel future development of the two indices. When the trend line of the infant mortality rate is traced, what can

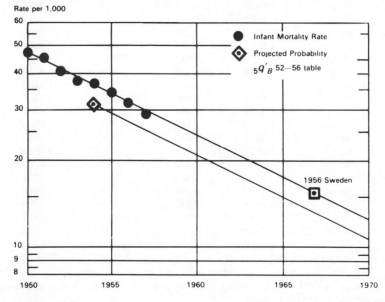

Figure 13.9a

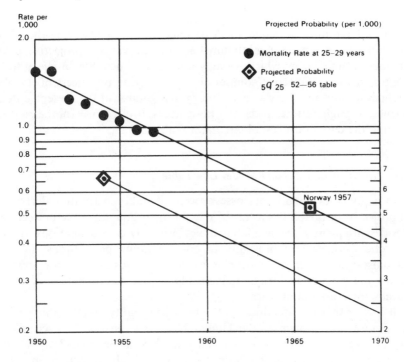

Figure 13.9b

be reasonably adopted for $_5q'_B$ is the parallel line leading from the point representing $_5q'_B$ during the period 1952–1956 (median year 1954). The mortality rates at 25 to 29 years can be similarly associated with the projective probability $_5q'_{25}$.

It might be feared that these future developments towards a declining mortality will lead to prediction of unreasonable levels of mortality 10 or 15 years in the future. The risk is the greater to the extent that the population studied already has a low mortality: might we not be led to make predictions about mortality that would assume implicitly the ability to fight effectively against some causes of death that at present cannot be overcome? Thus, the extrapolation concerning infant mortality (Figure 13.9a) leads to prediction of a female infant mortality rate lower than 9 per 1,000 after 1975; that is, a lower value than that contained in the table of biologically minimal mortality (J. Bourgeois-Pichat; see p. 129). With this method of prediction, for the most advanced countries, the threshold of 9 per 1,000 could indeed be crossed before that date.

We review the deficiencies of our overall extrapolation procedure and the impossibility of undertaking a genuine exploration of the future. The knowledge of the table of minimal mortality (in the present state of medical science) is the more valuable, for it permits tentatively orienting the extra-polations in specifying a minimum limit on the various projective prob-abilities, a limit below which we may not go. It is possible, in effect, to be limited in every projective computation to studying the effects of possible declines of mortality, as we have done with a glimpse at the present state of science, though setting aside all those necessarily risky hypotheses con-cerning the cure of cancer, of circulatory ailments, etc.[20]

Projective Probabilities and Model Life Tables

In many cases, we do not possess recent life tables permitting derivation of projective probabilities as of the date of the beginning of the projections. Besides, frequently the available tables are only approximations, as are all other measures of mortality in corresponding populations. In such circumstances, the measurement of levels and trends can be only approxi-mate, and all purely formal refinements in the determination of future development are out of place.

It is here that the usefulness of the model mortality tables elaborated by the Population Branch of the United Nations (which were discussed on pp. 148–152) reappears. Let us recall that these tables associate different sequences of specified probabilities (and survival tables) with given values of life expectancy. These associations are based on an analysis of 158 national tables representing diverse levels of mortality; they define the "mean struc-tures" of mortality by age and sex on the basis of the aggregate level measured by life expectancy at birth.[21]

The 48 tables (abridged) collected in *Population Studies* no. 25 include 24 male tables paired with 24 female tables; each pair corresponds to values of e_0 for the two sexes combined, going from 20 years to 55 years by intervals of 2.5 years, wherein e_0 equals 57.6, 60.4, 63.2, 65.8, 68.2, 70.2, 71.7, 73.0, 73.9. The levels thus defined are numbered 0, 5, 10, 15, ..., 110, 115. For each level there are given, besides the conventional elements (probabilities q_x, survivors l_x) the total numbers in the quinquennial age groups of the

20. Which does not prevent the possibility of interest in carrying out projective computations with life tables constructed on the assumption of the disappearance of cancer or some other causes of death: we are precisely in the domain of conditional forecasts, which seek to measure the effects of this or that factor (when it is not known whether or not they operate) on the structure of the population.

21. For full details on the way in which these "mean structures" have been determined, we return to the presentation of model life tables, which was given in the chapter on life tables. At the close of this section we cite the tables contained in *Population Studies, No. 25, Methods of Estimating Population, Manual III: Methods of Projecting the Population by Sex and Age*, issued by the United Nations.

corresponding stationary populations; from these totals are derived quinquennial survival rates for groups of cohorts, which are the complements
of the projective probabilities.[22] These survival rates are data that can be
directly used in computation of survivors.

When a computation of survivors must be made, this group of tables
permits: (a) choosing a table that corresponds to the present mortality

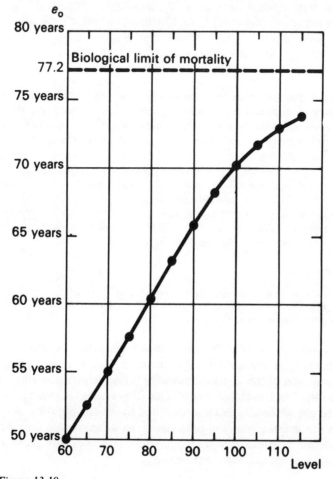

Figure 13.10

22. The survival rates given permit passing from birth to the age group 0–4 years, from the age
group 0–4 years to the age group 5–9 years, etc. The last group considered is the open-ended
group "80 years and over," for which survival rates are given in the group "85 years and over."
In the foregoing, we have not shown how to derive survival rates for open-ended groups from a
life table. For all practical purposes it will suffice to consider all the group up to ages 95–99 years
closed and to neglect survivors beyond 100 years.

level of the population one wants to project;[23] (b) choosing for the future the tables that represent the future levels of mortality.

Based on the expectation of life $e_0 = 55$ years, the levels taken from the United Nations' study correspond to variable progressions. If the progression from one level to the next were always accomplished in the same time interval, the corresponding change in mortality would be translated into an acceleration of progress toward the age of 60 years, and then a sizable slowdown beginning with $e_0 = 55.8$ (see Figure 13.10), which would indicate an asymptotic approach to the biological lower limit of mortality.

Moreover, in the opinion of those who constructed these model life tables, the group of 24 pairs of tables constitutes a valid chronological series:

> In view of past observations it was assumed that, where mortality is high or moderately high, favorable conditions in the future would bring about, on the average, a gain in expectation of life of about two-and-a-half years within each five-year period of time. . . . Where the expectation of life is already high, however, it cannot be presumed to go on increasing indefinitely at this pace. For high expectations of life, therefore, the sequence had to be further modified with a view to a gradual approach to minimum levels of mortality. . . . It was assumed that, in the time series of life-table death rates for any given sex-age groups, the maximum decline during a five-year period would be one-third of the difference between the present level and the minimum estimated by Bourgeois-Pichat.

But, naturally,

> this time sequence should merely be regarded as "normative," since in a given situation it may well be more realistic to expect that mortality will decline either more or less rapidly."[24]

In this way, the United Nations' model life tables constitute a useful set for arriving at computations of survivors for five-year periods. The careful gradation of the levels of mortality taken permits carrying out these computations with realistic hypotheses concerning declining mortality. In fact, the use of these tables is not limited to the computation of survivors as shown in the establishing of projections; as we cannot go into the details of the different possible uses, we will content ourselves with presenting one particularly elegant example of their use.

23. In principle, the projection concerns only the future, so that the mortality rate schedule to be taken for the initial population in the projection ought to correspond to an observed situation. In fact, the last available population estimates always refer to a date already in the past, and the first quinquennial period covered by the projections usually encompasses the present instant; thus it is the present mortality rate schedule that is best included in this case.

24. United Nations, *Population Studies*, No. 25, *op. cit.*, p. 71. "Minimum levels" refers to the level defined by the biological lower limit of mortality.

An Example of Computation of Survivors with Model Life Tables

The example treated is complex. It illustrates the double use of model life tables, which can calculate simultaneously *survivors* and *expectation of life*, when the available data are incomplete. We draw upon the computations of J-N. Biraben in his "Essay on the Demographic Development of the U.S.S.R."[25] The data are the following: (1) the (estimated) population of the U.S.S.R. by age and sex on January 1, 1951, is available; (2) the total number of births (24,860,000) and the total number of deaths (8,580,000) are known for the five-year period 1951–1955. Based on these, it is desired to derive the population by age and sex on January 1, 1956, and, secondarily, to estimate the expectation of life for this period.

First, the 24,860,000 births were distributed into 12,770,000 male births and 12,090,000 female births (sex ratio: 106 percent). Next, it was necessary to apply survival rates taken from the United Nations' model life tables to the population as of January 1, 1951, and to the newborn of the period 1951 to 1955. *The choice of the model type from which the survival rates should be taken was uncertain;* it was necessary to determine this by the condition that it would yield 8,580,000 deaths in this period, the only information available concerning mortality.

A first attempt, with a plausible expectation of life of 60.4 years (level 80 in the United Nations' classification) gave 9,504,000 deaths, an excessive number. A trial with a neighboring table (level 85: $e_0 = 63.2$ years) gave 8,388,000 deaths, a number considerably closer to the 8,580,000 deaths recorded. The adjustment was made by distributing proportionally the 192,000 deaths lacking among the deaths computed at different ages. This gives the distribution by age and sex of the Soviet population on January 1, 1956, as it is shown on p. 49 of the work referred to, and leads to the assumption, for both sexes, of an expectation of life at birth of slightly under 63.2 years, say, about 63 years.

An a posteriori confirmation of this estimate of the expectation of life is furnished by the data shown in the United Nations Demographic Yearbook for 1957. For the U.S.S.R. for the period 1954–1955, a mean expectation of life of 61 years for males and 67 years for females (a mean of 64 years) is found.

A Very Specific Example

In practice, we are led to undertake computations of survivors in many circumstances in which there is no question about classifying the problem or about automatically choosing the approach. Similarly, the techniques used vary according to the exact formulation of the problem and the quality

25. *Population*, No. 2a, June, 1958.

and completeness of the data available. What has been said in this chapter does not allow determining automatically the method to employ to resolve each of the exact questions that can arise. In detailing the manner in which the most common questions are posed, we intend simply to furnish the reader with a sufficient base to permit him, once he has acquired a certain statistical sense, to take the required initiatives in a particular case.

To illustrate these general considerations, we shall treat a specific problem that departs somewhat from that of computations of survivors, because it also concerns projections of newborn children brought in, it is true, very crudely.

TABLE 13.3. *France, Census of May 10, 1954, Département of Ain: Male Agricultural Population*

Year of Birth	Age on Jan. 1, 1955	Number	Year of Birth	Age on Jan. 1, 1955	Number	Year of Birth	Age on Jan. 1, 1955	Number
1950–54	0– 4	3,910	1920–24	30–34	3,500	1890–94	60–64	2,300
1945–49	5– 9	4,450	1915–19	35–39	1,480	1885–89	65–69	2,640
1940–44	10–14	3,820	1910–14	40–44	3,380	1880–84	70–74	2,420
1935–39	15–19	4,420	1905–09	45–49	3,600	1875–79	75–79	1,460
1930–34	20–24	3,640	1900–04	50–54	4,320	1874 and earlier	80 and above	1,260
1925–29	25–29	3,720	1895–99	55–59	3,440			
						1954 and earlier	All ages	53,760

Since a population census does not generally take place on January 1st, the classification by age that can be used on this occasion does not coincide with the classification by birth cohorts. In France, only the second classification, which is both easier to establish and more useful, is usually available. Thus, in the case of the male agricultural population (the male population in households in which the head is a farmer or agricultural worker), the statistics in Table 13.3 are available for the *département* of Ain at the census of May 10, 1954.

Figure 13.11 helps us grasp the meaning of these data. Having established a classification of total numbers enumerated by birth cohorts, the only classifications by age or by age groups that can be made to correspond are those for the January 1st dates before and after the census (January 1, 1954, and January 1, 1955).[26] Having chosen the second date, it is the movements across *AB, BC, CD* that give the totals on May 10, 1954, of persons 0–4 years of age, 5–9 years of age, 10–14 years of age, on January 1, 1955.

26. Naturally we exclude age classes on more distant January 1st dates, which offer no interest.

Now we are somewhat troubled by this single datum of the flow from *AB, BC, CD*, etc., the age groups at the corresponding dates being somewhat unusual (May 10, 1954). Thus, each time comparisons or projections must be made, we are required to estimate the movement across *OB′, B′C′, C′D′* on the basis of census data.

The movement from *AB* to *A′B′*, from *BC* to *B′C′*, from *CD* to *C′D′*, etc., requires that we take account of deaths[27] occurring in the groups considered between May 10, 1954, and January 1, 1955. Finally, the movement at *OA′*

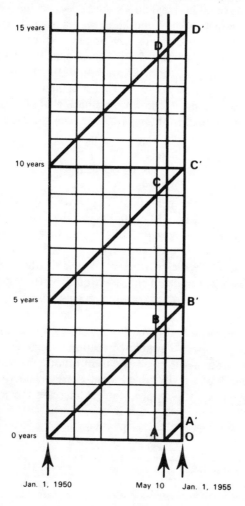

Figure 13.11

27. And, sometimes, migrations. We assume them to be negligible in what follows.

depends on the births at *AO* and on the deaths among newborn prior to January 1, 1955. In certain cases, these data may be obtained on the basis of vital statistics, and the estimate for January 1, 1955, then presents no problem. Usually, this estimate will depend upon approximate computations that aspire to furnish coherent figures for the January 1st in question, with, in any case, minimal errors if the computations were correctly carried out. It will then be a question of carrying out computations of survivors for the total of the age groups and, in addition, of carrying out forecasts of births for a fraction of a year. There is no question here of bringing too many formal refinements, inasmuch as the hypotheses we have made for mortality and natality can be only approximate. Let us direct our attention first to the estimation of the total numbers 5–9 years of age, 10–14 years of age, etc., on January 1, 1955, that is, to the estimation of the deaths in the parallelograms *BB'CC'*, *CC'DD'*, etc. With mortality comparable to that of France as a whole, and assuming a uniform distribution of deaths throughout the year, we estimate the deaths among 1,000 persons for each of the preceding parallelograms as being equal to

$$\frac{235}{365} = 64 \text{ per cent}[28]$$

of the corresponding rates (per 1,000). This is what was done in Table 13.4.

The population figures as of May 10, 1954, derive from inflation of a sample of one in twenty. For this reason, all the numbers are multiples of 20;[29] in addition, they are subject to random error. For these two reasons, it will be out of place to carry the corrections for the deaths to the nearest unit; working only with multiples of ten, we would better follow the degree of precision of the data with which we are working (and the computations are also somewhat easier).

Let us turn now to the estimate of the group 0–4 years of age on January 1, 1955. We shall propose a simple correction, which consists of assuming that the total number at *OB'* is to the total number at *AB* as the length of *OB'* is to the length of *AB*. But these lengths are proportional to 1,825 and 1,590.[30] Consequently, it is appropriate to increase the number at *AB* by

$$\frac{235}{1,590} = 14.8 \text{ percent.}$$

28. The period (May 11 to December 31) corresponds in effect to 235 days.

29. Except the first (5–9 year age group) which results, as do the numbers for the adjacent groups (0–4 years and 10–14 years) from estimates based upon the overall information for the group 0–14 years.

30. Five years (neglecting the cases in which leap years can be included) represent 1,825 days; subtracting the 235 days between May 10 and December 31, we find 1,590 days.

We accordingly increase the total aged 0–4 years in Table 13.3 by

$$\frac{3,910 \times 14.8}{100} = 580.$$

For the total of the population, the correction for moving from May 10, 1954, to January 1, 1955, is equal to

$$580 - 520 = +60.$$

TABLE 13.4. *Male Agricultural Population of Ain*

Age Groups	Mortality Rate, France 1954 (per 1,000)	Preceding Rate x 0.64[a]	Population, May 10, 1954[b]	Estimated No. of Deaths, May 10, 1954– Jan. 1, 1955	Estimated Population, Jan. 1, 1955
5– 9	0.545	0.3	4,450	—	4,450
10–14	0.478	0.3	3,820	—	3,820
15–19	0.983	0.6	4,420	—	4,420
20–24	1.51	1.0	3,640	—	3,640
25–29	1.83	1.2	3,720	—	3,720
30–34	2.30	1.5	3,500	10	3,490
35–39	3.24	2.1	1,480	—	1,480
40–44	4.68	3.0	3,380	10	3,370
45–49	7.71	4.9	3,600	20	3,580
50–54	12.0	7.7	4,320	30	4,290
55–59	17.6	9.7	3,440	30	3,410
60–64	25.8	16.5	2,300	40	2,260
65–69	37.8	24.2	2,640	60	2,580
70–79	73.6	47.1	3,880	180	3,700
80 plus	179	114.6	1,260	140	1,120
				520	

[a] $0.64 = \dfrac{235}{365}$.

[b] Age groups as of Jan. 1, 1955.

The correction is very small, which is normal. On May 10, 1954, this population had a total of 53,760; an increase of 60 in somewhat more than 7 months corresponds to an increase of slightly less than 100 for an entire year. The annual rate is then somewhat under 2 per 1,000, which is plausible in a fairly old population (the mean French rate was of the order of 6 per 1,000).

The small magnitude of the correction may make its necessity doubtful.

In reality, we do not seek a correction for the total number, but for the different groups of cohorts that form the conventional age groups on January 1, 1955. This latter correction is generally not negligible; it is indispensable for certain groups, especially the youngest ones. The fact that the balance of all the corrections may be virtually null only supports the necessity of the operations and approximations that were made.

Consequently, despite somewhat simplified hypotheses that are chosen at the same time by virtue of a lack of data and by the desire to avoid complicating the computations, we arrive at an acceptable estimate of the population by age groups on January 1, 1955. No refinement seems likely, in the present case, to lead to an estimate that could be considered, a priori, a better one.

Ease and Reliability of Computation of Survivors

It seems necessary to dwell upon the weak influence of mortality on short- and medium-term changes in the population totals for young age classes.

TABLE 13.5.   *France: Forecasts of Number of Youths Without Mortality*

Age in Completed Years	Jan. 1, 1958	Jan. 1, 1959	Jan. 1, 1960	Jan. 1, 1961	Jan. 1, 1962	Jan. 1, 1963
0	788.3					
1	781.3	788.3				
2	776.6	781.3	788.3			
3	778.1	776.6	781.3	788.3		
4	768.6	778.1	776.6	781.3	788.3	
5	785.5	768.6	778.1	776.6	781.3	788.3
6	778.8	785.5	768.6	778.1	776.6	781.3
7	816.9	778.8	785.5	768.6	778.1	776.6
8	827.1	816.9	778.8	785.5	768.6	778.1
9	822.8	827.1	816.9	778.8	785.5	768.6
10	819.3	822.8	827.1	816.9	778.8	785.5
11	792.1	819.3	822.8	827.1	816.9	778.8
12	595.3	792.1	819.3	822.8	827.1	816.9
13	578.3	595.3	792.1	819.3	822.8	827.1
6–13	6,030.6	6,237.8	6,411.1	6,397.1	6,354.4	6,312.9
Corrections for mortality*:						
per 1000		−0.40	−0.82	−1.27	−1.78	−2.37
—in thousands		−2.5	−5.3	−8.1	−11.3	−15.0

*For the total 6–13 years.

We have seen the paralyzing effect that determination of present mortality and its future change may cause the nonspecialist. The uncertainty surrounding the choice of procedure leads to certain reservations, though not necessarily discrediting the computation that has been undertaken. For many age categories in countries with low mortality, the effect of mortality on the change in the totals from year to year is very small; thus, even when making an error about the future change of mortality patterns, and in neglecting the influence of mortality, we still obtain projections that constitute good forecasts.

For example, Table 13.5 shows a forecast of the French school-age population (the group 6–13 years of age in complete years) that was conducted entirely without regard to mortality.

The errors are insignificant; in the present case, they risk being smaller than those caused by the absence of hypotheses concerning migration. Under these conditions, prediction is no longer a matter of technique, but only a state of mind.

These remarks hold for forecasts of the adult population, in which mortality cannot be neglected, but in which it suffices to include a plausible mortality level, without the difficulties of refined hypotheses, in order to arrive at acceptable figures that will not be too far from the actual number.[31]

Let us recall that, in either case, the level of the aggregate of mortality was assumed to be quite low, which leaves a rather minimal margin of future decline due to the diminishing of deaths avoidable in the present state of medical science. Finally, above all, the computation of survivors does not assume prior projections of births, which always constitute the most problematic part of demographic projections.

---

31. As much cannot be said for forecasts of elderly persons; although, on the average, this mortality varies but little (in contrast to the steadily declining mortality of youths and adults), it is, on the contrary, subject to sizable fluctuations in connection with epidemiological conditions (primarily influenza epidemics).

CHAPTER FOURTEEN

Projections of Births

THE STATISTICAL techniques involved in the computation of projections of births are generally more complex than those used in the computations of survivors. But to these formal difficulties are added others, which include, on one hand, the difficulty of appropriately translating, in terms of indices, whatever hypotheses are made concerning procreative behavior; and, on the other hand, the difficulty of predicting (when not simply a conditional forecast is required, but actual predictions), how this behavior will develop in the future.

We shall begin by examining the different techniques of computations for projections of births. After this, we shall discuss the choice of technique; for we shall see that in certain circumstances the use of different procedures can lead to very divergent results, while in different cases the hypotheses adopted will be formulated in identical terms.

Projections Using Fertility Indices by Age

The rate of fertility by age or by age groups is formally the equivalent of the corresponding mortality rate. We have seen previously that the projective probability of mortality (annual or quinquennial) was an index better adapted for the computation of survivors than was the mortality rate (by age or by age groups). We are similarly led to include projective probabilities of fertility (and not the conventional rate) each time we decide to carry out projections of births on the basis of a fertility measure by age of the woman. The definition of these indices is analogous to that of the projective mortality probabilities.

Here is an extract of the statistics for live births by year of birth and by age of mother in France for 1938:

Year of Birth of Mother	Age (in years)	Number of Births
1926	22	28,911
1925	22	29,963
1925	23	31,016
1924	23	30,712

The projective probability concerns a cohort or group of cohorts. With the preceding data, it is possible to compute the relevant probabilities for the 1925 female cohort, which reaches its 23rd birthday during the course of the year 1948. To do this, it is appropriate to relate the births that occur in this cohort to the initial total as of January 1, 1948, which is 326,181 women (see Figure 14.1). One finds:

$$\phi_{23} = 60{,}979/326{,}181 = 187 \text{ per } 1{,}000.$$

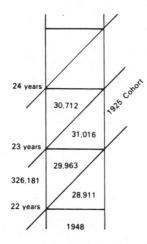

Figure 14.1

With a view toward setting up projections of births, it is necessary to choose a complete series of projective probabilities (by age or by quinquennial age group), such a series being able to be variable or fixed in time, depending on the case. It is generally useful to study the recent change in order to determine the future trend to adopt; however, the techniques of extrapolation can be quite different from those employed with mortality. We shall return to this point.

As an example, we give in Table 14.1 the full computations resulting from the application of fertility probabilities chosen by M. Febvay for his forecast

TABLE 14.1. France, Projected Births, 1960

Age in Completed years on Jan. 1, 1960	Female Population (thousands)	Projected Fertility Probability (per 1,000)	Number of Births (thousands)	Age in Completed years on Jan. 1, 1960	Female Population (thousands)	Projected Fertility Probability (per 1,000)	Number of Births (thousands)	Age in Completed years on Jan. 1, 1960	Female Population (thousands)	Projected Fertility Probability (per 1,000)	Number of Births (thousands)
15	288.6	4	1.2	26	304.6	170	51.8	37	322.6	45	14.5
16	287.6	12	3.5	27	318.6	156	49.7	38	337.5	37	12.5
17	265.8	30	8.0	28	321.7	142	45.7	39	342.3	30	10.3
18	243.0	59	14.3	29	328.0	128	42.0	40	207.8	23	4.8
19	257.1	96	24.7	30	311.8	116	36.2	41	187.1	17	3.2
20	284.0	134	38.1	31	315.7	108	34.1	42	165.6	11	1.8
21	285.8	167	47.7	32	313.6	93	29.2	43	157.0	7	1.1
22	287.9	186	53.5	33	320.6	83	26.6	44	194.3	4	0.8
23	293.4	192	56.3	34	321.6	73	23.5	45	296.4	2	0.6
24	296.4	190	56.3	35	317.0	63	20.0	46	298.4	1	0.3
25	306.2	180	55.1	36	321.3	54	17.4				
								15–46			784.8

of the size and structure of the French population as of January 1, 1960.[1]

The number obtained is 784,000 births anticipated for 1960. If we consider the probabilities of Table 14.1 as applicable during the subsequent years, then making projections of births (adequate choice of probabilities may be spoken of here as "forecasting") amounts to applying, each year, the projected probabilities in question to the projected number of survivors.

Very often, when we have decided to make projections of births on the basis of fertility characteristics by age, we do not have access to data allowing strict computation of projective probabilities for the past. This presents a different problem.

We may then have to estimate such probabilities for the future on the basis of other indices – necessarily approximate computations that will allow us to include the various data we do possess. Or, in addition, we may make use directly of other characteristics of fertility by age.

Rather frequently in the computation of projections of births, we employ directly the age-specific (or age group-specific) fertility rates, which are the usual descriptive indices of fertility by age. Care must be taken in applying these rates to corresponding mean populations.[2] Sometimes simple transformations of initial data are possible, permitting the substitution of more adequate indices for age-specific rates. Let us give an example.

We imagine drawing up projections of births, with constant fertility, for an underdeveloped country for which only rudimentary statistics are available; we estimate approximately the crude birth rate at 50 per 1,000. In the absence of age-specific rates, we can try to use those of a country with good statistics in which the crude birth rate is close to 50 per 1,000; this was the case for Taiwan in 1951 ($b = 49.9$ per 1,000). Table 14.2 gives a series of

TABLE 14.2.   *Taiwan, 1951, Age-Specific Fertility Rate (per 1,000)*

Age-Groups	Rates
15–19	68
20–24	287
25–29	350
30–34	311
35–39	226
40–44	132
45–49	34

1. See, for example, "Evolution naturelle de la population française jusqu'en 1975. Notes et documents, *Population*, No. 3, July–September, 1958.

2. Working in mean populations is less exact than making computations on cohorts or cohort groups, but the uncertainty that always accompanies projections of births justifies a lesser refinement in the formal conduct of computations.

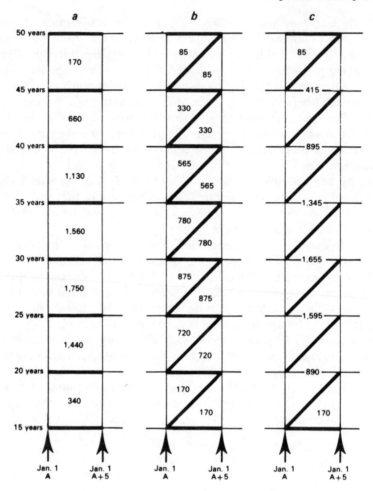

Figure 14.2

age-specific fertility rates for Taiwan. Let us see how to use this series to set up projections of births for five-year periods.

This concerns annual rates (that is to say, relating to a one-year duration) for quinquennial age groups. Multiplying them by 5, we obtain quinquennial rates, which are placed in a *Lexis* diagram, as in Figure 14.2a.[3]

By supposing that the births represented by these rates are equally distributed between the two groups of five cohorts that are involved in one square of Figure 14.2a, we arrive at Figure 14.2b. Naturally, such a simple hypo-

3. The products of the multiplications 287×5 and 311×5 were rounded to 1,440 and 1,560.

thesis introduces bias. But as we have in mind regrouping the groups in Figure 14.2c by cohort, and if we recall in addition how we came to choose the rate for Taiwan, we may easily suppose that the cohort rates thus obtained remain acceptable for carrying out projections of births in a country in which it is known, roughly, that the crude birth rate is on the order of 50 per 1,000.

Table 14.3 gives the details of the computations carried out. In the left part of the table are shown the numbers of the female totals by quinquennial age groups on January 1, A (date of the beginning of the projection); on January 1 $(A+5)$; on January 1 $(A+10)$; on January 1 $(A+15)$: this is a conventional computation of survivors. Let us notice that we cannot anticipate the female totals at the ages of procreation beyond the last date — January 1 $(A+15)$ — without drawing on the results of the projections of births we are planning to set up here.

The use of fertility indices by age is acceptable in many types of projective computations in which, with their help, the translation of hypotheses concerning procreative behavior is carried out with sufficient precision. In cases in which this is not so, it is generally appropriate to distinguish legitimate births and illegitimate births and to be most concerned with the projection of the former. But then it is necessary, as a preliminary step, to carry out projections of marriages.

Projections of Marriages

The computation of projections of marriages rests upon fairly crude methods; in particular, these computations are carried out for a single sex: thus, they cannot take account of the manner in which relationships may change in the future between the totals of the various male and female cohorts that are likely to contract marriages with each other. But we do know the importance for nuptiality of the relationship between the totals of marriageable persons.

The most common technique consists of choosing, in each cohort and for one sex (females, for example), the proportions marrying or of newly married persons at each age, and applying these proportions to predicted future totals.[4] These proportions can vary in time, but it is rare that we can legitimately hope to make hypotheses concerning probable future variations; so, generally, we choose constant proportions, trying to determine their values for the country in question during a period of stable nuptiality.

4. These are not real probabilities, which would have to be computed by relating the number of newly married women to the number of unmarried women only. Projections can be carried out with such probabilities only with difficulty, for their use would assume availability of population projections by marital status or, at least, including the distinction between the married population and the unmarried population.

TABLE 14.3. Projected Births Using Fertility Rates for Generation Groups

Age in Completed Years	Number of Women on:				Quinquennial Fertility Rates by Quinquennial Generation Groups		Time Periods					
							A to (A+5)		(A+5) to (A+10)		(A+10) to (A+15)	
	Jan. 1 A	Jan. 1 (A+5)	Jan. 1 (A+10)	Jan. 1 (A+15)	Age Attained by all Women in the Group	Rate (per 1,000)	Mean Number of Women	Births	Mean Number of Women	Births	Mean Number of Women	Births
0– 4	18,250											
5– 9	14,520	15,950										
10–14	12,280	13,720	15,190									
15–19	10,530	11,760	13,200	14,670	15	170	12,020	2,043	13,460	2,288	14,930	2,538
20–24	9,040	9,950	11,170	12,600	20	890	10,240	9,114	11,465	10,204	12,900	11,481
25–29	7,720	8,430	9,330	10,540	25	1,595	8,735	13,932	9,640	15,376	10,855	17,314
30–34	6,520	7,140	7,860	8,750	30	1,655	7,430	12,297	8,145	13,480	9,040	14,961
35–39	5,430	6,000	6,610	7,330	35	1,345	6,260	8,420	6,875	9,247	7,595	10,215
40–44	4,440	4,940	5,510	6,110	40	895	5,185	4,641	5,755	5,151	6,360	5,692
45–49	3,560	3,970	4,460	5,050	45	415	4,205	1,745	4,700	1,951	5,280	2,191
50–54	2,750	3,110	3,500	3,960	50	85	3,335	283	3,735	317	4,210	358
								52,475		58,374		64,750

For example, considering French female nuptiality in 1955 as representing a stable situation undisturbed by delays or postponement (which accompany wars and economic crises), we obtain the proportions given in Table 14.4 to characterize this nuptiality.

Applying these proportions to the female population estimated as of January 1, 1960, we obtain 292,403 as the number of marriages in 1960 in which the woman is under 50 years of age (Table 14.5). To take account of marriages in which the woman is over 50 years of age, it is appropriate to add to the preceding number by about 3 percent, the usual proportion (in France) of marriages of women above this age. In round numbers, we find 301,000 marriages for 1960.

We might wish to apply the same method to the males. To be satisfactory, the procedure ought to give the same total number of marriages or newly married persons in the two cases. In fact, the differences are sometimes fairly large (see Table 14.6).[5] It may then be appropriate to take the arithmetic mean of the two results.

TABLE 14.4. *France, Proportion of Newly Married in Female Cohort Groups, 1955*

Age*	Female Population on Jan. 1 (thousands)	Newly Married in 1955	Proportion Newly Married (per 1,000)
15–19	1,383.9	44,440	321
20–24	1,521.2	159,230	1,047
25–29	1,570.1	57,607	367
30–34	1,609.4	20,745	129
35–39	1,053.5	8,421	80
40–44	1,382.0	6,902	50
45–49	1,520.2	5,675	37

*Ages attained during 1955; the groups are thus cohort groups.

We see the uncertainty that surrounds this type of projection.[6] From such computations we can anticipate only some indications of the general trend in the annual number of marriages, as related to the variations in the total numbers of marriageable persons.

5. We must remark that in 1970, the year with the largest deviation, the effect of the passing of the demographic wave to the ages of most frequent marriages is very strongly felt inequality of the numbers of available marriageables in younger age groups.

6. Still, we could expect greater accuracy from a computation carried out by year of age, since the measurement and projection of marriage for the aggregate of a quinquennial group could be biased in the case of cohorts for which nuptiality varies considerably from one age to the next (for example, among women between 15 and 30 years of age) because of large inequalities that can obtain among the numbers of adjacent cohorts.

TABLE 14.5.   *France, Projected Marriages, 1960*

Age	Female Population on Jan. 1, 1960 (thousands)	Proportion of Newly Married (per 10,000)	Newly Married
15–19	1,380.5	321	44,314
20–24	1,408.2	1,047	147,439
25–29	1,547.5	367	56,793
30–34	1,589.7	129	20,507
35–39	1,620.0	80	12,960
40–44	1,059.8	50	5,299
45–49	1,376.0	37	5,091
15–49			292,403

It may seem hazardous to make projections of births on such bases. But it should not be forgotten that essentially the births to come in the near future will occur in marriages already contracted before the beginning of the projective computations. Besides, the differences existing between the computations carried out for each sex separately do not imply that actual deviations of such great size will be observed; further, compensations may occur among the years.

TABLE 14.6.   *France, Forecasts of Marriage (in thousands)*

Based Upon	1960	1965	1970	1975
Male Marriage Rates	314	301	352	385
Female Marriage Rates	301	314	378	391
Mean	307.5	307.5	365	388

In support of these remarks we can at least show some comparisons between past forecasts and observed results. Table 14.7 relates these two series of data for France, the projections of marriages having been computed in 1954 on the basis of female nuptiality of the years 1930–1932. But, independently of the prolonged continuation of military mobilization and service (factors that prevented or delayed certain marriages), a large-scale immigration took place, which could have had a noticeable effect on nuptiality.[7] As a total, the cumulative difference from 1955 to 1959 (+ 53,000) represents only 3.4 percent of the actual number of marriages contracted during this interval of time. Now, these five marriage cohorts contribute

7. Let us recall that the computation of these migratory movements remains outside the field of our projections.

about 5 percent of the legitimate births that take place in 1959. Thus, the uncertainty about forecasting the number of marriages in fairly unfavorable circumstances brings about an error slightly over 1.5 percent in the projections of legitimate births over five years.

TABLE 14.7. *France, Comparison Between Forecasted and Observed Marriages (in thousands)*

	1955	*1956*	*1957*	*1958*	*1959*
Forecasted	307	305	300	294	288
Observed	313	293	311	312	321
Deviations	+6	−12	+11	+16	+33
Cumulative Deviations	+6	− 6	+ 5	+21	+54

Projections of Legitimate Births by Duration of Marriage

Such projections are carried out on the basis of fertility rates by duration of marriage; as these projections concern births in different calendar years, the durations of marriage to be used are durations in calender year differences.

The rates are defined in relation to an initial total of marriages as of the time of their contraction. From an operational point of view, what is involved is multiplying the marriages of a single year by coefficients that vary from year to year, and then adding together all the births so deduced that relate to a given calendar year. This leads to the practical mode of presentation of computations shown in Table 14.8.

In this table the rates are kept constant, so that the same series of rates is applicable to six calendar years; to keep the rates constantly opposite the number of marriages to which they apply, it suffices to shift the series one line higher each year. Naturally, it is enough to carry out this shift mentally.[8]

The sum of the fertility rates leads to a total of 2,350 children (live-born) per 1,000 marriages. So, by this hypothesis, the projections have been guided from beginning to end.

Projections of this type could have been carried out with variable rates, hence with the mean number of live-born children per 1,000 marriages similarly variable. We could thus have kept a progressive decline that would

8. All the numbers of marriages are naturally related to the area for which we are making the forecasts of births. Also, if it were necessary to work from estimates for 1940 to 1945, the numbers registered in that period do not apply to the 90 French *départements.*

Let us remark, finally, that there is no disadvantage to working only with marriages in which the woman is aged 15 to 49 years, the only fertile ages; but in that case it is necessary to use fertility rates computed in the same way.

TABLE 14.8a.   *France, Projected Legitimate Births, 1955–1960*

Marriages		Fertility	Projected number of Births (in thousands)					
Year	Number in thousands	Rate (per 1,000)	1955	1956	1957	1958	1959	1960
Forecasted Marriages								
1960	283							36.8
1959	288						37.4	121.5
1958	294					38.2	124.1	78.2
1957	300				39.0	126.6	79.8	68.1
1956	305			39.7	128.7	81.1	69.2	59.2
1955	307	*130*	39.9	129.6	81.7	69.7	59.6	51.3
Observed Marriages								
1954	314.4	*422*	132.7	83.6	71.4	61.0	52.5	47.5
1953	308.4	*266*	82.0	70.0	59.8	51.5	46.6	38.9
1952	313.9	*227*	71.3	60.9	52.4	47.4	39.6	35.2
1951	319.7	*194*	62.0	53.4	48.3	40.3	35.8	30.4
1950	331.1	*167*	55.3	50.0	41.7	37.1	31.5	26.8
1949	341.1	*151*	51.5	43.0	38.2	32.4	27.6	23.2
1948	370.8	*126*	46.7	41.5	35.2	30.0	25.2	21.1
1947	427.1	*112*	47.8	40.6	34.6	29.0	24.3	20.9
1946	516.9	*95*	49.1	41.9	35.1	29.5	25.3	21.7
1945	393	*81*	31.8	26.7	22.4	19.3	16.5	14.1
1944	205	*68*	13.9	11.7	10.0	8.6	7.4	6.2
1943	219	*57*	12.5	10.7	9.2	7.9	6.6	5.5
1942	267	*49*	13.1	11.2	9.6	8.0	6.7	5.3
1941	226	*42*	9.5	8.1	6.8	5.7	4.5	3.6
1940	177	*36*	6.4	5.3	4.4	3.5	2.8	2.1
1939	258.4	*30*	7.8	6.5	5.2	4.1	3.1	2.6
1938	273.9	*25*	6.8	5.5	4.4	3.3	2.7	1.9
1937	274.5	*20*	5.5	4.4	3.3	2.7	1.9	1.1
1936	279.9	*16*	4.5	3.4	2.8	2.0	1.1	0.6
1935	284.9	*12*	3.4	2.8	2.0	1.1	0.6	0.3
1934	298.5	*10*	3.0	2.1	1.2	0.6	0.3	
1933	315.7	*7*	2.2	1.3	0.6	0.3		
1932	315.0	*4*	1.3	0.6	0.3			
1931	326.7	*2*	0.7	0.3				
1930	342.1	*1*	0.3					
		2,350	761.0	754.8	748.3	740.9	732.7	724.1

have moved regularly from 2,350 children in 1955 to 2,300 in 1960. It is possible that this decline in the total number could result from different declines of the rates at different durations, and that, to compute the projection, it is not enough to know the total cumulative fertility of 1956, 1957, etc.

Assuming that the overall decline results from strictly similar declines at all durations, it suffices to carry out a rule of three on the results of Table 14.8a, in order to arrive at projections deriving from a cumulative fertility of 2,340 children in 1956, 2,330 in 1957, etc. This is what is done in Table 14.8b.

TABLE 14.8b. *France, Projected Legitimate Births, 1955–1960*

	Projected Numbers of Births *(in thousands)*					
	1955	*1956*	*1957*	*1958*	*1959*	*1960*
Births based on 2,350 children per 1,000 marriages	761.0	754.8	748.3	740.9	732.7	724.1
Cumulative fertility of 1,000 marriages	2,350	2,340	2,330	2,320	2,310	2,300
Corresponding projected legitimate births	761.0	751.6	741.9	731.4	720.2	708.7

We thus assume that, for the different final levels of mean number of births per marriage, the distributions of births among the different durations are identical.[9] If it were known not to be strictly so, it is conceivable that, in a given country, at dates close to one another and for very similar total numbers of children, this hypothesis is acceptable: it furnishes a simple technical solution to the majority of projective computations of variable fertility carried out on the basis of fertility rates by duration of marriage. Naturally, in particular circumstances, we might be led to apply series of rates that are different from year to year and that do not correspond to the same distribution made according to duration of marriage.

It is useful to note that, when one assumes a distribution of births by duration of marriage that is constant over time, the computation of projections of births serves to construct a weighted mean of still-fertile marriages, a mean that is multiplied by the final mean number of births per marriage adopted. Thus, on the basis of Tables 14.8a and 14.8b, the number of legitimate births in 1960, under the hypothesis that 2,300 is the mean number of

9. The reader will observe that despite a terminology taken from cohort analysis the reference is to period analysis.

children per 1,000 marriages, results from:

$$2{,}300 \times \left[283 \times \frac{130}{2{,}350} + 288 \times \frac{422}{2{,}350} + 294 \times \frac{266}{2{,}350} + 300 \times \frac{227}{2{,}350} + \cdots \right].$$

The weighting coefficients,

$$\frac{130}{2{,}350} = 0.057 = 57 \text{ per } 1{,}000, \qquad \frac{422}{2{,}350} = 0.183 = 183 \text{ per } 1{,}000,$$

$$\frac{266}{2{,}350} = 0.116 = 116 \text{ per } 1{,}000, \qquad \frac{227}{2{,}350} = 0.099 = 99 \text{ per } 1{,}000, \ldots,$$

take account of the way in which 1,000 legitimate births are distributed by duration of marriage:

    57 are of duration 0 (in calendar year differences);
    183 are of duration 1 (in calendar year differences);
    116 are of duration 2 (in calendar year differences);
    99 are of duration 3 (in calendar year differences); etc.

We find 308.1 as a weighted mean of marriages (in thousands); it is to these 308,100 marriages that we apply the marital fertility rate, taken as 2,300 children per 1,000 marriages, or an average of 2.3 children per marriage. This procedure is closely akin to that adopted in carrying out projections of births by birth order.

Projections of Legitimate Births by Birth Order

These projections are set up by successive steps, the projection of births of the order $(n+1)$ being computed only after the projection of births of the nth order.

First-Order Births

Let us transpose rigorously the computation procedure employed in Table 14.8, substituting, however, the rate of fertility of the first order by duration of marriage for fertility rates (of all birth orders) by duration of marriage. These rates, which are shown in Table 14.9, derive from the computations in Table 8.17, p. 230, which correspond to the French situation of 1956.[10] Thus, in applying this series to recent marriages (we have each

10. There are slight deviations between the two series, that of Table 14.9 deriving from rounding carried out on the findings of Table 8.17, p. 230. We may remark, however, that the rate at duration 0 in Table 14.9 (thus relative only to first births), i.e., 132 per 1,000, is greater than the rate at duration 0 in Table 14.8 (relative to all births). This apparent anomaly results when we do not study the same year in both cases.

time taken 16 marriage cohorts) we arrive at the projections in Table 14.9.[11]

We have remarked, in connection with the computations of projections of Tables 14.8 and 14.8a, that the datum for the series of fertility rates by duration of marriage is equivalent to the datum for the final total fertility and the distribution of 1,000 births by duration of marriage. It is the same here; in order to reproduce the series of fertility rates of Table 14.9, it is enough to know that 1,000 marriages result in 826 first births, and that, when 100 first births are produced, there are:[12]

> 16 with duration of marriage 0 (in calendar year differences)
> 46 with duration of marriage 1 (in calendar year differences)
> 16 with duration of marriage 2 (in calendar year differences)
> 8 with duration of marriage 3 (in calendar year differences)
> 4 with duration of marriage 4 (in calendar year differences)
> 3 with duration of marriage 5 (in calendar year differences)
> 2 with duration of marriage 6 (in calendar year differences)
> 1 with duration of marriage 7 (in calendar year differences)
> 1 with duration of marriage 8 (in calendar year differences)
> 1 with duration of marriage 9 (in calendar year differences)
> 1 with duration of marriage 10 (in calendar year differences)
> 1 with duration of marriage 11 (in calendar year differences)[13]

to arrive at the projections of Table 14.9.

This observation takes its full weight in the computation of projections of births of orders higher than one. In effect, the existing statistics do not generally permit computation of fertility rates for births of orders higher than one.[14] We can simply determine, on the basis of indirect methods, the frequency of the coming of a child of order $(n+1)$ in cohorts[15] that have attained parity n (parity progression ratio); this frequency is none other than the sum of the fertility rates of the birth order considered (826 per 1,000 in the example of Table 14.9). For conducting projective computations, what

11. The example is purely illustrative, for in practice there would be no question of carrying out projections in 1954 on the basis of 1956 fertility rates.

12. This distribution was derived from the rates of Table 14.9 after some roundings, which explains the contraction to 12 years.

13. We again borrow terminology from cohort analysis, although this is a case of period description. Assuming, as we shall in what follows, that the period description is fixed in time is, for all practical purposes, equivalent to considering the distributions of births as identical whatever the cohorts and is similar to the description of the period analysis.

14. It is likewise sometimes impossible to compute fertility rates for first-order births; this is what happens when we do not have the statistics of first births by duration of marriage. Thus we do not know how to derive the rates to be adopted for projections of nonexistent retrospective series. In this case the remarks that will follow apply to projections of first-order births.

15. Referring to fictitious cohorts, since we are in a period analysis.

TABLE 14.9.   *France, Projected First Order Births, 1955–1960*

	Marriages	First Order Fertility Rate (per 1,000)	Projected First Order Births (in thousands)					
Year	Number in thousands		1955	1956	1957	1958	1959	1960
Forecasted Marriages								
1960	283							37.3
1959							38.0	110.3
1958	294					38.8	112.6	40.0
1957	300				39.6	114.9	40.8	18.6
1956	305			40.3	116.8	41.5	18.9	11.3
1955	307	*132*	40.5	117.6	41.8	19.0	11.4	7.7
Observed Marriages								
1954	314.4	*383*	120.4	42.8	19.5	11.6	7.9	5.0
1953	308.4	*136*	41.9	19.1	11.4	7.7	4.9	3.1
1952	313.9	*62*	19.5	11.6	7.8	5.0	3.1	2.2
1951	319.7	*37*	11.8	8.0	5.1	3.2	2.2	1.6
1950	331.1	*25*	8.3	5.3	3.3	2.3	1.7	1.3
1949	341.1	*16*	5.5	3.4	2.4	1.7	1.4	1.0
1948	370.8	*10*	3.7	2.6	1.9	1.5	1.1	0.7
1947	427.1	*7*	3.0	2.1	1.7	1.3	0.9	0.9
1946	516.9	*5*	2.6	2.1	1.6	1.0	1.0	0.5
1945	393	*4*	1.6	1.2	0.8	0.8	0.4	0.4
1944	205	*3*	0.6	0.4	0.4	0.2	0.2	
1943	219	*2*	0.4	0.4	0.2	0.2		
1942	267	*2*	0.5	0.3	0.3			
1941	226	*1*	0.2	0.2				
1940	177	*1*	0.2					
		826	260.7	257.4	254.6	250.7	246.5	241.9

is lacking is a knowledge of the distribution of births of order $(n+1)$ by duration elapsed since the births of order n (according to the analysis that we have done from the computations in Table 14.9).

The distributions to be used are the same ones used for the computation — by indirect methods — of parity progression ratios. What was said then (see p. 231) about the manner of choosing the appropriate type of spacing between births remains valid. Besides, a great analogy exists in the method of carrying out computations, whether it involves determining period parity progression ratios or determining projections of births by order.

We propose, by way of example, to compute projections of second-order births in France. Let us adopt for this a long type of spacing, that of France in 1907.[16] The computations are the subject of Table 14.10: the arrangement is analogous to that of Table 14.9. It is no longer the fertility rates that are involved, but, rather, the weighting coefficients. The various weighted means of first-order births are multiplied by the parity progression ratios, a_1, adopted for the projection. Here $a_1 = 0.750$.[17]

Total Live Births

Finally, projections for the aggregate of legitimate live births result from the addition of projections of births of the different birth orders.[18] In practice, we are limited in making the computations to the birth orders 7, 8, or even 9, the total of births of higher orders being estimated together by summary procedures. The resulting inaccuracy is negligible if we recall that in France, for example, births of an order higher than 9 represent no more than 1 percent of all legitimate births.

When one wishes to obtain projections for the total of live births (legitimate or not), it is appropriate to apply a percentage (generally varying little over the short term) to the number of legitimate births, in order to take account of illegitimate births.[19] Naturally, this observation is equally valid when the projections of legitimate births are conducted on the basis of the series of fertility rates by duration of marriage.

Choice of Methods and Hypotheses

The existence of many methods of computing projections of births poses a question of choice when confronting each particular problem.

An Example of the Use of Age-Specific Fertility Rates

The use of age-specific fertility rates[20] is most extensive; when projections of births were first introduced, they were made in this manner. In what

16. Exactly that resulting from an inquiry among government employees and workers carried out in France in 1907.

17. a_1 is therefore constant, but nothing prevents making the parity progression ratios vary in time.

18. Under certain circumstances we could hope to carry out projections of births by order using parity progression ratios that vary in time. The manner in which the computations are connected requires, even when a single ratio varies, that we recompute all the births whose order is higher than that corresponding to the variable parity progression ratio.

19. At the present time (1961) this percentage is around 6.5 percent in France.

20. Which, among all age-specific fertility indices, are best adapted to projective computations, like projective probabilities.

TABLE 14.10.   *France, Projected Second Order Births, 1955–1960*

First Order Births		Weighting	Projected Second Order Births (thousands)					
Year	Numbers in thousands	Coefficients	1955	1956	1957	1958	1959	1960
Forecasted Births								
1960	241.9							4.8
1959	246.5						4.9	54.2
1958	250.7					5.0	55.2	82.7
1957	254.6				5.1	56.0	84.0	40.7
1956	257.4			5.1	56.6	84.9	41.2	23.2
1955	260.7	2	5.2	57.3	86.0	41.7	23.5	15.6
Observed Births								
1954	243.0	22	53.5	80.2	38.9	21.9	14.6	9.7
1953	242.7	33	80.1	38.8	21.8	14.6	9.7	7.3
1952	247.5	16	39.6	22.3	14.8	9.9	7.4	5.0
1951	254.2	9	22.9	15.3	10.2	7.6	5.1	5.1
1950	276.3	6	16.6	11.1	8.3	5.5	5.5	2.8
1949	299.1	4	12.0	9.0	6.0	6.0	3.0	
1948	333.1	3	9.9	6.7	6.7	3.3		
1947	366.2	2	7.3	7.3	3.7			
1946	314.6	2	6.3	3.1				
1945	203.4	1	2.0					
Weighted Mean of First Order Births			255.4	256.2	258.1	256.4	254.1	251.1
Weighted Mean $\times a_1$(0.750)			191.6	192.2	193.6	192.3	190.6	188.3

follows, we shall see an example in which the use of this method is contraindicated. Nevertheless, it remains sufficient in many circumstances, for example, when the age compositions are only a little upset and fertility conditions are fairly stable. It is similarly adaptable to projective computations that are not encumbered by extremely cloudy hypotheses.

We have seen previously how to proceed in choosing fertility rates for quinquennial age groups in order to carry out projections for a country in which the crude birth rate is estimated at approximately 50 per 1,000 (see p. 405). It is then a question of projections with constant fertility.

By way of example, we propose to draw up, for the same country, projections with declining fertility. We are in the typical case in which projective computations have no pretensions to being forecast, but simply try to infer the consequences of a given modification in procreative behavior on the structure of the population. Naturally, the type of modification taken corresponds to a carefully made choice; it could be a case of extreme situations or, on the other hand, plausible "average" situations. Let us go into the details.

Let us imagine that special attention is given to the effects of as rapid a decline as possible in fertility; then it is appropriate to adopt the set of age-specific fertility rates at different dates, which translate this hypothesis and detail it as well. In consequence, it is necessary to decide (1) the pace of the decline, and (2) the level of stabilization.

Figure 14.3 presents a system of admissible hypotheses. Let us recall that, initially, the gross reproduction rate R is taken as equal to 3.5 (about 7 live births per woman); the rates given in Figure 14.3 represent female births occurring in 5 years in a quinquennial age group of women.[21] The level of stabilization was taken as that corresponding to strict replacement in a

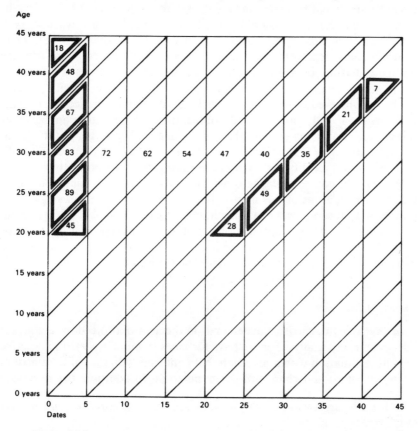

Figure 14.3

21. Their sum for a given period or a given cohort represents, by moving the decimal point, the gross reproduction rate of the period or cohort.

group of cohorts (net reproduction rate $R_0 = 1$), the first group to have this behavior being the quinquennial group giving birth in the first 5 years. Given the change adopted for mortality,[22] to obtain this net rate it is necessary that the gross reproduction rate R reach the value 1.4 in the cohort group considered. Once these initial and final rates are established, it suffices to interpolate to obtain the intermediate fertility rates. In Figure 14.3, the interpolated rates are shown for the age group 25 to 29 years of age in complete years at the beginning of each 5-year period.

The aggregate of this construction naturally leaves room for considerable arbitrariness, whether on the level of stabilization ($R_0 = 1$) of the cohorts that are first to attain this level[23] or the manner of interpolation. Let us note, however, that at the level of national populations it is rare that a net reproduction rate would be maintained with stability much below 1. Besides, the distribution of births by age of the mother, which is obtained when $R_0 = 1$, is derived from observed distributions in very Malthusian populations in which integral replacement of generations is just assured. Similarly, the decline of fertility by age that results from our interpolations is the greater the more it refers to more advanced ages, which is consistent with patterns of change observed in societies in which contraceptive practice has become widespread. Finally, it should be noted that fully Malthusian behavior should not be anticipated until the coming of age of cohorts not yet present at the beginning of the projection, that is to say, at a period in which conditions of natural fertility still exist in the aggregate of the population.

We may, of course, imagine other methods adapted to conducting projective computations of this nature. Here we have given only a single illustration of what can be done in using indices of fertility by ages — fairly global indices that find an appropriate domain of use in this type of projection, for they are well accommodated to the imprecision of the basic data and to the inevitably arbitrary part accompanying the choice of hypotheses.

Choice of Indices

In developed countries, the demands in the area of projections are generally greater; especially when we have forecasts in mind, we wish to describe the future situation with a precision that conforms with that of the statistics of the structure and change of the population. In addition, the situations

22. A change we may summarize crudely by the increase during 100 years from a life expectancy of 43.9 years to one of 70.3 years.

23. Let us observe that this level, defined by a net reproduction rate equal to unity, does not define a level of pure fertility but relates fertility to mortality; afterward, with mortality continuing to decline, fertility does the same, the crude rate approaching unity to the extent that life expectancy increases.

are often quite confused and sometimes poorly adapted to analysis of age-specific fertility rates only, which, for this reason, may be completely un-adaptable for projection purposes.

Finally, in similar cases, because of a certain wealth of available statistics, we are generally able to choose many types of data for analyzing the situation; for the same reason, when what is involved is the construction of projections that are often based on the continuation of recent trends, a problem of choice arises: what categories of indices to use in the formulation of hypotheses to be adopted concerning the future.[24] This problem of choice is all the more important in certain cases in which employment of one or another method is not a matter of indifference.

We shall illustrate these generalities in studying, following Louis Henry, the differences there may be among computed projections of births after fluctuations of natality, calling on different indices in the measurement of fertility.[25]

The example is that of France; it involves computing projections of legitimate births beginning with 1953. The author has used five categories of indices of measurement of fertility; and first of all the four following:

  I. Age-specific fertility rates.
 II. Fertility rates by age at marriage and by duration of marriage.
III. Fertility rates by duration of marriage.
IV. Fertility rates by birth order and by time elapsed since the preceding birth (or sometimes since marriage).

The deficiency of the statistics for analyses of this sort has necessitated the use of indirect methods in conducting the projections. As we have seen, these methods include categories of types of spacing between births. Two series of interval distributions were used here. One series is taken from a study carried out in France in 1907; it leads to projection IVa. The other series is taken from the prewar Czechoslovakian statistics relating to Sub-Carpathian Russia; it leads to projection IV_b.

These different indices were computed for France, and the means of their values for the years 1949–1952 were adopted for carrying out the projections.[26]

---

24. Let us observe, nevertheless, that detailed demographic information is often available only at the national level; so when we are led to work on subpopulations, we are reduced generally to the use of quite sketchy methods. This, however, can be justified by the fact that we work with fairly small groups in which random fluctuations are of considerable magnitude.

25. See Louis Henry, "Perspectives de naissances après une perturbation de la natalité," *Proceedings of the World Population Congress*, Rome, 1954, Vol. III, Session No. 13, pp. 55–66.

26. In the computations II, III, and IV, it was necessary to take explicit account of marriage. The projections of marriages were carried out on the basis of the female marriage rates of the period 1940–1952. By contrast, in I it was necessary to keep projections of births for legitimate births only; for this the illegitimate births were estimated at 6.9 percent of the total.

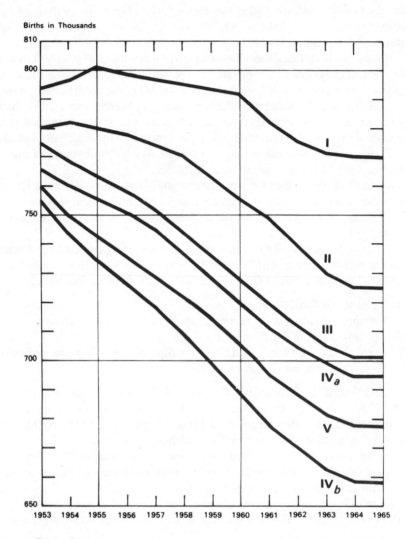

Births in Thousands

Figure 14.4

As L. Henry has indicated:

If one assumes that the principal effects of the disturbance of the war and of the postwar period were sufficiently attenuated some years after the end of the conflict, one can consider that the present behavior is appropriately translated for each series of rates by the mean of the observations of some recent years. Taking 1949–1952, one is far enough from the war, and one has access to a large enough number of years, so that the accidental fluctuations compensate one another, at least in a fairly large measure.

Subjected to the check of the projective computations, the preceding diverse series of rates lead to widely divergent results (see Table 14.11 and Figure 14.4), which would be inconceivable in a situation in which the different demographic characteristics remained fixed over time.

In fact, we have begun from a starting point in time, around 1949–1952; this starting point has allowed the isolation of different categories of cohorts (cohorts of women born the same year, married the same year, having their nth child the same year, etc.). The different series of rates that are associated with these different categories of cohorts have furnished us with different ways of characterizing French legitimate fertility in 1949–1952. But these categories of cohorts, according to the manner in which they are put together, reflect more or less the past conditions of fertility, mainly the fluctuations caused by World War II; this point was amply discussed in connection with the study of fertility. In carrying out projections of births with the different series of rates for the period 1949–1952, we extend for the future – to different degrees, according to the series – certain behaviors that in fact are only temporary and are explained by events occurring in a more or less distant past.

Without doubt, we are always on the brink of some period; but it is rare that the histories of different female fertile cohorts that we consider will be the same at a given moment. This lack of stability in conditions of fertility over time explains why the different series of rates for a given period, like those employed in establishing the results in Table 14.11, are never strictly equivalent. For a careful discussion of the preceding example, we refer to the article from which it is taken (see note 15). In reading this work, one can see that since the sequels of the past affect quite differently the diverse categories of cohorts considered, certain series of rates are preferable to others in computing projections of births under the hypothesis of a continuation of the conditions of a certain period.

Besides, it is also in connection with the determination of these current conditions that the question of appropriate measurement indices arises. It is when, wishing to make forecasts (not simply conditional projections), we intend to project certain current conditions, that we believe these conditions have some chance of continuing in the future. Such continuation will appear all the more probable to the extent that it prolongs a previous stability, but this stability cannot be assumed for just *any* series of indices. In the present example, it is in studying the cumulative fertility of recent marriages (subsequent to 1940) that we may most surely conclude stability of fertility: at the same duration of marriage, the different marriage cohorts have almost the same mean cumulative fertility. It is in a new situation with new behavior[27] that the future continuation constitutes a limiting hypothesis for making forecasts. This hypothesis is correctly translated by the series of rates utilized in III, in which for the higher durations of marriage we include the behavior of families formed prior to 1940, while we have inferred the stability of behavior only for the recent households. From this comes the idea of correcting the series used in III, by extrapolating the curve of cumulative fertility by duration of marriage, as was done in the chapter on natality and fertility (Table 8.8). It is in this way that we have carried out the projections numbered V (Table 14.11 and Figure 14.4), in which the fluctuations caused by the war are assumed to play no role in the future. Under these conditions one can logically assume that, during the coming years, the curve of annual births will progressively depart from III to rejoin V some time in the future.

TABLE 14.11.   *France, Projected Legitimate Births (in thousands)*

Years	Types of Computations					
	I	II	III	IV$_a$	IV$_b$	V
1953	794	780	775	766	755	760
1954	797	782	769	760	744	750
1955	801	780	764	756	735	743
1956	799	778	758	751	727	736
1957	798	774	752	746	718	729
1958	796	770	745	738	709	722
1959	794	763	736	729	698	714
1960	792	755	728	720	688	705
1961	783	749	719	711	677	696
1962	775	740	712	704	669	689
1963	771	730	705	699	662	682
1964	770	725	701	695	658	678
1965	770	725	701	695	658	678

We see in this example that the best way to carry out a diagnosis concerning fertility and, therefore, to formulate hypotheses for the future is to proceed by a cohort analysis. This is not to say that such a prognosis would always be easy.

The evidence of a past stability generates the supposition that it may be the same in the future, and this hypothesis is entirely reassuring since it is simple to formulate. But, if we have established a steep decline across each of the separate marriage cohorts, it would be much more difficult to make a

27. It may be noted that in the quotation from L. Henry (p. 422) allusion is made to "present behavior." The entire object of his analysis is precisely to show that if caution is not taken the translation of behavior in terms of fertility indices can be very bad.

decision: what rate of decline to adopt for the future and what point of stabilization to choose.

We have been more inclined to pose problems and to give warnings than to propose methods worked out for this or that case; this is because real situations are too complex and too diverse to allow setting standards in this area. In this regard, the fact that in our second example we have avoided the use of age-specific fertility rates does not indicate that this type of indices, so often employed in practice, should be rejected systematically.

CHAPTER FIFTEEN

The Use of Demographic Projections

PURELY demographic projections are rarely an end in themselves. They are typically sought because of their utility in making decisions in economic, social, and even political spheres. Some data on projective computations can be used towards this end without having to be transformed in any way. This is the case of annual projections of marriages, births, and deaths. It is equally so for the future numbers of particular age groups; thus, at the present time in France, the group 6–13 years of age in complete years comprises the total number of youths affected by the school attendance requirement.[1]

But, usually, strictly demographic projections must be prepared in order to lead to data directly usable by those responsible for economic and social action. Let us observe, finally, that even while it is possible to profit from conditional projections in which hypotheses are judiciously chosen, the users are more generally interested in actual forecasts.

Projections of the School-Age Population

When we are interested in the population affected by the school attendance requirements, it suffices, as has been said, to construct — on the basis of demographic projections — the appropriate age groups. At the ages at which the school attendance requirement does not apply (in France, before the 6th, and after the 14th birthdays), it is necessary to bring in the school attendance

1. In the same order of ideas, we may say that the group of demographic projections is already applicable just as it is. By furnishing precise indications (population size, age composition) of the consequences of some future development of natality and of mortality (or, sometimes, of migrations) it may move the legislator to one or another measure favoring or contrary to the realization of these consequences. We have seen that the first French projections, computed by A. Sauvy, eventually had this effect.

rates; this may involve over-all rates or rates by type of instruction (see pp. 292 and 294).

The choice of these rates depends on the particular circumstances of each projection, and we would not propose standards or norms in this sphere. However, the progressively stronger universal tendency toward education of youth leads us to take the rising school attendance rates for forecasts; projections using constant rates are presented, for this reason, as minimal projections deserving relatively little attention. In the past, predictive computations have not taken account of this spontaneous movement toward school attendance, or have notoriously underestimated them, and in this way permitted the anticipation of numbers of pupils much smaller than the actual numbers.

Like every extrapolation, those that can be undertaken on the basis of recent school attendance rates are always somewhat hazardous; they are even more so to the extent that the available chronological series of observations are of poor quality and for this reason make the determination of trends more difficult. Figure 15.1 shows that it is possible to do this with data available in France; the data concern 1953, 1954, 1957, and 1958. But the observations for the two first years are of doubtful quality; those for 1957 and 1958 are much more sure. In the diagram we have indicated the school attendance rates that can reasonably be anticipated for the beginning of the new school years 1960 and 1965.[2]

With these rates, and on the basis of population projections computed in 1958,[3] we have determined the school population between their 14th and 18th birthdays, as of the beginning of the school years 1960 and 1965 (see Table 15.1). It is seen how great an underestimate would be made in taking the 1958 rates purely and simply for the future (1,574,700 pupils instead of 1,897,500 pupils in 1965; an underestimate greater than 20 percent).

When one wants to develop separate rates by levels of instruction (first degree, second degree, technical) it is useful to extrapolate the corresponding school attendance rates, taking account of the anticipated increase in the over-all rates. Altogether this involves "exploding" the over-all rates. It can be assumed, for example, that the 81 children attending school at 14 years of age in 1965 are distributed in the following way:

> 15 children in first degree instruction;
> 40 children in second degree instruction;
> 26 children in technical instruction.

2. These extrapolations assume that there will be no changes in legislation concerning compulsory school attendance. If such changes were anticipated, it would be easy to take account of them in Figure 15.1.

3. See Évolution naturelle de la population française jusqu'en 1975", *Population*, 1958, No. 3, pp. 487–499.

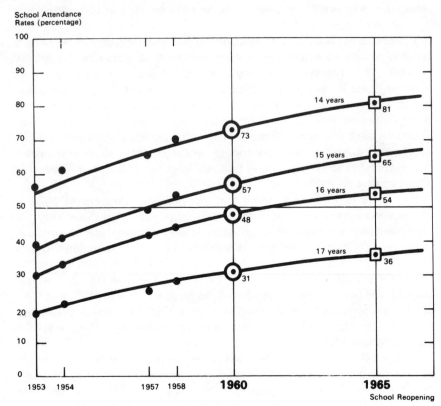

Figure 15.1. Projections of Change in School Attendance.

TABLE 15.1.   *Forecasts of Numbers Attending School (in thousands)*

Age in Completed Years*	1960 School Reopening			1965 School Reopening		
	Population	*Rate (%)*	*Pupils*	*Population*	*Rate (%)*	*Pupils*
14 years	791.0	73	577.4	776.1	81	628.6
15 years	594.3	57	338.7	814.0	65	529.1
16 years	577.3	48	277.1	824.0	54	444.9
17 years	578.1	31	179.2	819.3	36	294.9
14–17 years			1,372.4			1,897.5
Computations with 1958 rates			1,290.5			1,574.7
Deviations			81.9			322.8

*Age on Dec. 31, following the beginning of the school year.

The choice of the distribution is difficult and uncertain, and the division of pupils among the different types of instruction may vary in time for different reasons: a stronger interest of parents or children in one type of instruction rather than another; greater attendance facilities at one type of establishment because of a larger number of available places, etc.

A Different Method

This global manner of making the forecast of the total school populations may not suffice for those directly responsible for education in a country. On the one hand, the state may not carry the responsibility for instruction alone, and it is important to ascertain the total number of pupils attending the schools, public and private, respectively. On the other hand, in connection with the precise determination of the needs to be met (in buildings and in teachers), it is necessary to possess the details of future totals according to different grade levels, and those totals for each type of instruction. We will, then, wish to know the number of pupils attending school in a given school year — the first year of primary instruction, the second year, etc.

The use of school attendance rates, as we have defined them, is not adapted to this type of forecast. The students at a given level of instruction — to illustrate the idea, let us say the second year in *lycée* and college — belong to many age classes. In order to use forecasts by year of age (of the kind given in Table 15.1) to arrive at forecasts concerning this second class, the proper method is to carry out some laborious distributions: (1) between public instruction and private education; (2) between the various types of public education; (3) between the different classes within second-degree instruction that may possibly receive a child of the age considered, in order to retain finally only those in the second year.

This is why it is preferable, in the face of problems of this type, to proceed to direct analyses of the manner in which school attendance changes in the different years for different types of instruction. Let us take again the example of the second-year classes, in second-degree instruction.[4] It is known that for every 100 children attending these classes:[5]

4. In a narrow sense, i.e., including only the *lycées* and colleges and excluding the completion courses in the previous format.

5. See *Informations Statistiques*, supplement to *Bulletin officiel de l'Éducation Nationale*, January, 1959, No. 12. It concerns the distribution at the 1957 school reopening, the ages being those of December 31, 1957. Let us observe that this concerns a period or cross-sectional characteristic that thus reflects the effects of variations in behavior between cohorts. This is not serious for the use that we will make of the distribution, to the extent that these variations result from an aggregate change likely to continue in the future. The variations in number between cohorts can be more troublesome; fortunately, they are not very sizable here.

11 are 14 years of age (complete years)
36 are 15 years of age;
33 are 16 years of age;
17 are 17 years of age;
 3 are 18 years of age.

These results dictate the construction of an index of second-year attendance, by relating the pupils of this class to the weighted mean of the total number in the cohorts from which these pupils are recruited, the weighting coefficient being furnished by the preceding distribution.

At the beginning of the 1955 school year in France, 56,971 pupils attended the second-year classes in public secondary education. The cohorts liable to have some of their members in these classes were those born between 1937 and 1941,[6] for which the totals on December 31, 1955, are, respectively:

1937	*1938*	*1939*	*1940*	*1941*
576,600;	566,400;	563,600;	513,200;	484,400

With these totals we construct the weighted mean (numbers in thousands):

$$\frac{572.6 \times 3 + 566.4 \times 17 + 563.6 \times 33 + 513.2 \times 36 + 484.4 \times 11}{100} = 537.6.$$

Whence we have, as an index of school attendance:

$$\frac{56,971}{537,600} = 0.106 = 10.6 \text{ percent.}$$

A chronological series of values permits extrapolation of these indices (see Figure 15.2); forecasts of the total numbers in the second year are obtained products of the indices extrapolated by the weighted means of the future totals of cohorts from which the pupils are recruited.

Choice of Method

We would not expect these two methods to give strictly equivalent over-all results. The graphic extrapolation remains a quite synthetic forecasting procedure; in the second method, multiple repetitions of a procedure are used without the certainty of arriving at a coherent aggregate description by this procedure. Thus it is evident that the upward extrapolations (as in Figure 15.2), if carried out at all levels,[7] will fairly rapidly end in leading to

6. These truncations are evidently not exact; nor is the distribution of pupils in the second year by age.

7. This is what must be done above 14 years of age, where the progress of school attendance in the total group sets in motion an increase in school attendance indices in the different types of instruction.

the double enrollment of some children – that is, to forecast more pupils than there are children in certain cohorts.

The rather blind manner of carrying out the computations in the second method prohibits its use in our sense in long-term forecasts, although it is perfectly appropriate in the case of a description in some detail[8] of the situation of the school population a few years ahead. By contrast, the first method is perfectly adapted for carrying out long-term computations for very large numbers (by age and by type of instruction). We do not think that

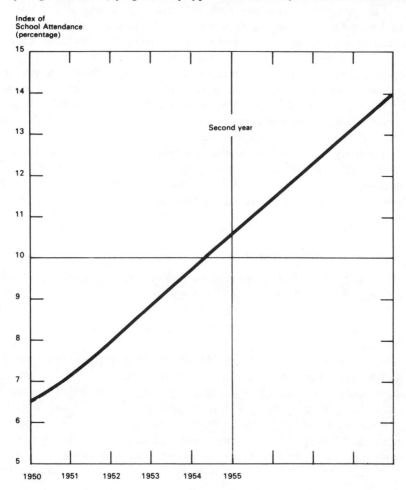

Figure 15.2. Projections of Change in an Index of School Attendance.

8. And most particularly with the details of concern to those in direct charge of seeing that school reopenings are properly assured.

it can be substituted for the second method in short-term forecasts requiring primarily detailed descriptions and, in addition, closely adapted to existing age compositions. But it remains the preferred procedure for forecasting the main line of development of the school population and for sketching the long-term forecasts that are indispensable in a sphere in which the needs must be expressed far in advance, since much time is required to satisfy them (especially with respect to training of teachers). We may add that this method assures us of coherent results.

Let us specify finally that any work on forecasting the total school population does not imply automatic recourse to one or the other of these methods. Special procedures can be worked out to be adapted to the resolution of quite specific problems. Thus, there is some advantage to associating the forecasts of the total numbers in higher education with the forecasts of the totals with newly acquired baccalaureate degrees, the latter being necessary (in virtually all cases) for registration in a faculty of higher education in France; besides, with this approach it is interesting to measure the progressive dropouts from one year to the next.[9]

In summary, if it is possible to derive a number of methods having a broadly universal validity, it is nevertheless always necessary to study carefully the composition and organization of education to extract the most appropriate modes of operation before proceeding to forecasts of the total school population.

Projections of the Labor Force

These projections rest on the application of the rates of labor force participation to the projections of populations by age or age groups. Consequently the formal analogy with projections of the school population using school attendance rates is complete. Our attention will thus be given to the choice of these rates.

The variations that can be considered (variations in relationship to the situation defined at the last census or survey) concern the extreme ages of economically active life: (1) In France, at young ages (essentially before 20 years of age), the progress of school attendance delays more and more the entry of the cohorts into the labor force; so, at a given age, 16 years, for example, the intensity of labor force activity and the rate that measures it are diminishing; (2) at the older ages (for all practical purposes, after 55 years of age), the variations in economic activity can take place in different direc-

---

9. At least the problem is posed when the accomplishment of higher studies results from progressive movement to different levels defined by years of study (for example, in French education, in law, and in medicine). It is different when no such progression is defined and when what is involved is obtaining a number of diplomas.

tions under the influence of the greater or lesser employment opportunities available to aged persons, legislation on the subject of retirement, the relative size of the agricultural population, etc.

On the other hand, at the various ages of adult life (from 20 to 55 years), participation in the labor force is almost complete, at least for the male cohorts (rates close to 100 percent), and in the projective computations the use of constant rates is the rule.[10]

In the last resort, the choice of hypotheses depends on the purpose at hand. Projections using constant rates at all ages have the merit of separating the effects of strictly demographic change on the numbers and the composition of the labor force.

If the probable future change of the labor force must be indicated, the choice of rates ought to be more realistic. In particular, it is necessary, as indicated above, to take into account declining rates at the young ages. To do this, we must be guided by the anticipated change in the rates of school attendance, remembering, nevertheless, that the rate of school attendance and the rate of labor force participation are not complementary, with only a fraction of the young persons entering the labor force immediately after leaving school.

For the older ages, no trend is imposed a priori, the anticipated future developments being clearly different among the different countries, under the influence of general economic conditions, social legislation, etc.

An example will clarify the preceding generalities. We wish to carry out, for January 1, 1960, forecasts of the labor force in France; in order to detail the changes resulting from the progressive entrance into the labor force of many cohorts born after 1945, we shall be concerned with the probable structure of the labor force in 1965 and in 1970 (as of January 1, to illustrate the ideas). We have access to the projections of the population by sex and age as of January 1, 1960, and the labor force participation rates from the 1954 census. To simplify the presentation somewhat, we shall be concerned only with computations for males.

The first data to be used are the forecasts of the population by sex and age that can be calculated for January 1, 1960. For the most part, the labor force participation rates of the 1954 census will be retained. In particular, we have no access to information permitting assessment of recent changes and of changes likely to occur in the coming years as far as labor force activity at advanced ages is concerned.

At young ages (prior to 20 years of age) the observed increase in the school attendance rates during recent years brings about a correlative

10. In the adult female generations, where the situation is different, it may be reasonable to assume future variations in extent of labor force participation. However, it is not generally easy to formulate hypotheses on this point.

diminution in the rates of labor force participation. Besides, it is anticipated that compulsory education will be increased to 16 years of age for the 1953 cohort and subsequent generations. Thus, a lowering of the rate of labor force participation by young persons is promised in the immediate future under the double influence of a spontaneous increase in school attendance and a modification of legislation concerning compulsory school attendance.

Figure 15.3 shows one of the procedures capable of giving plausible rates of economic activity for carrying out the forecast. The curve of rates by age at the census of 1954 yields a guide for extrapolation of these rates to January 1, 1969, the January 1 following the reopening of the first school year in which school attendance will be obligatory until 16 years of age.

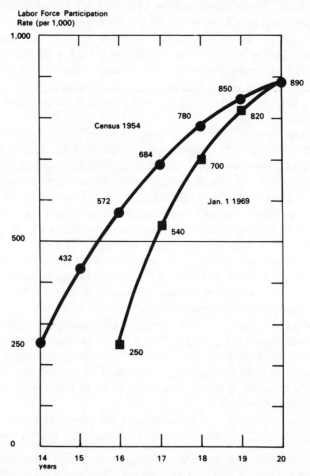

Figure 15.3.   Projections of Labor Force Participation Rates (males).

Consequently, at this latter date, the rates at 14 to 15 complete years will be zero. On the other hand, at 20 years of age, the decline in the rate of labor force participation will not be very great even if, as is probable, the rate of school attendance goes up quite noticeably.[11] In retaining the 1954 rates (890 per 1,000) for the forecast from here to 1970, we commit a systematic error, but one that remains negligible compared with the errors resulting from the uncertainty about other rates.

According to the graph in Figure 15.3, we have assumed that the rates of labor force participation at 16 complete years on January 1, 1959, will be equal to the rate at 14 complete years as of the census of 1954. We assume, in short, that in the year of age following the period of compulsory school attendance, the intensity of labor force activity is the same in 1954 and in 1960, even though, during the interval, the duration of school attendance has been prolonged by two years.[12]

On the basis of the two extreme points (250 per 1,000 at 16 years; 890 per 1,000 at 20 years), we determine, graphically, the rates at 17, 18, and 19 years. At the same time, by linear interpolation, we determine the rates for each of the intervening years (and by extrapolation, for 1970).

If we have gone into the complete detail of the operations leading to the determination of projected rates of labor force participation, it is not because we consider the method taken here as being of particularly general application. In fact, it is not possible to standardize methods of forecasting, and in the present state of our knowledge, each project of projective computation must be the subject of a particular study, from which will come appropriate projection procedures. In the example treated, we have tried, first of all, to introduce plausibility and coherence into a realm in which genuinely scientific procedures have not yet penetrated. Since there remains a certain element of arbitrariness in the decisions taken, the procedures advocated here are sometimes judged unfavorably by the nonspecialist. In our opinion, these reservations do not justify the negative attitude — still frequent — that consists in purely and simply continuing to use in the future indices that we know no longer represent the situation — far from it — at the start of computations.

The computations are presented in Table 15.2. Until 20 years of age, the quite large variations in rates of labor force participation from one age to the next require the treatment of data by single years of age, whereas beyond that age consideration of quinquennial groups suffices. In the study of

11. On January 1, 1959, this rate was 6.5 percent for the total of both sexes.

12. More precisely, the 1952 cohort, which will be 16 years old on January 1, 1969, will not be subject to the compulsory school attendance until 16 years; we believe, nevertheless, that its behavior will be close to that of the contiguous cohort (1953), which is the first covered by the new legislation.

Tables 15.3 and 15.4, we can evaluate the difference between computations at constant rates and those at decreasing rates.

TABLE 15.2. *France, Projected Male Population in the Labor Force (in thousands)*

Age (in completed years)	Jan. 1, 1960			Jan. 1, 1965			Jan. 1, 1970		
	Popula-tion	Labor Force Partici-pation Rate (per 1,000)	In the Labor Force	Popula-tion	Labor Force Partici-pation Rate (per 1,000)	In the Labor Force	Popula-tion	Labor Force Partici-pation Rate (per 1,000)	In the Labor Force
14	307.1	142	43.6	418.9	52	21.8	397.1	0	—
15	297.0	258	76.6	423.4	113	47.8	399.2	0	—
16	299.2	440	131.6	421.6	334	140.8	392.3	229	89.8
17	277.9	624	173.4	418.8	576	241.2	403.2	531	214.1
18	250.9	745	186.9	405.5	720	292.0	396.3	695	275.4
19	268.8	838	225.3	305.6	828	253.0	416.8	818	340.9
20–24	1,532.8	923	1,414.8	1,383.8		1,277.2	1,961.3		1,810.3
25–29	1,695.0	968	1,640.8	1,519.2		1,470.6	1,371.7		1,327.8
30–34	1,653.1	970	1,603.5	1,677.2		1,626.9	1,503.1		1,458.0
35–39	1,647.8	968	1,595.1	1,630.0		1,577.8	1,653.4		1,600.5
40–44	896.0	968	867.3	1,615.3		1,563.6	1,597.6		1,546.5
45–49	1,445.5	956	1,381.9	867.9		829.7	1,564.1		1,495.3
50–54	1,428.9	940	1,343.2	1,374.1		1,291.7	824.9		775.4
55–59	1,335.9	822	1,098.1	1,321.6		1,086.4	1,270.7		1,044.5
60–64	1,016.1	680	690.9	1,192.1		810.6	1,179.2		801.9
65–69	712.3	495	352.6	861.7		426.5	1,009.2		499.6
70–74	565.3	335	189.4	550.8		184.5	668.3		223.9
75 and +	661.1	180	119.0	650.0		117.0	636.9		114.6
All ages			13,134.0			13,259.1			13,618.5

Note: Above age 20 years the rates of labor force participation are the same in 1960, 1965, and 1970.

Some Remarks

Let us recall that the labor force, as defined in the census, includes at the same time the population effectively employed and the population seeking employment. To the extent that there is considerable unemployment, the rates of labor force participation do not measure the real employment but rather what would be the total if all demands for employment were satisfied.

The same holds true for projective computations that are carried out on the basis of labor force participation rates. The change undergone by these rates takes account of recent trends, trends that are related to the general development of the society. In the framework so sketched, the projections define, if one wishes, the change required in the number of employed so that there will be full employment in the population.

It is this interpretation of the computations that gives them real interest. Without dwelling on this, we see that the computations in Table 15.2 lead to forecasting a needed increase in male employment in France of 484,500 units during the period 1960–1970 (see Table 15.4).

In projections of the labor force, attention is more usefully directed to the *variations* in the volume of this population between one date and another than to the volumes themselves at different dates, since, as has just been said, one of the essential purposes of these computations is to determine the number of new jobs that must be created. This circumstance justifies the carrying out of projective computations with the aid of labor force participation rates, even though these rates can be determined only in an uncertain fashion. The relative error that will result from this, in thus determining the volume of the labor force, will be generally the same as that which will affect the variations in these volumes. But, if we cannot be satisfied by a single total number for the labor force, known only within 5 to 10 percent, we will generally find sufficient a projection of the variation in the labor force that does include such a margin of uncertainty.

Here is an example of computations in which this observation applies. If we wish to set up projections of the labor force in France for each *département* in the period 1960–1970, we can in principle apply the projections of the population by age for each *département* to the rates of labor force participation, possibly adopting a certain pattern of change for some of these rates. But the work thus conceived is too laborious to be carried out. In addition, the characteristics of economic activity in each *département* may not be known or may be accessible only with difficulty. Indeed, in France as of January 1, 1960, the 1954 census data necessary for computing the labor force participation rates had been published only for certain *départements*; the treatment of these data imposes, in addition, a rather long preliminary task.

From this comes the idea of applying the rates for France as a whole to the projections of the population in each *département* (which is done in Table 15.2); the national rates being mean rates that may deviate markedly from the rates in certain *départements* because of various factors (variable percentage of the agricultural population, greater or lesser opportunity for female employment, etc.).

As has been said, we may nevertheless expect from this type of computation a completely satisfactory degree of accuracy for assessing the variations in labor force participation. For the present, and from the point of view of projections, it is much more important to take account, even approximately, of the almost certain decline of labor force participation at young ages than to make use of all the regional rates in the computation.

We present, for the *départements* of Nord and Pas-de-Calais, the forecasts carried out by two methods[13] (see Table 15.5). We establish a substantial difference between the two figures for 1960,[14] which result from the smaller labor force participation rates in the two *départements* (especially among women) than in France as a whole.

TABLE 15.3. *France, Male Population Under 20 Years of Age in the Labor Force (in thousands)*

	Jan. 1, 1960	Jan. 1, 1965	Jan. 1, 1970
Constant Labor Force Participation			
Rates (1954 level)	990.5	1,391.4	1,435.4
Decreasing Rates	837.4	1,038.5	920.2
Difference	153.1	352.9	515.2

TABLE 15.4. *France, Changes in the Male Labor Force (in thousands)*

	1960–1965	1965–1970	1960–1970
Constant Labor Force Participation			
Rates (1954 level)	+ 366.8	+ 479.8	+ 846.6
Decreasing Rates	+ 167.0	+ 317.5	+ 484.5
Difference	199.8	162.3	362.1

The differences in the variations derive primarily from the hypothesis adopted concerning the labor force participation of young people. The disagreement is particularly marked for the period 1960–1965, when the first large cohorts arrive at the first ages of labor force participation. While this quinquennial period will see only a moderate increase in the labor force (due to the lengthening of required school attendance, which delays many young persons from entering the labor force), the computation with constant rates anticipates as large an increase in 1960–1965 as in 1965–1970.

This example well illustrates the importance in many demographic computations of distinguishing between indispensable adjustments and useless refinements.

13. Based, moreover, upon slightly different forecasts of population by age.

14. A difference that will be even greater if the national rates employed in 1960 were those of the 1954 census.

We are generally able to compute projections of the structure of the labor force, as we have just done. In this way, we may learn about the total number and about the age and sex composition of this population at one or another date, and under one or another hypothesis.

Nevertheless, there will always be an obvious interest in having similar projections of the *change* in the labor force; that is, projections (annual, for example) of entries into and departures from this population.

The entries take place at the completion of school attendance; among women, certain entries take place between 30 and 50 years of age, often occurring after a temporary interruption following marriage and child-bearing. The departures take place because of deaths and retirement; in the latter case, they occur most often after 55 years of age; among women, certain departures take place, as we have indicated, following marriage and the birth of children.

TABLE 15.5. *Forecasts of Labor Force for Northern Region of France (Nord and Pas-de-Calais Départements, in thousands)*

	1960	1965	1970
Forecasts with National Rates Decreasing at Young Ages	1,494	1,523	1,598
	+29	+75	
Forecast with Constant Regional Rates	1,376	1,462	1,551
	+86	+89	

Except among women, the periods of entries and of departures in the first half of adult life do not overlap. This fortunate circumstance permits using labor force participation rates to make projections of changes in the labor force. The method is that furnished by the Population Branch of the United Nations.[15] We shall summarize it in the simplest case, that in which the labor force participation rate does not vary in time. In this way, the history of a cohort can be followed more easily, and so we can see more easily the insight that can be drawn from the data on labor force participation rates. Let us work with the male rates of the French census of 1954 and, for the moment, assume that there is no mortality.[16]

15. "Les facteurs de variation de la population active," *Proceedings of the World Population Conference*, 1954, III, 597.

16. This assumption facilitates the presentation. In reality, the variations in rates of a given age below, which we shall show, apply to 1,000 persons attaining that age.

To say that there are for 1,000 persons in a generation:

> no persons in the labor force at 13 complete years of age;
> 250 persons in the labor force at 14 complete years of age;
> 432 persons in the labor force at 15 complete years of age;
> 572 persons in the labor force at 16 complete years of age; etc.,

is the same as saying that

250 persons *enter employment* between 13 and 14 complete years of age;
182 persons *enter employment* between 14 and 15 complete years of age;
140 persons *enter employment* between 15 and 16 complete years of age; etc.,

250, 182, 140 being the differences between the successive rates ($250 - 0$; $432 - 250$; $572 - 432$; etc.).

In the same manner, to say that there are:

> 880 in the labor force at 55 complete years of age;
> 840 in the labor force at 56 complete years of age;
> 812 in the labor force at 57 complete years of age;
> 794 in the labor force at 58 complete years of age; etc.,

is the same as saying that:

40 persons *leave employment* between 55 and 56 complete years of age;
28 persons *leave employment* between 56 and 57 complete years of age;
18 persons *leave employment* between 57 and 58 complete years of age; etc.

As for the exits from the labor force due to death, these are obtained by applying mortality rates to the labor force by age;[17] generally, in the absence of specific data, the rates for the general population are applied.

According to the structure of the population on January 1, 1960, and if the rates of 1954 had been applicable,[18] we would see during 1960 the entrances and exits (by retirement) resulting from the computations of Table 15.6.

It can be seen that, at the ages at which the entries and exits overlap, the variations in the rates of participation take account only of the net changes (balances of the entrances and departures) at each age; fortunately, we have seen that for all practical purposes this exists only among women at certain ages of adult life.

17. In proceeding this way, we double count exits from the labor force by retirement followed by deaths in the same year and exits from the labor force by deaths in the year when the exit by retirement was supposed to have taken place. But the error committed remains negligible.

18. Let us recall that these rates are particularly inappropriate to young ages. It is more appropriate to use decreasing rates, with which we can apply the present method, as shown below.

TABLE 15.6. *France, Male Population in the Labor Force Entrances and Departures (by Retirement) in 1960 (in thousands)*

Age on Jan. 1	Population	Changes in Participation Rates	Entrances	Age on Jan. 1	Population	Changes in Participation Rates	Departures
13 years	407.3	0.250	101.8	50 years	290.6	-0.040	11.6
14 years	307.1	0.182	55.9	51 years	289.1	-0.028	8.1
15 years	297.0	0.140	41.6	52 years	283.9	-0.018	5.1
16 years	299.2	0.112	33.5	53 years	284.4	-0.018	5.1
...	...	...	...	...	...	...	...

The method is quite naturally extended when the rates of labor force participation vary from year to year; it is necessary to follow the variations in rates in the cohorts, variations that this time will no longer be constant at a given age.

General Remarks Concerning the Use of Projections by Age

The study of a population by age and sex permits properly describing numerous social phenomena. This is why projections of population of the same type can be utilized for different purposes.

We have dwelled particularly on the manner of treating these purely demographic projections (or forecasts) to arrive at projections (or forecasts) of the school population and of the labor force. Here, rapidly reviewed, as examples, are two other spheres of use:

1. Certain projections of consumption, especially of needs,[19] can be sketched by using projections by age. Let us take the projections of over-all food needs, which may be computed for countries in which there is an acute subsistence problem affecting individuals by coefficients that vary with age. We would thus give the coefficient 1 to adults, the coefficient 0.7 to certain classes of youths or aged persons; and we may go further in going into detail about food rations according to protein composition, etc.

2. At the same time as the ageing of populations continues in France and elsewhere in the West, the support of aged persons is more and more frequently assured by the aggregate of the society, by means of various advance

19. We speak readily of *consumption* when the choice of the consumer can be exercised over a certain range of products, all offered in abundance; by *needs* we mean all that is appropriate to offer to individuals to satisfy quite elementary needs. With these nuances we may say the population projections by age assist especially in sketching projections of needs.

deductions taken from the labor force. So that this collective responsibility can be correctly assured, it is appropriate to set up forecasts concerning as much the cost of retirement as the development of certain specific needs of aged persons (medical assistance, homes for the aged). The forecasts of population by age are an essential datum that, related to other information (concerning retirement legislation, the structure of medical needs by age, etc.), permits specifying the future trend.

Finally, the use of projections by age always rests on a more or less refined weighting of the totals of different classes. The possibilities in this area are related to the preliminary statistical information that one possesses; in the absence of these data for past years or fairly recent years, the indices to apply during the period covered by projections could not be chosen properly. Let us recall that in France, until recently (1956), there was no school attendance rate available by age; then there was no question of making forecasts of the school population with the assistance of such rates.

But a projection by age is not always the best means for carrying out projections that ordinarily are related to demographic change. In this type of analysis, the individual is considered as having the characteristics of the age group to which he belongs, when, in fact, numerous aspects of his behavior (in the area of consumption, for example) depend on his way of life as a member of a household. So, in certain cases, the forecasts of a number of households, possibly classified by different criteria, constitute the best demographic base for arriving at forecasts in economic and social areas. Unfortunately, the methodology for forecasts of households is still quite poor, and, in the framework of this work, we cannot dwell on the little that does exist.

Use of Limiting Hypotheses

One form of the utilization of projections is based not so much on the treatment of purely demographic data as on the choice of hypotheses that are to be involved in their computation. We will illustrate this by an example.

If, when carrying out regional projections — for example, in France, the projections of the population by *départements* — we neglect to take account of possible migratory movements, we leave aside one factor of change that in the past was often predominant. Also, we may decide a priori that there is no interest of any kind in such computations. But, in France, internal migrations are poorly measured, and it would be very hard to formulate hypotheses for the future based upon continuation of previous movements that are altogether unknown or only poorly known.

Besides, for the future these geographical displacements are not inevitable, and it is even conceivable that we will be obliged to negate some of them.

It is here that the forecasts without migration come to play their role. We may imagine, in effect, that hypotheses entering into a projective computation are chosen in order to orient political, economic, and social action so that these hypotheses will be realized.

In the present example, making projections without migration, we estimate what would be, say, ten years from now, the present population of a *département* if this population is kept within its present boundaries.[20] As one of the motivations of emigration is the search for employment (or for better employment), it is important to enumerate the development of the desired number of jobs under this hypothesis of a closed departmental population. This involves making forecasts of the labor force in accordance with the previously explained technique and deducing from it the variations between 1960 and 1970.

Thus, working with the male population of the *département* of Ille-et-Vilaine, we find that the volume of employment should be augmented by (1) 4,700 units between 1960 and 1965, and (2) 6,700 units between 1965 and 1970 to satisfy the demands for employment coming from this population.

But the creation of jobs will take place only in the nonagricultural sector, the agricultural population being redundant. According to some hypotheses and some computation procedures (the details of which we cannot go into here), the economically active rural population of Ille-et-Vilaine will diminish by (1) 4,300 units between 1960 and 1965, and (2) 4,800 units between 1965 and 1970. Finally, it will be necessary to bring about the creation of (1) 9,000 new jobs between 1960 and 1965, and (2) 11,500 new jobs between 1965 and 1970 in the nonagricultural sector, so that the *département* will have some chance of retaining its population by offering employment to all.

20. Or at any rate had a null migration balance with the total of other *départements* and with foreign countries.

Part V
MATHEMATICS AND DEMOGRAPHIC ANALYSIS

CHAPTER SIXTEEN

Description of Demographic Events

THUS far we have used only very elementary mathematical concepts and techniques, which still have allowed us to present methods of demographic analysis with acceptable rigor, while not obliging us to depart from the conditions of concrete research. If we have depended on only the simplest rules of calculation, it was not intended as a concession to the general lack of mathematical sophistication among demographers, but was rather a result of the very "climate" in which demographic speculations are found — where the difficulties are other than formal.

However, the use of the elements of differential and integral calculus still is advantageous to the researcher, who can thereby establish certain results more rapidly and with greater rigor than he could by using only the four traditional calculation operations (addition, subtraction, multiplication, division).

The fruitfulness of this use of mathematics lies essentially in the resulting movement from the discrete terms, in which all demographic observations are given, to continuous terms, which are the domain of mathematical analysis. The majority of the difficulties of comprehension that arise from this "mathematization" originate in this formulation in continuous terms of problems whose foundations are in the domain of discrete quantities. Nevertheless, the absorption of the material that follows should be made easier by the fact that often the questions touched upon here have been treated previously with more modest mathematical equipment.

Let us consider first how the description of demographic phenomena is presented in the language of mathematical analysis.

Mortality

For the sequences of quantities in life tables, $[l_x]$, $[d_x]$ and $[q_x]$, we shall substitute functions of analogous meaning to which are imputed

447

all the properties (continuity, differentiability) that we shall need. Instead of introducing these functions a priori, we shall associate them with the sequences from which they are derived.

For the sequence $[l_x]$ we shall substitute a function $l(x)$, defined for all usual values of age x and identified at l_x for values of x, which are generally whole or integral numbers of years where this latter quantity is defined. From a practical point of view, this operates to fit a curve passing through all of the points where l_x is defined.

The deaths d_x, and more generally $_a d_x$, are attached to finite age intervals; we will substitute for these quantities a function $d(x)$, which allows definition of deaths over infinitely small intervals $(x, x+dx)$. For this we consider the quantity

$$d(x, x+\Delta x) = l(x) - l(x+\Delta x).$$

This quantity tends toward zero as Δx becomes smaller, but the ratio

$$\frac{d(x, x+\Delta x)}{\Delta x},$$

which represents the number of deaths that would be observed during the unit of time chosen (a year, for example), on the basis of observations in the period $(x, x+\Delta x)$, is never zero, however small Δx may be. We will thus substitute for the sequence $[d(x, x+1)]$ the function $d(x)$ defined by the passage to the following limit:

$$d(x) = \lim_{\Delta x \to 0} \frac{d(x, x+\Delta x)}{\Delta x}.$$

Consequently $d(x)$ has the same size as d_x, and its defining formula shows us that the deaths during an infinitely small interval $(x, x+dx)$ number:

$$d(x)\,dx.$$

Following the definition of $d(x, x+\Delta x)$, we have again the equality:

$$d(x) = \lim_{\Delta x \to 0} \frac{l(x) - l(x+\Delta x)}{\Delta x} = -l'(x)$$

and the deaths function $d(x)$ is equal, except for sign, to the derivative of the survival function $l(x)$ (see Figure 16.1). This relation between the functions $d(x)$ and $l(x)$ permits specification of the form of the survival curve: to the extremities m and M of $d(x)$ there correspond points of inflection I_m and I_M of $l(x)$ (see Figure 16.2).

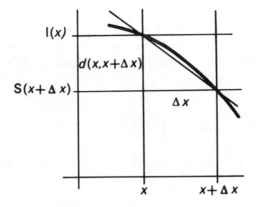

Figure 16.1

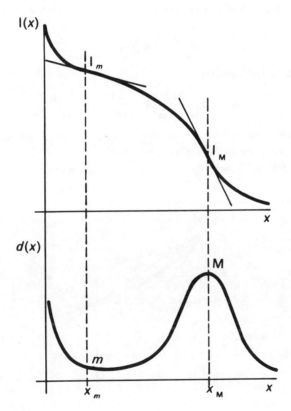

Figure 16.2

The mortality probabilities, q_x and more generally $_aq_x$, are associated with finite age intervals; to define analogous quantities for infinitely small intervals, we will again give to the measure over an interval $(x, x+\Delta x)$ the value that it would have during the time unit on an observation base lasting that interval, while we move to the limit. That is, we will consider the ratio

$$\frac{d(x, x+\Delta x)}{\Delta x \cdot l(x)}$$

and will introduce the *instantaneous mortality probability* $q(x)$ by moving to the following limit:

$$q(x) = \lim_{\Delta x \to 0} \frac{d(x, x+\Delta x)}{\Delta x \cdot l(x)} = \frac{d(x)}{l(x)}.$$

Consequently $q(x)$ has the same size as q_x, and its defining formula shows us that the probability of death during the infinitely small interval $(x, x+dx)$ is equal to

$$q(x)\,dx.$$

We have again the equality

$$q(x) = \lim_{\Delta x \to 0} \frac{l(x)-l(x+\Delta x)}{\Delta x \cdot l(x)} = -\frac{l'(x)}{l(x)}$$

and the instantaneous probability $q(x)$ is equal, except for sign, to the logarithmic derivative of the survival function.

Let us compare $q(x)$ with q_x. In the case of Figure 16.3,

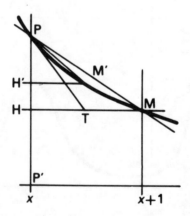

Figure 16.3

$$q(x) = \lim_{M' \to P} \frac{PH'}{M'H' \cdot PP'} = \frac{PH}{TH \cdot PP'} > \frac{PH}{PP'} = q_x;$$

so that, since the survival curve is concave upwards,

$$q(x) > q_x.$$

The converse inequality would occur in the opposite kind of figure.

From this point of view the survival curve is divided into three zones delimited by points I_m and I_M of Figure 16.2.

We have thus introduced the functions $l(x)$, $d(x)$, and $q(x)$, which can advantageously be substituted in the calculations for sequences of corresponding quantities, because they permit definitions over infinitely small intervals and, consequently, the formulation of problems in continuous terms. Here is the correspondence between these two types of representation:

	Discrete *(Using Finite Differences)*	*Continuous* *(Using Differentials)*
Survivors	l_x	$l(x)$
Deaths	$d_x = l_x - l_{x+1}$	$d(x) = \dfrac{l(x) - l(x+dx)}{dx} = -\dfrac{dl(x)}{dx}$
Mortality probabilities	$q_x = \dfrac{d(x, x+1)}{l_x} = \dfrac{l(x) - l(x+1)}{l_x}$	$q(x) = \dfrac{d(x)}{l(x)} = -\dfrac{dl(x)}{dx \cdot l(x)}$

We note again that in the continuous case the distinction between the probability and the rate disappears, and the instantaneous probability could as well have been called the *instantaneous mortality rate*.

We can pass naturally from the functions $d(x)$ and $q(x)$ to the quantities d_x and q_x.

We have immediately:

$$d_x = \int_x^{x+1} d(\xi)\, d\xi$$

Also, it follows, because of the equality

$$q(x) = -\frac{l'(x)}{l(x)}$$

that

$$\log l(x) = -\int q(x)\, dx + \text{constant}$$

$$l(x) = \text{constant} \times e^{-\int q(x)\, dx}$$

so that, insofar as the integral is defined,

$$l(x) = l(0) e^{-\int_0^{x+1} q(\xi) d\xi}$$

Assuming the entire x continuum, and dividing the two sides of the preceding equation by the two sides of

$$l(x+1) = l(0) e^{-\int_0^{x+1} q(\xi) d\xi},$$

we obtain

$$\frac{l_x}{l_{x+1}} = \frac{1}{1-q_x} = e^{\int_x^{x+1} q(\xi) d\xi}$$

whence

$$q_x = 1 - e^{-\int_x^{x+1} q(\xi) d\xi}.$$

Expression for Expectation of Life

Let us see again how the expectation of life at birth is expressed. The deaths at age x that take place during the infinitely small interval $(x, x+dx)$ number $d(x) dx$; they represent $xd(x) dx$ years of life. The total years of life lived by $l(0)$ newborns is then

$$\int_0^\omega xd(x) dx$$

from which, as an expectation of life at birth, $e(0)$ is:

$$e(0) = \frac{1}{l(0)} \cdot \int_0^\omega xd(x) dx.$$

We will transform the expression noting that

$$d(x) = -l'(x)$$

and integrating by parts:

$$\int_0^\omega xd(x) dx = -\int_0^\omega xl'(x) dx = [-xl(x)]_0^\omega + \int_0^\omega l(x) dx.$$

Finally,

$$e(0) = \frac{1}{l(0)} \int_0^\omega l(x) dx$$

and more generally,

$$e(x) = \frac{1}{l(x)} \int_x^\omega l(\xi) d\xi.$$

We have arrived at this formula somewhat laboriously, for we wished to be able to follow the computation of years lived carried out with discrete quantities. We could reach this much more rapidly noting that the total time lived by the survivors of $l(0)$ newborns between x and $x+dx$ is

$$l(x)\,dx.$$

Analytical Expressions for Mortality Functions

We have sought satisfactory analytical expressions for the functions $l(x), d(x)$, and $q(x)$. Let us cite, for example, the attempts of Bourgeois-Pichat to represent the mortality during the first year of life. He has obtained the expression

$$l(0) - l(x) = a + b \log^3(x+1),$$

which is a good approximation for the period from the end of the first month to the end of the first year (x having been expressed in days), permitting him to separate endogenous deaths from exogenous deaths; a represents the endogenous deaths.

But the most systematic attempts at analytical representation have concerned the function $q(x)$. Gompertz (1825) proceeded from the idea that the compound interest growth of human beings can be expressed as continuous growth, at a constant rate, of the instantaneous mortality probability which is given:

$$\frac{dq(x)}{q(x)} = k\,dx;$$

This results in

$$\log q(x) = kx + \text{constant}$$

and

$$q(x) = Ae^{kx};$$

The survival function thus reverts to the form

$$l(x) = Ca^{bx}.$$

Makeham (1860) introduced into the Gompertz formula for the instantaneous probability a parameter k' independent of age, to take account of accidental deaths (essentially, from infectious diseases):

$$q(x) = Ae^{kx} + k'.$$

We have then

$$l(x) = Ca^x b^{c^x}.$$

The Gompertz formula, like that of Makeham, can be applied only to those ages for which the function $q(x)$ is increasing (in practice, above the age of 20 years). Given the hypothesis upon which it is derived, the Gompertz formula seems *a priori* more likely to describe present mortality than mortality during the period in which it was formulated, when mortality from infectious diseases was of relatively greater importance. In fact, the fit of an experimental curve to the curve of finite mortality probabilities is better at advanced ages (over 80 years, for example) when deaths from old age are prevalent; it is similarly satisfactory for the quasi-total years of life when we consider only the probabilities relative to endogenous causes (such as heart diseases, circulatory ailments, cancer).

An Application

We end these considerations of mortality by an example of the application of our new concepts.

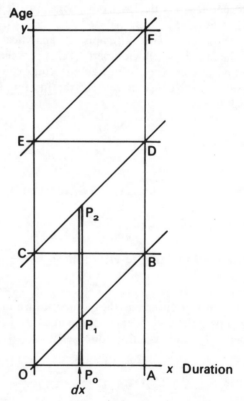

Figure 16.4

Let us refer to Figure 16.4, in which the line OA represents the time unit; suppose that the births that we have to consider are distributed uniformly over time and that the mortality conditions do not vary.

Thus the deaths at OAB, OBCD, CDEF, and so forth arise from the newborns in "equal" numbers. What proportions of deaths are found in the different areas?

The reader will recognize the problem that preoccupied us when it was necessary to weight correctly the different births involved in the infant deaths during a year, a quarter, or a month (see p. 55 to 58 and 84 to 86); the line OA may represent then, one year, one quarter, and one month respectively.

Let us take the births at OA as equal to unity, and calculate the number of deaths in the column, $P_0 P_1$ on an infinitesimal base, dx, with $OP_0 = x$. This number is

$$dx \int_0^x d(y)\, dy$$

and, consequently, for every triangle OAB we have

$$\int_0^1 dx \int_0^x d(y)\, dy \text{ deaths.}$$

But

$$d(y) = -l'(y)$$

$l(0)$ being the root of the life table taken equal to the births in OA, that is, to unity.

The preceding double integral is thus transformed to

$$\int_0^1 [l(0) - l(x)]\, dx = l(0) - \int_0^1 l(x)\, dx.$$

Let us turn to an evaluation of the number of deaths in the area OBCD; in the infinitesimal column $P_1 P_2$, the deaths number

$$dx \int_x^{x+1} d(y)\, dy,$$

and, therefore, for the entire parallelogram OBCD we have:

$$\int_0^1 dx \int_x^{x+1} d(y)\, dy \text{ deaths,}$$

a double integral that is transformed to

$$\int_0^1 [l(x) - l(x+1)]\, dx = \int_0^1 l(x)\, dx - \int_1^2 l(x)\, dx.$$

Similarly, we would find this expression as the number of deaths in the area CDEF:

$$\int_1^2 l(x)\,dx - \int_2^3 l(x)\,dx.$$

Thus the deaths in the age interval $(0, n)$ observed during the period $(0, 1)$ arise from the newborns of $(n+1)$ unitary periods, in the respective proportions that are those defined by the surfaces denoted $0, 1, 2, \ldots n$ in Figure 16.5.

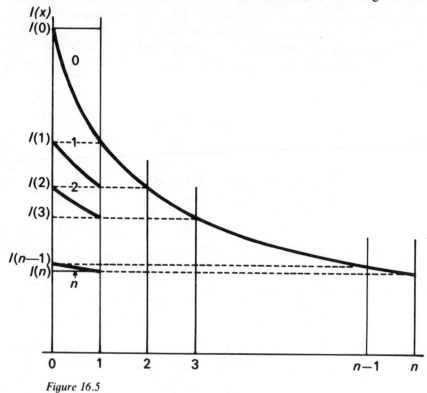

Figure 16.5

Using the French life tables for 1960–1964 and choosing successively the year, the quarter, and the month as the unitary period, we have computed – by graphic integration – the coefficients associated with the infant mortality rates centering around 20 per 1,000 (shown on p. 86).

Nuptiality

The functions $S(x)$, $m(x)$, $n(x)$ are introduced in the same manner as their homologues referring to mortality. The function $m(x)$ having only one extremity, the curve $S(x)$ has only one point of inflection. This time we have

$$S(x) = S(\alpha)\,e^{-\int_\alpha^x n(\xi)\,d\xi}$$

where α is the minimum age at marriage.

Let us calculate the mean age at marriage; with β being the maximum age at marriage, the sum of ages at marriage is

$$\int_\alpha^\beta xm(x)\,dx = -\int_\alpha^\beta xS'(x)\,dx = [-xS(x)]_\alpha^\beta + \int_\alpha^\beta S(x)\,dx$$

$$= \alpha S(\alpha) - \beta S(\beta) + \int_\alpha^\beta S(x)\,dx.$$

This sum must be divided by the number of persons ever marrying, $S(\alpha) - S(\beta)$; we find, thus,

$$m = \alpha + \frac{\displaystyle\int_\alpha^\beta S(x)\,dx - (\beta - \alpha)S(\beta)}{S(\alpha) - S(\beta)}$$

Using this formula we can clearly find those based on discrete measurement. Let us take, for example, $\alpha = 15$ and $\beta = 50$;

$$\int_\alpha^\beta S(x)\,dx = \int_{15}^{16} S(x)\,dx + \int_{16}^{17} S(x)\,dx + \cdots + \int_{49}^{50} S(x)\,dx$$

and inserting the surface represented by each integral in the right-hand side:

$$\int_\alpha^\beta S(x)\,dx = \tfrac12 S_{15} + S_{16} + \cdots + S_{49} + \tfrac12 S_{50}.$$

Taking this value in the expression for m and using 15 and 50 in place of α and β respectively, we readily arrive at:

$$m = 15.5 + \frac{S_{16} + \cdots + S_{49} - 34 S_{50}}{S_{15} - S_{50}}.$$

Relationships Between Events

The use of continuous notation greatly simplifies the problem of specifying relationships between events. Let us look at this in the case of mortality and nuptiality.

To simplify the presentation, we will take, in this paragraph,

$$l(0) = S(0) = S(\alpha) = 1.$$

The functions $l(x)$ and $S(x)$ are, respectively, the probabilities at birth of surviving to age x in the absence of nuptiality, and of remaining single at age x in the absence of mortality. Making the hypothesis that these two probabilities are independent, we find a total of $l(x)S(x)$ single persons at age x.

Let us analyze what happens during an infinitely small age interval $(x, x+dx)$. If only mortality were operating, there would be

$$l(x)S(x)\left[1-q(x)\,dx\right]$$

single persons at $x+dx$.

Consequently the marriages contracted between x and $x+dx$ are included between:

$$l(x)S(x)n(x)\,dx \text{ (if all the deaths take place at } x+dx)$$

and

$$l(x)S(x)\left[1-q(x)\,dx\right]n(x)\,dx \text{ (if all the deaths take place at } x)$$

which, in the infinitesimal interval, are equal to:

$$l(x)S(x)q(x)n(x)\,dx\,dx.$$

Thus between x and $x+dx$ there are:

$$l(x)S(x)n(x)\,dx = l(x)m(x)\,dx \text{ marriages of single persons}$$

and

$$l(x)S(x)q(x)\,dx = S(x)d(x)\,dx \text{ deaths of single persons,}$$

The second result is derived in the same way as the first. Altogether there are between x and dx,

$$l(x)S(x)\left[n(x)+q(x)\right]dx \text{ events,}$$

with the probability of single persons leaving the population written

$$\left[n(x)+q(x)\right]dx.$$

There is, then, *additivity of instantaneous probabilities*, a property that is interesting for the formulation of various problems. This property is, moreover, the same as the expression for differentiation of a product of functions:

$$d[l(x)S(x)] = -l(x)S(x)\left[n(x)+q(x)\right]dx$$

to which the previous type of calculation — following that made in the discrete case — would have led.

We note in conclusion that if we wish to compute the total number of marriages and of deaths of single persons, we must evaluate the integrals:

$$\int_\alpha^\beta l(x)m(x)\,dx \text{ and } \int_\alpha^\beta S(x)\,d(x)\,dx.$$

First Application

Let us use the continuous formulation to evaluate the annual probabilities relative to each category of vital events, using registered vital events within a given population size.

More concretely, let us put ourselves in the particular situation to observe deaths for a birth cohort. The deaths from a given cause are denoted by index 1, and the deaths from all other causes are denoted by index 2, in a unitary age interval denoted $(0, 1)$. We shall try to evaluate the corresponding finite mortality probabilities q_1 and q_2 on the basis of observed deaths d_1 and d_2.

For this we introduce (1) the instantaneous probabilities $q_1(x)$ and $q_2(x)$; and (2) the corresponding survival probabilities $l_1(x)$ and $l_2(x)$ with, consequently, $l_1(0) = l_2(0) = 1$. In addition, because of the assumption of the independence of the two types of causes, the probability of survival due to all causes together, $l(x)$, is

$$l(x) = l_1(x)l_2(x).$$

The actual number of deaths d_1, as we see, is expressed by

$$d_1 = \int_0^1 l(x)q_1(x)\,dx. \tag{R_1}$$

Since $l_1(0) = 1$, the mortality probability q_1 is equal to the deaths due to cause 1 acting alone:

$$q_1 = \int_0^1 l_1(x)q_1(x)\,dx. \tag{R_2}$$

Let us try to relate equations (R_1) and (R_2) to find an expression for q_1 involving d_1. Using the mean value theorem, we have

$$d_1 = \int_0^1 l_1(x)l_2(x)q_1(x)\,dx = l_2(\theta)\int_0^1 l_1(x)q_1(x)\,dx \qquad (0<\theta<1).$$

Thus

$$d_1 = l_2(\theta)q_1. \tag{R_1'}$$

But

$$l_2(\theta) > l_2(1) = 1 - q_2,$$

and consequently

$$l_2(\theta) = 1 - \lambda_2 q_2 \qquad (0<\lambda_2<1).$$

Finally, (R'_1) leads to

$$q_1 = \frac{d_1}{1 - \lambda_2 q_2} \qquad (0 < \lambda_2 < 1) \qquad\qquad (G_1)$$

We determine similarly that

$$q_2 = \frac{d_2}{1 - \lambda_1 q_1} \qquad (0 < \lambda_1 < 1) \qquad\qquad (G_2)$$

Let us specify the meaning and value of the coefficients λ_1 and λ_2. The actual number of deaths d_1 is equal to the number of deaths excluding those from all other causes represented by q_1, less the number of deaths from the group 2 causes, which prevented the occurrence of deaths from cause 1. If a succession of deaths were possible for a given person, we could then have $q_1 q_2$ persons who would die successively from the two causes. Denoting λ'_2 as the probability that a death from group 2 causes precedes a death due to cause 1, we see that

$$d_1 = q_1 - \lambda'_2 q_1 q_2,$$

and, by substitution in (G_1),

$$\lambda_2 = \lambda'_2;$$

λ_1 obtains an analogous meaning and, by symmetry of definitions, the necessary relationship follows:

$$\lambda_1 + \lambda_2 = 1.$$

By referring to the meaning of these coefficients, we will be able to express the value on the basis of mortality functions:

  a. On the one hand, regarding only cause 1 of death, the probability that a death from that cause will take place before age x is reached is

$$\frac{1 - l_1(x)}{q_1}.$$

  b. On the other hand, for only the group 2 causes of death, the probability that a death in this group will take place in the interval $(x, x + dx)$ is equal to

$$\frac{l_2(x) q_2(x)\, dx}{q_2}.$$

Because of the assumption of independence, the product of these two preceding quantities,

$$\frac{1}{q_1 q_2} [1 - l_1(x)] l_2(x) q_2(x)\, dx,$$

represents the probability that a death from cause 1 will occur before a death due to group 2 causes that would occur in $(x, x + dx)$. Summing this elementary probability from 0 to 1, we obtain λ_1:

$$\lambda_1 = \frac{1}{q_1 q_2} \int_0^1 [1 - l_1(x)] l_2(x) q_2(x) \, dx,$$

and similarly,

$$\lambda_2 = \frac{1}{q_1 q_2} \int_0^1 [1 - l_2(x)] l_1(x) q_1(x) \, dx.$$

Thus we can see that, because of the presence of the quantities λ_1 and λ_2 in formulas (G_1) and (G_2), knowing only the quantities d_1 and d_2 does not suffice for determining q_1 and q_2 precisely. Nevertheless, we arrive at specifically simple results if we can assume that the *survival functions are linear* (an assumption generally admissible for small intervals). We would then have:

$$l_1(x) = 1 - q_1 x$$

$$l_2(x) = 1 - q_2 x$$

$$q_2(x) = \frac{l_2'(x)}{l_2(x)} = \frac{q_2}{1 - q_2 x}$$

it then follows that

$$\lambda_1 = \int_0^1 x \, dx = \tfrac{1}{2},$$

and hence

$$\lambda_1 = \lambda_2 = \tfrac{1}{2};$$

and the formulas (G_1) and (G_2) can then be written

$$q_1 = \frac{d_1}{1 - (q_2/2)} \tag{G_1'}$$

$$q_2 = \frac{d_2}{1 - (q_2/2)} \tag{G_2'}$$

Substituting, in the denominators, q_1 and q_2 for d_1 and d_2, we arrive at the classical formulas:

$$q_1 = \frac{d_1}{1 - (d_2/2)} \tag{H_1}$$

$$q_2 = \frac{d_2}{1 - (d_1/2)} \tag{H_2}$$

Second Application

The question that we have just treated satisfies a concern for theoretical thoroughness. Let us now examine the same problem – the determination of a probability of mortality from a particular cause of death or in the absence of this particular cause – viewed from the practical angle.

In practice it is unusual to have as detailed a classification of deaths by age for deaths due to a particular cause as for the total of deaths from all causes. Usually, in the best of circumstances, we have information on the causes of deaths for quinquennial groups according to age at death. The problem, then, is to determine if, with only such information, it is possible to estimate mortality probabilities by causes of death isolated in this manner.

Let k denote the proportion (assumed constant) of deaths due to cause 1 taking place in each sufficiently small interval around age x. We have, then,

$$d_1(x, x+\Delta x) = kd(x, x+\Delta x),$$

an equality that, when both members are divided by Δx and taken to the limit, leads to

$$d_1(x) = kd(x)$$

and consequently to

$$q_1(x) = kq(x).$$

Because of the additivity of the probabilities – due to the assumption that the causes are independent – we can deduce the probability $q_2(x)$ in the absence of the cause of death considered by the formula

$$q_2(x) = (1-k)q(x).$$

In practice we are generally less interested in determining the cause-specific mortality probabilities themselves than in constructing life tables based upon the elimination of a certain cause of death (that is, to estimate expectation of life in the absence of, say, cancer or infectious disease or accidents).

In these instances, it is a matter of using the last formula to calculate the number of survivors corresponding to the probability function so defined.

As we cannot assume k to be constant for the entire range of ages, we make the assumption that it is constant over sufficiently small intervals, for example, over annual intervals; thus we would associate with each interval, $(x, x+1)$ a coefficient k_2, such that $q_2(x) = (1-k_x)q(x)$. We integrate between x and $x+1$:

$$\int_x^{x+1} q_2(\xi)\,d\xi = \int_x^{x+1} (1-k_x)q(\xi)\,d\xi$$

whence

$$\log_e \frac{l_2(x+1)}{l_2(x)} = (1-k_x) \log_e \frac{l(x+1)}{l(x)},$$

where, denoting $p_{2,x}$ and p_x as the annual probabilities,

$$\log_e p_{2,x} = (1-k_x) \log_e p_x.$$

This is to say, again,

$$\log_e (1-q_{2,x}) = (1-k_x) \log_e (1-q_x).$$

Using these formulas, we are then able to substitute for mortality probabilities reflecting all causes of death new mortality probabilities resulting from the elimination of the cause of death denoted 1. These formulas naturally hold true for all intervals for which the quantity k can be assumed constant.

Fertility

We are concerned here with measures of fertility not differentiated according to birth order, the measures by birth order leading to solutions of the type adopted for mortality and nuptiality.

Here the description is carried out with a table of cumulative fertility defined by the series of cumulative fertility rates $\{C_x\}$ at different birthdays of the women (for fertility of all women), or at different wedding anniversaries (for marital fertility). These cumulative fertilities are related, respectively to a fixed total number F, of women, or U, of married couples. In the case where $F = U = 1$, the births

$$b(x, x+1) = C_{x+1} - C_x$$

are identical to the fertility rate, f_x. In what follows we shall deal always with this situation.

For the sequence $\{C_x\}$ we shall substitute a function $C(x)$ identical to C_x for the values of x where the latter quantity is defined, and determined by interpolation for the other values of x.

We introduce the *instantaneous fertility rate* $f(x)$[1] by passing to a limit as follows:

$$f(x) = \lim_{\Delta x \to 0} \frac{C(x+\Delta x) - C(x)}{\Delta x} = C'(x).$$

1. As in the discrete case, there is no question here of speaking of a (instantaneous) probability. Moreover, the distinction between rates of the first and second categories remains for the case of instantaneous rates, and the relations that we have established in the discrete case between these rates and the probabilities and events of tables (or fertility charts) are transformed this time, as can be readily verified, by strict equalities.

This defining formula shows that the frequency of births in the infinitely small interval $(x, x+dx)$ equals $f(x)\,dx$.

The function $f(x)$ apparent in the sequence $\{f_x\}$ gives a maximum corresponding to a point of inflection of the curve of $C(x)$ (see Figure 16.6).

Among the possible equations permitting a satisfactory analytical representation of the fertility function $f(x)$, let us indicate the one related to the gamma function:

$$f(x) = C\phi(x-15; \alpha, p),$$

C being the final cumulative fertility, and

$$\phi(x-15; \alpha, p) = \frac{\alpha^p}{\Gamma(p)}(x-15)^{p-1}\,e^{-\alpha(x-15)} \qquad (x \geq 15; p > 0)$$

ignoring fertility at ages under 15 years; thus ϕ represents the calendar.

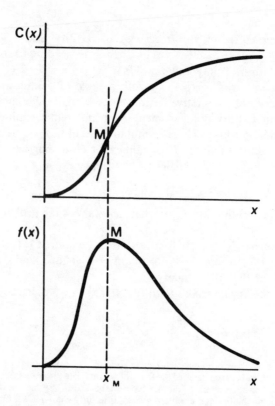

Figure 16.6

Two parameters are free for making adjustments; using the method of moments, we determine these parameters with the aid of the formulas

$$E(x - 15) = p/\alpha$$
$$\sigma^2(x - 15) = p/\alpha^2$$

the mean and variance being furnished by the observed calendar.

But there is another area of fertility analysis in which the introduction of continuously defined functions is particularly useful – the area involving the quantities introduced in the chapter "Fertility and Family," including fecundability, sterility, and intrauterine mortality. A fruitful exploration of the connections between these different parameters and certain measures of fertility is thus made possible.

CHAPTER SEVENTEEN

Populations

We shall now refer to calendar time (in the normal sense of the word), since the study of populations requires, above all, instantaneous observations.

General Relationships

We shall denote $P(t)$ as the size of a population at any arbitrary date t, the function $P(t)$ having all the properties that we shall need. Such a function can be conceived as deriving from an adjustment based on the points $\{t_i, P_{t_i}\}$ corresponding to the data available on the size of the population in question.

On this basis we define the *instantaneous rate of growth*, $r(t)$ by passing to the following limit:

$$r(t) = \lim_{\Delta t \to 0} \frac{P(t + \Delta t) - P(t)}{P(t)\Delta t} = \frac{P'(t)}{P(t)}.$$

It follows from this definition that the growth during the infinitesimal interval $(t, t + dt)$ is written

$$dP(t) = P(t)r(t)\, d(t)$$

and that

$$P(t) = P(0)\, e^{\int_0^t r(t)\, dt}$$

If the population in question is closed, the variation in size between instants t and $(t + \Delta t)$ results from births $B(t, t + \Delta t)$ and from deaths $D(t, t + \Delta t)$ that occur during the interval $(t, t + \Delta t)$:

$$P(t + \Delta t) - P(t) = B(t, t + \Delta t) - D(t, t + \Delta t).$$

To take account of infinitesimal variations in population, we introduce the functions

$$B(t) = \lim_{\Delta t \to 0} \frac{B(t, t + \Delta t)}{\Delta t}.$$

We have, then,

$$D(t) = \lim_{\Delta t \to 0} \frac{D(t, t + \Delta t)}{\Delta t}$$

$$dP(t) = [B(t) - D(t)] \, dt.$$

Introducing

$$b(t) = \frac{B(t)}{P(t)} \quad \text{and} \quad d(t) = \frac{D(t)}{P(t)},$$

which we denote respectively the *instantaneous crude birth rate* and the *instantaneous crude death rate*, we have this relationship (assuming the population to be closed):

$$\frac{dP(t)}{dt \, P(t)} = r(t) = b(t) - d(t).$$

Thus far we have brought only cross-sectional data to bear; in using longitudinal data we specify the manner in which populations are formed and the conditions under which the vital events occurring during any given period appear. For this we must refer at the same time to the calendar date t and to the duration x at date t for the infinitesimal fractions of the cohort that we are studying.

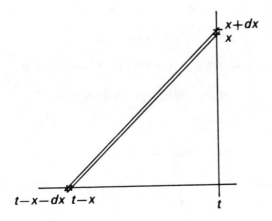

Figure 17.1

In this way we introduce the probability of survival

$$l(x, t)$$

from birth until age x for persons reaching age x at date t. We shall work actually with the infinitesimal fraction of the birth cohort whose ages are between x and $x+dx$ at date t an_ who, therefore, were born between $t-x-dx$ and $t-x$ (Figure 17.1). We have, then,

$$l(0, t-x) = 1$$

Let us denote as $d(x, t)$ and $q(x, t)$ the two functions related to $l(x, t)$.

Let us now introduce the fertility function $f(x, t)$, which gives the value of the instantaneous birth rate at date t for women aged x to $x+dx$. With this established, we shall express $P(t)$, $B(t)$, and $D(t)$ as functions of these longitudinal data.

The population $P(t)$ at date t is composed of survivors among the newborns of the period $(0, \omega)$. The newborns of the period $(t-x-dx, t-x)$ number $B(t-x)\,dx$, and survive in the proportion $l(x, t)$ to date t; at that date, they total then,

$$B(t-x)l(x-t)\,dx.$$

Consequently,

$$P(t) = \int_0^\omega B(t-x)l(x, t)\,dx.$$

Let us now look at the contribution of the newborns of the period $(t-x-dx, t-x)$ to the births and deaths of the period $(t, t+dt)$. As far as births are concerned, we must consider only the female newborns, whose number and survival function we denote $B_F(t-x)$ and $l_F(t-x)$. These being the

$$B_F(t-x)l_F(x, t)\,dx$$

survivors at date t, they will give during the period $(t, t+dt)$:

$$B_F(t-x)l_F(x, t)f(x, t)\,dx\,dt \text{ births.}$$

Thus

$$B(t)\,dt = dt \int_\alpha^\beta B_F(t-x)l_F(x, t)f(x, t)\,dx$$

or

$$B(t) = \int_\alpha^\beta B_F(t-x)l_F(x, t)f(x, t)\,dx,$$

α and β being the limits of the fertile period.

An analogous reasoning leads to

$$D(t) = \int_0^\omega B(t-x)l(x, t)q(x, t)\,\mathrm{d}x$$

or again:

$$D(t) = \int_0^\omega B(t-x)d(x, t)\,\mathrm{d}x$$

Let us now introduce an important cross-sectional datum: *the age distribution of the population.* We denote

$$P(t; x, x+\Delta x)$$

as the number in the population aged x to $x+\Delta x$ at date t; we set

$$\lim_{\Delta x \to 0} \frac{P(t; x, x+\Delta x)}{\Delta x \cdot P(t)} = c(x, t)$$

so that the frequency of persons in the infinitesimal interval $(x, x+\mathrm{d}x)$ is equal to

$$c(x, t)\,\mathrm{d}x,$$

and

$$\int_0^\omega c(x, t)\,\mathrm{d}x = 1.$$

It is clear that the function $c(x, t)$, which depends upon the variable x, is related to the longitudinal data; this can be shown explicitly by relating the following two expressions of the size of the population in age interval $(x, x+\mathrm{d}x)$:

on one hand,

$$P(t)c(x, t)\,\mathrm{d}x$$

and on the other,

$$B(t-x)l(x, t)\,\mathrm{d}x.$$

It follows from these that

$$c(x, t) = \frac{B(t-x)l(x, t)}{P(t)}.$$

In particular,

$$c(0, t) = \frac{B(t)}{P(t)} = b(t).$$

Let us note again that

$$d(t) = \int_0^\omega c(x, t)q(x, t)\,\mathrm{d}x.$$

Similarly,

$$b(t) = \int_\alpha^\beta c(x, t)f(x, t)\,\mathrm{d}x,$$

the function $c(x, t)$ referring this time only to the female population.

Some Population Examples

To explain further some of the functions that we have introduced thus far or to impose some conditions upon them, we shall define some population types. Thus, assuming the *instantaneous growth rate* to be constant, we can define the *exponential population;* in this case it is

$$P(t) = P(0)\,\mathrm{e}^{rt}.$$

There are, of course, as many particular exponential populations as there are possible values of r, i.e., infinitely many.

By assuming that the growth rate of the population diminishes in proportion to the size attained, Quételet (1835) and Verhulst (1838) were led to the equation:

$$r(t) = r - kP(t) = \frac{P'(t)}{P(t)};$$

that is,

$$\mathrm{d}P(t) = rP(t)\left[1 - \frac{k}{r}P(t)\right]\mathrm{d}t$$

$$\frac{(r/k)\,\mathrm{d}P(t)}{P(t)\left[(r/k) - P(t)\right]} = \frac{K\,\mathrm{d}P(t)}{P(t)\left[K - P(t)\right]} = \left[\frac{1}{P(t)} + \frac{1}{K - P(t)}\right]\mathrm{d}P(t) = r\,\mathrm{d}t;$$

Integrating

$$\log_e \frac{K - P(t)}{P(t)} = -rt + a \quad \text{and} \quad P(t) = \frac{K}{1 + \mathrm{e}^{a - rt}}\left(K - \frac{r}{k}\right),$$

we arrive at the *logistic population,* a model that once enjoyed great popularity — probably because of the upper bounds assigned by such a model to populations thus adjusted and the good description it provides of the growth of certain animal populations. It is possible, moreover that the growth of world population may obey some such mathematical rule, which seems to provide a good model of growth in a limited universe.

Exponential Populations with Fixed Age Distributions

More interesting extensions of the exponential population are obtained by adding to the assumption $r(t) = r$ an additional assumption concerning one of the several functions that we have considered:

$$c(x, t), \quad p(x, t), \quad d(x, t) \ldots$$

Let us make in this way the supplementary hypothesis that the age distribution is fixed over time, *i.e.*,

$$c(x, t) = c(x).$$

It then follows that

$$c(0, t) = c(0) = \frac{B(t)}{P(t)} = b(t) = b;$$

that is, the birth rate is constant and

$$B(t) = bP(t) = bP(0) e^{rt} = B(0) e^{rt}.$$

The death rate is also constant by virtue of the relationship

$$r(t) = b(t) - d(t),$$

and consequently

$$D(t) = D(0) e^{rt}.$$

The relationship

$$c(x, t) = \frac{B(t - x)l(x, t)}{P(t)},$$

which in this case is written

$$c(x) = \frac{B(0) e^{r(t - x)}l(x, t)}{P(0) e^{rt}} = b e^{-rx}l(x, t),$$

shows that $l(x, t)$ is independent of t; in other words, the survival function is fixed in time, and finally:

$$c(x) = b e^{-rx}l(x).$$

Integrating between 0 and ω the two sides of the equality, we have

$$1 = b \int_0^\omega e^{-rx}l(x)\,dx$$

or

$$b = \frac{1}{\displaystyle\int_0^\omega e^{-rx} l(x)\, dx}.$$

The general formula

$$d(t) = \int_0^\omega c(x, t) q(x, t)\, dx$$

becomes here:

$$d = \int_0^\omega c(x) q(x)\, dx = -b \int_0^\omega e^{-rx} l'(x)\, dx$$

$$= -\frac{\displaystyle\int_0^\omega e^{-rx} l'(x)\, dx}{\displaystyle\int_0^\omega e^{-rx} l(x)\, dx}.$$

In the chart below, we recapitulate the definition and the properties of the characteristic exponential populations that we have just considered:

Definition   *Properties*

$$P(t) = P(0)\, e^{rt}$$
$$b(t) = b; \quad B(t) = B(0)\, e^{rt}$$
$$d(t) = d; \quad D(t) = D(0)\, e^{rt}$$

$r(t) = r$ $l(x, t) = l(x)$
$c(x, t) = c(x)$ $c(x) = b\, e^{-rx} l(x)$

$$b = \frac{1}{\displaystyle\int_0^\omega e^{-rx} l(x)\, dx}; \quad d = \frac{\displaystyle\int_0^\omega e^{-rx} l'(x)\, dx}{\displaystyle\int_0^\omega e^{-rx} l(x)\, dx}$$

The limited list of properties is not exhaustive. But from this list we can already extract many pairs of *characteristic properties*, that is, properties that, when taken as assumptions, define populations characterized by all the other properties (those listed here as well as all the others), as well as the definitional relationships of the chart itself. The same result can be obtained by associating any appropriately chosen property with one of the two definitional relationships.

A. J. Lotka, who was interested in the class of populations with which we are now concerned, presented them starting with two definitional relationships:

$$c(x, t) = c(x) \quad \text{and} \quad l(x, t) = l(x).$$

We have here the combination of one definitional relationship and one property taken from our preceding chart. It is easily seen that, from these two equalities, $r(t) = r$; in effect:

$$b(t) = c(0, t) = c(0) = b; \quad d(t) = \int_0^\omega c(x, t)q(x, t)\,\mathrm{d}x = \int_0^\omega c(x)q(x)\,\mathrm{d}x = d$$

Since $b(t)$ and $d(t)$ are constants, $r(t)$, which is their difference, is also constant. Thus the equivalence between the two modes of definition is clearly demonstrated.

"*Malthusian*" *Populations*

Following Lotka, we shall call the particular exponential populations thus described *Malthusian populations*. As we have presented them, we see that these populations can be considered as forming many combinations, an endless number in two senses. In this way the first definition that we have chosen (in the chart above) leads to classification of Malthusian populations in terms of the value of the growth rate r and the form taken by the function $c(x)$. It is by taking all possible values of these two characteristics that we pair off the entire set of Malthusian populations, a set that we can denote $E[r; c(x)]$; but we can also arrive at such a systematic count of Malthusian populations by following Lotka, *i.e.*, by considering the doubly infinite set, $E[c(x); l(x)]$.

Let us look at still another way of classifying the set of all Malthusian populations: by considering the set $E[B(t) = B(0)\,e^{rt}; l(x)]$.

From

$$B(t) = B(0)\,e^{rt}$$

it follows that

$$P(t) = \int_0^\omega B(0)\,e^{r(t-x)}l(x)\,\mathrm{d}x$$

$$= B(0)\,e^{rt}\int_0^\omega e^{-rx}l(x)\,\mathrm{d}x = P(0)\,e^{rt}$$

and

$$c(x, t) = \frac{B(0)\,e^{r(t-x)}l(x)}{P(0)\,e^{rt}} = b\,e^{-rx}l(x)$$

and we are brought back to our first definition.

This manner of defining the set of Malthusian populations lends itself conveniently to the computation of these populations. This is the way in which we have developed and presented — albeit by a different name — stable populations (see p. 326).

Stable Populations

If the fertility function $f(x, t)$ is not used in the study of the possible definitions and the properties of Malthusian populations, it is because this function concerns only a single sex. Obviously we can introduce two fertility functions:

first, $f_M(x, t)$, describing male births as a function of the age of the fathers and of (calendar) time;

second, $f_F(x, t)$, describing female births as a function of the age of the mothers and of (calendar) time.

But then there is, in general, an incompatibility between the two necessary relationships:

$$B_M(t) = \int_{\alpha'}^{\beta'} B_M(t-x) l_M(x) f_M(x, t) \, dx$$

$$B_F(t) = \int_{\alpha}^{\beta} B_F(t-x) l_F(x) f_F(x, t) \, dx.$$

We can thus use the fertility function in Malthusian populations only by considering one sex alone. *In what follows we shall be considering only the female sex*, without specifying this in the formula by an index.[1]

In a quite general fashion, we have

$$B(t) = \int_{\alpha}^{\beta} B(t-x) l(x, t) f(x, t) \, dx$$

and, if a Malthusian population is involved, since $l(x, t) = l(x)$:

$$B(t) = \int_{\alpha}^{\beta} B(t-x) l(x) f(x, t) \, dx.$$

But we also have, in this case,

$$B(t) = B(0) e^{rt},$$

so that the preceding relationship is transformed to

$$\int_{\alpha}^{\beta} e^{-rx} l(x) f(x, t) \, dx = 1.$$

The verification of this relation is the condition that the function $f(x, t)$ must fulfill in the case of Malthusian populations. The name *stable popula-*

---

1. It is understood, then, that the fertility function $f(x,t)$ will refer only to female births.

tions is reserved for the particular Malthusian populations for which

$$f(x, t) = f(x).$$

The existence of stable populations corresponding to a given function $f(x)$ is then related to the possibility of finding $l(x)$ and r such that we have:

$$\int_{\alpha}^{\beta} e^{-rx} l(x) f(x)\, dx = 1. \qquad (E)$$

To discuss this point let us consider, with $f(x)$ and $l(x)$ jointly fixed, the function of r:

$$I(r) = \int_{\alpha}^{\beta} e^{-rx} l(x) f(x)\, dx.$$

Since

$$I'(r) = -\int_{\alpha}^{\beta} x\, e^{-rx} l(x) f(x)\, dx < 0$$

the function $I(r)$ is constantly decreasing. Moreover,

(a) if $r \to -\infty$, then $e^{-rx} \to +\infty$ and $I(r) \to +\infty$;

(b) if $r \to +\infty$, then $e^{-rx} \to 0$ and $I(r) \to +\infty$;

the curve representing the function $I(r)$ then has a form like those of Figure 17.2; this curve crosses the vertical axis at the ordinal point:

$$I(0) = R_0 = \int_{\alpha}^{\beta} l(x) f(x)\, dx.$$

It follows from this discussion that for $l(x)$ and $f(x)$ jointly fixed, there is only a single value of r that will satisfy equation (E), this value being positive or negative according to whether the quantity R_0 is greater or less than unity.

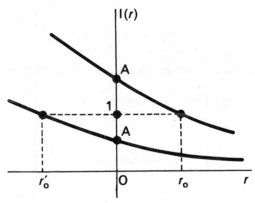

Figure 17.2

Stable Populations as Limit Populations

Interest in the notion of a stable population comes from the fact that the indefinite operation of fixed laws of mortality and fertility $l(x, t) = l(x)$ and $f(x, t) = f(x)$ makes *any population* tend toward a stable state. To prove this result[2] let us study what happens to the annual number of births $B(t)$ in an arbitrary population, starting with the moment that mortality and fertility become fixed over time. The function $B(t)$ then satisfies the equation

$$B(t) = \int_{\alpha}^{\beta} B(t-x)l(x)f(x)\,dx.$$

To solve this equation we can use any satisfactory analytical expression for $l(x)f(x)$ (an expression related to the gamma function, for example). Or we can proceed, as did Lotka, to consider very generally the form and the properties of solutions.

Lotka solved the equation by looking for solutions for form:

$$B(t) = Q_0\,e^{r_0 t} + Q_1\,e^{r_1 t} + \cdots$$

which, when this expression is substituted in the preceding equation, leads to this sequence of equations:

$$1 = \int_{\alpha}^{\beta} e^{-r_n x}l(x)f(x)\,dx \; (n = 0, 1, 2, \ldots).$$

The quantities r_n are then defined as roots of the equation

$$\int_{\alpha}^{\beta} e^{-rx}l(x)f(x)\,dx = 1 \tag{E}$$

which we encountered in the preceding section.

We have already seen that this equation has only one real root. It also has an infinite number of imaginary roots, their specification leading to the consideration of

$$\int_{\alpha}^{\beta} e^{-(u+iv)x}l(x)f(x)\,dx = 1,$$

which, when the real and imaginary parts are separated, breaks down into

$$\left.\begin{aligned}
\int_{\alpha}^{\beta} e^{-ux}\cos vx\,l(x)f(x)\,dx &= 1 \\[2em]
\int_{\alpha}^{\beta} e^{-ux}\sin vx\,l(x)f(x)\,dx &= 0
\end{aligned}\right\} \tag{E'}$$

2. This result can be proved with discrete quantities by representing the population and the fixed set of fertility and mortality projection probabilities in matrix form.

The values of u are, then, such that

$$\int_\alpha^\beta e^{-ux} l(x) f(x) \, dx > 1;$$

and since the real solution ρ satisfies

$$\int_\alpha^\beta e^{-\rho x} l(x) f(x) \, dx = 1,$$

we have

$$e^{-ux} > e^{-\rho x}$$

and consequently

$$u < \rho$$

Finally, by virtue of the equations (E'), if $(u_1 + iv_1)$ is a particular solution, $u_1 - iv_1$ is also a solution: the roots z other than ρ are pairs of conjugated imaginary roots. As for the coefficients of the two conjugated roots in the expression of $B(t)$, they must be identical to make real terms other than $Q_0 e^{\rho t}$ appear. In a general way, we would then have the term

$$Q[e^{(u+iv)t} + e^{(u-iv)t}] = 2Q_2 e^{ut} \cos vt$$

corresponding to the two solutions $u + iv$ and $u - iv$, and the general solution would be written

$$B(t) = Q_0 e^{\rho t} + Q_1 e^{u_1 t} \cos v_1 t + Q_2 e^{u_2 t} \cos v_2 t + \cdots$$

the quantities Q_i being dependent upon the initial conditions.

Since ρ is greater than all the u_i, when t increases, the term $Q_0 e^{\rho t}$ ends by being greater than all the others, and it can be shown that it becomes predominant relative to the sum of the others. Consequently, in a population in which mortality and fertility functions remain constant, the annual number of births tend to become, as time passes, an exponential function of time. This limiting form is attained after oscillations which reflect the terms in $\cos v_n t$.

The limiting population is, then, a Malthusian (stable) population, the conditions of (1) fixed mortality regime; and (2) exponential growth of annual numbers of births being fulfilled. The root ρ which, by reference to the limiting stable population, characterizes the rate of growth implied by the corresponding mortality and fertility functions, is called the *intrinsic rate of natural increase*.

By averaging approximations, we can prove a simple relationship between this rate and the quantity

$$R_0 = \int_\alpha^\beta l(x) f(x) \, dx$$

that is none other than the *net reproduction rate*. Let us, in fact, express the definitional relationship

$$\int_\alpha^\beta e^{-\rho x} l(x) f(x) \, dx = 1,$$

bringing in an age x_0 whose value will be specified later:

$$\int_\alpha^\beta e^{-\rho(x-x_0)} e^{-\rho x_0} l(x) f(x) \, dx = 1;$$

that is,

$$\int_\alpha^\beta e^{-\rho(x-x_0)} l(x) f(x) \, dx = e^{\rho x_0}.$$

But

$$e^{-\rho(x-x_0)} \simeq 1 - \rho(x-x_0)$$

if $\rho(x-x_0)$ is small; under this hypothesis, the preceding equality is written

$$\int_\alpha^\beta l(x) f(x) \, dx + \rho \left[x_0 \int_\alpha^\beta l(x) f(x) \, dx - \int_\alpha^\beta x l(x) f(x) \, dx \right] = e^{\rho x_0}.$$

Let us choose x_0 so that the quantity inside the brackets will be null, i.e.,

$$x_0 = a' = \frac{\displaystyle\int_\alpha^\beta x l(x) f(x) \, dx}{\displaystyle\int_\alpha^\beta l(x) f(x) \, dx},$$

where a' is the mean age (total) of mothers at the time of their children's birth.

This choice leads to the relationship[3]

$$R_0 = e^{\rho a'} \tag{1}$$

or

$$\rho = \frac{1}{a'} \log_e R_0$$

3. This relationship is equivalent, in continuous terms, to the formula $R_0 = (1+\rho)^x$ given on page 350.

a formula that permits an approximate calculation of the intrinsic rate of natural increase corresponding to the functions $l(x)$ and $f(x)$.

We see, with this formula, that ρ depends not only on the net reproduction rate, but also on a', which measures in its way the pace of replacement of generations (in the ordinary sense of this word).

Stationary Populations

Stationary populations are a special case of stable populations, those in which $r = 0$, which justifies their name. Annual numbers of births and deaths are constant and equal, as are the rates of birth and death.

Since

$$c(x) = b\,e^{-rx}\,l(x) = bl(x),$$

we see that the profile of the age pyramid is determined by the survival function and that

$$b = \frac{1}{\displaystyle\int_0^\omega l(x)\,dx} = \frac{1}{e_0} = d;$$

that is, the birth and death rates are equal to the inverse of the expectation of life at birth.

As for the constant total population size P, in view of the relationship $b = B/P$, the total population numbers $P = B/b = Be_0$, which is the product of the annual number of births times the expectation of life at birth. It is readily seen that stationary populations could as well be defined as stable populations in which

$$c(x) = kl(x) \qquad (k = \text{cte})$$

or, alternatively,

$$B(t) = B$$

and so forth.

Application

In the case of a stationary population, there is a relationship between the expectation of life at birth and the mean age of the population; the latter is expressed as follows:

$$\bar{a} = b \int_0^\omega x l(x)\,dx = b\left[\frac{x^2}{2}l(x)\right]_0^\omega - \frac{b}{2}\int_0^\omega x^2 l'(x)\,dx.$$

The quantity inside the brackets is null, and

$$-\frac{b}{2}\int_0^\omega x^2 l'(x)\,dx = \frac{b}{2}\int_0^\omega x^2 d(x)\,dx = \frac{1}{2e_0}\left[\int_0^\omega (x-e_0)^2 d(x)\,dx + e_0^2\right].$$

Finally,

$$\bar{a} = \frac{e_0}{2} + \frac{\sigma^2}{2e_0}$$

and, introducing the coefficient of variation,

$$v = \frac{\sigma}{e_0},$$

we arrive at

$$\bar{a} = \frac{e_0}{2}(1+v^2) > \frac{e_0}{2}.$$

Thus the mean age of a stationary population is greater than half the expectation of life at birth; the two quantities would be equal if age at death were uniform. Following L. Henry, we are led by this property to a general observation.

To calculate the mean age of a population is to calculate the mean time elapsed since a prior event – birth. Often in demography we are similarly led to carrying out calculations of mean time elapsed; it is thus that we will compute (a) the mean time elapsed in the country of a population of temporary immigrants; and (b) the mean time elapsed since the last menstrual period, in a female population.

There is a great temptation to evaluate in this way the mean duration of the sojourns of immigrants, the mean duration of the menstrual cycle, etc., by doubling the observed mean durations. However, our preceding formula shows that for persons in a stationary population, the doubled mean time elapsed since birth exceeds the mean duration of life, due to the variation in individual lengths of life.

Thus, with the assumption that the elapsed times observed, which, after all, can be most varied – vary among populations (in a broad sense) that are notably stationary, we see that it is not possible to evaluate the mean durations (of sojourn, of menstrual cycle, etc) associated with these elapsed times by doubling the mean values of the latter: the results thus obtained exceed more or less markedly the results that are actually sought.

Appendix

I. *Reed-Merrell Tables*

These tables, with the exception of Table 1, first appeared in *The American Journal of Hygiene*, Vol. 30, No. 2, September 1939. Permission by the editors of that journal to reproduce these tables here is gratefully acknowledged.

The formulae relating mortality rates and probabilities are as follows:

table 1: $_4q_1 = 1 - e^{-4_4m_1 - 0.008(4)^3_4m_1}$

table 2: $_5q_x = 1 - e^{-5_5m_x - 0.008(5)^3_5m_x}$

table 3: $_{10}q_x = 1 - e^{-10_{10}m_x - 0.008(10)^3_{10}m_x}$

TABLE 1.

$_4m_1$	$_4q_1$	Δ	$_4m_1$	$_4q_1$	Δ
		.00			.00
.000	.00 000	399	.020	.07 707	371
.001	.00 399	398	.021	.08 078	369
.002	.00 797	396	.022	.08 447	367
.003	.01 193	395	.023	.08 814	366
.004	.01 588	393	.024	.09 180	365
.005	.01 981	392	.025	.09 545	364
.006	.02 373	391	.026	.09 909	362
.007	.02 764	389	.027	.10 271	360
.008	.03 153	387	.028	.10 631	360
.009	.03 540	386	.029	.10 991	358
.010	.03 926	385	.030	.11 349	356
.011	.04 311	383	.031	.11 705	356
.012	.04 694	381	.032	.12 061	354
.013	.05 075	381	.033	.12 415	352
.014	.05 456	378	.034	.12 767	352
.015	.05 834	378	.035	.13 119	350
.016	.06 212	376	.036	.13 469	348
.017	.06 588	374	.037	.13 817	348
.018	.06 962	373	.038	.14 165	346
.019	.07 335	372	.039	.14 511	344
.020	.07 707	371	.040	.14 855	

1. For discussion of these tables, see pages 138–140.
2. For reasons indicated in page 138 we have ourselves computed Table 1. We give the values of $_4q_1$ to five significant figures (the Reed–Merrell tables give six), which suffices for all actual use.

TABLE 2. *Part A*

$_5m_x$	$_5q_x$	Δ	$_5m_x$	$_5q_x$	Δ	$_5m_x$	$_5q_x$	Δ
		.00			.00			.00
.000	.000 000	4 989	.050	.223 144	3 952	.100	.399 504	3 116
.001	.004 989	4 965	.051	.227 096	3 935	.101	.402 620	3 100
.002	.009 954	4 943	.052	.231 031	3 915	.102	.405 720	3 085
.003	.014 897	4 920	.053	.234 946	3 897	.103	.408 805	3 070
.004	.019 817	4 897	.054	.238 843	3 879	.104	.411 875	3 056
.005	.024 714	4 876	.055	.242 722	3 861	.105	.414 931	3 041
.006	.029 590	4 852	.056	.246 583	3 842	.106	.417 972	3 026
.007	.034 442	4 830	.057	.250 425	3 824	.107	.420 998	3 011
.008	.039 272	4 808	.058	.254 249	3 807	.108	.424 009	2 998
.009	.044 080	4 786	.059	.258 056	3 788	.109	.427 007	2 982
.010	.048 866	4 763	.060	.261 844	3 770	.110	.429 989	2 969
.011	.053 629	4 742	.061	.265 614	3 753	.111	.432 958	2 953
.012	.058 371	4 720	.062	.269 367	3 735	.112	.435 911	2 940
.013	.063 091	4 698	.063	.273 102	3 717	.113	.438 851	2 926
.014	.067 789	4 676	.064	.276 819	3 700	.114	.441 777	2 911
.015	.072 465	4 655	.065	.280 519	3 682	.115	.444 688	2 897
.016	.077 120	4 633	.066	.284 201	3 665	.116	.447 585	2 883
.017	.081 753	4 612	.067	.287 866	3 647	.117	.450 468	2 870
.018	.086 365	4 590	.068	.291 513	3 630	.118	.453 338	2 855
.019	.090 955	4 570	.069	.295 143	3 613	.119	.456 193	2 842
.020	.095 525	4 547	.070	.298 756	3 596	.120	.459 035	2 827
.021	.100 072	4 527	.071	.302 352	3 579	.121	.461 862	2 815
.022	.104 599	4 506	.072	.305 931	3 562	.122	.464 677	2 800
.023	.109 105	4 485	.073	.309 493	3 545	.123	.467 477	2 787
.024	.113 590	4 464	.074	.313 038	3 528	.124	.470 264	2 773
.025	.118 054	4 444	.075	.316 566	3 511	.125	.473 037	2 760
.026	.122 498	4 423	.076	.320 077	3 495	.126	.475 797	2 746
.027	.126 921	4 402	.077	.323 572	3 478	.127	.478 543	2 733
.028	.131 323	4 382	.078	.327 050	3 461	.128	.481 276	2 720
.029	.135 705	4 361	.079	.330 511	3 445	.129	.483 996	2 707
.030	.140 066	4 341	.080	.333 956	3 429	.130	.486 703	2 693
.031	.144 407	4 321	.081	.337 385	3 412	.131	.489 396	2 680
.032	.148 728	4 301	.082	.340 797	3 396	.132	.492 076	2 667
.033	.153 029	4 281	.083	.344 193	3 380	.133	.494 743	2 655
.034	.157 310	4 261	.084	.347 573	3 364	.134	.497 398	2 641
.035	.161 571	4 241	.085	.350 937	3 347	.135	.500 039	2 628
.036	.165 812	4 221	.086	.354 284	3 332	.136	.502 667	2 616
.037	.170 033	4 201	.087	.357 616	3 316	.137	.505 283	2 603
.038	.174 234	4 182	.088	.360 932	3 300	.138	.507 886	2 590
.039	.178 416	4 162	.089	.364 232	3 284	.139	.510 476	2 577

$_5m_x$	$_5q_x$	Δ	$_5m_x$	$_5q_x$	Δ	$_5m_x$	$_5q_x$	Δ
		.00			.00			.00
.040	.182 578	4 143	.090	.367 516	3 268	.140	.513 053	2 565
.041	.186 721	4 123	.091	.370 784	3 253	.141	.515 618	2 552
.042	.190 844	4 104	.092	.374 037	3 237	.142	.518 170	2 540
.043	.194 948	4 085	.093	.377 274	3 222	.143	.520 710	2 527
.044	.199 033	4 066	.094	.380 496	3 206	.144	.523 237	2 515
.045	.203 099	4 047	.095	.383 702	3 191	.145	.525 752	2 503
.046	.207 146	4 028	.096	.386 893	3 176	.146	.528 255	2 490
.047	.211 174	4 008	.097	.390 069	3 160	.147	.530 745	2 478
.048	.215 182	3 990	.098	.393 229	3 145	.148	.533 223	2 466
.049	.219 172	3 972	.099	.396 374	3 130	.149	.535 689	2 454
.050	.223 144	3 952	.100	.399 504	3 116	.150	.538 143	2 442

TABLE 2.   *Part B*

$_5m_x$	$_5q_x$	Δ	$_5m_x$	$_5q_x$	Δ	$_5m_x$	$_5q_x$	Δ
		.00			.00			.00
.150	.538 143	2 442	.200	.646 545	1 904	.250	.730 854	1 476
.151	.540 585	2 430	.201	.648 449	1 894	.251	.732 330	1 469
.152	.543 015	2 418	.202	.650 343	1 885	.252	.733 799	1 462
.153	.545 433	2 406	.203	.652 228	1 876	.253	.735 261	1 453
.154	.547 839	2 394	.204	.654 104	1 866	.254	.736 714	1 447
.155	.550 233	2 382	.205	.655 970	1 856	.255	.738 161	1 439
.156	.552 615	2 371	.206	.657 826	1 847	.256	.739 600	1 432
.157	.554 986	2 359	.207	.659 673	1 838	.257	.741 032	1 424
.158	.557 345	2 347	.208	.661 511	1 829	.258	.742 456	1 417
.159	.559 692	2 336	.209	.663 340	1 819	.259	.743 873	1 409
.160	.562 028	2 324	.210	.665 159	1 810	.260	.745 282	1 403
.161	.564 352	2 313	.211	.666 969	1 802	.261	.746 685	1 395
.162	.566 665	2 301	.212	.668 771	1 792	.262	.748 080	1 388
.163	.568 966	2 290	.213	.670 563	1 783	.263	.749 468	1 381
.164	.571 256	2 279	.214	.672 346	1 774	.264	.750 849	1 374
.165	.573 535	2 267	.215	.674 120	1 765	.265	.752 223	1 366
.166	.575 802	2 257	.216	.675 885	1 756	.266	.753 589	1 360
.167	.578 059	2 245	.217	.677 641	1 747	.267	.754 949	1 353
.168	.580 304	2 234	.218	.679 388	1 739	.268	.756 302	1 345
.169	.582 538	2 223	.219	.681 127	1 729	.269	.757 647	1 339
.170	.584 761	2 211	.220	.682 856	1 721	.270	.758 986	1 332
.171	.586 972	2 201	.221	.684 577	1 712	.271	.760 318	1 325
.172	.589 173	2 190	.222	.686 289	1 704	.272	.761 643	1 318
.173	.591 363	2 180	.223	.687 993	1 695	.273	.762 961	1 311
.174	.593 543	2 168	.224	.689 688	1 686	.274	.764 272	1 304

$_5m_x$	$_5q_x$	Δ	$_5m_x$	$_5q_x$	Δ	$_5m_x$	$_5q_x$	Δ
		.00			.00			.00
.175	.595 711	2 157	.225	.691 374	1 678	.275	.765 576	1 298
.176	.597 868	2 147	.226	.693 052	1 669	.276	.766 874	1 291
.177	.600 015	2 137	.227	.694 721	1 661	.277	.768 165	1 284
.178	.602 152	2 125	.228	.696 382	1 652	.278	.769 449	1 278
.179	.604 277	2 115	.229	.698 034	1 644	.279	.770 727	1 271
.180	.606 392	2 105	.230	.699 678	1 636	.280	.771 998	1 264
.181	.608 497	2 094	.231	.701 314	1 627	.281	.773 262	1 258
.182	.610 591	2 083	.232	.702 941	1 619	.282	.774 520	1 251
.183	.612 674	2 073	.233	.704 560	1 611	.283	.775 771	1 245
.184	.614 747	2 063	.234	.706 171	1 602	.284	.777 016	1 239
.185	.616 810	2 053	.235	.707 773	1 595	.285	.778 255	1 231
.186	.618 863	2 042	.236	.709 368	1 586	.286	.779 486	1 226
.187	.620 905	2 032	.237	.710 954	1 578	.287	.780 712	1 219
.188	.622 937	2 022	.238	.712 532	1 570	.288	.781 931	1 213
.189	.624 959	2 012	.239	.714 102	1 562	.289	.783 144	1 206
.190	.626 971	2 002	.240	.715 664	1 555	.290	.784 350	1 201
.191	.628 973	1 992	.241	.717 219	1 546	.291	.785 551	1 193
.192	.630 965	1 982	.242	.718 765	1 538	.292	.786 744	1 188
.193	.632 947	1 972	.243	.720 303	1 531	.293	.787 932	1 182
.194	.634 919	1 962	.244	.721 834	1 522	.294	.789 114	1 175
.195	.636 881	1 952	.245	.723 356	1 515	.295	.790 289	1 169
.196	.638 833	1 943	.246	.724 871	1 507	.296	.791 458	1 163
.197	.640 776	1 933	.247	.726 378	1 500	.297	.792 621	1 157
.198	.642 709	1 923	.248	.727 878	1 492	.298	.793 778	1 151
.199	.644 632	1 913	.249	.729 370	1 484	.299	.794 929	1 145
.200	.646 545	1 904	.250	.730 854	1 476	.300	.796 074	1 139

TABLE 2. *Part C*

$_5m_x$	$_5q_x$	Δ	$_5m_x$	$_5q_x$	Δ	$_5m_x$	$_5q_x$	Δ
		.00			.000			.000
.300	.796 074	1 139	.350	.846 261	874	.400	.884 675	667
.301	.797 213	1 133	.351	.847 135	869	.401	.885 342	663
.302	.798 346	1 128	.352	.848 004	865	.402	.886 005	660
.303	.799 474	1 121	.353	.848 869	860	.403	.886 665	656
.304	.800 595	1 115	.354	.849 729	856	.404	.887 321	653
.305	.801 710	1 110	.355	.850 585	850	.405	.887 974	649
.306	.802 820	1 103	.356	.851 435	847	.406	.888 623	646
.307	.803 923	1 098	.357	.852 282	842	.407	.889 269	642
.308	.805 021	1 092	.358	.853 124	837	.408	.889 911	638
.309	.806 113	1 087	.359	.853 961	833	.409	.890 549	635

$_5m_x$	$_5q_x$	Δ	$_5m_x$	$_5q_x$	Δ	$_5m_x$	$_5q_x$	Δ
		.00			.000			.000
.310	.807 200	1 080	.360	.854 794	828	.410	.891 184	632
.311	.808 280	1 075	.361	.855 622	824	.411	.891 816	628
.312	.809 355	1 070	.362	.856 446	819	.412	.892 444	625
.313	.810 425	1 063	.363	.857 265	816	.413	.893 069	621
.314	.811 488	1 059	.364	.858 081	810	.414	.893 690	618
.315	.812 547	1 052	.365	.858 891	807	.415	.894 308	614
.316	.813 599	1 047	.366	.859 698	802	.416	.894 922	612
.317	.814 646	1 042	.367	.860 500	798	.417	.895 534	607
.318	.815 688	1 036	.368	.861 298	793	.418	.896 141	605
.319	.816 724	1 030	.369	.862 091	789	.419	.896 746	601
.320	.817 754	1 026	.370	.862 880	785	.420	.897 347	598
.321	.818 780	1 019	.371	.863 665	781	.421	.897 945	594
.322	.819 799	1 015	.372	.864 446	776	.422	.898 539	592
.323	.820 814	1 009	.373	.865 222	773	.423	.899 131	588
.324	.821 823	1 003	.374	.865 995	768	.424	.899 719	585
.325	.822 826	0 999	.375	.866 763	764	.425	.900 304	581
.326	.823 825	0 993	.376	.867 527	760	.426	.900 885	579
.327	.824 818	0 988	.377	.868 287	756	.427	.901 464	575
.328	.825 806	0 982	.378	.869 043	751	.428	.902 039	572
.329	.826 788	0 978	.379	.869 794	748	.429	.902 611	569
.330	.827 766	0 972	.380	.870 542	744	.430	.903 180	566
.331	.828 738	0 967	.381	.871 286	739	.431	.903 746	562
.332	.829 705	0 962	.382	.872 025	736	.432	.904 308	560
.333	.830 667	0 957	.383	.872 761	732	.433	.904 868	556
.334	.831 624	0 952	.384	.873 493	728	.434	.905 424	554
.335	.832 576	0 947	.385	.874 221	723	.435	.905 978	550
.336	.833 523	0 941	.386	.874 944	720	.436	.906 528	548
.337	.834 464	0 937	.387	.875 664	716	.437	.907 076	544
.338	.835 401	0 932	.388	.876 380	712	.438	.907 620	541
.339	.836 333	0 927	.389	.877 092	708	.439	.908 161	539
.340	.837 260	0 922	.390	.877 800	705	.440	.908 700	535
.341	.838 182	0 917	.391	.878 505	700	.441	.909 235	532
.342	.839 099	0 912	.392	.879 205	697	.442	.909 767	530
.343	.840 011	0 907	.393	.879 902	693	.443	.910 297	526
.344	.840 918	0 903	.394	.880 595	689	.444	.910 823	524
.345	.841 821	0 897	.395	.881 284	686	.445	.911 347	521
.346	.842 718	0 893	.396	.881 970	682	.446	.911 868	518
.347	.843 611	0 888	.397	.882 652	678	.447	.912 386	514
.348	.844 499	0 884	.398	.883 330	674	.448	.912 900	513
.349	.845 383	0 878	.399	.884 004	671	.449	.912 413	509
.350	.846 261	0 874	.400	.884 675	667	.450	.913 922	

TABLE 3. *Part A*

$_{10}m_x$	$_{10}q_x$	Δ	$_{10}m_x$	$_{10}q_x$	Δ	$_{10}m_x$	$_{10}q_x$	Δ
		.00			.00			.00
.000	.000 000	9 959	.050	.405 479	6 391	.100	.660 404	3 920
.001	.009 959	9 874	.051	.411 870	6 332	.101	.664 324	3 879
.002	.019 833	9 792	.052	.418 202	6 273	.102	.668 203	3 840
.003	.029 625	9 709	.053	.424 475	6 214	.103	.672 043	3 800
.004	.039 334	9 627	.054	.430 689	6 156	.104	.675 843	3 762
.005	.048 961	9 546	.055	.436 845	6 098	.105	.679 605	3 723
.006	.058 507	9 465	.056	.442 943	6 041	.106	.683 328	3 685
.007	.067 972	9 384	.057	.448 984	5 985	.107	.687 013	3 646
.008	.077 356	9 305	.058	.454 969	5 928	.108	.690 659	3 610
.009	.086 661	9 225	.059	.460 897	5 872	.109	.694 269	3 571
.010	.095 886	9 147	.060	.466 769	5 816	.110	.697 840	3 535
.011	.105 033	9 068	.061	.472 585	5 762	.111	.701 375	3 499
.012	.114 101	8 990	.062	.478 347	5 706	.112	.704 874	3 462
.013	.123 091	8 913	.063	.484 053	5 653	.113	.708 336	3 426
.014	.132 004	8 836	.064	.489 706	5 598	.114	.711 762	3 390
.015	.140 840	8 760	.065	.495 304	5 546	.115	.715 152	3 355
.016	.149 600	8 684	.066	.500 850	5 492	.116	.718 507	3 320
.017	.158 284	8 608	.067	.506 342	5 439	.117	.721 827	3 285
.018	.166 892	8 534	.068	.511 781	5 388	.118	.725 112	3 251
.019	.175 426	8 459	.069	.517 169	5 335	.119	.728 363	3 216
.020	.183 885	8 386	.070	.522 504	5 284	.120	.731 579	3 183
.021	.192 271	8 312	.071	.527 788	5 234	.121	.734 762	3 149
.022	.200 583	8 239	.072	.533 022	5 182	.122	.737 911	3 116
.023	.208 822	8 167	.073	.538 204	5 132	.123	.741 027	3 083
.024	.216 989	8 095	.074	.543 336	5 083	.124	.744 110	3 050
.025	.225 084	8 023	.075	.548 419	5 033	.125	.747 160	3 018
.026	.233 107	7 953	.076	.553 452	4 984	.126	.750 178	2 986
.027	.241 060	7 882	.077	.558 436	4 935	.127	.753 164	2 954
.028	.248 942	7 812	.078	.563 371	4 887	.128	.756 118	2 923
.029	.256 754	7 743	.079	.568 258	4 840	.129	.759 041	2 891
.030	.264 497	7 673	.080	.573 098	4 791	.130	.761 932	2 861
.031	.272 170	7 606	.081	.577 889	4 745	.131	.764 793	2 830
.032	.279 776	7 536	.082	.582 634	4 698	.132	.767 623	2 799
.033	.287 312	7 470	.083	.587 332	4 652	.133	.770 422	2 769
.034	.294 782	7 402	.084	.591 984	4 605	.134	.773 191	2 740
.035	.302 184	7 336	.085	.596 589	4 560	.135	.775 931	2 710
.036	.309 520	7 269	.086	.601 149	4 515	.136	.778 641	2 680
.037	.316 789	7 204	.087	.605 664	4 470	.137	.781 321	2 652
.038	.323 993	7 139	.088	.610 134	4 425	.138	.783 973	2 623
.039	.331 132	7 073	.089	.614 559	4 382	.139	.786 596	2 594

$_{10}m_x$	$_{10}q_x$	Δ	$_{10}m_x$	$_{10}q_x$	Δ	$_{10}m_x$	$_{10}q_x$	Δ
		.00			.00			.00
.040	.338 205	7 010	.090	.618 941	4 337	.140	.789 190	2 567
.041	.345 215	6 946	.091	.623 278	4 294	.141	.791 757	2 538
.042	.352 161	6 881	.092	.627 572	4 251	.142	.794 295	2 511
.043	.359 042	6 820	.093	.631 823	4 209	.143	.796 806	2 483
.044	.365 862	6 756	.094	.636 032	4 166	.144	.799 289	2 456
.045	.372 618	6 695	.095	.640 198	4 123	.145	.801 745	2 429
.046	.379 313	6 633	.096	.644 321	4 083	.146	.804 174	2 402
.047	.385 946	6 572	.097	.648 404	4 041	.147	.806 576	2 376
.048	.392 518	6 511	.098	.652 445	4 000	.148	.808 952	2 350
.049	.399 029	6 450	.099	.656 445	3 959	.149	.811 302	2 324
.050	.405 479	6 391	.100	.660 404	3 920	.150	.813 626	2 298

TABLE 3. *Part B*

$_{10}m_x$	$_{10}q_x$	Δ	$_{10}m_x$	$_{10}q_x$	Δ	$_{10}m_x$	$_{10}q_x$	Δ
		.00			.00			.000
.150	.813 626	2 298	.200	.901 726	1 290	.250	.950 213	693
.151	.815 924	2 273	.201	.903 016	1 274	.251	.950 906	683
.152	.818 197	2 248	.202	.904 290	1 259	.252	.951 589	675
.153	.820 445	2 222	.203	.905 549	1 244	.253	.952 264	666
.154	.822 667	2 198	.204	.906 793	1 228	.254	.952 930	658
.155	.824 865	2 174	.205	.908 021	1 215	.255	.953 588	649
.156	.827 039	2 149	.206	.909 236	1 199	.256	.954 237	641
.157	.829 188	2 125	.207	.910 435	1 185	.257	.954 878	633
.158	.831 313	2 102	.208	.911 620	1 171	.258	.955 511	624
.159	.833 415	2 078	.209	.912 791	1 157	.259	.956 135	617
.160	.835 493	2 054	.210	.913 948	1 142	.260	.956 752	608
.161	.837 547	2 032	.211	.915 090	1 129	.261	.957 360	601
.162	.839 579	2 008	.212	.916 219	1 115	.262	.957 961	593
.163	.841 587	1 986	.213	.917 334	1 102	.263	.958 554	585
.164	.843 573	1 964	.214	.918 436	1 088	.264	.959 139	577
.165	.845 537	1 941	.215	.919 524	1 075	.265	.959 716	570
.166	.847 478	1 920	.216	.920 599	1 062	.266	.960 286	562
.167	.849 398	1 897	.217	.921 661	1 049	.267	.960 848	555
.168	.851 295	1 876	.218	.922 710	1 036	.268	.961 403	548
.169	.853 171	1 855	.219	.923 746	1 024	.269	.961 951	541
.170	.855 026	1 833	.220	.924 770	1 011	.270	.962 492	534
.171	.856 859	1 813	.221	.925 781	0 998	.271	.963 026	526
.172	.858 672	1 792	.222	.926 779	0 986	.272	.963 552	520
.173	.860 464	1 771	.223	.927 765	0 974	.273	.964 072	513
.174	.862 235	1 751	.224	.928 739	0 962	.274	.964 585	506

$_{10}m_x$	$_{10}q_x$	Δ	$_{10}m_x$	$_{10}q_x$	Δ	$_{10}m_x$	$_{10}q_x$	Δ
		.00			.00			.000
.175	.863 986	1 731	.225	.929 701	0 950	.275	.965 091	499
.176	.865 717	1 711	.226	.930 651	0 939	.276	.965 590	493
.177	.867 428	1 692	.227	.931 590	0 926	.277	.966 083	486
.178	.869 120	1 672	.228	.932 516	0 916	.278	.966 569	480
.179	.870 792	1 652	.229	.933 432	0 904	.279	.967 049	473
.180	.872 444	1 633	.230	.934 336	0 892	.280	.967 522	467
.181	.874 077	1 615	.231	.935 228	0 882	.281	.967 989	461
.182	.875 692	1 596	.232	.936 110	0 871	.282	.968 450	455
.183	.877 288	1 577	.233	.936 981	0 859	.283	.968 905	449
.184	.878 865	1 559	.234	.937 840	0 849	.284	.969 354	443
.185	.880 424	1 540	.235	.938 689	0 839	.285	.969 797	436
.186	.881 964	1 523	.236	.939 528	0 827	.286	.970 233	431
.187	.883 487	1 505	.237	.940 355	0 818	.287	.970 664	426
.188	.884 992	1 487	.238	.941 173	0 807	.288	.971 090	419
.189	.886 479	1 470	.239	.941 980	0 797	.289	.971 509	414
.190	.887 949	1 452	.240	.942 777	0 787	.290	.971 923	408
.191	.889 401	1 436	.241	.943 564	0 777	.291	.972 331	403
.192	.890 837	1 418	.242	.944 341	0 767	.292	.972 734	397
.193	.892 255	1 402	.243	.945 108	0 758	.293	.973 131	392
.194	.893 657	1 386	.244	.945 866	0 748	.294	.973 523	387
.195	.895 043	1 368	.245	.946 614	0 738	.295	.973 910	381
.196	.896 411	1 353	.246	.947 352	0 729	.296	.974 291	377
.197	.897 764	1 337	.247	.948 081	0 720	.297	.974 668	371
.198	.899 101	1 320	.248	.948 801	0 710	.298	.975 039	366
.199	.900 421	1 305	.249	.949 511	0 702	.299	.975 405	361
.200	.901 726	1 290	.250	.950 213	0 693	.300	.975 766	356

TABLE 3. *Part C*

$_{10}m_x$	$_{10}q_x$	Δ	$_{10}m_x$	$_{10}q_x$	Δ	$_{10}m_x$	$_{10}q_x$	Δ
		.000			.000			.0000
.300	.975 766	356	.350	.988 667	175	.400	.994 908	82
.301	.976 122	352	.351	.988 842	173	.401	.994 990	82
.302	.976 474	346	.352	.989 015	171	.402	.995 072	80
.303	.976 820	342	.353	.989 186	168	.403	.995 152	80
.304	.977 162	337	.354	.989 354	165	.404	.995 232	77
.305	.977 499	333	.355	.989 519	163	.405	.995 309	77
.306	.977 832	328	.356	.989 682	161	.406	.995 386	76
.307	.978 160	323	.357	.989 843	158	.407	.995 462	74
.308	.978 483	319	.358	.990 001	157	.408	.995 536	73
.309	.978 802	315	.359	.990 158	153	.409	.995 609	72

$_{10}m_x$	$_{10}q_x$	Δ	$_{10}m_x$	$_{10}q_x$	Δ	$_{10}m_x$	$_{10}q_x$	Δ
		.000			.000			.0000
.310	.979 117	310	.360	.990 311	152	.410	.995 681	71
.311	.979 427	306	.361	.990 463	149	.411	.995 752	70
.312	.979 733	302	.362	.990 612	147	.412	.995 822	69
.313	.980 035	297	.363	.990 759	145	.413	.995 891	68
.314	.980 332	294	.364	.990 904	143	.414	.995 959	66
.315	.980 626	289	.365	.991 047	141	.415	.996 025	66
.316	.980 915	285	.366	.991 188	139	.416	.996 091	64
.317	.981 200	282	.367	.991 327	136	.417	.996 155	64
.318	.981 482	277	.368	.991 463	135	.418	.996 219	63
.319	.981 759	274	.369	.991 598	133	.419	.996 282	61
.320	.982 033	269	.370	.991 731	130	.420	.996 343	61
.321	.982 302	266	.371	.991 861	129	.421	.996 404	60
.322	.982 568	263	.372	.991 990	127	.422	.996 464	58
.323	.982 831	258	.373	.992 117	125	.423	.996 522	58
.324	.983 089	255	.374	.992 242	123	.424	.996 580	57
.325	.983 344	252	.375	.992 365	121	.425	.996 637	56
.326	.983 596	248	.376	.992 486	120	.426	.996 693	56
.327	.983 844	244	.377	.992 606	117	.427	.996 749	54
.328	.984 088	241	.378	.992 723	116	.428	.996 803	53
.329	.984 329	237	.379	.992 839	114	.429	.996 856	53
.330	.984 566	234	.380	.992 953	113	.430	.996 909	52
.331	.984 800	231	.381	.993 066	111	.431	.996 961	50
.332	.985 031	228	.382	.993 177	109	.432	.997 011	51
.333	.985 259	224	.383	.993 286	107	.433	.997 062	49
.334	.985 483	221	.384	.993 393	106	.434	.997 111	49
.335	.985 704	218	.385	.993 499	104	.435	.997 160	47
.336	.985 922	215	.386	.993 603	103	.436	.997 207	47
.337	.986 137	212	.387	.993 706	101	.437	.997 254	47
.338	.986 349	209	.388	.993 807	100	.438	.997 301	45
.339	.986 558	206	.389	.993 907	098	.439	.997 346	45
.340	.986 764	203	.390	.994 005	096	.440	.997 391	44
.341	.986 967	200	.391	.994 101	096	.441	.997 435	43
.342	.987 167	197	.392	.994 197	093	.442	.997 478	43
.343	.987 364	194	.393	.994 290	093	.443	.997 521	42
.344	.987 558	192	.394	.994 383	090	.444	.997 563	42
.345	.987 750	188	.395	.994 473	090	.445	.997 605	40
.346	.987 938	186	.396	.994 563	088	.446	.997 645	40
.347	.988 124	184	.397	.994 651	087	.447	.997 685	40
.348	.988 308	180	.398	.994 738	085	.448	.997 725	38
.349	.988 488	179	.399	.994 823	085	.449	.997 763	39
.350	.988 667	175	.400	.994 908	082	.450	.997 802	

490

II. Model Distributions of Spacing Between Births

Duration	2nd Order					3rd Order				
	Fr.	Bo.	Mo.	Sl.	Ru.	Fr.	Bo.	Mo.	Sl.	Ru.
Years										
0	2	2	2	2	2	2	2	3	2	2
1	22	24	28	26	25	16	21	23	20	19
2	33	26	29	33	37	33	28	30	33	38
3	16	15	15	17	19	19	17	17	20	24
4	9	11	9	8	8	11	11	9	9	8
5	6	7	6	5	4	7	7	7	6	4
6	4	5	4	4	2	4	4	4	4	2
7	3	4	3	2	1	3	4	3	2	1
8	2	2	2	1	1	2	2	2	2	1
9	2	2	1	1	1	2	2	1	2	1
10	1	1	1	1	—	1	1	1	1	—
11	—	—	—	—	—	—	1	—	—	—
Total	100	100	100	100	100	100	100	100	100	100

Duration	4th Order					5th Order				
	Fr.	Bo.	Mo.	Sl.	Ru.	Fr.	Bo.	Mo.	Sl.	Ru.
Years										
0	2	3	3	2	2	3	4	3	2	2
1	16	21	23	19	18	16	22	23	20	18
2	33	28	32	35	37	33	29	33	36	37
3	20	17	17	21	27	20	17	17	22	27
4	11	11	9	9	8	11	10	9	8	8
5	6	7	6	5	4	6	6	6	4	4

6	4	4	4	4	2	4	4	4	3	2
7	3	4	2	2	1	3	3	2	2	1
8	2	2	2	1	1	2	2	1	1	1
9	2	1	1	1	—	1	1	1	1	—
10	1	1	1	1	—	1	1	1	1	—
11	—	1	—	—	—	—	1	—	—	—
Total	100	100	100	100	100	100	100	100	100	100

Duration	6th Order					7th Order					8th Order				
	Fr.	Bo.	Mo.	Sl.	Ru.	Fr.	Bo.	Mo.	Sl.	Ru.	Fr.	Bo.	Mo.	Sl.	Ru.
Years															
0	3	4	3	3	3	3	4	3	3	3	4	4	4	4	4
1	17	24	24	20	18	17	24	24	20	16	19	26	24	20	19
2	36	30	33	36	36	37	31	35	36	38	37	34	35	36	38
3	20	18	19	22	27	21	18	19	23	27	20	18	20	23	24
4	10	8	9	8	9	10	8	8	8	9	10	8	8	8	9
5	6	6	5	4	3	5	6	4	4	3	5	5	4	4	3
6	3	3	3	3	2	3	3	2	3	2	2	2	2	3	1
7	2	2	2	1	1	2	2	2	1	1	1	1	1	1	1
8	1	2	1	1	1	1	2	1	1	1	1	1	1	1	1
9	1	1	1	1	—	1	1	1	1	—	1	1	1	—	—
10	1	1	—	1	—	—	1	—	—	—	—	—	—	—	—
11	—	1	—	—	—	—	—	—	—	—	—	—	—	—	—
Total	100	100	100	100	100	100	100	100	100	100	100	100	100	100	100

Fr.: France; Bo.: Bohemia; Mo.: Moravia; Sl.: Slovakia; Ru.: Sub-Carpathian Russia.

For France the distributions are obtained from the survey of government workers and employees carried out in 1907; for Czechoslovakia they are taken from a study of 1925–1926 marriage cohorts. The durations are in terms of differences between dates.

1. Percent distributions of births of the specified birth order by time duration elapsed since the previous birth.

Index